Una Merkel

The Actress with Sassy Wit and Southern Charm

A Biography by
Larry Sean Kinder

BearManor Media

Albany, Georgia

Una Merkel: The Actress with Sassy Wit and Southern Charm
Copyright © 2016 Larry Sean Kinder. All Rights Reserved.

No part of this book may be reproduced in any form or by any means, electronic, mechanical, digital, photocopying or recording, except for the inclusion in a review, without permission in writing from the the publisher.

Published in the USA by
BearManor Media
P.O. Box 71426
Albany, GA 31708
www.BearManorMedia.com

Softcover Edition
ISBN-10: 1593939027
ISBN-13: 978-1-59393-902-1

Printed in the United States of America

Table of Contents

Acknowledgments — ix
Introduction — xiii

Chapter 1: Rising Star — 1
Chapter 2: Broadway Bound — 15
Chapter 3: Hollywood — 31
Chapter 4: Fox Studios — 47
Chapter 5: Marriage — 65
Chapter 6: One of the Busiest Gals on the Lot — 79
Chapter 7: Gold Diggers — 93
Chapter 8: Domesticity — 117
Chapter 9: Harold Lloyd — 131
Chapter 10: Mysteries — 141
Chapter 11: MGM Musicals — 155
Chapter 12: Cars, College, and Gin — 173
Chapter 13: Harlow — 185
Chapter 14: Good-bye, Mr. Mayer — 199
Chapter 15: Western Catfight — 217
Chapter 16: Free Agent — 227
Chapter 17: Entertaining the Troops — 239
Chapter 18: Tragedy — 257
Chapter 19: Phoenix Rising From the Ashes — 267
Chapter 20: Mothers, Matrons, and Companions — 277
Chapter 21: Pressing On — 291
Chapter 22: Tony Award — 303
Chapter 23: Mrs. Winemiller, Disney, and Television — 323
Chapter 24: Back Home to Kentucky — 341

APPENDIX — 355
Credits — 359
Selected Bibliography — 425
Index — 431
Photo Credits — 451
About the Author — 453

To God, my wife, family, and friends—
Without you, I am nothing.

Una Merkel modeling a tiered lace gown. (MGM, 1936)

Acknowledgments

This biography could never have been completed without the patient love and support of my wife and family, and I thank you for your perseverance and endurance while I completed this long, arduous adventure.

To my loving wife, Valérie—I cannot express my gratefulness to you for your unconditional and unfaltering love. You endured all my hours of frustration, exasperation, and stress with a gentle grace and amazing patience, and you were always there with a word of encouragement, a warm embrace, and an uplifting smile. This book certainly would not have come to fruition without you, and the countless ways you contributed to it. I thank you from the bottom of my heart, and I want you to remember always: *Je t'aime de tout mon cœur pour toujours!*

To my parents (Larry and Christine Kinder), and my sister, Markie—you were behind me 100 percent on this project, and I am so thankful for all the big and small ways you helped me along the way.

Dad, thank you for your patience, endurance, and incredible forbearance. You are a rock of strength and a staunch supporter of all that I do. Who could ask for more? You are the backbone of the family, and I remain awed and impressed by your fortitude, resourcefulness, dedication, and commitment to the family.

Mom, how can I ever adequately thank you for all that you contributed to this biography in terms of interest, loving support, and enthusiasm? You never failed to uplift me throughout the whole process, and for that, I am eternally grateful. I also appreciate the endless hours that you gave up so freely to pore over my manuscript, offering useful suggestions and tips, and even helping with the compilation of the theatrical credits.

Markie, can you imagine how much I need and appreciate your unwavering love and support, not to mention your belief in my abilities? You are one of my biggest fans, and you were a meaningful part of this journey. I thank you in particular for trudging through the legal documents connected with Una and for your valuable insights, opinions, and perspectives. Thanks for also indulging my love of old Hollywood and vintage films.

To the late Therese Duzinkiewicz Baker—I am so appreciative for all your help in the initial stages of this project, especially the endless hours that you devoted to finding, collecting, and organizing material. Thank you so very much! Please tell Una that I hope my biography has done her proud.

To Ben Ohmart, Allan Duffin, and BearManor Media—I thank you so much for believing in me and my manuscript and for giving Una and her story a chance to be heard.

My gratitude to my co-workers, colleagues, and associates at Western Kentucky University Libraries, including Dean Connie Foster, Dr. Brian Coutts, former Dean Michael Binder, and all my friends in the Department of Library Public Services and other library departments. Your encouragement made all the difference.

A special "thank you" to the incredible staff at WKU Libraries' Interlibrary Loan—those working now and previously, including the late Debra Day, Selina Langford, Ken Foushee, and Robin McGinnis. Please know how grateful I am for your assistance over the years. You always fulfilled my information needs with the utmost efficiency, competency, and courtesy. Bravo!

My student assistants over the years have been of immeasurable help. A big round of cheers for all their efforts and hard work: Rebecca L. Nimmo, Ruth Carman Britt, Ashley R. Jackson, Lindsey K. Meade, Dawn Rinehardt, Jonathan B. Russelburg, Christopher "Brent" Simmons, Daniel T. Lyons, Victoria (Tori) Brown.

To Clyde Day—You were my first interviewee, and I appreciate how gracious, patient, and kind you were. A hearty thank you!

To Susan Henning-Schutte—Despite not feeling your best, you granted me a wonderful interview. A heartfelt thank you for your efforts!

To Joan Krenzin—I appreciated your incisive comments on my manuscript. Thank you!

To Eve Golden—I've been a fan of your biographies for years. You were one of the inspirations for this book. Thanks!

The following individuals are recognized and acknowledged for their special contributions to my book. I am grateful for your support and assistance: Edward "Ned" Comstock (librarian extraordinaire!), Constance McCormick, and the wonderful staff at USC's Cinematic Arts Library; Richard Lamparski, Sarah Marshall, Joan Leslie, James Frasher, Richard Anderson, Paul Comi, Robert Morse, Joanna Barnes, Eddie Hodges, Carole Sharpe, James Gavin, Bob King, Louise Erickson, Patricia Carlin, G. D. Hamman, Ron Ringler, Dale Mott, "Cinevent" Larry, Mark A. Vieira, Herbert Abrams, Jerry D. Mayfield, Jan Brumagen, Bailey E. Johnson, Anna D. Dotson, Nancy Richey (your introducing me to the Cumulated Dramatic Index—the orange books—was a godsend!), Rosemary Meszaros (thank you for the information about Una and Ronnie from ancestry.com), Lea Whittington and the rest of the staff at Margaret Herrick Library; and the library faculty and staff at the Performing Arts Special Collections, UCLA.

There are certainly others whom I have inadvertently failed to acknowledge, and to all of you, I extend my heartfelt apologies.

Introduction

A columnist for the *St. Petersburg Times* once told the story of a male acquaintance she knew who had married a much younger woman. The marriage did not last, and the man later offered his explanation for the break-up. "How can I live," he asked, "with a woman who doesn't know who Una Merkel is?"[1] While the husband's pithy remark may elicit a hearty, "Here, here!" from fans who fondly remember the talented actress, many others, like the wife mentioned above, probably still wonder, "Just who *was* Una Merkel?"

Una Merkel was born in Covington, Kentucky, on December 10, 1903, and from an early age, this bashful, awkward, self-professed "wallflower" dreamed of becoming an actress. After appearing in numerous local theater productions and taking all kinds of lessons—acting, elocution, piano, dance—she landed work in silent films because of her physical resemblance to Lillian

Gish. In 1923, she appeared in an early, experimental two-reel sound film, *Love's Old Sweet Song*. A vaudeville tour and several plays both on and off-Broadway followed, but Una didn't really garner significant attention until 1928, when she appeared as Betty Lee Reynolds in the hit play *Coquette*, which starred her friend and idol Helen Hayes.

In 1930, D. W. Griffith lured Una to Hollywood to appear in his first all-sound feature, *Abraham Lincoln*. This film was the beginning of Una's most prolific period. She soon became one of the busiest actresses in Hollywood, appearing in sixty films by the end of the decade. In 1933 alone, she appeared in thirteen films! Possessing one of the most familiar faces on the silver screen and in movie magazines, Una was known for her "merry eyes," distinct Southern drawl, delicate blonde femininity, and witty way with a wisecrack. Although she never became a major star like Joan Crawford and Bette Davis, she did connect with moviegoers, who identified with her portrayals of helpful secretaries, confiding best friends, wisecracking sidekicks, and lovable second bananas. Fans flocked to her films, eager to see their beloved Una hold her own against—and often upstage—actors as diverse as Jean Harlow, Carole Lombard, Eleanor Powell, Loretta Young, Myrna Loy, Robert Taylor, Clark Gable, Jimmy Stewart, and Bob Hope.

Una was hardworking and extremely conscientious about her craft. She never wanted to disappoint her colleagues, so she strove to be the consummate professional, arriving on set punctually, well-prepared, lines completely memorized, and ready to work. From all accounts, Una was sweet, accommodating, and well liked, with never a harsh or unpleasant word about anyone. When pressed about her career, she was self-effacing and very humble, prompting author Richard Lamparski to note that "she had no ego at all...."[2]

As is the case with most modest and unassuming people, Una was neither comfortable nor interested in self-promotion or "tooting her own horn." With a few notable exceptions, she did not campaign or fight for parts. Instead, she was content to let her work, talent, and reputation speak for themselves. Filmmakers responded enthusiastically, but nearly always with character roles. Una accepted them graciously, acquitting herself with considerable aplomb and grace. These parts, however, typecast her and did little to stretch or showcase her abilities. Fortunately, she found more challenging and rewarding work on the stage, including memorable performances in *Summer and Smoke (1950)*, *Come Back, Little Sheba (1951)*, and *The Remarkable Mr. Pennypacker (1953–4)*. In 1956, her touching performance in Eudora Welty's *The Ponder Heart* wowed critics and audiences, earning her a Tony Award for Best Supporting or Featured Actress. In 1961, she reprised her stage role of Mrs. Winemiller for the film version of Tennessee Williams' *Summer and Smoke*. Once again, her acting won critical raves, and she was nominated for an Academy Award for Best Actress in a Supporting Role. She didn't win, losing out to Rita Moreno in *West Side Story*.

Una was pleased to see her work acknowledged, but these accolades did not change her. She remained just as unpretentious and down-to-earth as always. By her own admission, her career was never the top priority in her life. Family and friends always came first, and she did her best to create a fulfilling life outside the machinery of Hollywood and its glitterati. Early in her career in the 1930s, Una and her husband lived happily with her parents in a modest home (by Hollywood standards), and they often hosted dinner parties for friends. When not working, Una indulged in her favorite pastimes—writing, reading, cooking, bike riding, and badminton. From all appearances it was a prosaic life, but as this book will show, it was far from boring or uneventful. All seemed to bode well for the young actress, but little did she know that these idyllic years would be some of the best of her life, and all too brief. As time went on, Una would discover how cruel life could be when she faced disappointment, heartache, and great personal tragedy, some of which played out in the headlines of America's newspapers.

Despite all this sadness and upheaval, Una was a real trouper who showed remarkable spirit and resilience. Her story is about strength and perseverance, but also endurance and the constant struggle against life's challenges. She proved that she was not only a fighter, but ultimately, a survivor.

Una once wrote that all of us need to learn what kind of flower we are in life. "Everybody can't be an exotic, alluring flower, an ivory gardenia or a soft rose camellia," she observed.[3] "Some of us have to be the hardier variety . . . just plain everyday garden flowers."[4] Una may have thought she was ordinary, but those who knew her saw something special. While perhaps not the most beautiful or ostentatious flower in Hollywood, she was certainly one of the most lovable and endearing, and her legacy still lives on and "blooms" in the hearts of her fans who appreciate her talent, inimitable charm, and many accomplishments.

(ENDNOTES)

[1] Barbara L. Fredricksen, "Birthday Journal Goes Too Far . . . Back," *St. Petersburg Times*, May 2, 1998, 1.

[2] Richard Lamparski, interview with author, January 5, 2008.

[3] Una Merkel, "Wallflowers Can Bloom," *Cosmopolitan*, June 1942, 28.

[4] Ibid.

Chapter 1
Rising Star

In the summer of 1902, Arno Merkel said good-bye to his new fiancée and headed north to settle arrangements for an inheritance he would collect on his next birthday. This dapper twenty-year-old of German descent never minded traveling. In fact, he felt the yearnings of wanderlust at an early age. He ran away from his home town of Cincinnati as a teenager to join the British Merchant Marines, and while enlisted, he supposedly was so small that he had to stand on a soapbox just to wash dishes. Although short in stature, Arno made up for it with big dreams and aspirations. He was a born entrepreneur and was always on the lookout for his next business venture.

While in Cincinnati, he went to a dance and met Elizabeth Phares, a beautiful girl from Cincinnati who was of French and Irish extraction, but

(c. 1907) Merkel family portrait

who also claimed through her mother (née Hanks) some kinship to Nancy Hanks, Abraham Lincoln's mother. Like Arno, Elizabeth (Bessie) was also engaged, but her beau lived across the Ohio River in Covington, Kentucky, where she had grown up. When Arno and Bessie met that fateful evening, it was love at first sight, and they quickly forgot their respective fiancés. After only three days, the couple was engaged, but they didn't tie the knot until six months later on December 31, 1902. They set up housekeeping in Covington on the corner of Fourth and Greenup Street, and one of their neighbors was Dick Ernst, who would go on to be a Kentucky senator.

Bessie gave birth to a baby girl less than a year later on December 10, 1903. The delivery was so difficult that doctors told her that she would never

Una, age five, dressed in her Sunday finest and sporting an impish grin.

have another child. Before Arno could see his daughter for the first time, a superstitious aunt snatched her out of Bessie's arms and ran to a ladder to climb it, an act believed to bring good luck. When it came to naming the baby, everyone thought she should be named Mary Elizabeth after Bessie's mother, but the grandmother had other ideas. She had grown up in New Orleans living right next door to a little French girl called Una, and she liked the name so much she decided to bestow it on her granddaughter.[1] Una means "one" in Latin, and since Una would be the Merkels' one and only child, her name seemed particularly appropriate. The family did make a concession about how they pronounced it, eschewing the traditional pronunciation for the more sonorous "you nuh," because as Una explained it, "I like the soft 'U' better."[2]

When Una was born, the Merkels' financial situation was at an all-time low. Arno had staked much of his fortune on an invention that had not panned out, so he decided to take a job as a traveling salesman. With Una and Bessie in tow, he traveled all over the South, hawking calendars, candy, and the drink Cherry Smash, the latter two making Una very popular on the few days she actually attended school. Up until the age of nine, Una spent most of her time traveling and became very familiar with horses, buggies, trains, and boarding houses. Being around adults most of the time, she quickly learned to behave herself and gained a sense of filial obligation that belied her tender age. She recalled, "When I was still young enough to squeeze mashed potatoes through my fingers and drop them behind my chair when no one was looking, I felt the responsibility of managing the household. When my parents were out late, I worried constantly about what might happen to them until they returned safely, and when they had a domestic upheaval . . . I ran back and forth between them, scolding and cajoling until I had patched things up. I acted exactly as though I was the parent and they were the children."[3]

An advantage of her constant traveling was that it offered Una the chance to visit and learn about her extended family members. One place that left her endlessly intrigued and perplexed was her great-grandfather John Alexander's house in New Orleans, whose living room was wallpapered in worthless Confederate bills. During the Civil War, he had run the *New Orleans Times Picayune* from a flatboat on the Mississippi. Young Una was once a passenger on one of those boats and got the scare of her life when a terrible storm swept in and buffeted it all about. A group of nuns aboard started praying fervently, and not long afterwards, the storm subsided, allowing the boat to make it to its destination.

First United Methodist Church, Covington, Kentucky.
(Courtesy of the author and Therese Duzinkiewicz Baker)

In addition to traveling, Una's parents tried to enrich her upbringing by exposing her to culture and the fine arts. They especially loved the theater, so every time they made it back to Cincinnati, they would take her to a performance. She would sit between them expectantly, waiting, as she put it, for the "shade" to go up. Captivated by what transpired on stage, she would memorize some of the dialogue and invite family members over to watch her act it out. After having collected pins from the audience as the admission price, she would come out dressed in her mother's clothes, hold an oversized dictionary as a prop, and begin her performance. Woe be it to anyone who laughed at the wrong spot, as her cousin once did, because the blunder would elicit an indignant "There'll be no more show tonight."[4] Thinking back on this occasion, Una affirmed, "I think it was the only time I ever showed much temperament."[5]

Una's maternal grandfather died in the spring of 1909, so Arno brought the family back to Covington for the burial. While there, they were reminded how friendly the townspeople could be. A lady in the neighborhood, someone whom the Merkels had never met, came over regularly to prepare their meals. She also saw to it that Una had eggs and a basket of sweets on Easter morning, a touching act of kindness that the future actress would never forget.

Shortly thereafter, Una officially embarked on her acting career by playing a reindeer in a Sunday school pageant. In another production, she took on the part of Spirit of Spring, a role requiring her to don a Mother Hubbard dress and a daisy chain. "I was so proud of my costume that I paraded down the street long before show time," she said. "My elegant costume brought giggles from neighbor kids, and I was so mad I let them have it, daisy chain and all."[6] In an interview, Una further elaborated on the story, explaining that a mean-spirited boy had teased her unmercifully all the way home. She ran inside crying, and her father was at the door to greet her. "Una," he told her. "Why don't you go out there and give that kid a thrashing?"[7] Una hesitated, not sure what to do. She had always been taught that little ladies do not fight, so she looked questioningly at her father. When he nodded, she dutifully obeyed him by storming out of the house, lighting into the boy with a vengeance, blackening both his eyes, and receiving one in return. This altercation caused quite a scandal, and Una was the talk of her neighborhood for a month.

The Merkels didn't stay home in Covington for long. They continued their peregrinations, much to the detriment of Una's already piecemeal education, which Bessie tried to supplement by reading aloud a chapter of the Bible every night. As time went on, Una started reading the chapter herself. Prayers were also a part of her daily regimen, but her parents probably never suspected her plea at the end of each nightly prayer—that God would give her an exciting life even if it hurt her.

When Una was nine, the truant officer finally caught up with her, and she remained in Covington to attend school regularly. The next two years were difficult, not academically—she even skipped a grade—but due to all the illnesses she contracted: laryngitis, measles, diphtheria, double pneumonia, and whooping cough. Another unfortunate event had her sliding down a cellar door, which obliged many of the kindly neighborhood women to gather at the Merkel home for a "splinter-removing bee."

(2007) One-hundred-year-old Clyde Day, one of Una's childhood friends, stands on East Fifth Street in Covington, Kentucky, in front of the dwelling where the Merkels lived after moving out of Una's birthplace.
(Courtesy of the author and Therese Duzinkiewicz Baker)

Thinking back, Una described herself as a straight-laced girl, always scrubbed a bright pink and adorned with large hair ribbons. She rarely ventured outside to play. "I was shy," she explained. "I didn't make friends easily. I didn't know how to mix with people."[8] But Clyde Day, one of Una's childhood friends at the time, disagreed: "She had a lot of friends and was very popular in school," he countered. "She wasn't quiet . . . she was a typical girl."[9] Day said that his older cousin Virginia Day was Una's best friend, and the two girls often played together, sometimes with the nearly seventy dolls in Virginia's collection. He would sometimes tag after them and was even invited to Una's tenth birthday party.

Una had attended a Catholic church when she was younger, but she followed the Days to the Union Methodist Episcopal Church (later the First United Methodist Church), where she became an active member of the choir. Day also remembered that she used to come occasionally to the church's Sunday evening services that took place on the lawn when weather permitted. When asked about Una's distinctive Southern accent, which would become her trademark, Day confirmed that she had it even then, and it seemed natural and not some affectation.

Bashful or not, Una found that one activity brought her out of her shell—entertaining an audience. In January 1913, she recited a speech, "Youthful George Washington," which she wrote herself, at a meeting of the Mothers' and Teachers' Club. Several days later, at Covington's Odd Fellows Hall, she had the lead in an original musical play, *The Fairy and The Imp*, which had a cast of seventeen children. She was elated to win the leading role, but hadn't anticipated a few unpleasant side effects: "I got sick at my stomach with nerves and was scared to death. All dressed up—the fairy I was—with spindly legs and little knobby knees, and white stockings that lay in folds and looked more like long underwear on me than fairy garments."[10]

Now that she had a taste of acting, Una knew that she wanted to be a performer when she grew up. Her career choice was well received by her parents, who supported her vocation wholeheartedly. She began taking elocution, ballet, and acting lessons in Cincinnati from Helen Emma Reaume Power, better known simply as Patia Power or Tyrone Power, Jr.'s mother.

Bessie wanted her to play the piano, so a teacher was found in Covington.

Una, age twelve

Una once claimed she had as much talent for piano as a crawfish, but she applied herself to it with a steadfast devotion. "I practiced for hours and hours and hours," she noted. "I read the biographies of great musicians. I studied harmony. I went to recitals. And eventually I was able to render Bach and Chopin and MacDowell in a fashion that at least earned me the praise of accomplished musicians."[11] Despite her modesty about her playing ability, Una apparently left a very favorable impression on her teacher, who kept a large photograph of her prize student on her piano and spoke highly of her to other pupils.

If Una was blessed with musical talent, she didn't always enjoy the same favors from Lady Luck, who not only failed to smile down at her, but also seemed to laugh openly in her face. One time Una was in a little southern town and decided to try her luck in a church-sponsored raffle. "I was eleven at the time and skinny as a rail," she explained. "I bought a fifty-cent raffle ticket and won a hand-crocheted brassiere—size forty."[12]

***

On November 28, 1916, a Covington newspaper, the *Kentucky Post*, featured twelve-year-old Una on the front page in a photo that captured her trademark "merry eyes" and a floppy organdy bow atop her sandy blond hair. The occasion was the sealing of a "time capsule" inside the cornerstone of Covington's new Holmes High School. Following a parade led by the mayor, and with twenty thousand people in attendance, Una was an honored guest and participant in the day's events. After winning first prize for a written history of her school, Una had the honor of preserving her work for posterity. She was the youngest student to contribute to the capsule. Ever quick with a wry comment, she told a reporter that the chief requirement for placing the new school's cornerstone was "a great deal of walking."[13] She had walked thirty blocks to the event, but made it clear that she hadn't minded the effort because she hoped to attend the high school one day.

Una's poise at this public event came readily to her and could probably be attributed to her years of elocution, dance, acting, and piano lessons. A recent event may also have given her confidence. Just a few months earlier, she was one of the four hundred young girls who made up the ballet corps in the opening day performance of *The Big Show*, a Broadway revue that featured Anna Pavlova among other performers. Back home, however, Una's brief appearance on Broadway did little to impress her male classmates in the love department. "The boys didn't give me much of a tumble," she recalled. "I always longed to be popular with them. I wanted to be a different type—very beautiful and popular."[14] Her first crush was on Chokey Todd, a Boy Scout whom all the girls adored. Una lavished attention on him for several weeks, and he finally took notice, allowing her to wear his Scout pin for two "heavenly" days. "It was the shape of an anchor and pulled my dress down like the real thing," she recollected. "But I would have worn it proudly till Doomsday, until the weight of it had made me round-shouldered—if he hadn't sent another girl to ask for it back the following morning. I was probably just the unsuspecting instrument of a well-laid scheme to arouse jealousy in another feminine heart."[15]

Una survived this embarrassing moment and focused on what she did best—performing. In April 1917, she again graced the front page of the local paper, and the accompanying article reported that she had given a dramatic reading at a fundraiser to purchase a new piano for the Latonia Trinity Methodist Episcopal Church. Appearances like this one, along with her frequent roles in many local theatrical productions, caused some folks to jokingly ask if there were any talent shows or plays in the area that *didn't* feature the Merkel kid.

Una's life continued much the same until 1919. On January 6 of that year, the new Holmes High School opened its doors, but Una was not a student there as she had hoped to be. Instead, she learned that her family would be moving. After spending a few months with Arno's brother, Carl Merkel, in the Clifton neighborhood of Cincinnati, the family arrived in their new home—New York City. Their stay in the Big Apple, however, was short-lived. Arno wasn't convinced the family would be happy there, so they packed up their belongings and headed to Philadelphia, where Una enrolled in the Girls' Annex High School.

In the fall of the same year, Una's maternal grandmother came for a visit, and she and Una decided to go to a theater downtown to see Lillian Gish's latest film, *Broken Blossoms*. When they arrived at the theater, a man jumped out from behind the box office and came right up to them. "I wanted to say hello to you and tell you that you look a lot like my dear Lillian,"[16] he said. Una didn't recognize she was talking with D. W. Griffith, the director of the film, until he revealed his name. He was right about Una. At the time, she did bear a startling resemblance to Gish, having the same wide-set, china blue eyes, small mouth, and delicate features.

Una may have looked like a famous movie star, but she certainly didn't feel like one in high school. She realized it might be time to give up school altogether when she had no idea what the teacher was putting on the board when she saw her first algebra problem. Although it is widely reported that Una finished school in Philadelphia, the truth is she never graduated. She revealed this fact to a fan: "I only had six months in high school myself, and though I know I should not admit it, I am not sorry that I did not have more. There are so many ways in educating yourself besides attending daily classes."[17]

Nearly sixteen years old, Una broke the news to her parents that she didn't want to finish high school, but attend drama school instead. Again, her parents were sympathetic to her career aspirations. Arno, who was now traveling around promoting patents, moved the family to New York City, where Una would have more opportunities to pursue her dreams. According to many sources, it was around this time that Una supposedly worked as a stand-in for Lillian Gish in D. W. Griffith's *Way Down East*. Una, however, never once acknowledged appearing in the film. In fact, in a *Los Angeles Times* article appearing several years later, she publicly denied ever being Gish's double or understudy.[18] This confusion may have originally come about because both ladies worked together on a silent film called *World Shadows*.[19]

This film opportunity came about not long after Una enrolled in the Alviene School of Dramatic Art. There she met producer Jerome Storm, who was looking for a girl who looked like Gish to play a minor role in an upcoming film. When he saw Una, he knew he had his actress, but he still needed her to make a screen test. Una consented, but ended up not doing it because her maternal grandmother suddenly died, and she went back to Kentucky with her parents for the funeral. While she was away, Una learned that Storm would forego the test and hire her anyway. Thus, in the late fall of 1920, sixteen-year-old Una reported to the set of *World Shadows*, which was filming at the old Biograph studios. Another girl who had been hired didn't work out, so Una got her part, that of Gish's youngest sister who was blind. Una thought the film had a "marvelous story," but nobody ever got to see it because money for the project ran out, and filming was suspended.[20]

Nevertheless, the experience proved beneficial. Not only did it provide Una with her first taste of filmmaking, which she thoroughly enjoyed, but it also introduced her to Lillian Gish, who became a lifelong friend and confidante.

(ENDNOTES)

[1] Many online sources indicate that Una's birth name was Una Kohnfelder, which is categorically false. This error most likely came about from a misreading of the 1930 census, which indicates that the Merkel family was living at the Kohnfelder residence at the time. Una's birth certificate reveals that her birth name was indeed Una Merkel. Further proof can be seen in newspaper articles that appeared during her childhood. They all refer to her as "Una Merkel." For one example, see "Mothers Club Meets (Child, Una Merkel, Recited in Program at First Dist Sch, Covington)," *Kentucky Post*, January 10, 1913, 2.

[2] Richard Lamparski, *Whatever Became of. . . ?* radio interview with Una Merkel, WBAI, April 7, 1970.

[3] Weldon Melick, "Una Merkel's Untold Secret," *Picturegoer*, May 16, 1936, 8–9.

[4] Lamparski, radio interview with Una Merkel, April 7, 1970.

[5] Dallas MacDonnell, "Una Merkel," *Hollywood Daily Citizen*, June 29, 1931.

[6] Robert Fender, "Una Merkel—Picture Saver," *Movie Classic*, May 1935, 60

[7] Curtis Mitchell, "Ex-Sunday School Teacher," *Modern Screen,* September 1934, 101.

[8] Una Merkel, "Make Things Happen to You," *Movie Classic*, October 1936, 66.

[9] Clyde Day interview with author, March 12, 2007.

[10] Una Merkel, "Wallflowers Can Bloom," *Cosmopolitan*, June 1942, 28.

[11] Merkel, "Make Things Happen to You," 66.

[12] Liza (no last name provided), "The Opening Chorus" (A Letter from Liza), *Silver Screen*, February 1936, 4.

[13] "Little Folk Do Lots of Hiking in City Parade," *Kentucky Post,* November 28, 1916, 1.

[14] MacDonnell, "Una Merkel," June 29, 1931.

[15] Melick, "Una Merkel's Untold Secret," *Picturegoer*, May 16, 1936, 8.

16 Ray Neilson, radio interview with Una Merkel, Ray Neilson Celebrity Interviews Collection, University of Central Arkansas Archives, Sept. 1979.

17 Letter to Miss Avalon Benson (Author's collection), June 6, 1941.

18 Alma Whitaker, "What Chance Has Double?" *Los Angeles Times*, October 19, 1930, 9.

19 In at least one source, Una did acknowledge being Gish's understudy briefly in the initial days of production of *World Shadows* before being hired to play her blind sister.

20 Leonard Maltin, "FFM Interviews Una Merkel," *Film Fan Monthly,* January 1971, 4.

Chapter 2
Broadway Bound

If Una was making progress career-wise, she was still struggling personally and socially. She felt unattractive, awkward, and unconfident. In the summer of 1921, at the age of seventeen, she went to a Saturday dance at the Pine Grove Pavilion in Connecticut and was absolutely miserable the whole time, feeling very much the wallflower. While all the other girls had a special beau or two, Una didn't have any. She ended up dancing with her father and uncle, and some fathers of the girls she knew who came over and asked her to dance, out of kindness. "But I only felt more and more like a charity orphan," she recalled. The following year was only marginally better. This time she had a boyfriend, but her father, worrying that her date wouldn't remember to bring her a corsage, bought her one. "So there I was again. An escort of my own, but flowers by the family."[1]

Una had a better time at her drama school. She enjoyed herself there immensely and found it to be of inestimable value. She was careful to take copious notes of everything, reasoning that if her dream of being an actress didn't materialize, she could always become a drama teacher and pass along her extensive knowledge and experience to her future students.

School, however, didn't occupy Una's every waking moment. She also served as president of a Christian Endeavor Society and worked so diligently at her position that she raised the membership from sixteen to sixty-five. A religious college then offered her a scholarship, which she ultimately declined, but she did teach Sunday school in the Hamilton Grange Reformed Church, where a young Bette Davis was one of her pupils. Years later, thinking back on Una, Davis would say that she was a "lovely young person whom I liked."[2]

After *World Shadows*, Una found work in a few unimportant films made by the Lee Bradford Corporation, which one film scholar once described as never having produced a memorable film.[3] Those who worked for this company, which tried to film full-length pictures in only a few days, faced grueling schedules and inhospitable conditions. If directors went over schedule, they risked seeing their sets torn down the next day. It wasn't uncommon for the company to send cameramen home with actors to squeeze in extra footage. "I couldn't even get away for meals," Una recounted, "so my father used to come over every noon with a bucket of something—soup, I think it was."[4]

In late 1921, one of Una's drama teachers heard that a new production of *Hamlet* was being prepared for Broadway and suggested she try out for Ophelia. Una didn't know where to apply, so she asked her father to check with Earl Carroll, a famous composer, theatrical director, and producer. Arno reported back, saying, "I think you'd better go home and forget about this, Una. John Barrymore is to play Hamlet in that production."[5] Intimidated by working with someone of Barrymore's stature, Una abandoned the idea but made up her mind to start looking for acting jobs. She read the theatrical papers religiously, copied the names of all the Broadway producers from the phone directory, and began making daily rounds. Her father recalled, "That little girl went up and down Broadway rain or shine, from one end of the old street to another. Time and again she heard 'Nothing today!' But she stuck it out!"[6]

Una finally managed to snag a non-speaking role on stage as a cigarette girl in *Montmartre*, which played at the Belmont Theatre in the early part of 1922.[7] The following year she answered a newspaper ad from Lee de Forest, an inventor who had patented an optical sound-on-film process called Phonofilm. He was seeking actors for his one-reel sound films, so she went down to his studio. Everyone there was busily preparing to sing or dance, neither of which Una felt comfortable doing. She decided to recite one of her own poems and was subsequently given a small role in the film, which was called *Love's Old Sweet Song*. Una, who was uncredited, and a cast of six others participated in the story of an invalid woman (Helen Lowell) whose ownership of a marble quarry is threatened by a villainous bank clerk (Ernest Hilliard). Louis Wolheim played a tramp who foils the clerk's nefarious schemes. Una spent five days filming and received $100 for her efforts, but it wasn't an easy shoot. The rooms had to be padded, and the cameras were enclosed in cabinets to muffle their clicking. The sound recording process was complicated, requiring a constant readjusting of the recording apparatus to best capture the sound waves of each speaker. The resulting synchronized sound was limited and crude, but showed remarkable promise. The movie studios, however, were less than impressed, seeing it as little more than an imperfect novelty. Una was much more enthusiastic, and she excitedly spoke about it to her father, who took it to Canada, where he raised $250,000 for Lee de Forest. However, things didn't work out as planned, and Una lamented, "Neither de Forest nor my father had an ounce of business sense, so they lost the rights to the talking picture."[8]

Not long afterwards, D. W. Griffith hired her to be an extra in *The White Rose*, starring Carol Dempster and Neil Hamilton. Of her experience on this film, Una wrote, "A working extra has this advantage over a loafing star—she eats and enjoys life! I am happy to be working again after several days of doing just about nothing. Carol Dempster, Mae Marsh, and Neil Hamilton are in this film, and they all seem very nice . . . Neil is quite handsome and very, very polite!"[9]

Faced with sporadic jobs and inconsistent income, Una decided she could improve her prospects by becoming a model. Bernarr Macfadden hired her to appear in his *True Story Magazine,* where she was seen in a series of photos as an innocent country girl who comes to the city only to be betrayed by a young man she meets there. In some of the photos she held a baby in her arms, and she preferred those because they paid better: "Seems like a babe in arms is worth an even ten-spot!" she mused.[10]

Her modeling jobs ran the gamut from showing off the latest fashions to posing her beautiful hands. Some of her more unpleasant assignments involved modeling for an artist who refused to pay her. Then there was the time a foreign artist, a suave, worldly type, had more on his mind than artistic designs. Una recorded what happened in her diary:

> [The artist:] "Now, little gal, suppose you show me just how cute you look in a lil' bear skin an' also how nicely itty bitty girlsie can make love? You seem precious. I'm an affectionate soul, and I must have my little inspirations!"
>
> He got his little inspiration all right. As he came toward me, I clinched my fist hard and landed right on his jaw! He went down pronto, and I mean he *went down*. I grabbed my belongings and beat it up the street. Angry? I sure was, but as I write this, I am amused too. I never knew I packed such a wallop![11]

When she wasn't avoiding artists' amorous advances, Una was scouting for acting jobs, still hoping to make it big in motion pictures. She found her next opportunity in producer E. M. McMahon's sentimental, low-budget drama, *The Fifth Horseman*, in which she played female lead Dorothy, a girl with physical disabilities. The story revolved around Tom (Charles Brook), who turns his life around due to two men: John Franklin (Cornelius Keefe), a kind social worker who helps heal Dorothy; and Colonel Woodson (Leslie Stowe), a veteran of the American Civil War and current member of the Ku Klux Klan, who inculcates in his friend a love of God and country. This film, which was essentially a propaganda film for the Ku Klux Klan, was refused in certain first-run theaters throughout the country. *Variety* reported that when the film ran in Topeka, Kansas, not even the Klan came out to support it, and it was an unqualified flop, the worst that city had seen that season.[12]

Una in an unidentified production in the 1920s.

Realizing that she was getting nowhere in films, Una turned her attention to the stage, and redoubled her rounds at the casting offices. She later said that theatrical agents there, tired of seeing her loiter about so long, relented and gave her a job. True or not, in early 1925, she did get her first speaking role in a play, *Two by Two*, which starred Charlotte Walker. It was the story of an older lady (Walker) who falls in love with a young suitor, only to lose him accidentally to her bashful daughter. Una played an office clerk in a marriage license bureau and had only two lines, but she was grateful for the experience, which included befriending Walker, who took Una under her wing and taught her how to apply stage makeup correctly.

In the spring of 1925, Una was hired for Broadway's *The Poor Nut*. Her one and only scene found her up in a grandstand, yelling, "Come on, Wisconsin," as star Elliott Nugent raced past for his team. During each performance she got so caught up in the excitement of cheering that she would slap her legs enthusiastically, leaving them covered in bruises. Her twenty-dollar check each week helped soften the blows, and the job had another benefit: putting her in contact with other important producers, most notably John Golden. "I was learning by this time that if I were going anywhere, I'd have to adopt unusual tactics. So when I got a job as a super in *The Poor Nut* . . . I shrieked until John Golden's ears split. I'm sure he gave me a job in *Pigs* just to get me out of the grandstand so he could do some work in his office, which was within earshot."[13]

Una's yelling didn't get her the role in *Pigs*. She actually paid Golden a visit in his office one day and asked him if he might have a part for her. When he asked about her stage experience, Una was honest, explaining that she had very little. Golden, known for his "clean" and wholesome plays, saw something in Una that intrigued him. Maybe it was her candor, innocence, or distinct Southern accent, but he thought he might be able to use her one day in his productions. He gave her a ticket to attend a performance of *Pigs* and made her the understudy for the part of Lenore, then played by Rosemary Hilton. Golden's instincts were right. A few days later Hilton resigned, and Una took her place, continuing with the play for the rest of its run.

The public enjoyed this whimsical, moving tale of tenderhearted Thomas Atkins, Jr. (Wallace Ford), who tries to raise enough money to purchase two hundred fifty pigs that are ill with cholera so that he and his sweetheart Mildred (Nydia Westman) can nurse them back to health and resell them for a profit. The play was one of the most successful of the season, and when it closed in the summer of 1925, it had run for over three hundred performances.

Even though Una had been with the play for only a couple of months, she made a favorable impression on Golden, who signed a long-term contract with her. When Westman decided not to tour the play when it was revived in the fall of 1925, Golden gave her role to Una, who showed the public and critics that she could match or even surpass her predecessor's heralded portrayal. One New York newspaper critic commented that it was a privilege to experience Una's "meritorious" performance, witnessing her "moving through the entire performance with a sureness that delighted" the spectators.[14] The ease of her interpretation belied all the hard work that Una had put into the role. She told the press about being frightened to take on Mildred, but she loved playing her, being very sympathetic to her serious nature and determination.

Una was more coy about publicly discussing her growing attachment to Emerson Treacy, who played budding poet Spencer Atkins in the play. The two had plenty of time to get to know each other, traveling around for a year and a half until the play closed in early 1927. Their romance did not last much longer. It ended when Treacy decided to go to Los Angeles to write and perform with another theatrical company. Not long after arriving there, he fell in love with a young actress and got married.

In March of 1927, Una again replaced Nydia Westman. This time it was in Golden's hit play *Two Girls Wanted*, which was about a stenographer and her sister who hire themselves out as a cook and maid at a country estate where much business intrigue takes place. Una barely had time to get her feet wet in the show before Golden pulled her out to take the female lead in his farce, *The Gossipy Sex*. Lynne Overman had the starring role as an inveterate rumormonger who wreaks havoc in several marriages because of his unapologetic gossiping. This play met with mixed reviews, breaking Golden's string of hits, with most critics finding it only mildly amusing and lacking substance. The play was somewhat of a departure for Una, who was used to playing timid, ingénue roles. She had one powerful scene in which she had to give full vent to vehement emotion in an outburst of strength. Her emoting didn't merit a mention by most New York newspapers, including the *New York Times*, but a Brooklyn newspaper did find her portrayal "charming."[15]

Una, fifth figure from right, in *The Gossipy Sex*. (1927)

The Gossipy Sex fizzled after only three weeks, but Una got along so well with Overman that she decided to go on the road that summer with him and E. J. Blunkall in a vaudeville act. The six-week tour covered the Northeast but ventured west, with intended stops in Chicago and Louisville, Kentucky. Una was excited to perform in her home state, but Overman fell ill, and they had to cancel their appearance there.

In the fall, Broadway producer Jed Harris contacted her to see if she might be interested in playing Betty Lee Reynolds in his new play *Coquette*, which boasted Helen Hayes as the leading lady. Una was thrilled at the offer for many reasons, not the least of which was the possibility of playing opposite Hayes, one of her acting idols. She had seen Hayes in several shows and had admired her talent over the years. The only problem was that she had promised Golden just a few days before that she would take one of his plays on the road. She wrestled with what to do, spending a sleepless night before finally making up her mind. She went in to Golden the next day and told him that she didn't want to break her promise, so she was ready to go on tour for him. "Fine!" said Golden, pleased with her loyalty. "You will report immediately for rehearsal—with Helen Hayes in *Coquette*."[16]

Una Merkel, Broadway actress

Coquette tells the story of winsome flirt Norma Besant (Hayes), who gets pregnant by her boyfriend, Michael (Elliot Cabot), a shell-shocked war veteran. Furious over his daughter's lost virtue, Norma's father (Charles Waldron) shoots and kills Michael. Norma then must decide whether she will lie to protect her father by claiming Michael raped her. Andrew Lawlor, Jr. played Jimmie Besant, Norma's brother, while Una played a gawky Southern ingénue who wants to learn how to attract men.

In October 1927, the play opened in Atlantic City to tepid reviews. Hayes wanted out, but her mother, producer Harris, and playwright George Abbott believed in the play and persuaded her to be patient. Harris was in favor of pruning the text. The scenes with Una and Lawlor were the first ones on his chopping block, even though they were getting the biggest laughs, no doubt because the audience was desperate for some levity to relieve the dramatic tension. "Most of our scenes had to be cut," Una confirmed. "I didn't mind much because I realized it was necessary to the success of the piece, but if it hadn't been for Helen, much more of our roles would have been deleted. She insisted that they leave enough in to give us a chance to make individual hits."[17]

The troupe next traveled to Philadelphia, then on to New York, where the play was sold out for sixteen weeks. Una never forgot the mixed emotions she felt on opening night: "Neither Helen nor I could eat anything all day. We were perfect wrecks and kept wishing we were dead or could be magically transplanted to some place miles from there, so we wouldn't have to face that audience. Five minutes after we were out on the stage, we wouldn't have traded places with anyone in the world."[18]

The performance that night went without a hitch—no technical problems, missed cues, flubbed lines, or late entrances—and the audience gave the play a fifteen-minute ovation. Hayes came out for a curtain call and broke down in tears. The play took New York by storm and ran for three hundred sixty-six performances. Joseph M. Schenck, President of United Artists, and one of his producers, John W. Considine, Jr., saw the play and were summarily

Andrew Lawlor, Jr.

impressed, especially by Una's comic portrayal. In fact, Considine was so taken with both Una and the play that he wired Mary Pickford, urging her to buy it and to bring Una over to Hollywood to play in it. Pickford bought the play, but passed on Una, deciding to star in the film herself. (The film doesn't have Una's character of Betty Lee.)

Early in the run of *Coquette*, Una received a call from her father, who was still promoting films for Lee de Forest's production company. He told her that D. W. Griffith was at a nearby studio making screen tests, so she dashed over there and saw a number of actors, including Claudette Colbert, Sylvia Sidney, and Chester Morris. Una waited so long for her turn that she grew hungry. She bought a pastrami sandwich and was busy eating it when Griffith walked over. He mentioned having seen her before, and Una reminded him of their previous meetings. "I'd like to make a test of you for *Abraham Lincoln*, but I have to leave on the six o'clock train. Could you make a test without any make-up or anything?"[19] He also asked her to eat her sandwich for the test because he thought it would make for a pretty scene. Una agreed, but being so shy and self-conscious, she later admitted to worrying the whole time, thinking that she must have looked absolutely terrible.

As she stayed with *Coquette* and took it on tour, Una discovered that critics throughout the country loved the play as much as the public did, and she was getting their attention. Arthur Ruhl of the *New York Tribune* thought her performance was "one of those cases in which casting and directing are as much responsible as premeditated art, but, whatever the explanation, the result was just about as right as could be."[20] The *Los Angeles Times* reported that during a show the audience rewarded Una with special applause after her first exit from the stage. The review went on to say that she had "great personal facility and such perfect appreciation of the requirements of her ... character-drawing that it would be difficult to imagine her ever playing anything else."[21]

The cross-country tour provided Una and the other members of the company with very special memories. While in Pennsylvania, they performed in a town hit by a flood and were forced to walk on boards just to get to their dressing rooms. The spectators, meanwhile, were perched on undertakers' chairs to watch the show. In Boston, the players remembered two unusual incidents that took place during performances. One time a man became increasingly emotional as the play progressed. By the final act, he was sobbing and moaning so hysterically that the show had to be stopped long enough for him to be escorted to the exit. Another time an elderly pair of women in the audience caused an entirely different kind of disruption. During one of Hayes' particularly emotional scenes, one of the ladies leaned over to the other and asked loudly:

> "Hey, what did she say?"
> "She says she ain't."
> "Ain't what?"
> "Aw ... she says she ain't pure!"[22]

As the actors traveled throughout the country, they enjoyed picnics in

Wisconsin, parties in Chicago, shopping in San Francisco, trips to the cinema, and wonderful meals, sometimes in swanky restaurants, sometimes back in Hayes' hotel room. Romance was also in the air. Hayes met and married Charles MacArthur during the run, and Una became smitten with fellow troupe member Andrew Lawlor, Jr., a dark-haired Irish actor who had been a child star, the original Penrod in stage adaptations of Booth Tarkington's famous comic novels.

But all good things must come to an end. On July 20, 1929, a pregnant Hayes fainted after the matinee performance, and doctors warned that if she continued with the show, she risked losing her baby. The play closed immediately. It was a bittersweet moment for Una, who cried upon hearing the news, but she tried to put it in perspective: "I'm glad it ended that way," she said. "None of us realized it was our last performance, and it would have been a heart-breaking thing to all of us had we known."[23] Producer Jed Harris, however, didn't take the news so well. He refused to compensate Una, Lawlor, and three other actors in the cast for their two weeks' salary in lieu of notice, claiming that Hayes' pregnancy was an "Act of God," as stipulated in their contracts. The case was brought before arbiters who ruled against Harris, and he was forced to pay them an award totaling over $3,000.

In November of 1929, Una returned to John Golden for her next acting job in *Salt Water*. It's the story of John Horner (Frank Craven), a snack vendor on a night boat, who dreams of becoming a sea captain like his ancestors. Horner's pregnant wife, Pansy (Edythe Elliott), hoping to keep him around, buys the local ferry boat for him to operate. When it sinks, she must face his wrath and an uncertain future. Una's role was that of Marion Potter, a man-crazed adolescent who had her sights set on a dull-witted lifeguard (Alan Goode).

In her book *September Child*, Jean Dalrymple recounts Una's involvement in the production: "We had cast Una Merkel in "my" role ... I wanted the advantage of seeing the part played before I took it on. But Una Merkel made such a hit in the role that I never had the heart to take it away from her, and she went on to stardom."[24]

Reviews were mixed for this comedy, although most critics agreed it was well acted and reasonably funny in spots. The public, however, was more hesitant, and ticket sales were sluggish. The play lasted for only eleven weeks, a disappointing run for a Golden production.

Before it closed, Considine and Schenck caught Una's performance, and they were even more convinced of her cinematic potential. They telephoned Griffith and asked him to review the screen test that Una had done earlier. He liked what he saw, so Schenck called his friend John Golden to see whether he could secure Una for film work. Golden consented, bidding farewell to his young player, whom he called the "most even-tempered and most capable young actress on the stage."[25]

It wasn't long before Griffith offered her the part of Mary Todd, Abraham Lincoln's wife, in his upcoming *Abraham Lincoln*. He wasn't sure, however, that he made the right choice. He couldn't decide whether to cast her as Mary Todd or Ann Rutledge, Lincoln's first love. At one point he even confided to Una that he wished she could play both roles, but he finally assigned her Rutledge. United Artists tried to sweeten the deal by offering Una a year-long contract. She surprised everyone at the studio when she turned it down flat, explaining she was happy on stage and wanted to stay longer in New York. Studio officials argued that stage work was infrequent and the movie contract would assure her job security. But Una wasn't convinced. "Excuse me," she interjected, "but I have to contradict you. If anything, I've had too much work to do in my five years on the stage . . . what I really need is a holiday."[26] Studio officials assumed she was just wrangling for more money, so they countered with a more lucrative offer.

Una had a difficult decision to make. The money was certainly a factor, as well as the opportunities that films could provide, but her father's health was also a consideration. Arno had recently suffered a serious arm injury, and the general consensus was that the California weather would hasten his recovery.

Her relationship with Andrew Lawlor was more problematic. While she loved him, Una was beginning to question their future together. She saw that he had not made an easy transition from child to adult actor, and he was struggling to find work. Laden with all these conflicting thoughts and emotions, Una finally decided she would give California a try. She signed her contract with United Artists, gathered up her belongings, and left for the West Coast within twenty-four hours.

(ENDNOTES)

[1] Una Merkel, "Wallflowers Can Bloom," *Cosmopolitan*, June 1942, 28.

[2] Bette Davis, "Uncertain Glory," *Ladies Home Journal*, July 1941, 108.

[3] Anthony Slide, *The American Film Industry: A Historical Dictionary* (New York: Limelight Editions, 1990), 194.

[4] Kyle Crichton, "Something to Fight About," *Collier's Weekly*, April 2, 1938, 17.

[5] Madeline Glass, "Perky Merkel," *Picture Play Magazine*, May 1932, 26.

[6] "Film Star's Father Never Resents Being Called 'Una Merkel's Papa'," *The Times-Picayune*, December 19, 1946, 23.

[7] Una's participation in this play cannot be completely substantiated. For more information, see *Montmartre* under Una's stage credits.

[8] Leonard Maltin, "FFM Interviews Una Merkel," *Film Fan Monthly*, January 1971, 5.

[9] Una Merkel, "Up Pops the Past," *Screenland*, January 1936, 33. Note: The first page of diary entries are dated 1933, but they should read 1923. Subsequent entries seem to have the correct date.

[10] Ibid.

[11] Ibid.

[12] "Klux Film Real Cluck," *Variety*, January 14, 1925, 23.

[13] Wood Soanes, "Una Merkel Tells Why She Stays on Set When She Might as Well Be Taking Good Rest Elsewhere," *Oakland Tribune*, September 16, 1934, 7.

[14] "Love and Pigs Themes of Closing Play in Van Curler," *Schenectady Gazette*, December 18, 1926, 16.

[15] "'The Gossipy Sex' at Mansfield,'" *Brooklyn Standard Union*, April 20, 1927, 8.

[16] "There's Only One Una," *Picturegoer*, Oct. 19, 1935, 15.

[17] Laura Ellsworth Fitch, "A Goddess to Merkel," *Picture Play*, August 1933, 69.

[18] Ibid.

19. Maltin, "FFM Interviews Una Merkel," 5.
20. Arthur Ruhl, "Second Nights," *New York Herald Tribune,* December 25, 1927, 1.
21. Edwin Schallert, "Love-Honor Clash Thrills," *Los Angeles Times,* July 3, 1929, 7.
22. Maud Cheatham, "Four Girls," *New Movie Magazine,* November 1933, 86.
23. Ibid.
24. Jean Dalrymple, *September Child: The Story of Jean Dalrymple* (New York: Dood, Mead, 1963), 105.
25. "Roland West Brings Back Mystery Hit," *Washington Post,* December 7, 1930, 2.
26. Cedric Belfrage, "Shy and Sincere: Una Merkel Believes in Being Herself," *Motion Picture Magazine,* September 1930, 77.

Chapter 3
Hollywood

On February 10, 1930, Una arrived in Hollywood by train. Her parents did not accompany her (they would arrive shortly), so she knew virtually no one in the city, except for Emerson Treacy, her former sweetheart from *Pigs*. He and his new wife met her at the train station, got her settled in an apartment, and introduced her to their acquaintances, among them Dick Jordan, who quickly became a dear friend. Una recorded her thoughts about her new home in her diary: "Here I am in the world's most publicized city. It's a bit different from what I pictured it, but I like it and really think I am going to like it a whole lot more as time goes on."[1] She also wrote John Golden a long letter, expressing her excitement about her upcoming role, and included several poems she had written.

Una had little time to get acclimated to her new surroundings because filming for *Abraham Lincoln* began on February 24. Her role of Ann Rutledge was challenging because she wasn't sure how to play it. The character seemed unreal to her, one created on paper. (Una's intuition was perhaps more correct than she realized because some historians think that Ann Rutledge's relationship with Lincoln is more legend than fact.) Una expressed her concerns to Walter Huston, and he had an idea. They would rehearse their scenes together that evening, and while running their lines, they would use their real names instead of their character's names, making the scenes more believable.

When filming began, most of it was shot chronologically according to the script, but this was not true of Una's three scenes. Her first one before the cameras was her death scene. For a seasoned stage actress like Una, who was used to working into her character, polishing and refining it as a play progressed, shooting scenes out of sequence was disconcerting. "What I miss mostly on the stage," she told the *Los Angeles Examiner*, "is the continuity of emotion. You assume a character with the rise of the curtain, and you live with it until the curtain falls. In pictures, you may play your last scene first, or the big climax on your first day."[2] She predicted that motion pictures would eventually be filmed differently, more like plays, "in continuity," as she put it, allowing an actor to "grow in his or her character and give a performance that was doubly sincere because it was one . . . actually lived through."[3] Her reservations notwithstanding, Una manages a beautifully rendered death scene. It was so effective that many of the people on the set wept. Una nuanced the death with little flourishes and touches that were very reminiscent of her friend Lillian Gish, and years later Una revealed just how much Gish had influenced her characterization: "I began to imitate her in every possible way. I tried to make-up the way she did, aimed to affect the Gish style of acting, and came to behave very much as though I . . . were her shadow."[4]

In another scene, Una and Huston find themselves in a peaceful, bucolic

Walter Huston and Una Merkel in D. W. Griffith's *Abraham Lincoln*. (United Artists, 1930)

spot on a farm, sitting beneath a large tree and surrounded by lush vegetation, in what one film historian sees as a "typically romantic Griffith landscape."[5] This scene was reproduced for some of the posters used to promote the film, ostensibly to play up the romantic storyline, even though Ann Rutledge appears in only ten minutes of the film. This is the scene in which the amorous couple confess their love for each other, with Abe proposing marriage and Ann graciously accepting. Once again, both actors deliver a poignant performance, with Una showcasing her ability to vary the emotional register throughout the scene. She is intermittently sweet, innocent, earnest, and wistfully demure, all of which imbue the scene with emotional veracity and real pathos.

Una's third filmed scene was the rail-splitting one, in which she sits atop a woodpile and helps Lincoln study law as he tries to split logs. This scene, when it played before a preview audience in early May of 1930, was not well received, so Considine ordered it reshot, this time without Griffith's direction. This scene introduced Una's character to the audience, and she took full advantage of it. In perhaps her most memorable moment, she takes a very realistic and humorous tumble backward off the logs, screaming for Abe as she falls. In addition to this physical exploit, she gets a chance to show off her emotive ability, conveying Ann's naivety and childlike innocence with a masterful range of gestures, facial expressions, and modulations in the timbre of her voice. She injects just the right amount of tenderness and humanity into her appearance, lifting her above Huston's excessive makeup and the saccharine dialogue that strains the bounds of credulity.

Film historians over the years have had mixed feelings about Una's performance. Anthony Slide was brutal in his assessment, saying it is "the worst case of miscasting in the history of the cinema."[6] Peter John Dyer thought that she played her death scene "appallingly" and compared her to a "simpering nanny goat."[7] The majority of critics in 1930, however, were laudatory. One reviewer, waxing poetic, compared Una to Griffith's other actresses, saying she was as "spiritual as Lillian Gish, as lovely as Carol Dempster, with a quality of loveliness as intangible as the twilight mists which veil the rose bowers. . . ."[8] In the October 1930 issue of *Photoplay* magazine, Una's acting was recognized as one of the best performances of the month. Griffith certainly believed in Una, and he remained one of her greatest champions, hailing her at the time as the "greatest natural actress now engaged in pictures."[9]

Years later when discussing the film, Una spoke of Griffith's kindness and gentleness and described him as a "wonderful director and a wonderful man,"[10] but she also recalled his looking tired and not offering much direction. Griffith corroborated Una's memories in a statement given around the film's release: "I did not direct them. It would have been presumptuous for me to tell them what to do; to tell them how to act. I merely sat on the sidelines to give suggestions when requested."[11]

Throughout her career, Una rarely, if ever, had anything but words of praise for her colleagues or directors, but in one interview, she was a little more forthcoming. She spoke frankly about Griffith, and not all of it flattering. Maybe her candor came from knowing that the interview would appear in a Brazilian publication, or perhaps she was simply in a particularly loquacious mood: "I have never seen a director who is more demanding and more severe than he is," she began. "High-handed. Even selfish—but his selfishness is pardoned. Every great artist is selfish about his art . . . Griffith is not . . . personally selfish. He does not treat his artists with severity or even a certain brutality just for the work to end up being a Griffith film. . . . He loves the cinema. This is why he *kills* his artists. He makes them work long hours without a break, repeating, changing, and doing everything over again which, in his opinion, is not perfect. . . ."[12]

Despite these remarks, Una once stated that she didn't remember any tension on the set, but there was one incident she would have liked to have forgotten. While sitting on the set, watching scenes being filmed, Una suddenly felt her chair shaking and heard a voice whispering in her ear, "Come on and stretch, sister, we've got to hurry up this scene!"[13]

Una as Sybil in *The Eyes of the World*. (United Artists, 1930)

John Holland and Una in *The Eyes of the World*. (United Artists, 1930)

Hugh Huntley, Nance O'Neil and Una in *The Eyes of the World*. (United Artists, 1930)

Before she knew what was happening, a young man yanked her chair out from under her and dumped her unceremoniously onto the floor. The perpetrator, a prop man, was absolutely mortified to see it was Una who was sprawled out before him. "I sure am sorry about this, Miss Merkel," he exclaimed. "I thought it was just your stand-in for this scene that was sitting there airing herself!"[14]

Una had ample opportunity to get some fresh air in her next film, *The Eyes of the World*, an adaptation of a novel of the same name by the popular writer Harold Bell Wright. Director Henry King took a group of one hundred forty technicians and his cast to Santa Ynez Canyon, located about thirty miles from Santa Barbara, for several weeks of filming in the great outdoors. Una plays the leading female role of Sybil, a mountain girl who falls in love with a sophisticated city boy. The two struggle to reconcile their very disparate views of the world, but after some harrowing adventures, they learn to accept their differences and forge a conjugal life together.

While working on this second film, Una learned that she still had a lot to learn about the logistics and rigors of filmmaking. For one scene, King needed Una to jump from a steep embankment into a shallow pool of water. He asked if she wanted a double, but Una refused, explaining that she could swim. King explained that the stunt involved a certain risk, and if she injured herself, the production would lose time and money. Unmoved, Una did the scene herself. As filming progressed, she found it very taxing and much more difficult than her work on the stage, which at least let her rehearse. Of her experience in *The Eyes of the World*, she lamented: "we were compelled to employ our nights after a hard day's work studying the lines for the next day. One doesn't mind the labor at first, but when it continues for five or six weeks, it tells on one's nerves and health. I personally lost six pounds while making the picture."[15] She was equally unhappy about her wardrobe, wondering why they dressed a girl of her height in such short frocks. As the female lead, she also didn't like the emphasis placed on her physical appearance, nor the effort required to be photogenic for the camera. She grumbled, "I suppose this turning of one's face so as to get one's best camera angles is necessary . . . but I don't like it. I don't want even to think how I look. I just want to act a part."[16]

Although it was Una's second Hollywood film, *The Eyes of the World* premiered in New York on August 14, 1930, nearly two weeks before *Abraham Lincoln*, much to the chagrin of the *Los Angeles Times*, which thought that Una deserved a more credible role to introduce her to the filmgoing public. *New York Times* critic Mordaunt Hall found the film "muddled and lethargic," but praised the photography and settings.[17] He also extolled Una's performance, characterizing her as "wistful and charmingly natural in most of her scenes . . . with a pleasing spontaneity which is a contrast to some of the work of the other players."[18] Una, however, had no illusions about the film and called it "unfortunate."[19] Commenting about contemporary films and plays, she suggested the film's melodramatic and sentimental nature might have made it unpalatable to modern audiences: "People don't go to the theater merely to have their feelings combed out," she remarked. "They want something besides mere sobby entertainment."[20]

Even with two Hollywood films under her belt, Una was still having trouble getting used to life on the West Coast and her new film career. After *The Eyes of the World* came out, she told a reporter, "I suppose it is my big chance, and all that sort of thing, but I can't quite feel my feet on solid ground. It doesn't seem quite real."[21] After a short time, her parents moved out to California to live with her, but she was working so hard that she hardly had time to socialize. Plus, she was leery of the pernicious effect that Hollywood seemed to have on actors and their craft: "I think most of the people who come out here tend to run to seed. They very seldom increase in artistic stature, so to speak."[22]

Andrew Lawlor was one of many such actors who ventured west in search of work in Hollywood, but he also had an ulterior motive—to see and woo his beloved Una. He arrived shortly after the release of *Abraham Lincoln*. To someone as lonesome as Una, his arrival might have been a godsend, providing her just the impetus she needed to go out and make new friends, but just the opposite occurred. Una began pulling away from others, and she lavished all her free time, energy, and attention on Andrew. Family and friends began to worry about such singular devotion, but they didn't know that Una's actions were motivated less by love than by fear of hurting him. Una's time away from Andrew only confirmed what she had already known—he was not the man for her, and their love would never lead to marriage. Try as she might, Una could not bring herself to tell Andrew the sad truth, so she suffered in silence.

Una's next film did little to lift her flagging spirits. It was *The Bat Whispers*, directed by Roland West. It is a mystery-comedy that revolves around Cornelia Van Gorder (Grayce Hampton), a dowager who, accompanied by her personal assistant, Lizzie (Maude Eburne), and niece Dale (Una), spends the night in a sprawling manor that is menaced by a mysterious criminal called The Bat. Capitalizing on the public's fascination with sound pictures, the film was touted as "the picture of a thousand sounds," and these noises ran the gamut from shrieks, sinister whispers, shattered glass, and creaking doors, to sliding panels, thunder claps, and heavy footfalls.[23]

Not to be outdone by auditory elements, West also filled his film with striking visual imagery: spooky shadows, eerie lighting, vertiginous camera movement, and masterful cinematography. To make his final product even more grandiose, West even chose to film one version of his production on extra-wide 65mm, known as Magnifilm. He also filmed a standard 35mm version for those theatres (nearly all of them at the time) that were not equipped with the special projection equipment needed. While the wide film format ran in only a handful of theaters across the country, those who saw it were impressed. Los Angeles columnist Jimmy Starr recounted how audience members became so caught up in the action during a viewing that they screamed out warnings to the actors.

If filmgoers appreciated the wide-screen spectacle, the same could not be said for the cast during the arduous production. Someone targeted Una for a prank and hooked up electrical wires to her chair, zapping her when she sat down. The usually affable Una broke into tears but immediately apologized for her outburst, saying she was just tired. She then went on to lose fifteen (some sources say twenty) pounds during the seven-week shoot, much of it due to the heat of the Klieg lamps. Leading man Chester Morris didn't fare much better under the intense lights. His eyes became red, and they burned and watered excessively, telltale signs of "Klieg eyes." William Bakewell, who was Una's close friend and her on-screen boyfriend in the film, remembered director West as taciturn and idiosyncratic. He was not necessarily disagreeable, but definitely a taskmaster. "He would only work at night," Bakewell recalled. ". . . we would work from seven o'clock at night until seven in the morning. We went home like we'd crawled out from under a rock. . . . You'd shoot a scene, and he'd [West] walk away to the other side of the stage, and he'd say 'OK, Cut! Print it!' and he didn't look at it; he just listened to it."[24]

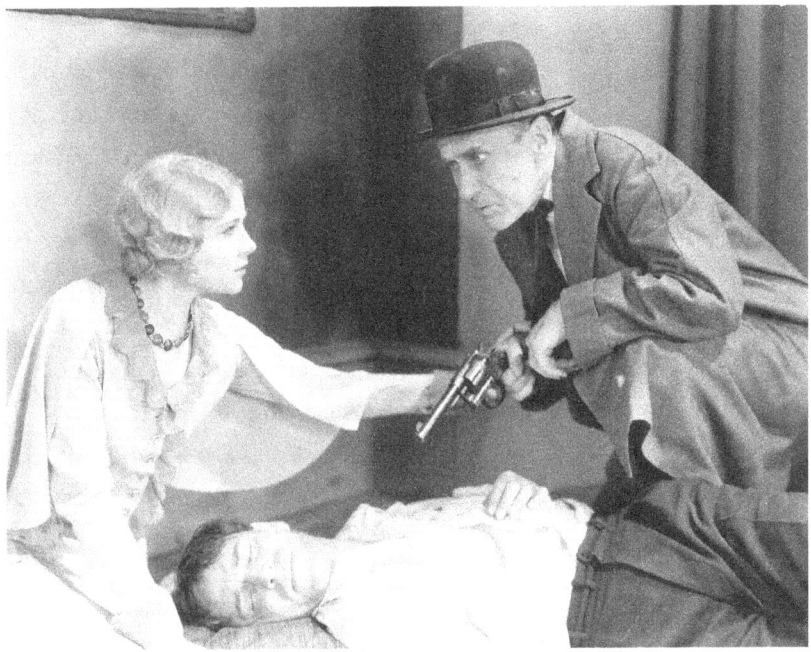

(Left to Right) Una, Ben Bard, and Charles Dow Clark in *The Bat Whispers*. (United Artists, 1930)

Una thought that West shot the film at night to avoid any interference from the studio, but newspapers at the time wrote that his decision was based more on his desire to conceal the identity of "The Bat" and create just the right atmosphere.

The *New York Times* was only lukewarm towards *The Bat Whispers*, saying it was "moderately effective," and "well directed," but also a "waste of time."[25] As in most of the reviews, Una is only briefly mentioned as a youthful beauty, which underscores just how little she had to do except look decorative. Chester Morris gives a competent, if somewhat overplayed performance, but his sharp, chiseled features are what really take center stage. They are spookily illuminated by cinematographers Ray June and Robert H. Planck, who worked on the 35mm and 70mm versions, respectively. Grayce Hampton played the wealthy grande dame to perfection. Her imperious mien and cultivated demeanor are a welcome contrast to Maude Eburne's nervous shrieks and silly behavior, which are humorous, but quickly become tiresome.

In the early fall of 1930, Andrew was called back to New York, where he was given a small part in a play that was to open in December. Una wished him well, thinking this new role might revive his career, but at the same time she hoped it might be the start of a new life for him, one without her. She still didn't see a marriage with Andrew in her future, so she knew she would have to do the inevitable—break off the relationship. But how?

Una didn't have much time to consider her options because United Artists loaned her out at the end of November to play the female lead in *The Command Performance*, a film directed by Walter Lang and distributed by Tiffany Productions, which one film scholar labeled the "MGM of the independents."[26] The film takes place in two mythical kingdoms, Sherblandt and Kordovia, supposedly somewhere in the Balkans. The prime minister of Sherblandt hopes that a marriage between prince Alexis (Neil Hamilton) and Princess Katerina (Una) of Kordovia will unite the two countries and stave off conflict with a rival kingdom. The problem is that Alexis has no desire to woo the princess, especially after several of her previous suitors have died mysteriously. Hamilton also plays Peter Fedor, an actor who resembles the prince and is persuaded (after being threatened with imprisonment in the salt mines) to impersonate the prince and win Katerina's hand in marriage.

Una and Neil Hamilton in *The Command Performance*. (Tiffany, 1931)

Helen Ware, Vera Lewis, Una, and Albert Gran in *The Command Performance*. (Tiffany, 1931)

The film is breezy entertainment that capitalizes nicely on its romance, humor, and suspense. Albert Gran, who plays the king to Una's princess, supplies many of the laughs, while Hamilton handles his dual roles with necessary aplomb. In one beautiful outdoor scene, Una is seen walking across her palatial estate, accompanied by a pair of Afghan hounds. She meets Hamilton under a tree for a romantic rendezvous. In this scene and many others, she looks appropriately regal in her many costumes, which include a stunning velvet evening gown and a pearl-studded bridal gown of ivory chiffon and satin.

While the film's dialogue is occasionally trite, Una improves upon it by infusing her lines with gentle drollery and charm, both of which allow the audience to see a part of Una that had been sorely lacking in her earlier films—her sense of humor and natural ebullience. Most critics liked the film and Una's contribution to it. The *Los Angeles Times* found her "particularly outstanding,"[27] while *The International Photographer* noted that "Miss Merkel ... supplied the high spot of the production...."[28]

* * *

Una celebrated her twenty-seventh birthday on December 10, 1930, and one of her belated birthday presents was the news that she would soon start production on a new film, this time for the Fox Film Corporation. John W. Considine, Jr., who had worked with Una on *Abraham Lincoln*, was largely responsible for her new job. He had left United Artists a month earlier and was now working at Fox Studios. He remembered Una's fine comedic performance in *Coquette* and thought she would be perfect as a Southern girl in *All Women are Bad*, a film that would hit theaters under the title *Don't Bet on Women*. Because there were problems with the script, Una didn't receive it until a few days before shooting began. That same evening she received word from New York that Andrew was gravely ill in the hospital, suffering from complications from an appendectomy. Una tried to focus on learning her lines, but she had a terrible sense of foreboding that would not go away. She became so worried that she felt compelled to send him an urgent telegraph. She confided that it contained "everything I knew he wanted to hear. Even though some of the things by then were not wholly true. It's not fair to press upon people the unhappy truths when they're having a bad time. Later on, if they get themselves in hand, [it] is time enough."²⁹

Andrew received the telegram shortly after midnight, and he reportedly lay there smiling, holding it tightly in his hand. He was too weak to read it, but he refused to let anyone else read it to him. He died on December 13, 1930, surrounded by his family members. He was only twenty-two years old.

(ENDNOTES)

1. Una Merkel, "Up Pops the Past," *Screenland*, January 1936, 76.

2. Jerry Hoffman, "Miss Una Merkel Studies Stars," *Los Angeles Examiner,* August 24, 1930.

3. "Una Merkel Tells of Difficulties that Face the Stage Star in the 'Talkies,'" *The Eyes of the World* pressbook (Inspiration Pictures, 1930), n.p.

4. W.H. Mooring, "My Dizzy Dame," *Film Weekly*, October 18, 1935, 10.

5. Arthur Lennig, "There is a Tragedy Going on Here which I Will Tell You Later:" D. W. Griffith and Abraham Lincoln," *Film History: An International Journal* 22 (2010): 55.

6. Edward Wagenknecht and Anthony Slide, *The Films of D. W. Griffith* (New York: Crown Publishers, 1975), 252.

7. Peter John Dyer, "Death of a Mandarin—D. W. Griffith," *Sight and Sound* 28 (1958–9): 46.

8. Robbin Coone, "Hollywood Sights and Sounds," *Oswego Palladium-Times,* March 17, 1931, 3.

9. "The Show Window," *Hartford Courant*, December 11, 1930, 17.

10. Ray Neilson, radio interview with Una Merkel, Ray Neilson Celebrity Interviews Collection, University of Central Arkansas Archives, June 1978.

11. "Stop Us If We're Wrong," *Motion Picture News*, September 6, 1930, 93.

12. Gilberto Souto, "Una Merkel," *Cinearte* 404 (December 1, 1934) 32. (Translated from the Portuguese)

[13] Merkel, "Up Pops the Past," 76–7.

[14] Ibid.

[15] "Una Merkel Tells of Difficulties that Face the Stage Star in the 'Talkies,'" *The Eyes of the World* pressbook (Inspiration Pictures, 1930), n.p.

[16] Cedric Belfrage, "Shy and Sincere: Una Merkel Believes in Being Herself," *Motion Picture Magazine,* September 1930, 77.

[17] Mordaunt Hall, "The Screen" (*The Eyes of the World*), *New York Times*, August 15, 1930, 22.

[18] Ibid.

[19] W.E. Oliver, "Una Merkel Fits Needs of Role," *Los Angeles Evening Herald,* December 13, 1930.

[20] Ibid.

[21] Belfrage, "Shy and Sincere," 77.

[22] Ibid, 106.

[23] *The Bat Whispers* pressbook (Joseph M. Schenck Productions, 1930), n.p.

[24] William Bakewell, *Hollywood be Thy Name* (Metuchen, NJ: Scarecrow Press, 1991), 102.

[25] Mordaunt Hall, "The Screen" (*The Bat Whispers*), *New York Times*, January 16, 1931, 27.

[26] Michael R. Pitts, *Poverty Row Studios, 1929–1940* (Jefferson, NC: McFarland, 2005), 223.

[27] Whitney Williams, "Journey to the Balkans," *Los Angeles Times,* January 25, 1931, 3.

[28] George Blaisdell, "Looking in on Just a Few New Ones," *The International Photographer,* January 1931, 18.

[29] Caroline Somers Hoyt, "The Unknown Love of Una Merkel," *Movie Mirror*, December 1935, 73.

Chapter 4
Fox Studios

Una was supposed to begin working on *Don't Bet on Women* not long after Andrew's death, but she was too distraught to work. She explained her situation to director William K. Howard, and he granted her some time to compose herself. The film marks Una's first real comedy, and it is a bright, sparkling, sophisticated concoction that teeters on the brink of farce. Roger Fallon (Edmund Lowe) has soured on love and says that all women are bad. His attorney friend, Herbert Drake (Roland Young), thinks the fair sex are simply overgrown children who need to be reined in. Despite his cynical attitude, Fallon remains so confident of his ability to woo ladies that he bets $10,000 that within forty-eight hours he can kiss the next female he sees.

Drake takes him up on the offer, but his enthusiasm quickly cools when his wife Jeanne (Jeanette MacDonald) arrives, becoming the object of their wager. The film follows a crazy trajectory, keeping viewers engaged and guessing until the very end, wondering if Jeanne will succumb to Fallon's charm or remain faithful to her increasingly worried husband.

Una plays Tallulah Hope, a flapper of questionable intelligence, who makes a real splash in her opening scene, when she goes for a swim, flounders, and has to call out for help. Fallon rescues her, brings her back to his yacht, and gives her a drink to steady her nerves. She gulps some down and begins coughing. "What was that awful stuff I just drank?" He tells her it was some very good gin, but Tallulah shoots back, "Don't you believe it. It's been cut to ribbons." Una didn't think the line was funny at all, but during a showing, she was surprised at the audience's favorable reaction. "It got more laughs than any other line in the picture," she recalled.[1]

Other funny lines followed in the same scene when Fallon puts his hand on her stomach to see if he can feel the live fish she thinks she has just swallowed. His hands drift a little lower than anticipated. "That's not my stomach," she scolds. "That's my abdomen . . . I don't think you're interested in fish, anyhow!" If the public laughed heartily, some of the censors did not. Several found the whole fish scene objectionable and ordered it deleted, while others just asked that the suggestive dialogue be removed.

Like the censors, Jeanette MacDonald was not amused. She wrote a friend, stating that the film really wasn't her picture, and she also complained about looking "unpretty."[2] Perhaps her insecurity about her looks stemmed from not having her favorite cinematographer, Charles G. Clarke, but some of the blame might be placed on her wardrobe. In one scene, she appears in unflattering jodhpurs, while in another, she dons an ill-fitting dress that draws unfavorable attention to her bust line. These sartorial issues notwithstanding, several critics commented on her screen presence and fine acting, which was all the more impressive since she did not sing a single note. MacDonald was right, however, in thinking the film was stolen away from her. Most reviewers singled out Una and Roland Young as the film's most effective players. In describing Una, the *New York Times* said she aired an "adolescent philosophy with marvelous assurance, all of which is done in a Covington (KY) drawl, accompanied by capital acting."[3] The *Hollywood Daily Citizen* asserted that she provided the best humor of the picture, noting she was attractive and clever, and "her childlike simplicity is touched with just enough piquancy to make her thoroughly interesting."[4] Una, it seems, had found her niche—comedy—and the critics and public were uniformly impressed, none more so than the studio heads at Fox, who definitely saw her potential.

Don't Bet on Women wrapped in the middle of January of 1931, when Una had around a month left on her contract with United Artists. The studio became increasingly frustrated because they had tried to fashion her into a serious dramatic actress, but with little success. Una diagnosed the problem—her squeaky voice. "They thought I was the Gish-y type," she began, "fluttering through the night, sort of a waif in the storm. Nobody laughed at me then. Even at home, nobody laughed at me because they were used to my voice. I suppose I never meant to be funny. I was going to be a great dramatic star. But then talkies came, and I opened my mouth and everybody began to laugh."[5]

United Artists loaned her out to Warner Bros. for two films. The first was *The Bargain*, which stars Lewis Stone as Maitland White, a man who gave up his dream of being an artist to marry Nancy (Doris Kenyon) and manage the family's soap-manufacturing business. Greatly distressed at seeing his artistic son, Roderick (John Darrow), also renounce art, Maitland reevaluates his own missed opportunities and decides to take up painting again. He needs a model, and Ella (Una), the family's ambitious housekeeper, reluctantly obliges. Charles Butterworth plays Maitland's friend Geoffrey, a witty doctor who also sacrificed his dream—becoming a writer—for his medical practice.

During production, two minor nuisances, both of the animal variety, disrupted filming. First, while shooting a garden scene, the crew heard strange recurring noises off stage. A search was done, and the culprit turned out to be a wayward frog. The second incident involved a group of flies that kept buzzing relentlessly around Butterworth everywhere he went. Nothing seemed to deter them until someone figured out they must be attracted to the

J. M. Kerrigan and Una in *Don't Bet on Women*. (Fox, 1931)

Lewis Stone and Una in *The Bargain*. (Warner Bros., 1931)

oil he used in his hair. Studio hands concocted a paste of sugar and water and placed it around the room, drawing the flies away from the exasperated actor.

Robert Milton directed *The Bargain*, but did so with such impassivity that the actors were never quite sure what he thought of their interpretation. It is debatable whether his "hands-off" approach had any substantive effect on the finished film, but what is certain is that critics were generally unimpressed with the results, one of them calling the film "bloodless" and "pale."[6] Nevertheless, most of them had positive remarks for Una. The *New York Times* reviewer stated she capitalized on her part and reduced the audience to tears of laughter, especially when trying to convey various emotions as a makeshift model.

One evening after a day's filming of *The Bargain,* Una was going over her lines when a messenger from Warner Bros. delivered her a script for another film, *The Maltese Falcon*. Una sent the script back, instructing the messenger to tell the studio they made a mistake. She was already doing a film. As Una remembered, studio officials "got a kick" out of her naivety, and they sent back a note explaining that the script was indeed hers[7]; she was expected to film two films at the same time. Una was incredulous. "It had never occurred to me," she said, "that I could be that much in demand."[8]

The first film adaptation of Dashiell Hammett's *The Maltese Falcon* (1931) has been eclipsed by director John Huston's classic 1941 version, but it has much to recommend it and makes for intriguing viewing, with its plot twists, suspense, excellent pacing, and fine characterizations. Ricardo Cortez is a convincing Sam Spade. Slick, suave, and flashing an unctuous smile, he plays the detective with relish. He even impressed Hammett who said that Cortez was "perfect" and showed "keen judgment and cool courage—making Spade human under temptation and altogether normal in his reactions to all sorts of trying situations."[9] Ruth Wonderly (Bebe Daniels) is a beautiful woman who initially enlists Spade's help in finding her missing sister, but eventually embroils him in the search for the eponymous jewel-encrusted statuette. Daniels plays the alluring Wonderly with considerable finesse, wearing a blond wig, which she and the studio believed would draw softness out of her features, helping to convey the cool, hardened uncertainty of her character.

Una plays the small but notable role of Effie, Sam Spade's steadfast secretary. With her fair complexion and blue eyes, she doesn't exactly match Hammett's physical description of Effie in his book (she is described there as sunburned and brown-eyed), but she makes the role her own and does an admirable job of communicating the ambiguity of Effie's and Spade's special rapport, especially any past or present physicality. In the film, it's almost as though the two engage in a complicitous dance, sallying back and forth near each other, almost but never quite meeting as real dance partners should. Spade kisses the back of Effie's neck, calls her "honey," comments on her physique, and holds her hands so fervently that she nearly has to wrench them away at times. In return, Effie responds with playful teasing, knowing glances, fidelity, and utter obeisance, but she stops short of becoming Spade's latest conquest or possession. This interplay with Cortez is captivating and leaves viewers wishing for more scenes with them together.

Una playing the alluring secretary Effie to Ricardo Cortez's Sam Spade in the first film version of *The Maltese Falcon*. (Warner Bros., 1931)

Apparently, Cortez had hoped their on-screen chemistry would translate into something more romantic off-screen. He was attracted to Una, and one of the things that drew him was her tentative nature and palpable fright during filming. "I felt sorry for her," he confided, "for I thought her one of the sweetest girls I had ever met. I wanted to invite her out, but hesitated."[10] He finally mustered the courage to ask her, and they had an enjoyable time at dinner. The relationship, however, never developed further because of their respective insecurities. "I could never ask her out again, for I was sure she was disappointed in me," Cortez explained.[11] He was afraid she would expect him to be more like his womanizing persona on the screen, while Una later told him she had tried to be sophisticated, thinking he would prefer someone more worldly, seductive, and exotic.

Una's next assignment at Fox was the screen adaptation of the hit Broadway play *Six Cylinder Love*, which had starred Ernest Truex. In this version, Truex's role of Gilbert Sterling was essayed by the slight, but earnest Lorin Raker, who played the film's dramatic moments well, but was less impressive in the comedic ones, lacking Truex's light touch. In the film, Gilbert and his wife, Marilyn (Sidney Fox), face financial ruin when they buy an expensive car from a silver-tongued salesman (Spencer Tracy). Panned by most critics, the film desperately needs, as one newspaper noted, "oil, gas, sparkplugs, and six more cylinders."[12] Una plays Margaret Rogers, one of the Gilberts' sponging "friends," and aside from her oversized hats, she is hardly mentioned in the reviews. The atmosphere during production was tense. Spencer Tracy had been granted top billing, but he had a small role and didn't disguise his anger at having to do the picture. He argued frequently with director Thornton Freeland and castmate Edward Everett Horton, and the latter remembered him as unfriendly and "terribly nervous" during production.[13] The film ended up losing more than $25,000 and did nothing for Una's career or that of her colleagues.

Not knowing what to do with Una, United Artists decided not to renew her contract. Fox Studios snapped her up, hoping to capitalize on her distinct voice, accent, and comedic abilities. Her first film for them under contract was

Daddy Long Legs, which turned out to be one of the studio's most financially successful films of 1931. By this time, the story was a stale chestnut, having been performed on Broadway two different times by Ruth Chatterton and adapted to screen by Mary Pickford. Nevertheless, Fox Studios knew the story had great family appeal, so they decided to update it a bit, all while keeping the story's simple charm intact. Janet Gaynor plays Judy Abbott, an orphan whose college education is paid for by a mysterious benefactor (Warner Baxter), whom she affectionately calls Daddy Long Legs. The film is a sentimental love story, but wins over viewers with its engaging characters, humor, pathos, and wholesome entertainment values. As antiseptic as it is, it still ran afoul of some censors, who objected to seeing Gaynor change a diaper on screen. These same censors were inexplicably silent, however, about Baxter's dubious line in which he says he would spank Gaynor except he was afraid she might enjoy it too much.

Gaynor is a pleasure to watch in this film. She is so endearing that she wins over viewers' attention and sympathy right away, although her infantile voice can initially be jarring and distracting. Una plays Sally McBride, Judy's socially awkward best friend, to perfection. She is given great lines to showcase her characterization, delivering them in a southern accent so thick you could cut it with a knife. One memorable scene has her exclaim, "thrilling, sadistic delight," to describe what she feels as she holds a reluctant male admirer in her grasp. Una capitalizes on her scenes and succeeds in stealing away a few moments of the spotlight. At one point, Fox executives even talked about making a sequel that would feature Una's role, but it never happened.

As for the men, Baxter demonstrates he is the consummate professional. He handles his scenes with poise and a smooth assurance, but it is John Arledge who proves even more impressive in his role as Jimmy McBride, brother to Una's Sally and handsome beau to Gaynor's Judy Abbott. At times there are fleeting vestiges of theatricality in his acting, but more often, something very modern and natural emerges. It also doesn't hurt that he delivers some of the funniest lines in the film. At one point he is asked what he will be when he

Una and Janet Gaynor in Fox's *Daddy Long Legs*. (1931)

finishes college, and he grins and replies, "An old man," and then he bleats like a billy goat, drawing his fingers together in front of his chin like a beard.

Daddy Long Legs was Arledge's first major film at Fox, and it was during this film that he first met Una. It didn't take them long to realize they had much in common. Arledge's Southern accent was every bit as prominent as

Una's, and he got it naturally, being born in Crockett, Texas. His family, like hers, had no connection to the entertainment field. His father supported the family as a grocer. Arledge, who was very musical, played the piano very well and dreamed of being a professional musician. His musical talent had brought him to Hollywood, where he first made a name for himself in local theatrical productions before finding bit roles in films. He was amicable and down-to-earth, but could also be quiet, retiring, and somewhat of a loner. He became one of Una's best friends, and he and Dick Jordan were her most frequent escorts to Hollywood functions. Arledge also became Una's favorite lunch partner, and they were seen so often together that they became the subject of gossip. Newspapers hinted at a possible romance, but Una squelched such rumors, maintaining that Arledge was just a friend. She cited her strenuous work schedule as keeping her far too busy to date seriously.

John Arledge

Fox Studios certainly did work Una hard, barely giving her an idle moment. John Considine, Jr. placed her in another film he was producing—*Wicked*, starring Elissa Landi. It is a weeper about a young lady (Landi) who endures everything from a robbery, accidental shooting, imprisonment, motherhood, and kidnapping in a film that clocks in at a meager fifty-seven minutes. When asked about the fast pace of the film, director Allan Dwan joked that he must have had a date at the time and was in a hurry to finish it. When pressed further, he blamed it on impatience, saying, "I don't like things dragged out. People catch on, and it spoils the picture for them. It's better to get along with it."[14]

 Una proves to be a bright spot in the otherwise gloomy proceedings, providing much needed comic relief as Landi's friend, a fast-talking Southern gal who, as one critic described her, "runs on and on in a high, vague voice, never stopping for breath or an idea and never seeming to miss either."[15] If her performance as a ditzy lady was convincing on screen, Una's ignorance about certain filmmaking practices sometimes called into question her own intelligence. After working on the film for a while, she was sent home and told she would not be needed for a few days. After three days and no word from the studio, Una began to panic. She rushed to the set to speak to Dwan: "With sinking heart I asked why I had been taken out of the cast and what I had done that was wrong. They all looked at me as if I had suddenly had a brain storm."[16]

In early July, Dick Jordan introduced Una to one of his good friends, Ronald Burla. Born in Montana, a graduate of Harvard Military School and later Oregon State University, where he studied mechanical engineering and business law, Burla was a dark-haired aviation engineer, whose good looks often got him mistaken for a movie star. Una was immediately attracted to him, finding him not only handsome but also very dignified. She later admitted that it was love at first sight.

Ronald also felt a spark when he met Una, but his amorous feelings were nearly extinguished before they even caught flame, when, during one of their early meetings, he accidentally dropped her puppy, breaking one of its ribs.

Flowers and apologies helped to make amends, and the couple kept seeing each other at home, but they never ventured out for a single date. Both were guarded and had certain reservations about their blossoming romance. Una resorted to her standby defense mechanism: "I tried to hide it," she recalled. "I didn't think he liked me. I had been in Hollywood for a while then, and I had got used to being kidded and called 'darling' and 'sweetheart' whether they meant it or not. And Ronnie didn't act that way at all."[17] As for Ronnie, he was a bit intimidated by Una's success and still unsure about her sincerity, so when she agreed to a second date, he never followed through. They remained on good terms, but their relationship simply coasted along, not developing any further. Ronnie went out with other girls, while Una continued making public appearances with her family, Dick Jordan, John Arledge, and other colleagues.

That same month Una began work on her second picture with Spencer Tracy, *She Wanted a Millionaire*, which recounts the story of William Kelley (Tracy), a railroad worker, who falls in love with beautiful Jane Miller (Joan Bennett), only to be spurned in favor of Roger Norton (James Kirkwood), a wealthy suitor. Una is Mary Taylor, Jane's wisecracking journalist friend, who's not afraid to throw back a couple drinks to help William commiserate. Tracy didn't like the material, which swings radically from light romance to lurid melodrama, and he was peevish and a bit distant when filming began. Gradually, as shooting progressed, he settled down and proved to be a fine partner to Bennett, whom he enjoyed teasing unmercifully between takes. Their working relationship didn't last long, though. On July 28, Bennett was seriously injured after being thrown from a horse while filming a scene, and production ground to a stop. It wouldn't resume for six months.

Fox Studios, hoping to squeeze a bit more work out of Una, soon loaned her out to appear in *The Secret Witness*, a mystery comedy that was produced by Famous Attractions Corporation, a Poverty Row studio, but it was distributed by Columbia Pictures. It's the story of a young woman who commits suicide from a penthouse balcony, and the complications that follow: the penthouse owner's murder, and the mounting evidence that points to the woman's brother as the main suspect. Amateur detective Lois Martin (Una) doesn't believe the brother's guilty, so she sets out to find the real killer.

Seeing Una investigate the spooky crime scene, one is reminded of her scouting out the dark, mysterious mansion in *The Bat Whispers*. This time, however, she has much more to do than simply look decorative. As the film's leading player, she carries the film admirably, putting in a pleasing, yet intelligent performance that complements the suspenseful, well-written story and its clever ending. Playing it straight, she doesn't get any laughs, which fall to ZaSu Pitts, a fluttering telephone operator. Screenwriter Sam Spewack uses Pitts' on-screen naivety to sneak in a clever joke. Describing a book she is currently reading, Pitts explains to a friend that it's about some sort of well, but she doesn't quite understand it. The audience then sees her book—Radclyffe Hall's *The Well of Loneliness*—a real book that had gained some notoriety at the time for its treatment of lesbianism.

* * *

Around this time, Una paid a visit to her dear friend Lillian Gish. Una's contract with Fox was about to expire, so it's possible that she sought Gish's advice about whether or not to stay with the studio. She may also have been entertaining offers from other studios. Whatever the case, not long after their meeting, a casting director at Fox spoke to her about her future at the studio, and their exchange was a lively one:

> "We'd like to keep you, Una, at just what you're making, but we can't give you the raise that your contract calls for."

> "What, after making seven pictures in six months?"

> "Well, it's better to be on the inside looking out than the outside looking in."

Robert Montgomery (Elyot) and Una (Sibyl) tying the knot at the beginning of *Private Lives*. (MGM, 1931)

"You mean that if I didn't sign with you, I wouldn't get a job any place else?"

"No," he said, "but you're here."[18]

The casting director was leaving to go on vacation, and he told Una to think about his offer while he was away. In the meantime, MGM called saying they wanted to test her for a part in a film adaptation of Noel Coward's *Private Lives,* which he had performed so successfully on Broadway. She agreed to audition, but was still committed to *The Secret Witness.* The day before her big MGM screen test, she reported to work on *The Secret Witness,* worked until two in the morning, returned home, and went straight to bed. She didn't get a wink of sleep, though, being so wound up and nervous. When morning arrived, she made her way over to Metro to make the test. She waited two days before learning she got the part, but MGM had even bigger news for her. The studio wanted to offer her a seven-year contract. Not hesitating a bit, Una signed on the dotted line to become part of the most prestigious, most glamorous studio in all of Hollywood. Lil' Una had finally arrived!

(ENDNOTES)

[1] Katherine Albert, "Modern Screen's Dramatic School," *Modern Screen*, September 1935, 91.

[2] Edward B. Turk, *Hollywood Diva: A Biography of Jeanette MacDonald* (Berkeley: University of California Press, 2000), 105.

[3] Mordaunt Hall, "Screen News" *New York Times*, March 7, 1931, 23.

[4] Marjorie Ross, "Don't Bet on Women," *Hollywood Daily Citizen*, February 20, 1931.

[5] Winifred Aydelotte, "They didn't Mean to be Funny," *Photoplay*, February, 1935, 55.

[6] Relman Morin, "The Bargain," *Los Angeles Record*, September 18, 1931.

[7] Jerry Asher, "Una Merkel Scorns Sad Offstage Mask of Most Comedians, *Brooklyn Times-Union* (*Screen & Radio Weekly* Supplement*),* January 12, 1936, 3.

8. Ibid.

9. Dashiell Hammett, "*The Maltese Falcon* Author Defends Much Maligned Detectives," *The Maltese Falcon* pressbook (Warner Bros., 1931), 4.

10. Jerry Martin, "Hollywood's Most Sensitive Actor," *New Movie Magazine*, September 1934, 93.

11. Ibid.

12. Relman Morin, "Six Cylinder Love," *Los Angeles Record*, July 3, 1931.

13. Larry Swindell, S*pencer Tracy: A Biography* (Cleveland, OH: New American Library, Inc., 1969), 91.

14. Peter Bogdanovich, *Allan Dwan: The Last Pioneer* (New York: Praeger, 1971), 94.

15. Winifred Aydelotte, "Wicked," *Los Angeles Record*, October 23, 1931.

16. Jerry Asher, "Una Merkel Scorns Sad Offstage Mask of Most Comedians," *Brooklyn Times-Union* (*Screen & Radio Weekly* Supplement*)*, January 12, 1936, 3.

17. Gladys Hall, "Twenty-three Men—and Never Been Kissed," *Motion Picture Magazine*, November 1933, 83.

18. Leonard Maltin, "FFM Interviews Una Merkel," *Film Fan Monthly*, January 1971, 6.

Chapter 5
Marriage

Even though Noel Coward and Gertrude Lawrence played the leads in *Private Lives* to rave reviews in London and on Broadway, the two did not reprise their parts in MGM's film. Instead, the roles went to Robert Montgomery and Norma Shearer. Rehearsals for the film began in September of 1931, but Una was not available the first week because she was still finishing up work on *The Secret Witness*. Contract player Mary Carlisle read Una's part during her absence.

In *Private Lives*, an English couple—Amanda and Elyot Chase—divorce and marry Victor and Sibyl, respectively (Reginald Denny and Una). Both couples go to the French Riviera for their honeymoon and, unbeknownst to the other, accidentally end up in neighboring suites in the same hotel. Once Amanda and Elyot see each other again, they realize that they're still in love. They abandon their new spouses and steal away together, trying to rekindle their romance. It isn't long before their old problems begin to resurface, not to mention Victor and Sibyl, who track them down to settle things once and for all.

Una's Sibyl is a far cry from the kooky, off-beat Southern gals she had played at Fox. Decked out in glamorous gowns designed by Adrian, including a wedding dress in the opening scene of the film, she is very much the posh, European sophisticate. To play the part, Una affects a British accent, but not entirely successfully. She sounds, as one writer puts it, like a "spoiled plantation belle," and like her character's namesake, her words are "sibilant—the vocal equivalent of frilly doilies."[1]

Although Sibyl's accent is inconsistent and her voice a bit odd, they are not enough to make her an engaging character, nor does her character win any favor with wisecracking quips or one-liners. What makes her memorable and sets her apart is her uncanny ability to cry, and to do so loudly—if not shrilly—and very often. When silly, vacuous Sibyl starts bawling, look out! You're in for quite a spectacle, which probably accounts for Robert Montgomery's wry comment that MGM offered Una a contract because she cried so effectively in her first film at the studio.

Sibyl seems to appeal to two different dimensions of viewers' psyche or perhaps a combination of them: the first that sympathizes with her as a poor, unfortunate, put-upon target of others' scorn; and the other that sees her as a sniveling, over-wrought ninny, deserving all the contempt she gets. Viewers in the first camp acknowledge that, while she is not totally innocent, she does seem to get more than her fair share of slurs, insults, and barbs. Amanda, for instance, describes her as "insipid" and "shallow." Victor calls her an "ass," and her own "loving" husband says she is as "obstinate as a mule" and threatens to decapitate her with a meat ax. He even tells her to go and choke herself. Those who fall in the second camp, join in and perhaps even revel in her misery, waiting expectantly for her next blubbering meltdown. With viewers both for and against her, Sibyl emerges as a compelling character worth watching, and Una's interpretation generates much of that interest.

That Una portrays Sibyl so effectively might be attributed to a few similarities between actress and character. First, both were highly sensitive women who wore their feelings on their sleeve and were able to cry and emote easily. Sibyl is superstitious, just like Una, who had lucky numbers and wore a pair of black shoes as good luck charms. Both were skilled piano players, but not natural-born dancers. Finally, Sibyl admits having a talent for organization, not unlike Una, who reportedly was very organized and methodical off-screen.

Overall, reviews for *Private Lives* were very positive, with most critics agreeing that Shearer and Montgomery put in first-rate performances. Denny and Una were often cited for their sterling support. The *Los Angeles Times* particularly enjoyed Una's portrayal, claiming she was the "brightest" part of the film.[2] Her greatest validation, however, came from Noel Coward himself. Nearly four years after the film's release, he attended an important MGM luncheon and made a point of looking up Una. He wanted to tell her how much he had enjoyed her performance. Understandably moved, Una could only gush, "To think he remembered that!"[3]

* * *

Ronnie Burla decided he would host a Halloween dinner party that year. His date for the evening was actress Rochelle Hudson, and he invited five other couples, one of them his good friend Dick Jordan, who came with Una. During the course of the evening, Una and Ronnie danced together, and they discovered that their special feelings for each other had not diminished. Ronnie asked Una out again, and she accepted. As much as she wanted to date him, she didn't feel comfortable doing so until she got her father's blessing. Una had to wait until Arno returned home from his job in Europe. He gave his consent, but she still didn't get to see much of Ronnie due to her grueling

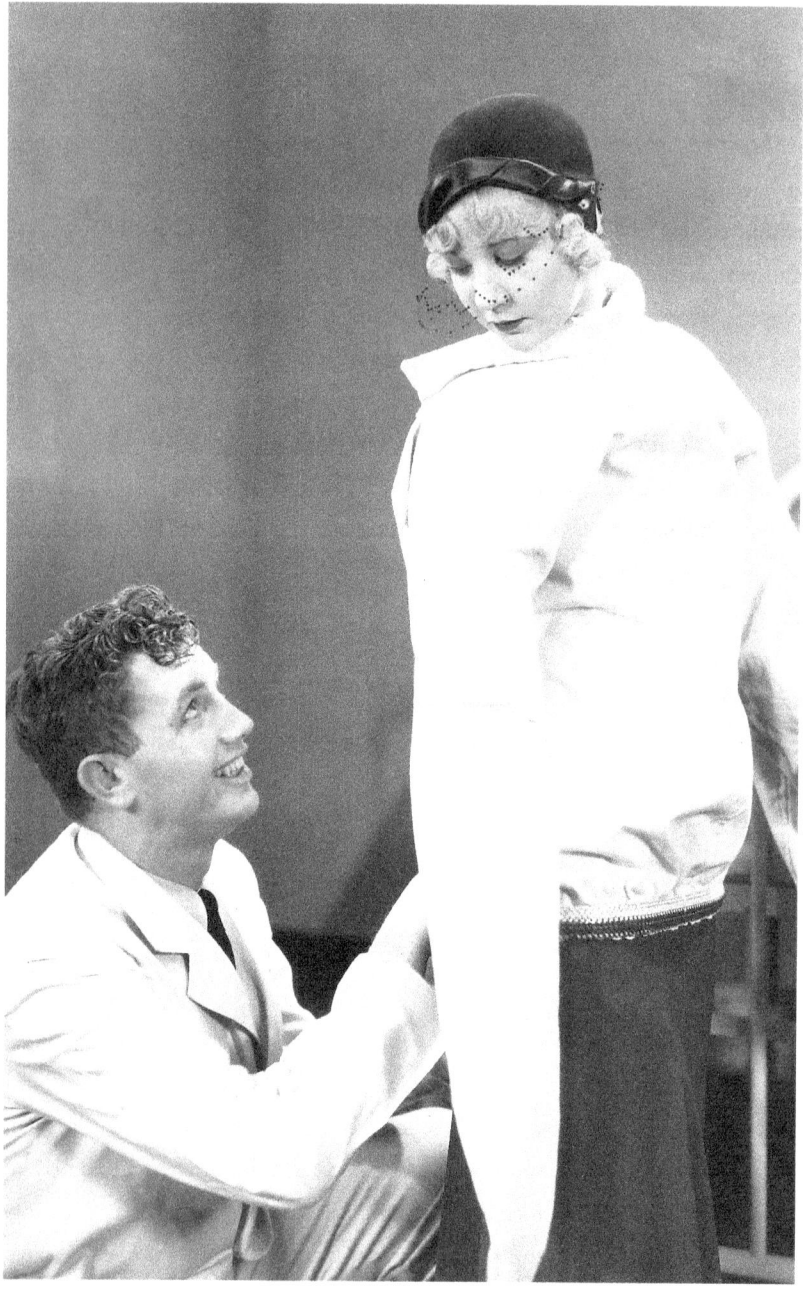
Una testing out Andy Devine's new zipper straightjacket in *The Impatient Maiden*. (Universal, 1932)

studio schedule. When the couple finally went out on their next date, they solidified their commitment to each other by getting engaged.

In early November of 1931, Una went to the hospital to have her tonsils removed. The procedure gave her some time to catch up on her reading and to relax a little before starting her next picture, which was slated to begin the following month. In her diary at this time, Una noted that she was really starting to like Hollywood—everything, that is, except the rain. She recorded the story of her coming home one evening from the store and seeing a "Road Closed" sign. It was getting late, and knowing her mother was waiting for her, Una plunged ahead anyway, thinking that the road couldn't possibly be that bad. Before she knew it, her car was stuck in a muddy embankment. Then a "lovely-faced" lady walked up to the car and asked if she could be of some assistance.[4] Una explained her predicament, and the woman called a nearby garage. Not wanting the woman to be out in the cold, Una suggested that she go back inside her home, but the woman refused. "Oh, I wouldn't dream of leaving you out here all alone," she insisted. "I shall remain until I see you safely on your way."[5] Una thanked the woman profusely and the lady kept talking, asking Una about her acting and Broadway plays. It was only then that Una recognized her gracious rescuer—Mrs. Leslie Carter—a renowned actress known as the "American Sarah Bernhardt."

Una returned to work in December, and MGM loaned her out to Universal for *The Impatient Maiden*, directed by James Whale, whose successful *Frankenstein* had premiered just weeks earlier. Not a horror film, *The Impatient Maiden* relates the burgeoning romance that develops between a medical intern (Lew Ayres) and a cynical secretary (Mae Clarke). Una was back to form as Betty, a sassy flower shop girl who is so mouthy that she is accused of having "sunburned tonsils." As Clarke's best friend and love interest to Andy Devine's "gentleman" nurse, Una's Betty is delightful, and she adds piquancy and infectious energy to every scene she's in. Her valuable contribution, however, was not enough to redeem the film for Andre Sennwald, reviewer for the *New York Times*, who was unimpressed, discounting it as something that "nestles naïvely on the back stairs of cinema."[6] The film

The Burlas and Merkels: (clockwise) Bessie Merkel, Ronald Burla, Una, Arno Merkel.

didn't do much better with the *Los Angeles Times*, which found it "tedious" and "unconvincing," but extolled Una, stating that her harebrained character gave the film its only vitality.[7]

The critic was no doubt referring to Una's hilarious scene in an insane asylum, where she foolishly tries on Devine's newly designed zipper straightjacket only to get stuck inside. As he leaves to find something with which to cut her out of it, she struggles to free herself, ranting and raving with increasing agitation, arousing everyone's suspicions that she's probably a mental patient herself. The scene stretches on a bit long, and Una comes perilously close to overacting. "The director told me not to rehearse the scene," she remembered. "I was just to imagine myself in that predicament and try to get loose. That scene lasted for five minutes, and I struggled, screamed, and wrenched. I was black and blue when it was over, but the scene got a lot of laughs."[8]

Una's parents' wedding anniversary was on January 1, so when New Year's Eve rolled around, Arno and Bessie decided to celebrate in Agua Caliente, an entertainment center in Tijuana, Mexico. They knew how hard Una had been working, so they invited her to accompany them, thinking it would do her good to get out and relax a little. Arno even suggested that she invite "that nice young chap, Ronnie Burla, to go along," which she did.[9] On the way down, Una and Ronnie discussed marriage, and they decided they would marry that spring. They weren't sure, however, how to break the news to Una's parents. Sensing what was in the works, Arno gave them the opening they needed:

> "Now your mother and I can see you two want to get married. Why don't you help us celebrate our wedding anniversary and do it?"
>
> "And wait a whole year?" Una asked.
>
> "It will be our wedding anniversary in five minutes."[10]

Knowing that it would take three days to obtain a license in California, the couple headed to Mexico, with Una's parents serving as witnesses. "We didn't like that Tijuana touch," Una conceded, "but it couldn't be avoided, if we were to be married on January 1st."[11] Una didn't even have a trousseau and didn't stop to buy one, but she was more demanding about her corsage. She had always dreamed of having orchids and wasn't willing to compromise. Ronnie tried to convince her that it would be difficult to find orchids on New Year's Day, but Una was adamant. He came up with a possible solution and raced into the Agua Caliente Casino, finding a woman who had a few of the elusive flowers. Ronnie persuaded her to lend them to him for the brief wedding ceremony, and he returned them to her afterwards. Being in such a hurry, he didn't even catch her name.

Una and Ronald lived with Una's parents in this home in Outpost Estates, a hillside residential area above Hollywood.

If Ronnie was a little put out with the orchids, he managed to keep his sense of humor about the actual ceremony. He joked that it must have looked like a shot-gun wedding, with three Merkels noted on the wedding license.

Una, too, had fun telling about their accommodations: "We had a bungalow at Coronado [California], and mother and I had one room, and father and Ronnie the other. And, when we came back from Tijuana, we had to change our luggage all around."[12]

Although Una had just gotten married the day before, she knew that a honeymoon was out of the question. She was required to report to Fox Studios at 9:00 a.m. to resume shooting on *She Wanted a Millionaire*, the film that had been started the previous summer but suspended after Joan Bennett's injury. She and Ronnie got in their car and left Coronado early in the morning. They stopped momentarily on their way to get some fruit and were surprised to see the news of their wedding splashed across the newspaper. They were, as several newspapers reported, the first Hollywood couple to marry in 1932. They resumed their journey, but had to turn round not long afterwards when Una discovered that she had left one of her wedding gifts behind. After retrieving it, they were back on the road, racing back to Hollywood as fast as they could. Una knew that time was of the essence, so she went ahead and did her own makeup and hair on the way, using the car mirror as a guide. They sped into the studio without a moment to spare, and Una spent the morning introducing her new husband to the cast.

When *She Wanted a Millionaire* finally appeared in theaters, it met with only a lukewarm reception. Most critics liked the actors' performance, but didn't care for the storyline, which started out promising, but got progressively dark and implausible. One reviewer said it "slugs itself right on the chin and at the finish is still on the floor. Result is a talker yarn that . . . will have to struggle for its returns everywhere."[13]

Una's experience and skill are clearly evident in her few scenes with Tracy. She has no problems keeping up with him, and they complement each other very well. Una's presence and comedic talents prove to be real assets, offsetting the film's more sober moments and improving an otherwise uneven story. Bennett, radiant and sumptuously attired, is beautiful, sincere, and appealing, and she puts in a convincing performance that skillfully expresses her character's timidity and fear.

Una poolside with her dear friend Madge Evans.

Una was again loaned out to Warner Bros. for her next film, *Man Wanted*, which has the distinction of being Kay Francis' first film at that studio. Francis plays Lois Ames, a successful magazine editor married to a womanizing playboy (Kenneth Thomson), who prefers polo and the jet-set life to her. She compensates by burying herself in work and is smitten with her handsome secretary, Tom (David Manners), who is engaged to a feisty flapper (Una). Andy Devine plays Manners' intellectually challenged best friend. It is difficult to know, as film historian Jeanine Basinger points out, whether this film is "a romance, a plea for female equality, or a celebration of the work ethic, but it *is* an example of role-reversal, and a positive one for the most part."[14]

Although driven along by a paper-thin plot and little action, the film is slight, but strengthened by some fine performances. Francis' acting is insightful and polished, and she oozes charm and allure as she parades around in her stunning designer gowns. If she liked her attire, she cared little for her co-workers' unprofessionalism. "Andy Devine and I behaved very badly," Manners confessed. "We were whooping it up one day, and Kay Francis walked off the set. She sent back word that she'd return when those two 'apes' quieted down."[15]

While her male colleagues were channeling their inner monkeys, Una was playing the thankless role of Ruth, who gets engaged to Tom when he is "swanked" on alcohol. Ruth is excited about the impending nuptials, but Tom has second thoughts but can't verbalize them. He becomes even more estranged from her as he falls deeper and deeper for Lois. He conveniently "forgets" about Ruth, stands her up on dates, refuses to take her calls, and avoids her whenever possible. Confused, but still very much in love, Ruth pursues Tom until she discovers the awful truth. Then her love turns sour, and she confronts Tom and Lois in a memorable scene of jealous fury. The *Los Angeles Times*' Philip Scheuer felt that Una, despite her zeal, was miscast. Devine fared better with critics, capitalizing on his squeaky voice and dull-witted shenanigans to emerge as an endearing character. He, not Una, elicits most of the film's laughs.

***

Una told a reporter that she and Ronnie would be living at her home because she didn't have time to choose a new house and furnish it. The couple's abode, which they still shared with Una's parents, was in Outpost Estates, a modern hillside residential area above Hollywood that boasted concrete sidewalks, decorative street lamps, and underground utilities. Their beautiful Spanish-style house was spacious, but sparse on accoutrements—swimming pool, tennis court, or sunken garden—that were commonly found at the homes of other Hollywood luminaries.

The couple settled down to a happy existence, and married life seemed to agree with Una. She explained to a reporter, "If I couldn't have had a marriage as sweet as that of my parents, I wouldn't want to have married. And even if I have never had a 'fling' except vicariously on the screen, I wouldn't change one thing in my life. I have found happiness."[16]

(Endnotes)

[1] Steve Vineberg, *High Comedy in American Movies* (Lanham, Md.: Rowman & Littlefield, 2005), 19.

[2] Edwin Schallert, "Private Lives Unfolded," *Los Angeles Times*, Dec 14, 1931, 7.

[3] Cal York, "Cal York's Gossip of Hollywood," *Photoplay*, June 1935, 37.

[4] Una Merkel, "Up Pops the Past," *Screenland*, January 1936, 77.

[5] Ibid.

[6] Andre Sennwald, "A Naive Melodrama," *New York Times*, March 4, 1932, 17.

[7] Norbert Lusk, "*Impatient Maiden* Wanders With Little Vitality," *Los Angeles Times*, March 13, 1932, 9.

[8] Katherine Albert, "Modern Screen's Dramatic School," *Modern Screen*, September 1935, 91.

[9] Ruth Biery, "I Bet I Stay Married," *Modern Screen*, May 1935, 84.

[10] Ibid.

[11] Madeline Glass, "Perky Merkel," *Picture Play Magazine*, May 1932, 64.

[12] Biery, "I Bet I Stay Married," 84.

[13] Unidentified clipping, production file, *She Wanted a Millionaire* (Fox Film Corporation, 1932), Academy of Motion Picture Arts and Sciences.

[14] Jeanine Basinger, *A Woman's View: How Hollywood Spoke to Women, 1930–1960* (New York: Knopf, 1993), 274.

[15] James R. Parish, *The Hollywood Beauties* (New Rochelle, NY: Arlington House Publishers, 1978), 79.

[16] Ben Maddox, "Don't Gamble With Love," *Romantic Movie Stories*, Sept. 1934, 92.

Chapter 6
One of the Busiest Gals on the Lot

"Here I am. A bride," Una told a writer. "And I'm wearing the same three nighties I always had. No romance about me, I guess."[1] Perhaps no romance, but Una's accent was still there, and it was the talk of the town and local newspapers. Una was reportedly the star attraction at one of Jeanette Macdonald's parties, with everyone clamoring to hear her Southern drawl. One reporter highlighted her accent in one of his columns, quoting her phonetically, "Ah sutinly wouldn't talk this way unless Ah wuh brought up down thair!"[2] Another journalist equated her conversations to a "Baptist Sunday school picnic down in Alabama."[3] Even columnist Louella Parsons couldn't resist jumping on the bandwagon, confessing how much she enjoyed listening to Una's "intriguing" accent: "We have had so many affected Southern accents," she began, "but Una's is the real thing."⁴ True, but Una supposedly loathed it—at least throughout the 1930s—and she was dismayed that it hadn't diminished since her arrival in Hollywood. She also knew, though, that her accent got her noticed, and it may have been what initially led Warner Bros. to consider her for the role of Madge Norton, daughter of a cotton plantation owner in *The Cabin in the Cotton*. Ultimately the coveted part went to Bette Davis, whose performance caught critics' attention.

After *Man Wanted*, Una was back on the MGM lot in *Huddle*, a Ramon Novarro vehicle that featured the Mexican actor as a young Italian-American steelworker who leaves the Midwest to attend Yale, where he becomes a star football player. Physically, Novarro is not right for the part, but he manages to eke out a mostly credible performance, fueled by the sheer determination and fortitude required of his on-screen character. He is on more secure footing in the film's one musical scene, in which he plays the guitar and shows off his fine tenor voice. The lovely Madge Evans plays his sweetheart and is winsomely charismatic. She also plays Una's bosom buddy, something that foreshadowed the two women's real-life friendship that began during filming. John Arledge also appears in the film, and it is the last one in which he and Una worked together. He is Novarro's best friend and infuses his role with a genuine naturalness that is both refreshing and appealing. As a Southern vamp hoping to snare some college boys, Una supplies humor and valuable support to her fellow thespians. Her role is not a very substantial one, which might explain her carelessness on the set one day when she arrived without her much needed makeup case. Ever resourceful, she showed some real Yankee (or in her case Southern) ingenuity when she simply picked up a football helmet lying around and used it as a makeshift carrier.

It didn't take long for Una and Madge Evans to become close friends. Una had seen her several times on the New York stage and greatly admired her talent. Evans had congratulated Una on her recent marriage, and this nice gesture made Una even more disposed to her friendship. They were comfortable in each other's company, and theirs was a rapport based on authenticity, not pretense or ceremony. They could simply be themselves, and that included endless teasing back and forth. The first time that Evans invited Una and Ronnie over to her house, Ronnie was embarrassed by the way the two women spoke to each other. He took Una aside later and admonished her: "You were positively rude to that girl. I know you hurt her feelings terribly."[5] Una was greatly amused and couldn't wait to tell Evans how their innocent ribbing had been misinterpreted. Ronnie came to see that the banter was all in fun, and he grew to like Evans, whom he affectionately called "Eyetonic," because she was so "good for sore eyes!"[6]

Just three short months after their wedding, Ronnie had to leave for a five-month business trip to Europe. His departure must have been difficult for Una, although she realized from her own experience in stock theater that traveling is unavoidable in certain jobs. She must have hoped, however, that Ronnie wouldn't emulate her father, who, according to Una's calculations, had been away from home a combined total of almost ten years during his first thirty years of marriage. Determined to stay close to Ronnie, Una decided to write to him as often as she could. "Lose contact under this circumstance?" she explained to an interviewer, "Not a bit of it! Our letters kept us together. And, actually, the separation proved that we were rightly mated."[7]

In July of 1932, Una found that she had to do some traveling of her own. MGM sent her, along with some other contract players, to New York City to make personal appearances at the Capitol Theatre in a stage revue called "Hollywood on Parade." Jack Benny served as master of ceremonies, while Anna May Wong, Lew Cody, Armida, Abe Lyman, and Jean Hersholt displayed their various skills in different kinds of numbers—acting out skits or scenes from their recent movies, telling anecdotes and jokes, reciting poems, or performing musical numbers. The critic from the *New York Mirror* was impressed by the show, describing it as "brisk, tuneful, colorful, loaded with laughs, rich in personalities."[8]

After New York, Una traveled to Washington D.C. to continue the tour. She and Wong roomed together, and the latter recounted the experience: "Una and I were ... staying at the same hotel in Washington. My room was

Jean Harlow and Una in *Red-Headed Woman*. (MGM, 1932)

right at the back of the suite; the telephone was outside the bathroom. My friends kept ringing me up, and every time I had to dash across, through doors and across rooms, to the phone. Eventually, Una said, "Say, Anna, you oughta take yo' baggage and go live in the bathroom!" Which is precisely what I did for the rest of my stay in that hotel!"[9]

Their friendship was particularly close during the 1930s, and Wong referred to Una on several occasions as either her best friend or special Hollywood friend. In the *Hong Kong Sunday Herald,* she called her a "darling girl, sympathetic, sincere, and as natural off the screen as on."[10] Una held

Wong in equally high esteem: "She is an amazing personality. Entirely by her own efforts, she had made herself a woman of poise, culture, and refinement ... [she] is one of the finest, truest women I ever knew. She has taught me to smile and to remember that there is such a thing as courage."[11]

While in Washington, Una's first film with Jean Harlow, *Red-Headed Woman*, came out in theaters. Una plays Sally, a beautician prone to gasping for air when she's shocked, and as the best friend of titian-haired Lil Andrews (Harlow in a red wig), poor Sally runs the risk of hyperventilating. Lil is a relentless, cold-hearted gold digger, and she sets her sights on her boss, Bill Legendre, Jr. (Chester Morris), thinking he will be her entrée into wealth, respectability, and social prominence. Harlow wasn't thrilled about making the film. She didn't like Lil, who was her polar opposite in real life. Nevertheless, she knew it was a great role, full of potential, and much more demanding than her previous characterizations. One challenging aspect of it was making Lil more likable, but Harlow was up to the task. When she saw the film, she was pleased with her performance. She confessed to the *Los Angeles Times* that for the first time in her film career she actually enjoyed watching herself on the big screen. There were some filmgoers, however, who were not amused, and they were downright outraged at Lil's highly sexual, licentious behavior, not to mention the fact that she goes unpunished at the conclusion. The film was banned in parts of the country, and letters of protest against it poured into the Hays office. Reviews were positive, though, and box-office business brisk. One Los Angeles paper called it one of the "smartest, gayest, and funniest comedies that has ever reached the screen."[12] This same review had plaudits for Una: "next to Miss Harlow, Una Merkel gives the outstanding performance. Her dry wit ... is priceless. Let's see Miss Merkel more often."[13] Another review stated that Una "has a valuable part in this picture with her smart-cracking. She saves the day in a few places where the film might drag a bit. . . ."[14]

Anita Loos' witty dialogue lifts the story, yet Una made it her own and even ad-libbed a few lines. Her barbs, comedic timing, and delivery greatly enhance the film, keeping it buoyant, punchy, and moving along at a jaunty pace. One example occurs when Lil and Sally are walking toward Legendre's house, and Lil confesses how nervous she is about seeing him. "I'd be nervous myself," Sally tells her, "if I didn't have any more brains than you've got." Later, Lil discovers that Sally is wearing Lil's new pajamas, so she makes Sally take them off immediately. Lil justifies her actions, saying, "I'm too important these days to sleep informally! What if there was a fire?" Sally retorts: "You'd have to cover up to keep from being recognized!" These scenes demonstrate only too well what Harlow biographer Eve Golden wrote about the two women: "Merkel's personality shouldn't have meshed well with Jean's, as they were both tart, wise-cracking blondes; but somehow they avoided canceling each other out and made a fine pair."[15]

Sometimes, however, this duo's camaraderie got them in trouble. During the filming of one scene, the gals were asked to play a record of "Frankie and Johnny," which they did all too willingly. After the scene was over, they kept playing the record over and over until director Jack Conway couldn't take it anymore. He walked over, seized the record, and smashed it to smithereens, much to the delight of the giggling girls. However, they didn't laugh for long when he announced they'd have to come back that night to complete the scene.

＊＊

After her return to California, Una embarked on another trip, this time to Del Mar with Ronnie for a long overdue honeymoon. Once back, she found a letter from Louis B. Mayer awaiting her. He had sent a similar letter to all MGM contract employees, and it asked them to consider taking a pay cut due to the country's harsh economic climate. He encouraged them to show "loyalty and devotion" to the organization.[16] As could be expected, this request was not well-received by the majority of recipients, most of whom thought it preposterous that MGM, still running in the black, should ask for such a cut. Many employees answered "no," including Una. It was undoubtedly a very sensitive issue for her, considering she had left Fox Studios a year earlier due to a salary dispute. She wrote Mayer, explaining that it was an honor and privilege to be with the studio, and she was sincere in her desire to "be fair and loyal."[17] She asked to schedule an interview with him: "There are things I want very much to discuss with you," she wrote.[18] Appealing to Mayer's paternal instinct, she continued, "I should like your opinions and your advice. . . ."[19] Overall, it was a more diplomatic refusal than Mayer received from most of Una's more outspoken colleagues. (As to Una's and Mayer's eventual meeting, no record or written account has been uncovered that details the specifics of what exactly transpired.)

* * *

At the end of August 1932, MGM loaned out Una to play a supporting role in *Men are Such Fools,* an independent film distributed by RKO. Leo Carrillo headed the cast and was paired with Vivienne Osborne. Carrillo, whom one film historian described as a "one-man ethnic unit in himself," was of American and Spanish extraction, but he was often called upon to play Italian characters, many of them stereotypical and possessing fiery personalities and raging tempers.[20] His role as the violinist Tony Mello was no exception. His character falls in love with Lilli (Osborne), an aspiring singer, and the couple settle in San Francisco to begin their music careers. Una plays Molly, a sweet hatcheck girl who befriends the couple. It isn't long before Tony suspects Lilli of cheating, and when his suspicions are confirmed, his anger gets the best of him, with disastrous results.

The film, despite some impressive production values in certain scenes, seems stale, uninspiring, and even a little depressing. Osborne's beautiful operatic voice, Carrillo's humorous malapropisms, and the storyline's drama and tension, do little to lift the film from its hum-drum doldrums. Even Una's character doesn't supply much needed humor. Instead, she is the kind, solicitous type, always there to comfort and uplift. While it is refreshing to see her play a role where she can just be cheery and good-natured, one can't help

Una was loaned out to RKO to appear in *Men Are Such Fools*. (1932)

but feel a bit cheated, waiting for the usual verbal barbs and saucy wisecracks that never come.

In December of 1932, Una and Ronnie went to Long Beach to see a preview of *A Farewell to Arms*, starring Gary Cooper and Helen Hayes. Una was impressed and thought Hayes was just as good on-screen as she had been on stage: "There's some inner quality in her that brings out sincerity in people. Everyone I know has given his best performance working with her. . . . Gary Cooper had never before made you believe in him as he did in *A Farewell to Arms*."[21] Unfortunately, Hayes, who was also in attendance, didn't share Una's positive opinion. She left the theater in tears, and Una later recounted how Hayes called her up at two o'clock in the morning, sobbing about how terrible she thought her performance had been. Una tried to console her, but with no success. "She [Hayes] went to Paramount and offered her services for free if they would remake the ending," Una recalled. "She never has confidence in anything she does. I can't understand it."[22] The irony of this last statement was lost on Una, who suffered from the same insecurities as her friend.

Despite her own success and celebrity status, Una was still insecure and very much the incredulous, awestruck fan she always had been, especially toward Hayes. One evening both Ronnie and Hayes' husband, Charlie MacArthur, were out of town, so Una invited her friend over for dinner. Hayes arrived and began to make herself at home right away. She let her hair down, kicked off her slippers, and sprawled out on the sofa. Una looked at her guest and couldn't help but think, "Is this real? Is this the great Helen Hayes here in *my* house, lying on *my* sofa?"[23]

That year Una enjoyed a quiet Christmas with Ronnie and her parents. Her diary captures her state of mind and records the special gift she received:

> I think today was the merriest Christmas I've ever spent. I don't think I deserve so many lovely things. One gift in particular I was so thrilled and happy to receive—a gorgeous beaded necklace with a tiny cross attached, and it was mailed to me from the Sisters at the convent in Kentucky where I attended in my growing-up days. They had heard, they wrote, about my success on the screen and sent the gift in 'loving appreciation and remembrance of a good little girl who made good in the world.' I'll treasure it always and wear it every chance I get. Think of those dear convent Sisters remembering me all these years! Weren't they sweet?[24]

After Christmas, Una put the finishing touches on *Whistling in the Dark*, a production she began at the beginning of December. This film offered her a part almost tailor-made for her unique on-screen persona, and it let her work opposite Ernest Truex, another of her Broadway idols. Truex plays Wallace Porter, a writer of murder mysteries, and Una is his fiancée, Toby Van Buren. Both find themselves trapped in a house with a gang of criminals who, knowing Porter's ability to think up ingenious crimes for his books, coerce him to concoct the perfect murder for their nefarious purposes.

(Left to right) Ernest Truex, Nat Pendleton, and Una in *Whistling in the Dark*. (MGM 1933)

One day Una and Truex were running lines as director Elliott Nugent watched.

>Truex: "You lie down there, and I'll keep watch."
>Una (departing from script): "I wouldn't trust you."
>Truex: "What do you mean by that?"
>Una: "I wouldn't trust you to keep your eyes open."

Nugent loved the ad-lib and told them to keep it in the script. An even funnier exchange between them came a little later when they sought refuge in a bedroom and locked themselves inside. Considering the precariousness of their predicament, the couple wonders how much longer they will survive. Will they even live through the night? If not, this might be the last chance for them to consummate their love. At this point, the sexual tension between the two becomes palpable, and it is hilarious watching them trying to maintain

A portrait that captures Una's winning personality—warm, engaging, and personable. (MGM)

their self-control and composure. Truex walks away from the bed, saying he has a lot of thinking to do.

> Una: "Why don't you think about me?"
>
> Truex: "I am, dear. Don't you suppose that I have any elemental impulses?"
>
> Una (pouting): "Oh, don't use big words at me! Can't you be human?"
>
> Truex: "I am human, darling. You have no idea how human I am!"

The film's clever dialogue, nuanced characterizations, suspense, and Nugent's smooth direction make the film an enjoyable treat. The film was Una's first release of 1933, and critics raved about her and Truex and their rapport together. Una even had *Variety* effusing that she "had not been seen to better advantage."[25] Unfortunately, Metro never capitalized on the couple's potential by pairing them again. The studio did see, however, Una's usefulness and put her in no less than thirteen films in 1933, making her one of the busiest actors on the MGM lot that year.

(ENDNOTES)

[1] Sara Hamilton, "She Wants to Be Funny," *Photoplay,* June 1932, 108.

[2] Jimmy Star, *Los Angeles Evening Herald Express,* March 3, 1932.

[3] Edwin Martin, "Cinemania," *Hollywood Citizen News,* May 27, 1932.

[4] Louella Parsons, *Los Angeles Examiner,* May 26, 1932.

[5] Elizabeth Wilson, "Madge Talks about Una and Una Talks Right Back," *Screenland,* February 1935, 97.

[6] Ibid.

7. Ben Maddox, "Don't Gamble With Love, Says Una Merkel," *Romantic Movie Stories*, Sept. 1934, 92.

8. Bland Johansen, "Hollywood on Parade," *New York Mirror,* July 15, 1932, 2.

9. "Anna May Wong Has Never Been to China," *Film Pictorial,* May 27, 1933, 7.

10. Philippa (no last name given), "Almost in Confidence," *Hong Kong Sunday Herald*, March 22, 1936, 3.

11. J. Eugene Chrisman, "She Learned About Living from Them," *Romantic Movie Stories*, April 1935, 54.

12. Louella O. Parsons, "Red-Headed Woman," *Los Angeles Examiner*, June 25, 1932.

13. Ibid.

14. "Red-Headed Woman Entertaining Film," *Eugene Register-Guard*, July 4, 1932, 6.

15. Eve Golden, *Platinum Girl: The Life and Legends of Jean Harlow* (New York: Abbeville Press, 1991), 90.

16. M-G-M Legal Department collection, Salary Reduction Correspondence, 1932, Folder 354; Special Collections, Academy of Motion Picture Arts and Sciences.

17. Ibid; Una's handwritten letter, n.d.

18. Ibid.

19. Ibid.

20. Roger Dooley, *From Scarface to Scarlett: American Films in the 1930s* (San Diego: Harcourt Brace Jovanovich, 1981), 566.

21. Laura Ellsworth Fitch, "A Goddess to Merkel," *Picture Play*, August 1933, 53.

22. Ibid.

23. Ibid, 69.

24. Una Merkel, "Up Pops the Past," *Screenland*, January 1936, 78.

25. Abel Green, "Whistling in Dark," *Variety*, January 31, 1933, 12.

Chapter 7
Gold Diggers

Gold diggers were practically omnipresent in the films of the 1930s, and Una played her fair share, her interpretations being some of the most memorable of her career. One of her first came in Warner Bros.' *They Call It Sin*, starring Loretta Young. It is a charming love story about Marion (Young), a church organist in a small town, who is swept off her feet by Jimmy (David Manners), a New Yorker passing through town on business. Marion eventually follows Jimmy to the Big Apple, but is heartbroken to learn that he is already engaged to a society lady. Not knowing what to do, she tries to find work in the theater and becomes involved with unscrupulous, skirt-chasing producer Ford Humphries (Louis Calhern), much to the chagrin of

Una caught in a whimsical mood. (MGM)

Jimmy's best friend, Tony Travers (George Brent), who has fallen in love with her. Una is Marion's roommate, Dixie Dare, a featured dancer known for her show-stopping cartwheels.

While the *New York Times* panned the film as an "unimportant offering," it has some fine acting, punchy dialogue, humorous scenes, and great pacing, all of which culminate in an entertaining, unpretentious film.[1] Young plays the demure Marion with appropriate innocence and vulnerability. Manners acquits himself well as Marion's suave and charismatic love interest, while Calhern is appropriately despicable. Most critics raved about Una's performance, saying, among other things, that she was "superb,"[2] "fast becoming one of the screen's comediennes,"[3] and worthy of sharing acting laurels with Young. *Variety* was a notable exception, strangely focusing attention on Una's supposed weight gain and its unflattering effect on-screen. However, Una looks as slender and lithe as she did in her previous pictures, and her dance sequences particularly call into question this dubious remark. With her dance training clearly in evidence, Una moves with grace and self-assured fluidity. In one scene, she even peppers her dance routine with no less than a dozen high kicks over her head. Her only concession to the demanding scene was not performing her character's famous cartwheels, which were done by a body double, filmed in long shot.

Those cartwheels actually turn out to be a source of great amusement in the film. They are supposed to be Dixie's bread-and-butter trick, but she seems surprisingly reluctant to show them off, which perhaps suited Una just fine. In her first dance scene, Dixie conveniently wears a confining dress, which, she tells Humphries, is simply too tight for cartwheels. Then she complains about getting splinters. During another dance scene, Dixie goes through the motions, but never actually does the required cartwheels, provoking the ire of the choreographer:

"Would you mind really doing those cartwheels for a change?"

"Why should I?" she pipes back. "I did cartwheels before you were born."

Una showing a bit of her mischievious side. (MGM)

"I don't doubt that!" he sneers, prompting an angry bulldog look from Una. "Maybe you better not do those cartwheels," he suggests. "I'd hate to have you get any dizzier!"

Some of Dixie's other humorous moments center around her irrepressible gold digging. At one point she advises Marion not to take men too seriously, but to cash in on them. "Say," she begins, giving Marion the once over, "if I had your looks, I would have ermine underwear." Later, Humphries, who was no stranger himself to taking advantage of others, sidles up to Dixie and tries to get her to dance with one of his wealthy friends. Sensing her resistance, he informs her, "That's not fat around his middle; that's the belt he carries his money in." Suddenly Dixie has a change of heart. "Oh, well," she gushes, "then maybe he needs me."

Una's final moment to sparkle happens in the last thirty seconds of the film. Dixie spies through a keyhole to see who Marion has chosen for her future husband. Elated, Dixie clasps her hands together, does a cartwheel, dives onto her bed, throws a heart-shaped pillow up in the air, lets it fall on her face, and hugs it tightly, kicking her legs in the air with wild abandon. It's a delightful ending to an amusing film.

In February of 1933, Louella Parsons, famous newspaper columnist, wrote about a recent event that had left two of her aunts in tears. Another journalist, Relman Morin, reporting on the same occurrence, described a lot of gurgling and sniffling taking place and a massive unfurling of handkerchiefs in all directions. What tearful occasion could have inspired such an outpouring of emotion? A funeral? Tragic accident? War? Nothing quite so dramatic—just a screening of the latest Irene Dunne picture, *The Secret of Madame Blanche*. In this modified *Madame X* story, Dunne plays an American entertainer who travels to Europe on tour. While there, she falls in love, marries, and gets pregnant by an English ne'er-do-well (Phillips Holmes). After their happy conjugal life ends tragically, Dunne finds herself alone and totally rejected by her father-in-law (Lionel Atwill), who wrestles custody of his grandson away from her, leaving her inconsolable and on the path to despair and self-destruction.

Dunne is transcendent in her tour-de-force performance. The role allows her to showcase not only her beautiful, shimmering soprano voice, but also her skillful acting and delicate sensibility, which, despite the sentimentality of the plot, never become maudlin. In fact, her sincere, heartwarming interpretation was so impressive that there was talk she might win a Best Actress Academy Award, but she didn't even receive a nomination.

Una plays chorus girl Ella, one of Dunne's friends, and she only appears near the beginning of the film. She makes her entrance as a tipsy passenger, staggering up a gangplank to board a cruise liner bound for Europe. In another scene, she shows up briefly, using her gold-digging wiles to cozy up to a rich passenger. With barely two minutes of screen time in the whole film, Una's part almost seems superfluous, yet she does provide some much needed levity in this otherwise dolorous melodrama.

Douglas Walton, who plays Leonard, Dunne's long-lost son in the film, deserves a mention for his sensitive portrayal. This was only the second film for which the Canadian-born actor received on-screen credit, yet he was intuitive, perceptive, and displayed fine emotional range. It was not all smooth sailing for this Hollywood neophyte, though. Like Una, his role called for him to act intoxicated, but he found it was harder than it looked. His voice was his stumbling block, and he just couldn't get it to sound right. Frustrated, director Charles Brabin put a lettuce leaf down Walton's throat, and that did the trick.

Clear All Wires! was special to Una for one important reason—she claimed it was the first film in which she received an on-screen kiss! Actually, she had already received an apathetic smooch from Robert Montgomery in *Private Lives*, but her embrace in *Clear All Wires!* was clearly more substantial, and it happened with Lee Tracy, no less. He plays Buckley Joyce Thomas, a fast-talking war correspondent who steals Dolly (Una), a gold-digging chorus girl, away from his publisher boss. Buckley gets sent to Russia on assignment, where he bullies fellow journalists, manipulates friends and foes, fakes sensational stories, and dumps Dolly for someone new—the beautiful

Benita Hume in her Hollywood film debut.

As self-serving Buckley, Tracy is far from likable, but he makes the character come alive with his frenetic energy, quick delivery, gift for gab, and unrepentant conniving. Hume makes a fine debut, showing she is photogenic, intelligent, and competent. Una gets some laughs, especially in one scene in which her character takes a singing lesson and belts out some real clunkers. With her musical background, it was not easy for Una to sing off key, so she had to be coached on the right way to sing the notes incorrectly to best comic effect. On more familiar ground with quips, her Dolly delivers a good one when describing her stint in Siberia, confessing that she hasn't taken off her girdle for three days.

For Una, the most anticipated moment on set was her kissing scene. Usually she was the consummate professional, but this scene threw her off-kilter. Or did it? She laughingly told how she repeatedly blew her lines on purpose to kiss Tracy over and over again. "The director finally lost all patience with me. He had heard that I was a rather bright girl. He said, 'What the so-and-so's the matter with you, Una?'... Could I tell him that I could get the scene into my head all right, that it was my heart that was eating it up . . . gumming up the works?"[4]

* * *

Just before six o'clock in the evening on March 10, 1933, Una was on the phone with her mother-in-law when something extraordinary happened. Una recorded the event in her diary: "'Excuse me,' I cried, 'but something must be the matter with me for I'm shaking like a leaf!' But the matter wasn't with me (even though my knees were shaking merrily), 'twas with old mother earth! Everything was doing the shimmy—it was a real earthquake!"[5] The earthquake that Una experienced measured 6.4 on the Richter scale, and its epicenter was in nearby Long Beach. Although the quake was destructive, homes in Hollywood's film colony, including Una's, were largely spared major damage, as were the film studios.

Dick Powell and Bebe Daniels take center stage in Warner Bros.' *42nd Street* (1933). Una, who is wearing pants, can be seen at far right.

The day after the earthquake struck, Hollywood was rocked by something nearly as seismic for the film industry—the wide release of the hit musical *42nd Street*. Musicals had been widely popular since the advent of sound films, but they began losing popularity soon afterwards when studios flooded the market with them. Many were ill-conceived, hastily produced, and full of silly plots, static cinematography, and creaky sound quality. Nevertheless, they still had their champions, most notably Darryl F. Zanuck. In 1932, he was Warner Brothers' production chief, and with his encouragement, the studio announced plans that fall for a new musical called *42nd Street*. Mervyn LeRoy was slated to direct a stellar cast including Warren William, Kay Francis, Loretta Young, and Joan Blondell, but for various reasons, none of those performers was able to participate in the film. Warner Baxter, Bebe Daniels, and Ruby Keeler replaced William, Francis, and Young, respectively, while LeRoy encouraged his then girlfriend, Ginger Rogers, to take over for Blondell as 'Anytime Annie' Lowell, the chorus girl who "only said 'No' once, and that was when she didn't hear the question." Rogers said "yes" to the part and stayed on, even after LeRoy had to leave the production due to tonsillitis. He was replaced by director Lloyd Bacon. Before leaving, however, LeRoy brought another important person aboard—Busby Berkeley—whose innovative dance routines contributed greatly to the film's overall success.

Una replaced quipster Glenda Farrell, who had been scheduled to play Lorraine Fleming, a chorine described in the film as someone who's been "hitting the bottle," while someone else retorts, "Yeah—the peroxide bottle!" Blond, but far from dumb, Lorraine is a feisty dame armed with more than her share of sass and wisecracks. It was a role seemingly perfect for Una. It let her try her hand at musicals and introduced her to Ginger Rogers, who would become a close friend. Critics greeted the film with nearly unanimous praise. Mordaunt Hall of the *New York Times* called it the "liveliest and one of the most tuneful screen musical comedies that has come out of Hollywood."[6] An exhibitor in *The Motion Picture Herald* opined, "At last we have a picture to offer the public that gives them real entertainment, and how they go for it. No musical made so far compares with this one."[7]

If critics were impressed, it certainly wasn't by the originality of the plot, which finds Julian Marsh (Warner Baxter) as an ailing producer who hopes to put on one last show before retiring. Marsh's job is complicated when his star performer, Dorothy Brock (Bebe Daniels), breaks her ankle just before opening night, and he is forced to replace her with an unknown ingénue (Ruby Keeler).

Despite its rather trite storyline, *42nd Street* is no run-of-the-mill musical. It distinguishes itself from its predecessors by its exceptional music, innovative dance numbers, and trenchant dialogue. The songwriting team of Al Dubin and Harry Warren created memorable ditties, which one writer labeled "middle-brow and fun," and their catchy rhythms, hummable melodies, simple words, and upbeat messages struck a chord with Depression-era audiences.[8] Three of them, "Shuffle off to Buffalo," the eponymous "42nd Street," and "You're Getting to Be a Habit," each spent eleven weeks on *Variety*'s Top Ten list.

Choreographer Busby Berkeley demonstrates his mastery of space, pattern, design, and perspective in his number "Young and Healthy," during which Dick Powell croons to a nubile chorus girl (Toby Wing), before focus shifts to a bevy of beautiful chorines on revolving platforms. Berkeley uses unusual camera angles, particularly overhead shots, to film the dancers, whose synchronous movements, props, and gleaming costumes come together to produce a kaleidoscopic effect on screen that dazzled moviegoers and helped to revitalize the moribund Hollywood musical.

Una and Rogers both appear in "Young and Healthy," but viewers will have to watch carefully to spot them. They show up again in the playful "Shuffle Off to Buffalo" routine, in which Keeler and Clarence Nordstrom are a newlywed couple on a Pullman car bound for Niagara Falls. As the train car splits open, the passengers tease the amorous couple, but none more heartily than Una and Rogers, who, perched like cackling hens in an upper berth, make fun of marriage in a song of rhyming couplets. Both women sing their parts well, with a winning combination of cheek and insouciance. Near the end of the song, Una gets a quick opportunity to use her eyes effectively when she looks aghast when Rogers intones, "He did right by little Nelly, with a shotgun at his bel-," nearly saying "belly" (a vulgarity at the time), before substituting the word "tummy" instead. The girls don't reappear until the end of the scene when they are surprised in their bunk, getting ready to retire to bed, cold cream slathered on their face.

Berkeley's dance productions certainly provide rich visual imagery and appeal, but the film's screenwriters prove equally adept at creating interest by introducing a different type of chorine, one not satisfied with her lowly position, but motivated to confront it. Film historian John Kobal describes this new chorus girl: "once a demure non-participant, she now becomes a predatory calculator, deceptively soft in garters and silk. Her crude, gutsy, and very funny line of repartee made her eminently capable of coping with the wolves and sugar daddies, swapping fast lines . . . and generally casting a caustic look at the world around her."[9]

Una's Lorraine Fleming embodies this description perfectly, as her sassy

In MGM's *Reunion in Vienna* (1933), Una proved that she didn't have to elicit laughs to be effective. This photo shows her in a serious, more pensive mood. (MGM)

attitude and retorts attest. "You got the busiest hands!" she fumes, when her bottom is repeatedly pinched as she is hoisted from boy to boy during a number. Even more revealing is a scene in which Una is sitting on a fellow's lap. The young man suddenly turns toward her to ask, "Where ya sittin'?" and she replies, "On a flagpole, dearie. On a flagpole!" With comebacks like that one and her unrivaled screen presence, Una was certain to make an impression; therefore, it is not surprising that one reviewer said that "it seems hardly necessary to say that Una Merkel is good. She never misses. More footage on her would have been a decided asset."[10] Una's growing number of fans couldn't have agreed more.

Una broke her string of gold-digger roles with two films during the summer of 1933—*Reunion in Vienna* and *Her First Mate*. The first reunited her with Sidney Franklin, who had directed her in *Private Lives*, her first MGM film. *Reunion in Vienna* was an adaptation of the hit Broadway play that Alfred Lunt and Lynn Fontanne had performed to such acclaim only a few years earlier. In the film, the leading couple's roles were played by John Barrymore and Diana Wynyard, respectively. The story centers on Elena (Wynyard), who attended court during Emperor Franz Josef's reign and had a tempestuous affair with the Archduke Rudolf Maximilian von Hapsburg (Barrymore). Now married to a famous psychiatrist (Frank Morgan) in Vienna, she is invited to a reunion organized by former royalty who want to reminisce and commemorate the fallen Hapsburg Empire. She decides not to attend, fearing that Rudolf might appear. Her husband, however, persuades her to go, hoping it may provide the psychological closure she needs to permanently dismiss the Archduke from her mind.

Barrymore is perfect as the mischievous Rudolf. His unbridled verve and energy are engaging, and it is obvious that he enjoys playing the character. In a scene with the venerable character actress May Robson, he cheekily raises her skirt to peek at her knickers, playfully tweaks her nose, and saucily slaps her backside. In contrast, Wynyard brings a quiet dignity and strength to her subdued performance, and her interpretation is enlivened by her gentle radiance.

Una played Ilse, a strange girl who recounts her odd dream about the Archduke to Morgan's Doctor Krug.[11] It was a small part, but it offered her one of her few serious roles at MGM. "I loved doing that," she remembered. "I only had one scene in it, with Frank Morgan, but it was a very long scene. It ran seven or eight pages. I was in another picture when I did that. But the director asked me if I would do this, and I was delighted...."[12] Una played the scene confidently and with no discernible Southern drawl, proving her skill at manipulating her accent if needed. The part also demonstrated that she was capable of a broader repertoire, not one limited to Southern sidekicks or daffy best friends.

With its opulent sets, sophisticated dialogue, and fine acting, the film has many redeeming qualities, although it is a bit slow and ponderous. Reviews were favorable overall, but the film didn't seem to resonate with the public and was a box-office failure. The owner of a small theater in Lebanon, Kansas, gave her assessment of the film, explaining why it didn't fare well: "Another of those super-sophisticated society shows that drags along over eleven reels and leaves the audience, what you have left of them, yawning and wondering how it came out ... [it] would no doubt go over big in a city but no good for the small town ... they don't want foreign shows."[13]

Una made *Her First Mate* on loan-out to Universal, and it was the only time in her career that she worked with director William Wyler. Una was a natural choice for the film because it was an adaptation of *Salt Water*, the Broadway play she had done back in 1929. This time around she played Hattie, the acid-tongued sister of John Horner (Slim Summerville). The principal female role went to ZaSu Pitts, who was playing opposite Slim Summerville in their fourth pairing. The duo was a bit more restrained this time, leading one critic to say the fun in this film is "more legitimate and less horsey than usual for this team."[14] All the major players shine. In Summerville's big scene, he takes frenzied delight in smashing all of his mother-in-law's dishes. Pitts generates considerable laughs during a hilarious boat-christening ceremony that goes terribly awry, while Una's memorable sequence takes place at the beach, where she nearly "drowns" in the presence of her harebrained lifeguard boyfriend (Warren Hymer).

Una during the shoot for *Her First Mate*. (Universal, 1933)

Wyler's personal assistant, Freda Rosenblatt, witnessed no real friction on the set and described the atmosphere as "light and fluffy," something that Hymer might have disputed.[15] Una was supposed to hit him with a water pitcher in the film, and as she recalled, the "pitcher was . . . supposed to break like an egg shell when brought in contact with a solid surface. However, somebody must have used too much cement or something in making the pesky ole thing, and as a result, profuse bleeding and seven stitches in the hospital was the price poor Mr. Hymer had to pay. Now, everyone is taking great delight in teasing me and asking why I don't pick on someone near my own size!"[16]

Una clowning around with Slim Summerville in *Her First Mate*. (Universal, 1933)

Although Una had appeared with Pitts a few years earlier in *The Secret Witness*, they hadn't really gotten to know each other during that production. *Her First Mate* allowed them to become better acquainted, and they hit it off right away. Una remembered, "We had many long talks together . . . and I never came away from one of them without feeling lifted up."[17] She went on to say that while most people only thought of Pitts as a rather sad-eyed comedienne with fluttering hands, she had discovered her to be so much more. "She is," Una revealed, "one of the most remarkable women I ever knew."[18]

With *Midnight Mary*, Una was back to her successful run of gold diggers. The film, which reunited her with David Manners, Andy Devine, and Ricardo Cortez, permitted her to stretch her acting muscles and play something uncharacteristic: the bad girl. The film opens with the beautiful title character, Mary Martin (Loretta Young), looking bored during her murder trial for killing a notorious gangster (Ricardo Cortez). She is escorted into the court clerk's office to await the jury's verdict, and while there, she sees some legal tomes with years printed on them. These years conjure up memories for Mary and lead to a series of flashbacks in which she tells her sad story. The first one shows her and her best friend, Bunny (Una), as nine-year-old girls, rummaging around a city dump. Director William Wellman could have hired two youngsters to play the scene, but he let Una and Young, who were twenty-nine and twenty years old, respectively, do it. They are surprisingly convincing, which is a testament to their acting, but also Hollywood's bag of tricks and legerdemain. Wellman had the women dressed in appropriate children's clothing, scrubbed their faces of extraneous makeup, pulled their hair back in youthful pig tails and pony tails, and made them look even smaller by "slightly elevating the camera's gaze to look down on them."[19] He went one step further by asking them to speak unnaturally high and weak. Sound engineers altered their voices further to make them sound even more childlike, thus making the illusion all the more complete.

As film historians Jeffrey Vance and Tony Maietta point out, this first flashback scene provides subtle but significant clues to Mary's and Bunny's innate nature. In the dump, Bunny shrieks with delight when she finds a dirty, old tire, while Mary is attracted to a piece of sculpture.[20] This scene sets up the dichotomy that exists between Mary and Bunny throughout the rest of the film. Mary is drawn to what is beautiful, refined, and cultured, whereas Bunny, as her name suggests, is more animalistic, driven by the more basic drives of survival. This attitude becomes all the more blatant later when Bunny justifies her gold-digging ways to Mary, saying, "A girl's gotta live, don't she?"

Even though Bunny and Mary fall in with ruffians and enjoy the easy lifestyle their gangster boyfriends provide them, the two women have divergent attitudes toward it. To Mary, art, culture, learning, and knowledge are the means by which she will grow and improve herself. They represent the trappings of a better, more fulfilling life. She dresses with style, improves her accent, reads about the great French society lady Madame Récamier, and even waxes longingly about a Corot painting she remembered seeing as a child.[21] Bunny, on the other hand, remains the crass, undignified, self-serving gal she always was, despite her money. When her boyfriend, Angelo (Warren Hymer), brings her six orchids (which he calls "orchards"), she slaps them away, screeching, "That's vulgar. I never wear more than four!" Poor Angelo also never stands a chance when Bunny's lap dog, Queenie, is around. She lavishes more love and affection on her pet than she ever does on Angelo, whom she calls a "big ape" and "gorilla."

In this MGM fashion photo, Una shows off a new hairstyle.

Loretta Young and Una in *Midnight Mary*. (MGM, 1933)

One of the ways that Bunny escapes is through alcohol, and in a hilarious scene, Una once again shows her deft touch at playing inebriated characters. She and Young are seated at a table, and as Una pours herself some wine, some of it splashes up and hits her in the eye. She wipes it away and then brings her fingers up to her nose in total bewilderment. Una then squints at Young, speaks to her in slurred speech, hiccups, excuses herself with a giggle, all while accenting her words with wide-sweeping gestures. She concludes her befuddled rant by breaking down into sobs. This scene is a delight to behold because in just ninety seconds, Una demonstrates so many of the fine qualities that made her such an accomplished actress: inventive bits of stage business, voice modulation, comedic timing, emotional range, and expressive body language. MGM publicists took notice of Una's work and promoted it, inviting comparison with Marie Dressler's outstanding performance as the sloshed Marthy Owens in *Anna Christie*.

"They had beauty to sell to women . . . and to give to men!" This catch-line was just one of the more suggestive examples used to promote *Beauty for Sale*, released in September of 1934. The film centers on Una and her two friends, all three of whom work in a posh New York City beauty salon. In some ironic casting, Madge Evans, a real-life New Yorker, plays Letty, a young lady from Paducah, Kentucky (who incidentally doesn't speak with a Southern accent), while Una abandons her Southern accent to play Carol Merrick, a cynical, hard-nosed New York gal. Florine McKinney, the third member of this female triumvirate, has the role of Jane, a quiet, tenderhearted girl smitten with Burt Barton (Phillips Holmes), the son of the beauty salon owner. Like Jane, Letty is also in love, but the object of her affection is Mr. Sherwood (Otto Kruger), husband of a loquacious client (Alice Brady). Una's Carol, on the other hand, is disillusioned with love, having decided a long time ago that "if there was any more tag gonna be played, the men were going to be *it*." Gold digging is her game, and she shamelessly pursues a married sugar daddy, who is "crawling with personality."

To create the modern salon in the film, MGM spared no expense, decorating the set in pastel colors, bringing in lots of glass, beautifying equipment, and other trappings to create the perfect contemporary look. They even used a powder box as a model for the design of the salon's main reception room. This exacting attention to detail extended to the cast, and Una might have been happier if they had been a little less concerned with realism. In one of her scenes, they added and removed a permanent wave in her hair several times, just to accommodate a shot from various camera angles.

While *Variety* found the film "a bit trashy" and "strictly pulp material," the trade paper also thought the comedic elements lifted the film, especially the "capital vein of incidental comedy provided by Una Merkel doing a breezy gold digger in her most persuasive manner, and another by Alice Brady functioning as a skittish blond wife...."[22] The review went so far as to state that the "picture really belongs to Misses Brady and Merkel."[23] The *Los Angeles Times* had equally laudatory remarks about Una, saying she was of "great help in making the picture entertaining and raising it from mediocrity on the strength of her rare ability to make a stock character human and appealing."[24]

(Left to Right) Madge Evans, Una, and Florine McKinney in *Beauty for Sale*. (MGM 1933)

Una scintillates throughout the movie, but there is one scene that really lets her show her special appeal—her "wooing" scene—in which she tries to persuade, cajole, wheedle, and sweet-talk her much older suitor into taking her to Paris. Una sits on her "Daddy's" lap, feeds him, resorts to some baby talk, and readies herself for her big emotional spiel, all to no avail. Realizing she must up the ante, she pulls out all the stops, using all her feminine wiles to convince him, even striking the same seductive pose as a nearby statue (one hand on hip, chest pushed out, and the back of her other hand held histrionically at her forehead). Next, comes some insincere blubbering and crying, which finally convince her benefactor. Una, conscious of what the scene requires, lapses into some good old-fashioned scenery chewing, and the results are hilarious.

Another sidesplitting scene ensues when Letty goes to Mrs. Sherwood's house to perform beauty treatments on her, which include exercises to improve her figure. Mrs. Sherwood lies down on her back while Letty pushes the older lady's legs over her head. Sherwood writhes and screams in pain, and apparently the screams were real. Alice Brady, who reportedly hated exercise of any kind, disclosed that her favorite sport was sleeping on a feather bed, and had she known about the "gymnastics" scene, as she called it, she would have refused the role.[25]

Unlike Brady, Una rarely, if ever, thought of turning down a part. It just wasn't her nature to complain, make demands, or lobby for roles. Shortly before working on *Beauty for Sale*, though, she was given a part that she really disliked, so much so that she asked to be released from it. She never revealed the name of it, but it could have been *Stage Mother*, starring Brady and Maureen O'Sullivan. Instead of reproaching her, the studio actually listened and assigned her another film, and it proved both challenging and distinctive, giving Una a chance to show her "true colors."

(ENDNOTES)

[1] Mordaunt Hall, "Loretta Young and David Manners in a Story of Small-Town Infatuations and Big City Temptations," *New York Times*, October 21, 1932, 25.

[2] Jimmy Starr, "Preview: *They Call it Sin*," *Los Angeles Evening Herald Express*, September 10, 1932.

[3] Jerry Hoffman, "They Call it Sin," *Los Angeles Examiner*, December 9, 1932.

[4] Gladys Hall, "Twenty-Three Men—and Never Been Kissed," *Motion Picture Magazine*, November 1933, 82.

[5] Ibid.

[6] Mordaunt Hall, "Putting on a Show (*42nd Street*)," *New York Times*, March 10, 1933, 19.

[7] Steve Farrar, "What the Picture Did for Me: *Forty-Second Street*," *Motion Picture Herald*, April 1, 1933, 35.

[8] Roy Hemming, *The Melody Lingers On: The Great Songwriters and Their Movie Musicals* (New York: Newmarket Press, 1986), 258.

[9] John Kobal, *Gotta Sing, Gotta Dance: A Pictorial History of Film Musicals*. (New York: Hamlyn, 1971), 112.

10. "42nd Street," *Los Angeles Record*, January 14, 1933.

11. Some sources mistakenly indicate her name was Ilsa.

12. Leonard Maltin, "FFM Interviews Una Merkel," *Film Fan Monthly*, January 1971, 8.

13. "What the Picture Did for Me," *Motion Picture Herald*, October 14, 1933, 50.

14. "Her First Mate," *Illustrated Daily News* (Los Angeles), August 12, 1933.

15. Jan Herman, *A Talent for Trouble: The Life of Hollywood's Most Acclaimed Director, William Wyler* (New York: Da Capo Press, 1997), 113.

16. Una Merkel, "Up Pops the Past," *Screenland*, January 1936, 78.

17. J. Eugene Chrisman, "She Learned About Living from Them," *Romantic Movie Stories*, April 1935, 54.

18. Ibid.

19. Frank T. Thompson, *William A. Wellman* (Metuchen, N.J.: Scarecrow Press, 1983), 145.

20. Jeffrey Vance and Tony Maietta, commentary, *Midnight Mary* (DVD, Forbidden Hollywood Collection), Turner Entertainment Co., 2009.

21. Ibid.

22. "Beauty for Sale," *Variety*, Sept 19, 1933, 13.

23. Ibid.

24. Norbert Lusk, "Alice Brady in Minor Role Real Star of 'Beauty for Sale,'" *Los Angeles Times*, Sept. 24, 1933, 2.

25. "Exercise Gives Alice Brady a Decided Pain," *Beauty for Sale* pressbook (MGM, 1933), 2.

Una and her mother, Bessie, at home.

Chapter 8
Domesticity

After a brief uncredited role in *Broadway to Hollywood*, in which she had a few close-ups as a flirt in the audience, Una began work on *Menu* (1933), a two-color Technicolor short that was part of MGM's "Oddities" series. At the beginning of the action, viewers are introduced to Mr. Omsk (Franklin Pangborn), who is shown taking a large dose of sodium bicarbonate to alleviate his incessant indigestion caused by his wife's (Una) terrible cooking. The scene then switches to the Omsk household, where Una is undertaking the daunting task of preparing a stuffed duck for dinner. It doesn't take long to see she is the embodiment of culinary ignorance and kitchen clumsiness. She ponders cracking an egg with a nutcracker, but accidentally drops it instead, getting a reprimand from the narrator, Pete Smith, well known at the time for his own series of "Pete Smith Specialty" shorts. Una then does the unthinkable—she breaks the sacrosanct silence usually imposed on the actors in these shorts—and gives Smith a piece of her mind, saying, "What do you think I am, a magician?" He retorts: "I do all the talking in this picture. Do you understand?" She meekly nods her head and doesn't utter another syllable for the rest of the film. Utter chaos ensues, with her making a total mess of the kitchen, while Smith makes wisecracks about her appearance and intelligence, underscoring how ditzy she is at every turn.

Soon, an expert "chef" played by Luis Alberni arrives to help, but first, the kitchen has to be cleaned. The task is accomplished by running the film footage backwards, whereby all spilt and dropped items return to their pristine state. Alberni continues his lesson and Una, his attentive protégée, is reduced to stock pantomime responses: smiling pertly, nodding compliantly, covering her eyes in surprise, clasping her hands together in delight, etc. Despite all of Smith's put-downs, Una looks cute in Technicolor, and she makes the most of her fluttery character. She confided afterwards that the part was fun to play, but the set was very warm, with more intense lighting needed to film in color. Neither she, Pangborn, nor Alberni is listed in the credits, but all contribute to making an entertaining short that is notable for its humor, clever narration, and cinematography. The film made such an impression on the Academy that it was nominated for Best Short Subject Novelty of 1933, but it didn't win, losing out to a documentary about the Krakatoa volcano in Indonesia.

If Una appeared as a bumbling neophyte in the kitchen in *Menu*, nothing could have been further from reality. She enjoyed spending time in the kitchen and cooked a variety of different foods. "I like to putter around the kitchen, and I pride myself on the knowledge of frying chicken as it should be fried," she remarked. "Mother taught me that when I was a little girl."[1] Una also had no compunction about receiving more formal instruction, even if it meant going to the world's finest cooks. She once went to the famous Trocadero restaurant, where she coaxed a few favorite recipes and culinary secrets from the head chef.

Jean Harlow and Una facing off in MGM's *Bombshell*. (1933)

Una didn't need to know how to cook for her second Harlow picture, *Bombshell*, a satirical look at Tinseltown full of inside jokes and composite characters inspired by real Hollywood denizens. Harlow plays Lola Burns, a famous movie star modeled primarily after Clara Bow, although there are a few elements from Harlow's own career thrown in for good measure, such as a scene from *Hold Your Man* (1933) and *Red Dust* (1932), the latter passed off as retakes from her character's last film. Lola is tired of her stressful, whirlwind existence, and the image she must maintain to satisfy the demands of her family and studio. She decides that some changes are in order, so she attempts to adopt a child, briefly gives up her career, and even contemplates getting married. Her manipulative, fast-talking press agent (Lee Tracy), however, has other ideas, as do her parasitic father and brother, played respectively by Frank Morgan and Ted Healy.

Una plays Miss Mac, Lola's exploitive secretary, who is more interested in raiding her employer's clothes closet than doing her job. Miss Mac was inspired by Clara Bow's friend and secretary, Daisy DeVoe, who was charged with theft and extortion (and according to most legal experts, wrongfully convicted). Aside from the illegal activity, Una and Daisy bear some striking similarities to each other—both were blond, born in Kentucky (just one year apart), and neither one finished high school. Una manages to channel a bit of Daisy's feistiness in her portrayal of Miss Mac, but she doesn't get much time to shine. Nevertheless, *Variety* appreciated her efforts, noting that she and a few other supporting players contribute to the film with "excellent results."[2]

Bombshell was shot very rapidly, and editor Margaret Booth cut it just as quickly. "Nobody had ever cut a film that fast," she remembered.[3] Tracy and Harlow add to the frantic pace due to their characters' frenzied behavior and lightning-fast banter, which is often spewed at ear-splitting decibels. Lola's romping sheepdogs—yet another allusion to Clara Bow, who owned several rambunctious Great Danes—contribute to the film's high-octane energy. Harlow seemed to enjoy working with her canine colleagues, and she kept them in her dressing room when they weren't required on the set. Una, a dog-lover in her own right, discovered that Harlow's four-legged friends weren't always the best acting partners: "My jolly contribution," she recalled, "was to be pummeled by three sheepdogs during several scenes. Very funny, ha, ha, ha. Those dogs each weighed a hundred pounds and were so affectionate. But if you think it was funny, just try three hundred pounds of rampant canine affection some time."[4]

Lee Tracy proved to be the critics' darling, and they were nearly unanimous in their praise of his over-the-top performance. Harlow also won over the critics, with Richard Watts, Jr. of the *New York Herald Tribune* writing that she "proves her right to the title of the screen's First Comedienne by taking rich and hearty advantage of her fullest film opportunity."[5] Many film historians feel it is among her best work, and Harlow once acknowledged it as her favorite film.

Una's cooking skills are much better served in *Day of Reckoning*, in which she plays Mamie, maid to John and Dorothy Day, played by Richard Dix and Madge Evans, respectively. John adores his wife and wants nothing better than to provide her all the material things she desires. Unfortunately, his

Clockwise: George "Spanky" McFarland, Stuart Erwin, Mary Ann Harper, and Una in *Day of Reckoning*. (MGM 1933)

meager income cannot keep pace with her extravagant taste, so he resorts to embezzling money to finance his spending. It isn't long before John is convicted and sentenced to prison, and Dorothy is seduced by a wealthy businessman. Mamie, now playing surrogate mother to the Day's two children, tries to keep the family together despite mounting difficulties and an uncertain future.

This B film was shot in only two weeks and turned out to be Dix's only assignment for MGM. Although Dix's character is weak-willed and overindulgent with his wife, he remains likable. Perhaps it's his vulnerability, sensitivity, and genuine devotion towards his family that endear him. This charisma notwithstanding, Dix can only lift this film so far, and it remains little more than a blip on his career trajectory.

As the unsympathetic wife, Evans is classy, sophisticated, and beautiful, and she lends able support to Dix, albeit within a limited range of emotions. She didn't remember the film with much fondness and once joked to Una that they were lucky to find work after they did it. Una, however, never echoed Evans' negative feelings, and with good reason. She knew, despite her fourth billing, that this modest film offered her an excellent role that would even let her dominate certain scenes. She deftly plays both comedic and serious moments with equal amounts of grace and naturalness, often opposite her love interest, Stuart Erwin. Una not only opens the film, but she is in the final frame, with "Mamie" the last word uttered in the film. *Motion Picture Daily* recognized Una's contribution, stating that she gave a "grand performance in a role that calls for much more than a display of her comedy talents."[6] The reviewer went on to say that she nearly stole the picture, a sentiment shared by other critics, including one who lauded Una as the "most interesting person in the picture."[7]

Una had some competition in the scene-stealing department, though, in the form of two child actors, one being George "Spanky" McFarland of *Our Gang* fame. In one scene, Una and Erwin have their hands full improvising, trying to keep up and react to the boundless energy and unpredictability of two toddlers. Erwin confessed just how difficult it had been to shoot the scene with them: "But am I tired! That was a lot of work. Una Merkel and I have been wearing side arms all day trying to keep Mary Ann Harper and Spanky, both under four, from stealing our scenes. . . . Our director, Charles Brabin, says we might just as well be working in *The Invisible Man*."[8]

Compared to *Day of Reckoning*, Una could have been invisible for all her screen time and importance in *The Women in His Life*. She played saucy Simmons, secretary to Otto Kruger's Barry Barringer, a successful, but disillusioned criminal lawyer who is more interested in chasing women and downing alcohol than pursuing his cases. Una exchanges a few zingers with love interest Roscoe Karns, but she doesn't really have much to do, despite her second billing. Kruger puts in a persuasive performance, as do Isabel Jewell and Irene Hervey, but the story is melodramatic and beleaguered by heavy-handed doses of suspense. The film does have one claim to fame: it is thought to be one of the first major productions to feature a pinball machine.

Although it's not known whether Una was fond of playing pinball, she was certainly known to love other games. She had a badminton court constructed at her home and organized tournaments among her friends. At her dinner parties, she would cook her friends' favorite dishes or have them grill their own on her backyard barbecue. Afterwards, everyone would gather around for the latest parlor games. At one party, it was reported that Una had organized a lot of intellectual games, but they were soon forgotten when some male guests found some dice and started shooting craps. Fortunately, Una was prepared for such an eventuality, having withdrawn hundreds of pennies from a bank for betting purposes. Before she could distribute them, the players had already spread out bills of all denominations on the table, leaving Una to collect her coins and slink away.

At this same party, Helen Hayes held court in the kitchen while John Arledge tickled the ivories, with Jean Harlow and Andy Devine singing along. The unexpected highlight of the evening came from an inebriated Ramon Novarro. Sometime during the festivities, he made his way to an upstairs bedroom, where he took off all his clothes, except for a bandana wrapped around his head. He then proceeded to jump up and down on the bed, screaming repeatedly, "I'm Queen Victoria on her deathbed."[9] After sobering up, Novarro apologized to Una, who just shrugged off the incident and told him he was the hit of the evening. She even invited him back to her next get-together.

Una's first film of 1934 was *This Side of Heaven*, a heartwarming feature that charts the trials and tribulations of the Turners, a typical American family. Like in *Day of Reckoning*, Una plays another sweet, hard-working maid, but this time she's Birdie, and true to her name, she flutters around, solicitous to her employers' every need. Lionel Barrymore is very affecting as patriarch Martin Turner, who, like the father in *Day of Reckoning*, gets involved in embezzling. He keeps it hidden from his wife and children, who are dealing with their own problems. Fay Bainter, in her screen debut, plays wife Francene, a writer whose principal concern is seeing her book adapted to the screen. His son, Seth (Tom Brown), is determined to get into a fraternity, while his two sisters, Peggy and Jane, played by Mary Carlisle and Mae Clarke, respectively, have boyfriend issues. It is only when some nearly tragic events occur that family members start to understand the gravity of their dad's plight and rally behind him and one another.

This film was a sleeper hit of early 1934 that resonated with critics and filmgoers alike, who appreciated the fine acting, believable characters, and honest depiction of an American family facing difficulties during the Great Depression. Mordaunt Hall of the *New York Times* waxed favorably about it, saying that it "possesses modified sentiment . . . a tenderness that escapes the boundary of hokum and which because of its truth is apt to catch a cynic unawares."[10] Critics were particularly impressed with Barrymore, whose interpretation was earnest, dignified, and poignant.

Una's character distinguishes herself from the others in a significant way: she is the only one who doesn't personally experience much hardship—aside from misplacing an ice pick. Floating above her employers' stress, turmoil, and heartache, she tempers some of the more sentimental scenes with her customary humor. Not everyone, however, liked her interpretation; one critic dismissed it as too derivative of ZaSu Pitts. This opinion, however, was an anomaly, as most other critics found her portrayal funny and a welcome boon to the production. What the critics didn't know is that Una had already drastically changed her approach and interpretation of the character since first receiving it. Studio officials had originally conceived the part as an African-American housekeeper, but changed their minds. They brought in Una and decided to enlarge her part. Edgar Allan Woolf and Florence Ryerson reworked the screenplay, but forgot to change the character's description in the script. When Una first read it, she thought she was supposed to play an African-American, so she came to the set the first day in blackface.

***

When *Paris Interlude* hit the theaters in the summer of 1934, one Miami newspaper review stated that "you have to peer through a maze of aperitif glass to find the plot," an assessment difficult to refute.[11] Alcohol does flow freely, with characters imbibing often, but this isn't terribly surprising in a film that takes place mostly in a bar. This Parisian watering hole is the favorite meeting place for a coterie of Americans, the most famous of whom is Sam Colt (Otto Kruger), a one-armed news correspondent whose appetite for women and alcohol are legendary. He is in town to cover Lindbergh's transatlantic flight and is aided in his efforts by fellow journalist Pat (Robert Young), who idolizes him. Julie (Madge Evans) succumbs to Sam's charms and is devastated when he proposes to her and then skips town to cover another assignment. Una is Cassie, a cynical fashion illustrator who has a caustic wit, but also a heart of gold, and a sincere desire to help her lovelorn friends.

In director Edwin L. Marin's capable hands, the film unspools effortlessly, and the action moves along at a fast clip. As the bartender, Ted Healy contributes some humor, as do Una's crackling one-liners. A *Chicago Tribune* critic cited Una as having made the most favorable impression in the film, and he praised the way she "knows her way around and deals out verbal cuffs to all the little boys and girls in her circle when they get out of line."[12] At one point, her character Cassie says to one of the miscreants who claims to be

In *Paris Interlude* (MGM, 1934), Una plays Cassie, a fashion illustrator who might have designed something as chic as this caracul coat with leg o' mutton sleeve.

ready to marry and settle down, "You couldn't settle down with a ton of lead in your pants!"

Kruger shows consummate skill in his portrayal of Sam Colt, a character whose physical disability proved a challenge to the seasoned actor. It took him a great deal of practice just to acquire a normal walking stride, during which he had to constantly recalibrate his movements, using his body to compensate, and his concentration to recalculate space and distance. Despite all his hard work and preparation, he didn't always manage successfully. In rehearsals, for instance, he nearly fell over each time he had to shake hands with someone. As he aptly put it, "Anyone who tries to keep one hand in a coat pocket for an hour can appreciate the strain."[13]

There was no strain, however, between Madge Evans and Una on the set. This film was their fifth and final one together, and their friendship was still intact, having never wavered. An interviewer caught up with them and asked them about their special camaraderie. Una, who felt at home with Evans, said, "Around her I am just Una Merkel, average girl and hopeful young actress, and I don't have to pretend to be anything I'm not. And Madge herself has no pretenses. You know exactly where you stand with her, and exactly where everybody else stands. I've never known such a sincere and delightfully frank person in my life."[14] She went on to describe Evans' eternally happy disposition and uncanny ability to raise others' spirits whenever depression set in.

For her part, Evans thought that Una had the "grandest sense of humor of anyone that I have ever known. And in this nerve-wracking business you certainly like to have someone around who can laugh and see the ridiculous side of things. Of course Una has her blues and worries just like all of us do, but if I say 'Let's play, Una,' she can jerk herself right out of her darkest mood and suddenly be the craziest, funniest person in the world. Una is such a comfortable person to know, too; no airs, no swank, no British accent, and when you go to her home, there is no ballyhoo. You're there because you're you, and Una likes you."[15]

Una Merkel, featured player. (MGM)

(c. 1934) The photo that Una routinely sent out to her many fans.

(ENDNOTES)

1. "There's Only One Una," *Picturegoer*. October 19, 1935, 15.

2. "Bombshell," *Variety*, October 24, 1933, 17.

3. David Stenn, *Bombshell: The Life and Death of Jean Harlow* (Raleigh, N.C.: Lightning Bug Press, 2000), 140.

4. Reine Davies, "Una Merkel Tells Me," *Los Angeles Examiner,* May 23, 1934.

5. Richard Watts, Jr., "Bombshell," *New York Herald Tribune*, October 21, 1933.

6. "Day of Reckoning," *Motion Picture Daily*, November 4, 1933, 2.

7. "Merkel Steals Erie Film From Dix and Evans." *Schenectady Gazette*, November 27, 1933, 9.

8. Stuart Erwin, "Movie He-Man is Tough Customer, Stu Erwin Finds," *Calgary Daily Herald*, October 24, 1933, 5.

9. Allan R. Ellenberger, *Ramon Novarro: A Biography of the Silent Film Idol, 1899–1968* (Jefferson, NC: McFarland, 2009), 121.

10. Mordaunt Hall, "Loyalty of a Family," *New York Times*, February 18, 1934, 5.

11. Miriam Bell, "Manners not Morals Theme of New Dramatic Comedies," *Miami Daily News*, July 24, 1934, 7.

12. Anna Nangle, "Una Merkel Seizes Chance in Fast Film," *Chicago Tribune*, August 11, 1934.

13. "A Role in Which One Arm Must Always Remember What the Other is Doing," *Paris Interlude* pressbook (MGM, 1934).

14. Elizabeth Wilson, "Madge Talks about Una and Una Talks Right Back," *Screenland*, February 1935, 97.

15. Ibid.

Chapter 9
Harold Lloyd

The early part of 1934 found Una working at General Service Studios with Harold Lloyd, former silent film comedian, who was now starring in his fourth talking picture, *The Cat's-Paw*. Over the years Lloyd had parlayed his "Glass Character" into much acclaim, with audiences readily identifying with his clean-cut, all-American persona, complete with horn-rimmed glasses and amiable personality. His films were known for their gags, sometimes at the expense of a strong storyline. With *The Cat's-Paw*, however, Lloyd thought he would change things up a bit. He bought an original story and had it adapted for the screen. The main character, Ezekiel Cobb, son of an American missionary in China, returns to the United States to find a wife, but discovers he is ill-equipped for the American way of life. Despairing, he meets Jake Mayo (George Barbier), a corrupt political boss who senses Cobb's naivety and decides to make a cat's paw, or patsy, out of him by encouraging him to run for mayor. Mayo thinks that he and the rest of the town's political machine will win easily now that Cobb has been set up as a straw man. What they don't count on is Cobb's popularity with the townspeople, who appreciate his integrity and honest campaign. Cobb wins the mayoral election. As the new mayor, Cobb confronts the town's criminals, and it takes all of his cunning wit to outsmart them and restore order.

Una and Harold Lloyd in *The Cat's-Paw* (Fox, 1934)

Just before production began, Lloyd vacillated between falling back on his usual gags or letting the strength of Clarence Budington Kelland's screenplay carry the film. He let chance decide by placing two slips of paper in a hat—one marked "the old way" and the other "the new way"—and he drew out the latter.[1]

If Lloyd had any doubts about what style the film should take, he was certain about his choice of female co-star: "Una Merkel is the best of the young comediennes in Hollywood," he told an interviewer. "The minute I decided upon *The Cat's-Paw* for my next picture I knew I was going to turn heaven and earth to get her to play the part of my girlfriend, Petunia Pratt. It's a natural for her. The author must have had her in mind. Every time I see Una going through her scenes I burst out laughing—and so will the audience. She's a swell kid to work with, and a well-nigh perfect actress."[2]

The feeling was mutual, and Una passed up three other films to work with him. She was very excited when he called her about the role. "This was one job," she explained, "I wouldn't have turned down if I had to leave a hospital bed. . . ."[3] In addition to the honor and prestige of working with Lloyd, she took the part hoping to learn something new and wasn't disappointed. Una remained on the set long after she was needed, just to watch him work. She considered Lloyd a "one-man show" and marveled at how he oversaw everything from start to finish.[4] She was equally impressed by his sensitivity to his colleagues. "I have never seen a man," she began, "who is so unceasingly solicitous of the underdog. He's a human dynamo himself, and there seems to be no exhausting his energy, but let an actor, even a bit player, show the first signs of fatigue, and he calls a halt on the day's work. Few directors are that considerate, and no producers I have met."[5] Lloyd and his cast and crew continued their considerate ways, right up until the end of shooting, when they gave Una a beautiful parting gift—a gold chain with miniature figures hanging from it, including a tiny stage coach studded with pearls.

The Cat's-Paw previewed in July of 1934, and Una attended, along with Ronnie and her parents. As was the case with other previews of her films, this one caused Una much anxiety. One of Una's friends there reported that as soon as Una sat down, she clasped her hands tightly together and offered up a plea to Heaven that the audience would laugh in the right places. She was so nervous when the picture began that Ronnie had to reach over and take hold of her hands to prevent her from biting her nails incessantly. If Una had any fears, they were dispelled when a female fan showed such great appreciation that she shrieked with laughter each time Una appeared. This woman kept elbowing her husband repeatedly, saying how cute Una was. Finally, after many nudges and sniggers, the badgered husband could stand it no longer. He leaned over to his wife and said, "I don't think she's as funny as all that."[6]

When the film was released the following month, critics were mostly complimentary. Faithful Lloyd fans, however, were dismayed at how different this film was from his previous ones, and box-office receipts reflected their disappointment. *The Cat's-Paw* still made a profit, but in comparison with his earlier films, it turned out to be Lloyd's first commercial failure. Be that as it may, the film still has its staunch defenders. Film historian and author Annette D'Agostino Lloyd (no relation to Harold Lloyd) argues that *The Cat's-Paw* is his best talking film, citing its highly developed storyline and most credible romantic couple. Of this last element, D'Agostino Lloyd has nothing but praise for Una Merkel, saying that "she portrayed the finest of Lloyd's talking female foils, and brought out the best in Lloyd's character."[7]

Around the last day of filming on *The Cat's-Paw*, Una received word to report to the casting office to pick up the script for her next film, *Bulldog Drummond Strikes Back*, which would be the sixth time the adventurer appeared on screen. "I started reading it," Una stated, "and the opening shot, I was supposed to be a bride, Charlie Butterworth's bride, but Ronald Colman was the best man, and he was kissing the bride. I said, 'My goodness, I've never met him and I'm going to get kissed!' and I got a big thrill out of that."[8] Una may have enjoyed kissing Colman, but her character Gwen soon grows angry with him. Each time she and new husband Algy want to enjoy their wedding night, Drummond interrupts them, calling Algy away. This recurring joke is just one of the funny examples in the larger storyline, which has Drummond pitted against Prince Achmed (Warner Oland), a villain who sends a shipload of cholera-contaminated furs to England.

With its high production values, comic situations, quick pacing, and engrossing plot, *Bulldog Drummond Strikes Back* was a big hit with moviegoers,

Vernon Steele, Una, and Charles Butterworth in *Bulldog Drummond Strikes Back*. (United Artists, 1934)

grossing over a million dollars. Una and Butterworth also contributed to the film's successful reception, with their scenes garnering big laughs. The *Los Angeles Examiner* praised the couple, saying that "no one can play sap roles better than these two, who can be funny without seeming to make the slightest effort."[9] But Joseph Breen of the Production Code Administration didn't like the references to the couple's unconsummated wedding night and complained the scenes were "objectionable," and "marred" an otherwise excellent film.[10]

* * *

Una described *Have a Heart* as "a simple and unpretentious film. There are no luxurious surroundings—but what is the value of all that when we have a story that will speak to the hearts of everyone?"[11] This love story relies heavily on emotional and sentimental appeal, and various reviewers labeled it as "unadulterated hokum"[12] and "hokey-pokey melodramatics."[13] The film tells the poignant story of Sally Moore (Jean Parker), a young woman who seemingly has it all—a promising career and loving fiancé—but loses it all after a debilitating accident. Emboldened by her friend Joan O' Day (Una) and Joan's browbeaten boyfriend (Stuart Erwin), Sally rallies and makes a new life for herself. She even catches the eye of a kindhearted ice cream vendor (James Dunn), and their relationship flourishes. Fate, however, steps in once again, forcing Sally to make some life-altering decisions.

Jean Parker, Una, and Stuart Erwin in MGM's *Have a Heart*. (1934)

Despite its tragic overtones, *Have a Heart* is not without humor, mostly supplied by Una and Erwin, who stave off the film's more maudlin moments. In fact, this clean, wholesome film has a little something for everyone. Based on reports from theater owners in *Motion Picture Herald*, it was a big draw for families, especially in rural areas. It even boasted the handiwork of cinematographer James Wong Howe, who didn't let the film's humble status stop him from lavishing considerable talent and skill on it. Director

Una sits among dolls used as props in *Have a Heart*. (MGM, 1934)

David Butler remembered that in "every scene he [Howe] wanted to have the shadows of Venetian blinds over the characters ... and then put the light on and have it wave a bit, like the wind was blowing. He was always that kind of artistic guy."[14]

Next up for Una was MGM's *Evelyn Prentice*, starring William Powell and Myrna Loy. It was the studio's attempt to cash in on the Powell and Loy pairing that had been so popular in *The Thin Man* series. *Evelyn Prentice* does not deliver the same punch because, unlike *The Thin Man*, it is not a witty, urbane comedy, but a serious melodrama. Loy plays the title character who, thinking that her lawyer husband has strayed, has a flirtation of her own. She ends the relationship, but her spurned lover threatens to blackmail her with incriminating letters. Evelyn confronts him, and things take a dangerous turn for the worse.

While it didn't exactly enthrall critics, the film is still enjoyable and suspenseful, with fine portrayals by the leading players, especially Isabel Jewell in a pivotal court scene. Una is Amy, Evelyn's good friend, and she plays the role with her usual panache, scoring some laughs in a scene in which she pretends to be French and affects a preposterously thick Gallic accent.

While making *Evelyn Prentice*, Una was also working on MGM's *Biography of a Bachelor Girl*. Norma Shearer was slated to play the female lead, but she was pregnant and needed some rest. The studio gave the part to Ann Harding, a beautiful, patrician blond from RKO. Harding plays Marion Forsythe, a bohemian artist with a scandalous past, who is approached by magazine editor Richard Kurt (Robert Montgomery) to write her autobiography. Marion is in financial straits, so she agrees, but her decision upsets one of her former flames—Leander Nolan (Edward Everett Horton)—who fears Marion's revelations might ruin his political aspirations. His jealous fiancée, Slade (Una), is not happy either. She rightly suspects that Nolan still has feelings for Marion, so she confronts them, intent on learning the truth.

When individuals from the Hays Office reviewed *Biography of a Bachelor Girl*, they were not pleased about Marion's promiscuous past. Irving Thalberg tried to appease them by giving the character a few more lines that painted her in a more positive light, minimized her past indiscretions, and showed her regret about them. Even these additions weren't enough to satisfy the International Federation of Catholic Alumnae, which was particularly outraged over Marion's remark: "You were always interesting, even fornicationally."[15] Upon review, however, officials determined the line in question had been misquoted, and it actually read, "You used to be quite a nice boy—even fun occasionally."[16]

As if the censors hadn't been bad enough, film reviews were not any more generous in their assessments. The general consensus was that the film was verbose, dull, and insignificant. Leads Montgomery and Harding were thought to be miscast and unconvincing, and Andre Sennwald of the *New York Times* went so far as to describe theirs as the "most unfortunate miscasting of the season."[17] Horton, on the other hand, did garner some positive comments, while Una was deemed competent or simply forgotten altogether.

One positive aspect of the production was its beautiful setting—Lake Arrowhead. Montgomery, Harding, and Horton seemed to enjoy themselves there, and they even engaged in childish hijinks between takes, such as painting mustaches on one another. Una's experience wasn't nearly as leisurely. Her daily routine consisted of working on *Evelyn Prentice* and another MGM film in Hollywood in the morning, and then traveling to Lake Arrowhead to shoot *Biography of a Bachelor Girl* in the evening. Needless to say, it was a grueling experience, and as Una recalled, "I got so I didn't know which set of clothes to put on!"[18]

While Una was trying to keep her wardrobe straight, some of her colleagues thought she should give more thought to the types of roles she was playing. "One day a certain star advised me I should never try to play comedy, and that very same afternoon another star told me I never should play anything else. So what's a poor girl to do?"[19] Una's question was not merely rhetorical but an issue she found herself pondering more and more frequently. For the time being, she dutifully played the characters that MGM offered her, but she was starting to tire of them, hoping that more diverse ones were in her future.

(ENDNOTES)

[1] William Cahn, *Harold Lloyd's World of Comedy* (New York: Sloan and Pearce, 1964), 160.

[2] Patricia Keats, "Una," *Silver Screen*, April 1934, 62.

[3] Wood Soanes, "Una Merkel Tells Why She Stays on the Set When She Might as Well Be Taking Good Rest Elsewhere," *Oakland Tribune,* September 16, 1934, 7.

[4] Ibid.

[5] Ibid.

[6] Elizabeth Wilson," Going to Previews," *Screenland*, January 1935, 87.

[7] Annette D'Agostino Lloyd, *Harold Lloyd: Magic in a Pair of Horn-Rimmed Glasses* (Albany, GA: BearManor Media, 2009), 279.

[8] Leonard Maltin, "FFM Interviews Una Merkel," *Film Fan Monthly*, January 1971, 9.

9. Louella O. Parsons, "Bulldog Drummond Strikes Back," *Los Angeles Examiner,* September 20, 1934.

10. "Bulldog Drummond Strikes Back," *AFI Catalog of Feature Films*, accessed January 17, 2015, http://www.afi.com/members/catalog/.

11. Gilberto Souto, "Una Merkel," *Cinearte* 404 (December 1, 1934), 33. (Translated from the Portuguese)

12. "Have a Heart," *Daily Variety*, August 11, 1934, 3.

13. "Have a Heart," *Variety*, October 27, 1934, 18.

14. David Butler and Irene K. Atkins, *David Butler* (Metuchen, NJ: Scarecrow, 1993), 119.

15. Mark A. Vieira, *Sin in Soft Focus: Pre-Code Hollywood* (New York: H. N. Abrams, 1999), 203.

16. Ibid.

17. Andre Sennwald, "A Spotlight for the Film Writers," *New York Times*, March 10, 1935, 3.

18. Maltin, "FFM Interviews Una Merkel," 7.

19. "Off-Screen Chat About Film Stars," *The Sun* (Baltimore), September 9, 1934, 7.

Chapter 10
Mysteries

In the 1930s, Una was able to gratify her love of mystery novels by appearing in several crime and murder mystery films. One opportunity came in a melodramatic farce called *Murder in the Private Car*, with Charles Ruggles as the male lead who is a *deflector* (not detective) of crime. He gets to practice his special skills, although none too effectively, in a private car attached to a train speeding to New York. Several passengers along for the ride are Ruth (Mary Carlisle), an heiress; Georgia (Una), her smart-alecky friend, and Blake (Russell Hardie), Ruth's boyfriend. The tormented passengers endure everything from a kidnapping, hidden panels, spooky voices, a gorilla, and a dead body. If that weren't enough, their car, which is filled with dynamite,

Una and Charles Ruggles in *Murder in the Private Car.* (MGM, 1934)

becomes disconnected from the main train and careens down a steep grade at breakneck speed, making for a pulse-quickening finale.

Ruggles may not successfully deflect crime in the plot, but he most certainly deflects laughs and attention his way. With his singular characterization, funny lines, and quirky presence, he commands attention and truly makes the film his own. His only competition in scene-stealing is Una, who "lobs back sardonic comments and wisecracks with a deadpan drawl that manages to straddle the distance between worldly experience and innocent sweetness."[1]

If the chemistry and repartee between Ruggles and Una aren't enough, there is also the fast-paced action, suspense, and excitement of the film's last fifteen minutes. Una and Carlisle contribute to the mounting tension by supplying a steady stream of screams. Una's screaming prowess was confirmed by Douglas Shearer, Chief of the Sound Department at MGM, who once stated that she and Isabel Jewell provided the studio with some of its most reliable and bloodcurdling screams. Carlisle should also be on Shearer's list because her horrendous shrieks rival and even surpass Una's at times. They took their toll, however, on Carlisle's throat, which she wrapped with a cold towel between takes.

The majority of Una's mysteries came out in the spring of 1935, and the first, *One New York Night*, was released in April of that year. She is Phoebe, a hotel telephone operator who is smitten with Foxhall (Franchot Tone), a rancher who has come to New York to find a wife. When her Russian countess friend (Steffi Duna) loses a valuable bracelet, Phoebe enlists Foxhall's help, and the two find themselves embroiled in the mysterious death of a stockbroker.

Like so many times before, Una's character is harebrained, but this time there's a major difference. The producers promised her that she would supply more than comedy relief. She would actually be the leading man's love interest, but Una was worried. She wasn't sure moviegoers would accept her squeaky-voiced, slow-witted character ending up with the handsome hero. "I'd characterized this girl," she began, "until I felt that whether she was just a dumbbell or a smartie, she had no sex-appeal at all and couldn't get away with any man if she tried. I rather wished they'd let me play her a little differently. But they said *no*, they wanted the same girl. So I played her just as I had always done before, except that I made her a little more cocksure than usual...."[2]

Unlike *Murder in the Private Car*, this film doesn't rely as much on over-the-top theatrics, shock value, and nail-biting tension as it does the humorous unfolding of events that lead to a satisfying, if somewhat predictable conclusion. According to *Variety*, the film is set apart from more routine comedy murder mysteries by the "spruce dialog [sic], the breezy dovetailing of their parts by Franchot Tone and Una Merkel, and the nifty treatment the film has received from the manipulator of the scissors."[3] Una's concern about Phoebe's romantic appeal was unfounded, and her portrayal is sound, believable, and very well executed. She was helped by Edward Childs Carpenter, the author of the play on which the film was based. He visited the set, took her aside and coached her, helping her to understand the feelings underlying the text.

Tone carries off his scenes with considerable flair, and he and Una play off each other effectively, forming a most agreeable couple. He thought very

Franchot Tone and Una in *One New York Night* (MGM, 1935). Tone said of Una that he had "never worked with an actress who was so conscientious and anxious to give her best every moment."

Una played Phoebe, a lively telephone operator in MGM's *One New York Night*. (1935)

highly of Una and her professionalism and had nothing but unqualified praise for her. He told a Hollywood reporter that he had "never worked with an actress who was so conscientious and anxious to give her best every moment."[4]

During a preview of the film, director Jack Conway sat down in the audience next to a young man he did not know. Hoping to get an average filmgoer's reaction, Conway would frequently nudge his neighbor and solicit feedback about the film. Right before the murderer was about to be revealed, Conway asked the man if he knew who it was. The filmgoer turned to Conway and replied, "I hope to tell you. My wife rehearsed the dialogue with me night after night."[5] Unbeknownst to Conway, he had been sitting next to Una's husband, Ronnie, the whole time.

Una was paired up with one of her favorite comedians—Charles Butterworth—in *Baby Face Harrington*, a story that had been adapted with them in mind. They had met on previous films, but this was the first time they both had the leading roles. Una was interviewed and waxed enthusiastically about the funny storyline and her co-star, whom she described as a "lamb."[6] The main character is Willie Harrington, a timid, ultra-naive clerk, whom Butterworth plays with his characteristically dour expression. He is married to Una's Millicent, a supportive woman who loves him, but would like to see him make a name for himself and be successful. Harrington becomes famous, but for all the wrong reasons. After several mishaps, he is mistaken for a dangerous gangster and winds up in jail, where he is eventually sprung by real henchmen. Held prisoner in their hideout, he tries to find a way to alert the authorities while avoiding his captors' murderous intentions.

"There may have been more pretentious ones," the newspaper publicity said of *Baby Face Harrington*, "but there has never in years been a better comedy filmed."[7] This praise is certainly overstated, yet there is some validity in the accolades heaped on this gem of a B film. Butterworth and Una make a stupendous comic pair, and a *London Times* reviewer explains why: "Each possesses a keen sense of humour; each knows precisely how to give edge to the most conventional situation, and each can conjure out of the most ordinary line a wit which would not be perceptible in print."[8]

While it is certainly difficult to convey the full effect of the film's humor without the benefit of Butterworth's deadpan delivery, enough of its intrinsic wit is still discernible in some of the dialogue. Take Willie's near-fatal collision with a passing train, after which he quips, "I bet there was a woman driving that!" A little later he goes into a bank to cash in an insurance policy, and the clerk, wondering which bills to give back, asks him, "How do you want it?" Willie responds, "Very badly, I mean ... in cash." Another time he is pondering what to say before a judge and thinks aloud, "I could plead insanity, but the judge might believe me."

Una's funny moments come less from specific lines and more from funny stage business and situational comedy. One priceless moment is when she takes a pistol out of a drawer, sneaks up behind Butterworth and surprises him, saying, "Stick 'em up!" She then takes the gun and uses it as a comb to smooth down his tousled hair. Another risible moment comes when Millicent visits Willie in jail, determined to see that he is being treated for his nasty cold. Armed with a hot water bottle, nose drops, thermometer, mustard baths, and whiskey, she fusses around him like a doting mother, even asking the police chief to make sure her husband's blankets are tucked in properly at night. Despite being considerably older than his wife, Willie has reverted to the helpless state of a dependent child, while Millicent has taken on the role of nurturing, ever-resourceful, parent. This role reversal is but one aspect of the pair's unique relationship. In fact, it is built on a couple of contrasts: age and temperament. Whereas Willie is gullible, slow, dilatory, and unassertive, Millicent is clear-sighted, swift, ebullient, and ambitious. He is lumbering into old age, while she is still young and energetic. The film derives much of its humor from these contrasts, and Una and Butterworth exploit them with singular skill and finesse.

Less successful in many ways is *Murder in the Fleet*, which came out in May 1935. This whodunit takes place on a U.S. Navy cruiser and revolves around a top-secret firing mechanism that is being installed on the vessel during a visiting day for civilians. When a saboteur resorts to murder to compromise the new equipment, the captain prevents anyone from leaving the ship, and an official investigation begins.

Nat Pendleton and Una in *Murder in the Fleet*. (MGM, 1935).

Much of the action was filmed on an actual cruiser, so it receives high marks for authenticity. At the same time, the restricted setting feels claustrophobic and stifling. The film offers some suspense and a satisfying resolution, but these positives are mitigated by inconsistent pacing and a sometimes monotonous plot. Acting throughout is solid, with a capable Robert Taylor showing he is up to the rigors of the role. The most impressive performances, however, come from those providing the comedy relief—Ted Healy, Nat Pendleton, and Una. The first two steal the show as squabbling buddies, but Una's scenes also register very well. Her Toots Timmons is hard to forget. She is decked out in a loud polka-dot ensemble, crowned with a hat and oversized bow. This hard-boiled gold digger, who chomps gum like it's going out of style, never sees an expensive engagement ring or a sugar daddy she doesn't like. She has Spud (Pendleton) and Gabby (Healy) wrapped around her little pinky, fighting for her affection. She's not afraid to spar with either one of them—verbally, that is.

While Una was busy playing mysteries on screen, Hollywood insiders were more interested in the "mystery" of how she and Ronnie managed what one writer described as "the most daring and sophisticated of all Hollywood unions."[9] People were surprised about a number of things about their marriage, especially the news that Dick Jordan, Una's former suitor, had moved in with the couple. Una dismissed any gossip, stating, "Ronnie knows I love only him, or we'd never have been wed—so why should he be jealous?"[10] She explained that she and Jordan had indeed gone out before her marriage, but it had never been serious. In fact, it was Jordan who had introduced her to Ronnie. Una also justified his living in their home for practical reasons: "As we all enjoy each other's company, and Dick hasn't a home here, we just naturally decided it would be grand for everyone concerned if he lived with us, not as a guest but as a member of the family. A large house like ours is made to share with friends. It's nice for Mother, too, Dick's being there, as Father is often out of town and I don't like to leave her alone."[11]

As Una's statement indicated, her parents were still living with her. When asked whether this living arrangement was a detriment to her marriage, Una shrugged it off, replying, "Not at all! I'd never have married, much in love as I am, if my husband wouldn't live with my parents. . . . They say that living with your relatives and third persons have caused break-ups in screen marriages, but honestly, they've only made ours more complete! Life is a give-and-take proposition, and the more you give out, the more you receive, whether it's grief or happiness."[12]

From all indications, Una and Ronnie got along very well and were happy in their marriage. Una confided that it didn't hurt that her husband had the disposition of an angel and didn't like confrontation: "It's awful hard to quarrel with Ronnie. He won't! He just goes out and slams the door as a climax, when he's had enough of what I'm saying."[13] But even Una acknowledged that they were opposites in many respects. Ronnie, for instance, liked movies, but wasn't interested in filmmaking. He didn't ask about her various film productions, nor did he visit her on the set. Likewise, Una didn't ask Ronnie about his work as an engineer, the technical aspects of which were beyond her comprehension anyway. For example, when asked about Ronnie's work activities, Una struggled to answer: "It has something to do with blueprints and things. I mean I know what he's talking about, but it's hard to explain."[14] Work was not a topic of conversation in the Burla home, and the couple preferred it that way. "Just because two people are married," Una pointed out, "is no reason for them to spend their leisure moments together discussing their private business headaches."[15]

Una with Shanty, her sad-eyed Scottie.

The two had different interests as well. Ronnie enjoyed the outdoors—swimming, golf, tennis, boating, and polo. He and Jordan also frequently went on hunting and fishing trips. Una, however, aside from an occasional swim or game of badminton and croquet, wasn't much for physical exercise. She preferred more sedentary pursuits, such as writing poetry and tending to her many collections, which included Dresden figurines, miniature perfume bottles, and handkerchiefs. A prized possession was an autographed copy of John Galsworthy's play *The Silver Box*. As might be expected, reading was one of her favorite pastimes, and it was an activity shared by the whole family: "I read so consistently," she said, "that mother often accuses me of being simple-minded. But reading runs in the family—mother, father, Ronnie, and myself—settle in our respective corners, and we read until bedtime. This occurs three or four times a week."[16] Reading also sustained Una during her frequent bouts of insomnia, and it was reported that sometimes she would stay up all night to finish an engrossing book, even when she had an early appointment at the studio. While she read for sheer enjoyment, Una also read with acting in mind, trying to imagine characters that she and her colleagues could play. She conceded that there was one major drawback to being chosen for a movie role that you had already read in a novel—you go into filming with a preconceived notion of the role, which might not be compatible with the cinematic version.

Una devoted much of her spare time to her dogs. She had gotten Shanty, her very affectionate Scottie, before she met Ronnie. Patsy, her wire-haired terrier, came along a little later, and her favorite pastime was crunching ice cubes. As much as she loved and doted on her pets, Una hoped one day to have children: "My father is German, and my mother is French and Irish from New Orleans. Ronnie's mother and father were Swedish, Spanish and French. His grandfather was really a Basque, so I don't know what our children will be. Probably explosions! And Ronnie says we've got to have triplets so there'll be one left over for us. My mother and father will have to have one, and his mother and father. So I've just got to have triplets, but not until I can give them a little personal attention."[17]

Although she once stated that she was reluctant to talk too much about her marriage because she didn't want to jinx it, she did share her belief that the best way to approach a marriage is with humor, reasonable expectations, and unselfish love. Despite the fact that she and Ronnie were very different, she remained confident about her relationship and their marriage, saying, "We don't fit, exactly, as people are supposed to who stay married. But if I weren't so superstitious, I'd bet we are going to stay married...."[18]

(ENDNOTES)

[1] Sean Axmaker, "Murder in the Private Car," *Turner Classic Movies*, accessed April 23, 2014, http://www.tcm.com/this-month/article/193618%7C0/Murder-In-the-Private-Car.html.

[2] W. H. Mooring, "My Dizzy Dame," *Film Weekly*, October 18, 1935, 10.

[3] "One New York Night," *Variety*, May 8, 1935, 45.

[4] Jerry Asher, "Una Merkel Scorns Sad Offstage Mask of Most Comedians," *Brooklyn Times-Union* (Screen & Radio Weekly Supplement), January 12, 1936, 3.

[5] George Shaffer, "$35,000 Week Rental Paid for a Barrymore: Studio Gets the Money, Though, Not He," *Chicago Tribune*, March 11, 1935, 15.

[6] "Avalon Program for Coming Week," *Journal and Republican* [Lowsville, NY], July 18, 1935, 1.

[7] "Couple Produces Laughs in Comedy," *Lodi News-Sentinel*, August 14, 1935, 5.

[8] "New Films in London," *London Times*, May 20, 1935, 12.

[9] Richard English, "Una Merkel's Amazing Marriage," *Movie Mirror*, October 1934, 43.

[10] Ibid.

[11] Ibid, 95.

[12] Ibid.

[13] Ruth Biery, "I Bet I Stay Married," *Modern Screen*, May 1935, 84.

[14] Harry Mines, "A Gal Who Worries is Una Merkel," *Illustrated Daily News* (Los Angeles), January 15, 1937.

[15] Harry Evans, "Sure, I know About Hollywood, too," *Family Circle*, March 27, 1936, 9.

[16] "There's Only One Una." *Picturegoer*. October 19, 1935, 15.

17 Biery, "I Bet I Stay Married," 85.

18 Ibid.

(Left to Right) George Barbier, Una, and Maurice Chevalier (MGM, 1934)

Chapter 11
MGM Musicals

Una's early foray into musicals was amplified at MGM studios. Since her experience in *42nd Street* (1933), she was eager to do more, and she got her wish. Near the end of 1934, Una appeared in the musical romance *The Merry Widow*, which was based on Franz Lehar's famous operetta of the same name. It was the first of several musicals that she did in the mid-1930s, and unlike *42nd Street*, it did not require her to sing or dance. Directed by Ernst Lubitsch, *The Merry Widow* starred Maurice Chevalier as the dashing Count Danilo and Jeanette MacDonald in the title role as Madame Sonia. Edward Everett Horton played Ambassador Popoff, and Una portrayed Queen Dolores to George Barbier's King Achmed II, royalty of a small (almost miniscule, in fact) country in Europe called Marshovia. The plot centers on one of the country's wealthiest citizens, Sonia, a rich widow who owns "fifty-two percent of every cow." When she decides to leave her country to live in Paris, the king is greatly alarmed, knowing her departure will spell financial ruin for his kingdom. After the king catches the queen and Danilo *in flagrante delicto*, he orders Danilo to report to Paris to woo Sonia back home. Once there, Danilo dutifully tries to carry out his mission, but he finds that Sonia is not as obliging as he had hoped.

Boasting sumptuous sets, incandescent music, beautiful dancing, luxurious costumes, sparkling wit, and fine portrayals, *The Merry Widow* was an unqualified success and struck a winning chord with critics and moviegoers alike. The *New York Times* opined that "it is a good show in the excellent Lubitsch manner, heady as the foam on champagne, fragile as mist, and as delicately gay as a good-natured censor will permit."[1] In reality, the censors had not been overly indulgent. They had demanded thirteen cuts, including one of Una's line: "I know what to do, but am too old to do it," which her character reads from a telegram. The line was eventually pared down to the abrupt and confusing, "I know what to do but—BUP!"[2]

Despite all the censors' cuts, Una's Queen Dolores remains a provocative and titillating character. Of all the characters, she is perhaps the one who embraces her sexuality most freely and unabashedly. Her first time on screen she is decked out in an alluring negligee and is sitting up in a large, extravagant bed. Perched right above her head and crowning the ornate headboard is a sleek, metallic head of a horned animal, most likely a ram. Lubitsch deftly plays on the sexual connotations of horns and their association with cuckoldry to provide a clue to Dolores' illicit sexual proclivities with Danilo. She has a cavalier attitude toward her indiscretions and never seems very repentant about them, despite the king's admonishments. Near the end of the film, a still infatuated Dolores sends Danilo one last token of her esteem—a pair of engraved handcuffs—a naughty parting gift or perhaps a brazen promise of more amorous adventures to come.

Notwithstanding these and other undeniable sexual elements, *The Merry*

Widow does not sink into tawdriness or vulgarity. Lubitsch uses his masterful touch to convey sexuality through sprightly dialogue, but also through subtle use of innuendo, symbolism, music, lighting, and delicate humor. Una was very fond of him and remembered his unique style: "He did all the parts for you; it's a wonder every part in the picture didn't sound like Lubitsch. He was a beautiful actor himself."[3] MacDonald also had a good rapport with Lubitsch, who enjoyed teasing her unmercifully, but on one occasion he took things a bit too far. He deliberately left a magazine lying around the set that contained an article about soprano Evelyn Laye, who was a possible threat to MacDonald. When the latter saw it, she became distraught and left the set in tears.

MacDonald's potential rival, one of the most popular musical stars in her native England, was not only an attractive, charming, and accomplished performer, but she was also blessed with an exquisite voice. MGM asked her to co-star with Ramon Novarro in *The Night is Young*, with Una, Charles Butterworth, and Edward Everett Horton rounding out the cast. The timeworn plot recounts the story of Archduke Paul Gustave (Novarro), who is betrothed to Countess Rafay (Rosalind Russell in a minor role), but falls in love with a lowly ballerina (Laye). He must then decide whether to follow the dictates of his heart or those of his official duty.

With its European setting, royal characters, opulent costumes, and remarkable set designs, *The Night is Young* invites comparison with the more lavish *The Merry Widow*, but comes up short, lacking the latter's delicate humor, risqué suggestiveness, and Lubitsch's masterful handling. If judged on its own merits, however, the film is a pleasing and entertaining diversion. Laye and Novarro are not completely convincing as a couple, but they are nevertheless charismatic and full of appeal. Of the two, Laye gets more opportunities to demonstrate her fine emoting skills, especially in the final scene, which she plays most movingly. Novarro is competent and engaging, despite some fleeting moments of awkwardness. Horton plays his flustered baron to great comic effect, while Butterworth is largely wasted, with the exception of one memorable scene with Una, who thinks he is singing a love

(Left to Right) Charles Butterworth, Una, and Evelyn Laye in MGM's *The Night is Young*. (1935)

song to her, but realizes midway through that he's actually serenading his horse.

Una doesn't really sing in the film, although in one scene she vocalizes some lines while impersonating a bandit, holding one of her detachable curls over her lips like a mustache. Her "wiggily" curls, as she calls them, make an earlier appearance when one flies off and hits a grande dame in the audience during a ballet routine. During this scene, Una reveals some of her dancing ability, and she supposedly learned a traditional Viennese ballet number for the production. For another dance scene, she traded in her tutu for a frilly dress, fancy hat, and feather boa.

Una's next musical, *Broadway Melody of 1936*, was released in the fall of 1935, and it has the distinction of being the film that gave dancer Eleanor Powell her first leading role. The simple plot has Powell, a small town girl named Irene, coming to New York to look up her former boyfriend, George Brown (Robert Taylor), now a successful Broadway producer. She wants to be in his show, but he sends her away, not wanting her to be disappointed, but also not knowing how truly talented she is. Brown's receptionist, Kitty Corbett (Una), takes Irene under her wing and capitalizes on a scheme concocted by columnist Bert Keeler (Jack Benny) to pass her off as a famous French singer—Mademoiselle Arlette.

Robert Taylor, Una, and Nick Long, Jr. in *Broadway Melody of 1936* (MGM, 1935). Taylor said that "Una Merkel is another that I greatly admire, both as an artist and as an individual."

In spite of its hackneyed story, *Broadway Melody of 1936* is an impressive film with first-rate music, dancing, and acting. At the time of its release, columnist Walter Winchell thought it was the finest musical he had ever seen. Another newspaper claimed it set a "new standard by which musical productions will be judged."[4] There's no denying that Nacio Herb Brown's and Arthur Freed's music is exceptional, and several of their songs became instant classics, eased along by Frances Langford's velvety delivery. In the dance department, the film gleams just as brightly, earning an Oscar for Best Dance Direction. Buddy Ebsen, who dances with sister Vilma, shows a natural ease in front of the camera and some definite star quality, but it is Eleanor Powell who steals the show with her innate grace, beautiful extension, remarkable flexibility, and incredible tap dancing. As for acting, Taylor oozes charm and charisma and even gets to sing a little. June Knight is fiery as the unsympathetic benefactress of the play, while Benny, Sid Silvers, and Una supply the comic relief.

A reporter invited to the set to have lunch with Una provided an interesting behind-the-scenes account of his day. He saw Una called back after her scenes to do some close-ups. She stood there wilting underneath a slew of hot lights, as her stand-in, whose job it was, sat nearby, leisurely rifling through a magazine. Apparently the young lady was excused because she simply didn't take light very well. He reported other mundane events—Una's having a sandwich and beer for lunch, making her daily mid-day phone call to her mother, and playing cards to relax. Perhaps the most interesting tidbit was Una's sometimes fastidious nature. He saw it first-hand when she became unsettled by something on the window pane in her dressing room. She immediately went over to investigate. A photographer captured what happened next, and the resulting photo ran in several newspapers across the country. It showed Una—hand caught in the blinds, head swathed in a kerchief, face scrunched in complete concentration—scrubbing away at a speck of dirt. It wasn't a terribly flattering shot, and Una looked more like a charwoman than a well-known Hollywood actress, but such was the publicity machine at the studio.

Fortunately, Una did enjoy a few perks on the set. Powell's mother kept the cast and crew well stocked in homemade candy. Ginger Rogers, knowing Una's love for games of all sorts, dropped off a new one—a miniature football game, which everyone, including director Roy Del Ruth, enjoyed playing.

Una's last film of 1935—*It's in the Air*—opened in the fall of that year. It starred Jack Benny and Ted Healy as two shysters on the run from a government employee (Nat Pendleton) who is pursuing them for tax evasion. They meet up with Benny's wife (Una) at a desert resort, where she had settled after having left Benny, exasperated by his endless

Jack Benny and Una in *It's in the Air*. (MGM, 1935)

shenanigans. Benny hopes to win her back and sees a way to do so, but it involves getting embroiled in yet another scheme—a stratospheric balloon flight.

Described by *Liberty Magazine* as a "pleasant time waster," this film was MGM's attempt to build on Benny's success in *Broadway Melody of 1936*.[5] Benny plays the straight man to Healy, and the result is comedic gold. Pendleton provides more hilarity, playing his forte, the buffoon, while Una

Una and Jack Benny played husband and wife in MGM's comedy *It's in the Air*. (1935)

acts as an effective counterpoint to all the absurdity by showing an earnest, more serious side. While the *Hollywood Reporter* characterized her as a "dependable little trouper," not everyone cared for her staidness.[6] One reviewer missed her wisecracking characters and felt she was a "softy and duck out of water" as Benny's tearful wife.[7]

As 1935 came to a close, Una and her mother hoped to return to New York City for the Christmas holidays, and the studio acquiesced by excusing Una from her next scheduled picture, *Small Town Girl*, which starred Janet Gaynor and Robert Taylor. When she realized what a nice part it was, Una almost cancelled her trip, but her desire for a respite won out. A year earlier she had confided to a reporter that she hadn't had a vacation in three years and needed at least three months to "brush the cobwebs" from her brain.[8] Now free, she busied herself making all the necessary preparations, including buying and wrapping all her Christmas gifts by late October. In November, she and Madge Evans even spent a few days in Palm Springs, a trip they had planned eighteen months earlier.

Around mid-December, Una and Bessie boarded a train bound for New York City. Ronnie and Arno stayed behind at the Outpost Estates home. Una's departure without Ronnie started the Hollywood rumor mill going, and there was talk of marital problems. Oddly enough, Arno's and Bessie's marriage escaped any such scrutiny, even though, they too, were apart for the holidays. If there were any truth to the gossip, Una hid it well. She did, however, burst into tears on the train and told a reporter that she wouldn't be enjoying New Year's Day away from home because it marked a double wedding anniversary—thirty-three years for her parents, and four for her and Ronnie.

When Una's train made a stopover in Chicago, she and screenwriter Ben Hecht, one of her fellow passengers, disembarked and were greeted by reporters. Hecht started railing against California and its residents, saying, "Everybody in California is nuts or drunk."[9] The reporters then turned to Una, who responded succinctly: "Mr. Hecht and I don't travel in the same crowd."[10]

After Una arrived in New York, she was a bit taken aback by what she found. Five years in Southern California had changed her, and she was now dismayed by the Big Apple's noise, stress, and frantic pace. "I don't know how you stand it," she said, commenting on the city's hustle and bustle. "It's a grand place, but it wears you to a frazzle in no time."[11] She couldn't fathom the motion picture industry moving back East, where it would be difficult for cast members to make it to the studio on time, much less locate someone on short notice. "Out in Hollywood," she explained, "everyone knows where everybody else is. And you get time to relax and rest. It is true that we work like blazes, but at the end of the day you have a home away from everything in a quiet spot."[12]

Una also couldn't abide New York traffic, and she and her mother had a particularly bad experience one evening when they hailed a taxi to take them to a play. At first, all went well in the cab, with the driver treating them like royalty, even spreading a rug over their knees to keep them warm. Things quickly degenerated though when he realized he had mistaken Una and Bessie for two other women he was supposed to pick up. Fit to be tied and spewing expletives, he demanded they exit his vehicle immediately. They refused, not wanting to get out in the sleet and snow until they were sure of getting another ride. Just then, another taxi pulled up behind them. Una turned around and motioned at the driver, but he misunderstood her intentions, thinking her cab was stuck in the snow. He gently tapped her cab with his bumper. Una yelled back at him to stop and back up. Thinking her protestations meant they needed a bigger, more forceful push, he backed up and rammed them. Una's driver, now absolutely livid, jumped out and began yelling at the other driver. Meanwhile, Una and Bessie, seeing a chance to escape, crept out of their cab and hailed another one. They finally made it to the theater, but not without missing the entire first act.

Things didn't go much better for Una when she agreed to appear with Conrad Nagel on Rudy Vallee's radio show. "I had been on the radio before," she said. "I don't know whether it was the thought of all those millions who listen . . . but I got so worked up over the whole thing, that the day of the broadcast I ate nothing but aspirin."[13] Fortunately, just before the show began, she ran into an old friend, who spoke with her and steadied her nerves.

Una's trip wasn't all unpleasant. She spent time with relatives in Connecticut, and Helen Hayes organized a luncheon in her honor. Lillian Gish was in attendance, so Una was able to catch up with her dear friends. Una also got to indulge another of her interests—dancing. A few of New York's top dancers saw her tripping the light fantastic, and they had nothing but favorable comments about her style and sense of rhythm. When Una heard them, she gushed, "I couldn't be more pleased if they had said I was the funniest woman in the movies."[14] She went on to say how much she loved dancing and hinted that she might be seen "hopping around in a picture very soon."[15]

Sid Silvers, Una, and James Stewart in *Born to Dance*. (MGM, 1936)

She wasn't mistaken. In the summer of 1936, she was reunited with much of the cast of *Broadway Melody of 1936* for a follow-up film—*Born to Dance*. In this film, she plays Jenny, a hostess in the New York Lonely Hearts Club and mother of three-year-old Sally (Juanita Quigley). She is married to Gunny

(Sid Silvers), whom she met in a dance marathon four years earlier. He left a few days after their wedding to join the navy, and he doesn't even know he's a father. Jenny tells him when he comes home on leave, accompanied by two of his buddies, Mush and Ted (Buddy Ebsen and James Stewart, respectively). While Mush is entrusted to deliver an important letter, Ted falls in love with dance hopeful Nora (Powell), but their relationship is threatened by Lucy (Virginia Bruce), a beautiful musical comedy star who wants him for herself.

Like *Broadway Melody of 1936*, *Born to Dance* has the flimsiest of plots, but it is more than redeemed by its other features. One strong point is the snappy dialogue, which brims with funny one-liners: When Nora tells Jenny that she's a dancer, Jenny looks at her suspiciously, wondering what kind of dancer: "You don't use a fan?" On another occasion, Sally asks her mom what Uncle Sam does for a living, and Jenny answers, "He's a collector." But some of the funniest cases are reserved for the repartee between Una and Silvers. A prime example occurs when Gunny first walks into the club, and Jenny fails to recognize him. She mistakes Ted for her husband and showers him with kisses.

Gunny: "Hey, hey, hey! Wait a minute, wait a minute. *I'm* Gunny."

Jenny (sizing him up): "I couldn't have been *that* tired."

Gunny: "But, Jenny. Ain't you glad to see me?"

Jenny: "I don't know yet."

Gunny: "But I'm your husband!"

Jenny: "Don't remind me...."

Variety applauded the strength of the film's dialogue and Una's contribution to it, saying she "adds plenty to every line, as usual...."[16] The *New York Times* concurred: "The dialogue that matters is left in capable hands, with Una Merkel carrying the thread of the story along in her typically worldwise way."[17]

Jack McGowan and Silvers wrote the screenplay, and the latter made no secret of his fondness for Una: "I got a sort of a schoolboy crush on her . . . we wrote in big parts for Merkel and Langford, but they cut them down. Well, of course, there can't be but one star in a picture...."[18] Silvers had hoped one day to write a show just for Una, but he never did. He had a good comedic ear and seemed to have an innate sense of how to write for her. She knew it and once described him as her favorite comedy writer.

Una and Sid Silvers (MGM, 1936)

Raymond Walburn, Una, and Eleanor Powell in *Born to Dance*. (MGM 1936)

Cole Porter wrote the film score, and it was very well received. Of particular note is "I've Got You Under My Skin," which Virginia Bruce sings exquisitely. It received an Oscar nomination for Best Song, but failed to win. Frances Langford is back, enhancing the fine music with her luscious tone and impeccable phrasing. Stewart warbles a few songs and actually acquits himself quite well. Powell is again dubbed by Marjorie Lane, as she was in *Broadway Melody*, but Una gets a rare opportunity to sing and dance on the catchy "Hey, Babe, Hey." Her lilting voice is both delicate and pleasing. Those who caught her appearance on Bing Crosby's radio show a few months earlier would not have been surprised. He had jokingly asked her to vocalize a few notes and was surprised to learn she could actually sing. This discovery led to her spending a few sessions with Roger Edens, MGM's vocal coach.

It is the dancing, however, that takes center stage, and it proves to be the high point of the film. Powell is outstanding in all of her routines and shows exceptional skill in combining the strength, power, and athleticism of her tapping with her softer, more graceful ballet moves. *Variety* lauded this deft combination, saying she "offers the most versatile display of solo hoofing that motion pictures have yet produced."[19] Her most impressive number is the finale, "Swinging the Jinx Away." Introduced by Langford's singing, Powell dances across the front of a gleaming white battleship and is supported by hundreds of extras who sing, dance, and play instruments, all to grandiose effect. As Edens pointed out, the number was an "embarrassment of bad taste. But the audience loved it...."[20]

Una was not a part of the finale, but as mentioned before, she did some hoofing during "Hey, Babe, Hey," alongside Powell, Stewart, and Silvers. She worked tirelessly to prepare the number and lost weight during rehearsals and the shoot. "I've been working on my dances so long this time," she began, "that it feels as if I'd been at it for months. Maybe all you'll get of it will be a few tiny flashes on the screen, but you'd think to hear all of us go on about it that we were premier ballerinas or new Pavlovas at the very least!"[21] Una's hard work paid off handsomely. Her dancing is nimble and confident, and she evinces a sure sense of rhythm and musicality.

During one of her days off from filming *Born to Dance*, Una took a visitor back to the studio for a visit. He was struck by how chummy she was with cast and crew. She knew all the employees' names and took time to inquire about some aspect of their job. Her congeniality so impressed him that he remarked that he had never met anyone who evoked such friendly greetings from so many people. Hollywood reporter Jimmie Fidler corroborated this story, stating that Una was the "most popular" gal at the studio.[22] Once, during a visit to MGM, he casually asked random workers to name the most likable actors on the lot. Una was the winner with seven out of fourteen votes, followed by Jean Harlow, who received four.

When Una was back at the studio working on the film, she and Powell would sometimes go to one of the aquatic sets in between takes. They would spend their time there sailing little toy boats, which must have reminded Una of Ronnie, who was away in Hawaii at that time, participating in a real-life boat race. As was her custom, Una kept in touch with him by writing, and she reportedly sent him more than two dozen letters during his absence.

While wearing this white satin Empire evening gown, Una reportedly said, "I feel like Empress Josephine." (MGM)

On Monday, September 16, 1936, Una's happy time on the set was tempered by the sad news that Irving Thalberg had died. Sound stages went dark, filming was suspended, and the studio went into mourning. His death was only a foretaste of another tragic death that the MGM family would face in less than a year.

(Endnotes)

1. Andre Sennwald, "A Lubitsch Production of 'Merry Widow,' with Jeanette MacDonald and Maurice Chevalier," *New York Times,* October 12, 1934, 33.

2. Mark A. Vieira, *Sin in Soft Focus: Pre-Code Hollywood* (New York: H. N. Abrams, 1999), 203.

3. Leonard Maltin, "FFM Interviews Una Merkel," *Film Fan Monthly*, January 1971, 10.

4. "Broadway Melody is One of Greatest Pictures Made," *San Jose News*, November 6, 1935, 4.

5. "It's in the Air," *Liberty*, Nov. 16, 1935, 23.

6. *Hollywood Reporter*, Oct. 4, 1935, 3.

7. Kaspar Monaghan, "Healy and Benny Teamed in Warner's Film Comedy," *Pittsburgh Press,* November 29, 1935, 55.

8. Wood Soanes, "Una Merkel Tells Why She Stays on the Set When She Might as Well Be Taking Good Rest Elsewhere," *Oakland Tribune,* September 16, 1934, 7.

9. "Disagree about Californians," *Cornell Daily Sun,* December 17, 1935, 3.

10. Ibid.

11. Harry Evans, "Sure, I Know About Hollywood, Too," *Family Circle*, March 27, 1936, 9.

12. Ibid.

13. Tom Kennedy, "Hollywood in New York," *Screenland*, March 1936, 79.

14. Evans, "Sure, I know About Hollywood, Too," 9.

15. Ibid.

16. "Born to Dance," *Variety*, December 9, 1936, 12.

17. John T. McManus, "The Capitol's 'Born to Dance' with Eleanor Powell," *New York Times,* December 5, 1936, 16.

18. Paul Harrison, "Never Went to School and He Writes Movie Scenarios," *Ogden Standard Examiner*, November 22, 1936, 37.

19. "Born to Dance," *Variety*, December 9, 1936, 12.

20. John Kobal, *Gotta Sing, Gotta Dance: A Pictorial History of Film Musicals.* (New York: Hamlyn, 1971), 122.

21. Betty Boone, "Inside the Stars' Homes," *Screenland*, December 1936, 92.

22. Jimmie Fidler, "Hollywood Shots," *Reading Eagle*, April 7, 1936, 15.

Chapter 12
Cars, College, and Gin

In early 1936, a Hollywood agent met with Una and tried to convince her that she was working too hard and getting too little pay. Una listened to him politely before telling him that he may be right, but she didn't mind a bit. "As long as they give me good parts and my health holds out," she began, "I don't mind how many pictures I do. I'm sure that I would eventually get more money if I wanted to fight with the studio. But I don't want more money. They have been very fair with me . . . I'm not a bit unhappy or discontented, and no one can make me that way. I don't want to borrow trouble, and I don't want to be one of those grasping persons who are always trying to get all they can."[1]

(c. 1936) Una looking classy in a studio portrait. (MGM)

A few months later a journalist caught up with a decidedly different Una, who was stressed and overwhelmed with work and personal responsibilities. Her kitchen was being repainted and was in total disarray. She was fighting a toothache, trying to memorize lines for her upcoming film *Speed*, and suffering the ill effects of a harsh permanent wave that left her looking like Edgar Kennedy. Adding to her concerns were nearly two dozen outfits she had to model for director Edwin Marin for her part of Josephine "Jo" Sanderson, a former secretary turned high professional executive. In the film, Jo loves Frank Lawson (Weldon Heyburn), an automobile plant engineer, but he seems to have eyes only for Jane Mitchell (Wendy Barrie), the plant's publicist. Frank's rival for Jane's affection is Terry Martin (James Stewart), inventor of a new carburetor and hopeful contender for setting a new world's speed record.

Speed was MGM's attempt to cash in on Malcolm Campbell's recent breaking of the world's land speed record in Utah's Bonneville Salt Flats in September 1935. It also has the distinction of being the first film in which James Stewart had top billing. Filmed partly at the Chrysler plant in Detroit and using footage from an Indianapolis 500 race to enhance the production, the film is mildly entertaining, but weak on plot and not very imaginative or distinguished. The *Christian Science Monitor* describes it best, saying it "has the air of a good short educational subject mistakenly padded into a feature."[2]

As earnest, businesslike Jo, Una performs competently, but her trademark spark and sass are conspicuously absent, prompting one critic to conclude that "comedy roles are much more to her fitting."[3] Another part, Fanny Lane, a lady from the Deep South, would have been better suited to her, but Una chose not to play it, leaving it for radio personality Patricia "Honey Chile" Wilder, whose broad Southern accent and charismatic screen presence make a real impression. Una explained her decision, saying that she hoped to diversify her on-screen persona: "I like comedy, but I do get tired of playing dumb girls who never have a thought in their heads, never say anything but the wrong thing. I'd like to appear to be at least normally intelligent now and again, which is why I did the bit part in *Speed*. I don't suppose it did me much good or much harm. But I wanted to prove that I could walk onto the screen without getting a laugh. And I did prove that. I hope, having made this happen to me by doing it when I didn't really have to, it will be the opening wedge for better parts happening to me."[4]

Una's serious-minded characters were not a far cry from the real Una. A newspaper article written about her at the time named her as "one of Hollywood's most consistent worriers."[5] The piece related how "she worries about everything and anything. If caught short on having any problems to ponder over, she will take on the troubles of her friends."[6] One way Una dealt with her nervousness and ultra-conscientiousness was to carry around a little black notebook in which she made lists of things to do. Some days she wrote up to eight tasks to finish before the end of the day. Her meticulousness carried over into her housekeeping. It was reported that everything was so methodically arranged in her house that she could wake up in the middle of the night, not turn on a single light, and still walk right over to something and find it.

As if to distance herself even more from her silly characters, Una once told a reporter that the "dizzy dame" persona she played on screen was the extreme opposite of who she really was.[7] This protestation notwithstanding, Una did have a few "dizzy dame" moments in real life. There was the time she was walking down Hollywood Boulevard when she suddenly felt something fall around her ankles. She looked down and was horrified to see her panties. She stepped out of them, scooped them up, and ran into the nearest store, which happened to be a men's haberdashery. She asked to use a dressing room, where she quickly put them back on. She then skulked out of the shop as soon as possible, the owner eyeing her suspiciously.

Another story circulated how she pulled her car up in front of a street corner where a young man was standing, a newspaper folded underneath his arm. She called out to him, "Boy, boy. *The Herald-Examiner*, please."[8] He went over to her, and before he could say anything, she thrust some change into his hand and snatched the paper. "Lady," the youth said, "I'm not a newsboy. I'm a bank clerk. But you can have a newspaper off of me anytime."[9] Embarrassed by her gaffe, Una apologized profusely and sped off.

In *We Went to College*, Una wasn't exactly cast as a scatterbrain, but she was back playing comedy relief as Susan Standish, wife of college professor Ellery (Hugh Herbert), who hosts some of his former classmates during a class reunion. One of his guests is friend Phil Talbot (Walter Abel), Susan's old college sweetheart. Phil arrives at the school, accompanied by his wife, Nina (Edith Atwater), but he's not there to reminisce. He wants to secure a business contract. Susan tries, with hilarious results, to take advantage of his visit to rekindle their relationship.

The *New York Times* review was very positive, describing the film as "pleasant a comedy as we have seen this season."[10] Other reviews were more sparing of praise. They acknowledged some funny moments, but dismissed the film's rather pedestrian storyline. For the most part, the cast escaped criticism, but Una was a rare exception. One critic considered her somewhat miscast, while another complained that the waste of her talents "might easily call for a Congressional investigation."[11]

Despite the naysayers and limited material, Una still manages to create an unforgettable character. The part affords her significant screen time, and she takes every advantage of it. Her most memorable scene is one in which she plays Desdemona to Frank Sully's Othello in the school play. (The film's screenplay had originally called for the play to be *Romeo and Juliet*, but MGM was currently producing an extravagant adaptation with Norma Shearer and Leslie Howard and didn't want it inadvertently ridiculed.)

As Desdemona, Una dons a luxurious blond wig and affects a semi-posh accent. She holds Othello's blackened face tenderly and recites her Shakespearean lines with great élan, but little nuance or subtlety. Then, in utter despair, she pulls her hands away, and buries her face in them. When she looks back up, her face is covered in brown splotches, a result of the shoe polish she has unwittingly removed from Othello's face. Next, Othello takes a pillow and smothers her with it. As he does so, he accidentally rips it open, spilling white feathers over her face and mouth. She spends the next few seconds spitting them out, even though she is supposed to be dead. In a grossly exaggerated Southern accent, Sully bellows out, "Not dead . . . not yet quite dead? I would not have thee linger in thy pain. . . ." He then proceeds to stab her repeatedly in a histrionic manner, before slumping over her stomach. She responds to his weight by letting out a very audible grunt in pain.

Una has a few other memorable moments to savor in the film. At one point she dresses up as Venus and cavorts alongside Abel's Neptune on a parade float. In another scene, she and Abel become sloshed, drift leisurely on a moonlit lake, and get soaked when their canoe capsizes during a passionate embrace. Near the end of the film, she is even thrown across Herbert's knees and spanked like a naughty child. Hers is a role that requires a bravura performance, and Una delivers, enhancing a film already notable for its excesses.

* * *

Just before the end of 1936, someone expressed interest in purchasing Una's house. She had just made the final payment on it a year earlier and was ambivalent about moving: "You don't know whether to be pleased with the compliment or to feel that nothing will induce you to part with the place. We've done several things to it that we're proud of, and we have more planned."[12] Some of the improvements included converting a side veranda into a sun room, planting a rose garden, building a backyard barbecue (which Ronnie did himself), and outfitting a summerhouse with an oven, grill, bars and seats, so that guests could enjoy eating outside. She and Ronnie also wanted to level a hill behind their house and build an outdoor sitting room, but it all hinged on whether or not they would sell. "The more I look at the things we've done," Una explained, "the more I don't see how I can part with the place!"[13] Una's statement became a self-fulfilling prophecy, and she and Ronnie decided to postpone selling—at least for the time being.

At the beginning of 1937, MGM assigned Una to appear in *Personal Property*, but she balked. The studio had wanted her to play a cockney maid, but Una struggled with combining the cockney twang with her own Southern accent. "Of course, I could have done it, but the mixture would have been something."[14] The studio then loaned her out to RKO to appear in the comedy *Don't Tell the Wife*. The cast was comprised of several actors on loan-out, including Lynne Overman from Paramount and Guy Kibbee from Warner Bros. The film's plot centers on Steve (Lynne Overman), a reformed scam artist who backslides into bad habits when his criminal friends convince him to take part in a stock scheme. In order to convince Nancy (Una), his suspicious wife, that everything is legitimate, he hires innocent Malcolm (Guy Kibbee) as a front for the phony venture. When Malcolm learns the truth, he endeavors to turn the tables on the racketeers.

To give the film a more realistic feel, RKO received permission to shoot certain scenes near a ranch just outside the city. When director Christy Cabanne began production, he anticipated a quick three-week shoot. Unfortunately, a few cast members fell ill, and he soon found himself nine days behind schedule. On a positive note, his actors were hardly neophytes. They were a highly accomplished lot, and they rallied to finish the picture. Una and Overman were reunited for the first time since working together on Broadway years earlier in *The Gossipy Sex*. In *Don't Tell the Wife*, they contribute very authentic performances, radiating both warmth and genuine affinity for each other. They also exude a collaborative spirit that is based on selfless give-and-take. Critics picked up on this rapport, with *Box Office* noting the film was "lifted far above the commonplace by the performances of Lynne Overman and Una Merkel."[15] *Variety* affirmed that the acting is "dominated by extraordinarily fine performances by Lynne Overman and Una Merkel."[16]

In the following repartee, Steve tries to finance his scheme by convincing Nancy to part with her hard-earned money. Their exchange provides a glimpse into their on-screen chemistry:

> Steve: "Some of the best people in Wall Street are interested in this deal."

Nancy: "Who?"
Steve: "Who?"
Nancy: "Who? . . ."
Steve: "Who?"
Nancy: "Say, we're beginning to sound like a bunch of owls!"

Besides Una and Overman, a few other performers distinguish themselves. Thurston Hall is suave but cunning in his portrayal of the gang's illustrious leader. Lucille Ball shows real promise in her bit part as a dutiful secretary, while Guinn Williams elicits a large share of laughs as a food-obsessed idiot. It's the talented Guy Kibbee, though, who truly stands out with his well-rounded characterization. Add to these fine performances the smooth, controlled direction of Christy Cabanne, and you have a film that never achieves any real profundity, but remains entertaining and worthwhile.

Wallace Beery and Una in *Good Old Soak*. (MGM, 1937)

Una suggested her next film be entitled *After the Gin Man*, but the studio went with something closer to the original title of the Broadway play—*The Old Soak*—but added the adjective "good" (and removed the article "The"), hoping to emphasize a more kindly side of the leading character Clem Hawley.[17] "I've been criticized so much for drinking," he says in the film, "that it seems to take all my willpower to keep on drinking." Wallace Beery was wisely chosen to incarnate this lovable, but lazy drunkard who nearly tears his family apart. The *New York Times* touted Beery as being "without a peer for the part,"[18] but another newspaper wryly said that he was most likely playing himself.

For this film, Una shed her recent spate of serious characters to play Nellie, the Hawley's housekeeper, who can't easily pass up the occasional swig of booze. Una is delightful in the role and wrings many laughs from her small but memorable part. She is aided and nearly upstaged by Peter, a parrot who appears with her in several comedy sequences. Peter was no rank amateur. He had appeared in an earlier MGM production—*Treasure Island*—and for *Good Old Soak*, he was trained to speak on cue. The press claimed he was the first bird to ever have a speaking role written into a picture. He and Nellie share several funny scenes, but she has the last laugh when she hilariously imitates the poor bird after it overindulges in hooch. According to the *Los Angeles Evening Herald Express*, the preview audience loved Una in the scene and rewarded her with a burst of spontaneous applause.

Less showy, but still noteworthy is Ted Healy's appearance as Clem's bootlegger. He and Beery work well together, but they experienced a minor hiccup while filming a scene together. Healy unconsciously kept shuffling his feet while reading his lines, ruining take after take. Fuming, Beery pointed to to Healy's shoes and told him to take them off. Healy complied, and Beery summarily nailed them to the floor, saying, "Now get your feet in them and try to shuffle."[19]

***

One day Una was having lunch at the Wilshire Brown Derby when she overheard a conversation that had profound repercussions on her career. A well-known talent scout was talking about her: "Look at Una Merkel over there," he began. "What description occurs to you when her name is mentioned? The answer is just two words, 'dumb' and 'southern'... she couldn't

Peter the parrot proved to be as adept at scene-stealing as Una in *Good Old Soak*. (MGM, 1937)

be anything else if she tried. . . ."[20] Crushed by what she heard, Una made up her mind then and there that she'd prove the scout wrong: "I began to pay attention to the eighteenth letter in the alphabet—"R." I also began to place G's where they belonged, and to talk faster and more clearly than I had before. I wasn't going to be 'typed' if I could help it! I even began to dream of dramatic roles such as Garbo or Helen Hayes might play."[21]

(ENDNOTES)

[1] Jerry Asher, "Una Merkel Scorns Sad Offstage Mask of Most Comedians, *Brooklyn Times-Union* (Screen & Radio Weekly Supplement), January 12, 1936, 3.

[2] "Monitor Movie Guide," *Christian Science Monitor,* June 13, 1936, 17.

[3] "Invention Trouble in Speed Film," *Los Angeles Evening Herald Express,* May 23, 1936.

[4] Una Merkel, "Make Things Happen to You," *Movie Classic*, October 1936.

[5] Harry Mines, "A Gal Who Worries is Una Merkel," *Illustrated Daily News* (Los Angeles), January 15, 1937.

[6] Ibid.

[7] W. H. Mooring, "My Dizzy Dame," *Film Weekly,* October 18, 1935, 10.

[8] Patricia Keats, "Una," *Silver Screen*, April 1934, 62.

[9] Ibid.

[10] Frank S. Nugent, "The Rialto's 'We Went to College' Gayly Examines a National Phenomenon, the Alumni Reunion," *New York Times,* July 27, 1936, 20.

[11] "We Went to College," *Hollywood Reporter,* June 20, 1936, 2.

[12] Betty Boone, "Inside the Stars' Homes," *Screenland*, December 1936, 12.

[13] Ibid.

[14] Mines, "A Gal Who Worries is Una Merkel," January 15, 1937.

[15] "Don't Tell the Wife," *Box Office,* January 30, 1937, 25.

[16] "Don't Tell the Wife," *Daily Variety,* January 20, 1937, 3.

[17] In some sources, the film's title is listed as *"The" Good Old Soak*, but lobby cards and other promotional material omit the article.

[18] John T. McManus, "Good Old Soak," *New York Times*, April 23, 1937, 25.

[19] "Had to Nail His Shoes to the Floor," *Mt. Adams Sun* (Bingen, WA.), July 23, 1937, 3.

[20] Marian Rhea, "Una: The Kentucky Bell Ringer," *Radio Mirror*, February 1939, 78.

[21] Ibid.

Chapter 13
Harlow

Jean Harlow died on June 7, 1937, from acute nephritis, and screenwriter Harry Ruskin remembered the day, saying, "There wasn't one sound in the MGM commissary for three hours."[1] Two days later the studio closed for her funeral, and at nine o'clock that same morning, all the Hollywood studios observed a moment of silence in her honor. Her funeral took place at Forest Lawn Memorial Park in Glendale in the Wee Kirk o' the Heather chapel, which was packed to capacity with some two hundred fifty friends, family members, and colleagues. Outside, nearly a thousand fans lined the streets in a show of love and respect for the fallen actress. Una was among the first

Wearing minimal makeup and a 98¢ dress, Una played Lil, Jean Harlow's sister, in *Riffraff*. (MGM, 1936)

group of visitors to arrive, and she was accompanied by her friend Madge Evans.

Like so many others in Hollywood, Una was greatly saddened by Harlow's death, but she had happy memories of her. "It was a joy to work with Jean Harlow," she wrote to a fan. "She was generous, kind, and a truly dear person."[2] Elsewhere, Una mentioned that Harlow could be "rather shy," although apparently not around Una, who spoke about the two of them sitting in rocking chairs on a movie set, rocking back and forth, talking for hours.[3] Una worked four times with Harlow as did May Robson, making them the two actresses in Hollywood who appeared in the most Harlow films. In addition to working together, Una and Harlow would occasionally socialize off-screen, and Harlow even came to one of Una's famous dinner parties. Una gave her an autographed photograph, which Harlow hung, along with the others in her collection, in her Palm Drive home.

On the surface, Una and Harlow may have seemed very different, but in fact, they were more alike than what people imagined. Besides their blond hair, both were known for their unpretentious, down-to-earth demeanor, pleasant disposition, sincerity, generosity, and professionalism. Both reportedly were voracious readers (especially detective novels) and had a special fondness for dogs. Both women had an extremely close (some would say unhealthily close) relationship with their family, from whom they could never separate themselves to live independently, even after their respective marriages. Both felt the acute loss or absence of their father, albeit in different ways. Harlow rarely saw her father after her parents divorced when she was a child. Una did have her father during her formative years, but as she grew older, Arno was rarely around. His work often kept him away for months at a time.

Perhaps the single most important similarity between Una and Harlow was their deep-rooted insecurity. During the filming of *Dinner at Eight*, Marcella Rabwin, one of producer David O. Selznick's assistants, recalled that Harlow was very insecure about working with her co-stars and even timidly asked one day, "Do you think I can talk to Mr. Selznick?"[4] Rabwin also remembered doing a small favor for Harlow and receiving an expensive gift in return, one indication of the actress' "severe inferiority complex."[5] Rabwin went on to say that if "anyone did anything for her, she'd give them a present. She was expressing gratitude for practically nothing."[6]

Una was also known for her gift-giving, and she openly spoke about her insecurities. She said she was "one of those unfortunate souls born with an inferiority complex" and never thought she was successful in doing herself over.[7] "Even after several years on stage and seven in pictures," she explained, "I get rattled easily, suffer agonies before each new picture, and have my bad moments sometime during every day."[8] Nevertheless, Una was grateful for acting, and the defenses it gave her against the world.

Harlow also recognized these benefits, but she struggled with losing herself too much in her on-screen persona: "If I could put on the Harlow personality like a mask while I was working, and then take it off when the day was done, that would be heaven."[9] But she couldn't, possibly because, as biographer David Stenn suggests, "She never knew who she was."[10] Una, on the other hand, knew exactly who she was and voiced a statement of self-awareness that Harlow might have applied to herself had she lived longer: "We should know when we are acting and when we are not—else, we would lose track of ourselves altogether. And no amount of good impressions or success is worth that."[11]

* * *

Una's favorite film with Harlow was *Riffraff*, which came out in January 1936. It was the production that she and Harlow had the most fun making together. The story centers around Hattie (Harlow), a tuna cannery worker who marries Dutch (Spencer Tracy), a proud fisherman who sows discord in his household when he encourages his fellow workers to strike against Nick (Joseph Calleia), their smarmy, no-good boss. As Hattie's sister, Lil, Una plays a first in her film career—a mother with children.[12] She recounted how she came to get the part. Irving Thalberg had called her into his office to discuss the character of Lil. "I don't believe you look like the mother of five," he announced. "We'll cut it down to three."[13] (When the film came out, she had two children.) Una enjoyed this meaty role and the new acting opportunities it offered her, but she also had a practical reason for liking it so much: it let her sleep in and report to the studio a little later than usual. As the drab Lil, who, as her character says, "married for love and found herself with two children and lumbago," Una did not require the usual prepping for the cameras—time in the makeup chair, people fussing over her hair, and tedious costume fittings. She simply arrived at the studio a little before nine, right before her scenes. "I didn't have any make-up on; I screwed my hair back, wore a dowdy old dress. I love that kind of part,"[14] she reminisced. When Una says dowdy, she wasn't exaggerating. The dress was reportedly bought on sale for 98¢ and was torn and stained to make it look aged and well used.

Like Una, Harlow also surprised her fans with a different look. She gave up her trademark platinum blond tresses to replace them with a "brownette" (brownish-blond) wig. Bowing to pressure from the Production Code Administration, studio officials pushed the new hair color to soften Harlow's image, and they got no complaint from her. She was ready for a change (as were her hair and scalp, which were suffering from years of harsh bleaching). Harlow's fans were probably flustered by the film's serious tone, dismal waterfront setting, and her hard-boiled, rough-and-ready character, but they rallied behind her and were treated to what one reviewer called her "most sincere and convincing performance."[15]

As for the other performers, Tracy shows himself an able and complementary partner to Harlow, acquitting himself admirably in a difficult, mostly unsympathetic role. Calleia is a breath of fresh air. He injects humor and unctuous charm into his scenes and shows a deft touch of characterization. Una fleshes out the earthy, down-trodden Lil convincingly, playing her with an inner strength and honesty that is achingly true. The *Los Angeles Times* thought Una deserved better and lamented her being "practically wasted in her role,"[16] while *Variety* extolled her interpretation, stating she "nearly makes off with the works on several occasions."[17] Even Spencer Tracy was impressed, telling a writer that Una was "one of the finest actresses in the business."[18]

Una's last film with Harlow was *Saratoga*, the film that Harlow was working on when she died. In this film, Harlow plays Carol Clayton, an important horse farm owner's daughter, who is engaged to stuffy New York stockbroker Hartley Madison (Walter Pidgeon). As time goes on, she realizes that the man she really loves is roguish, down-to-earth bookmaker Duke Bradley (Clark Gable). In a departure for her, Una plays Fritzi, a rich, sophisticated lady married to Jesse Kiffmeyer (Frank Morgan), a cosmetics tycoon.

Grace Wilcox conducted a lighthearted interview with Una at the actress' home, but the journalist received a bonus—Arno—who interjected his two cents whether it was solicited or not. Throughout the interview, the special father-daughter bond is evident in their good-natured jibing and repartee, and they show that if they had been so inclined, they might have made a real comedy duo. Una makes the first salvo in the comedy "routine," effusing that in *Saratoga*, she will kiss Clark Gable, marry Frank Morgan, get to wear new clothes, and look and feel glamorous and beautiful.

(Left to Right) Frank Morgan, Una, and Clark Gable in MGM's *Saratoga* (1937), Jean Harlow's last film.

Her father brings her back to earth, reminding her that a "... Merkel is only a Merkel regardless of how many diamonds she clamps into her tiara. Get into your overalls," he bellows, "and clear out this petunia bed."[19] But Una will not be subdued. "I've never had a really romantic Romeo-type of lover," she confesses. "I've always been handed clever men, in amusing situations and comedy roles. When I learned that I was to be given a chance to kiss Gable, I grabbed the script and ran home to find out more."[20] Her father sheepishly responds, "How d'you come to kiss him; are you playing post office?"[21] Ignoring him, Una announces she needs a swimming pool to match her new glamorous status, and Arno shoots back, "What's the matter with the Pacific Ocean? Hasn't dried up, has it?"[22]

All kidding aside, Una initially welcomed playing a beautiful, refined, and worldly wife after the homely woman she portrayed earlier that year in *Good Old Soak*. Although she appeared on-screen in only a third of the twenty-four different costumes that

Even though she didn't like glamorous roles like Fritzi in *Saratoga* (MGM, 1937), Una always looked elegant and sophisticated in her fashion shoots. (MGM)

early publicity boasted she would wear, Una showed that she could hold her own with some of the most accomplished clotheshorses in Hollywood. After seeing her new look, Dorothy Manners of the *Los Angeles Examiner* wrote that Una "looks so pretty that she'll probably develop into a 'glamour girl.'"[23]

But Una was more than beautiful window dressing in the film; she offered up some comedic flair, most notably in the scene on the train in which she and others sing a rousing version of "The Horse with the Dreamy Eyes." When it's Una's turn to sing, she punctuates her words at the end of certain musical phrases with a little body language: she clasps her hands together behind her head and pops her body forward in a quick, thrusting movement. The effect is priceless and contributes greatly to the scene's humor. The song's levity, however, belies the sadness that the whole cast felt as they continued filming after Harlow's unexpected death. "It was an unhappy time," Una remembered, "because I loved her very much."[24] The film's late filming schedule didn't help matters either. The scene in question wasn't filmed until two in the morning, and Una recalled that the studio distributed pills to keep her and the others awake. "Don't give me any," she pleaded with them. "I'll never go to sleep," but they insisted, offering her a half of one.[25] She took it and didn't sleep for another three nights.

Harlow had much more than insomnia to worry about during filming. Her failing kidneys caused her to be weak, exhausted, and in pain throughout much of production. Colleagues noticed that her skin had lost its beautiful translucence, and her face was puffy and her body swollen. She was also sweating profusely. On several occasions she arrived late to the set, a rare occurrence for her, as she was usually so professional towards her work. Director Conway teased her about her tardiness, and she answered back uncharacteristically, "You're lucky I'm here," indicating something was terribly wrong.[26]

As if this weren't enough, Harlow was not comfortable filming around horses, and she even wrote to a fan that she was "scared to death of them."[27] Her scenes with horses were shot without incident, but her uneasy feelings about them were not totally misplaced. During the production, a fuse box suddenly blew up, startling several horses that bolted for the nearest exit. Una was standing right in the path of one of them, paralyzed with fear. Thinking quickly, Clark Gable leaped up to grab the horse's halter, but missed. He was able, however, to divert the animal's direction, seize Una, and move her to safety at the last moment. She escaped death, but her friend Harlow was not as fortunate. She ultimately lost her life a few weeks later at the tender age of twenty-six.

Harlow's few remaining scenes on *Saratoga* were filmed using Mary Dees and Geraldine Dvorak as body doubles. Paula Winslowe dubbed Harlow's voice. The film was released on July 23, 1937, and moviegoers flocked to see Harlow one last time, making it one of MGM's most profitable pictures that year. Critics were gracious and mostly laudatory about Harlow, but it is not her best performance. She performs competently, but the telltale signs of her illness are visible, and they seem to cast a pallor over her scenes, robbing them of their usual sparkle and charm.

Una's interpretation received many complimentary remarks. The *Glasgow Herald* thought that she and Clark Gable stole the film, while the *New York Times* asserted that *Saratoga*'s "pleasantest side is presented by Una Merkel and Frank Morgan, with their plaintive sort of comedy."[28] Despite her positive reviews, Una admitted that she didn't really enjoy playing the rich, glamorous sophisticate. In fact, she said that Fritzi was one of the only roles that she hadn't like playing. For her, being glamorous was too much of a strain. "As a feather-brained blonde on the screen, I can act a bit balmy in real life and people will think nothing of it—in fact, they'd probably laugh along with me. But if a glamour girl isn't right up to par during every minute of her life, she promptly loses some of her glamorous prestige."[29] She concluded that she wanted to "have some fun out of life and out of my work. So I'll dodge the glamour stuff and stick to my comedy roles."[30]

But Una wasn't doing much laughing that same month when she discovered a mass underneath her arm. It was around the size of a pigeon egg, and while it didn't cause her any pain, her family and friends were concerned and persuaded her to have it removed. "Even the doctor didn't think much of it," Una told reporter Grace Wilcox, "but when he got going, he found it needed to come out. Everybody was very kind and made a great fuss over me, but I couldn't do anything but sleep."[31] Wanting to show that the operation had left her sense of humor intact, she hastily added, "I wish it had happened while we were making *Born to Dance*. I could have used it so nicely along with that song, 'I've Got You Under My Skin.'"[32]

After *Saratoga*, Una got another chance to work with horses in her last film of 1937, *Checkers*, a heartwarming drama starring Jane Withers as the eponymous character, an orphan raised by Edgar (Stuart Erwin), her horse-loving uncle. The problem is that Edgar's fiancée, Mamie Appleby (Una), doesn't share his affection for horses. She wants him to give them up and settle down and get married, but Ed can't part with them, especially his prize colt, Blue Skies, who has become injured and must be nursed back to health on Mamie's farm. When a wealthy banker starts to woo Mamie, Ed realizes he might lose her for good, so he decides to win her back with a little ingenuity and help from Blue Skies and Checkers.

With its thrilling race scenes, quick pace, and humor, the film is a delightfully entertaining romp. Withers, who had just been ranked the sixth most popular performer in Hollywood, is given ample opportunity to pull on the heart strings, but also amuse, beguile, and charm. Una was impressed with her and the other two children in the cast, and she marveled at how they were able to juggle their acting responsibilities with their on-set schooling: "I don't see how the poor little things can stand it.... The children are jerked from the teacher to the camera and back again to their lessons so fast it's a wonder they don't start reciting their lines to the teacher and their lesson to the microphone."[33]

As Withers got used to her busy schedule, Stuart Erwin had to deal with overzealous acting. In one scene, Withers was supposed to give him an inconspicuous kick to get his attention. All went well in rehearsal, but when the scene was actually shot, Stuart was stunned when the anticipated kick arrived with such force that it knocked him to the ground. Erwin couldn't blame Withers, though, because the one who kicked him was the horse

Una Merkel in *Checkers*. (20th Century-Fox, 1937)

chosen to play Blue Skies. "Why did you have to fall?" demanded Director H. Bruce Humberstone. "We could have used that if you had stayed upright. We'll never be able to get that colt to kick you at the right moment again."[34] Erwin looked over at him and answered: "Don't let's even try."[35]

As usual, Una provided excellent support, acting with her customary naturalness and sincerity. Her scenes with Withers are illuminated by a shared understanding and warmth, and those with Stuart ring true and never false. According to one review, she was "at her prettiest and her comedy as winning as ever."[36] It also noted her lack of accent in the film, asserting that she was always "just a wee bit more fascinating when she has to use that 'southern' accent of hers."[37]

Stuart Erwin, Jane Withers, and Una in *Checkers*. (20th Century-Fox, 1937)

(Endnotes)

1. David Stenn, *Bombshell: The Life and Death of Jean Harlow* (Raleigh, N.C.: Lightning Bug Press, 2000), 210.

2. Una Merkel, letter to Ron Ringler, August 21, 1978.

3. Richard Lamparski, *Whatever Became of. . . ?* radio interview with Una Merkel, WBAI, April 7, 1970.

4. Stenn, *Bombshell: The Life and Death of Jean Harlow*, 121.

5. Ibid.

6. Ibid.

7. Barrett Kiesling, "Una Merkel is 'Surprise Girl' of Movie Colony," *Pittsburgh Press*, July 30, 1937, 12.

8. Ibid.

9. Neal Gabler, "The Original Blonde," in *Best Sex Writing 2013: The State of Today's Sexual Culture*, ed. Rachel Kramer Bussel, (Berkeley, CA.: Cleis Press, 2013), 220.

10 Stenn, *Bombshell: The Life and Death of Jean Harlow*, 220.

11 Kiesling, "Una Merkel is 'Surprise Girl' of Movie Colony," 12.

12 Una played another mother later that year in *Born to Dance*, which was released on November 27, 1936.

13 Leonard Maltin, "FFM Interviews Una Merkel," *Film Fan Monthly*, January 1971, 10.

14 Ibid.

15 Louella O. Parsons, "Riffraff," *Los Angeles Examiner*, February 2, 1936.

16 John Scott, "Riffraff presented on Two Screens," *Los Angeles Times,* February 17, 1936, 19.

17 "Riffraff," *Variety*, January 15, 1936, 18.

18 Spencer Tracy, "I Arrive in Hollywood," *Picturegoer*, June 11, 1938, 7.

19 Grace Wilcox, "Glamor? I've Got It, Says Miss Merkel," *Milwaukee Journal* (Screen & Radio Weekly Supplement), July 25, 1937, 23.

20 Ibid.

21 Ibid.

22 Ibid.

23 Dorothy Manners, "Saratoga," *Los Angeles Examiner*, July 22, 1937.

24 Maltin, "FFM Interviews Una Merkel," 9.

25 Ibid.

26 Stenn, *Bombshell: The Life and Death of Jean Harlow*, 191.

27 Eve Golden, *Platinum Girl: The Life and Legends of Jean Harlow* (New York: Abbeville Press, 1991), 205.

28 John T. McManus, "Saratoga," *New York Times*, July 23, 1937, 16.

29 "Hollywood Parade," *Los Angeles Examiner,* December 16, 1937.

30 Ibid.

31 Grace Wilcox, "The Hollywood Reporter," *Long Island Sunday Press* (Screen & Radio Weekly Supplement), August 8, 1937, 2.

32 Ibid.

33 "Pictures on Fire," *Silver Screen*, January 1938, 59.

34 *Checkers* (Twentieth Century-Fox, 1937), Production File, Academy of Motion Picture Arts and Sciences.

35 Ibid.

36 "Juvenile Star Supported by Comic Actors," *Schenectady Gazette*, February 19, 1938, 8.

37 Ibid.

Chapter 14
Good-Bye, Mr. Mayer

In 1937, the Bernstein cinema circuit in the United Kingdom conducted a questionnaire among its filmgoers, and they selected Una as their favorite character actress. When the survey had been taken three years earlier in 1934, she also topped the list. Like many of his fellow countrymen, Val Gielgud, brother of famous actor John Gielgud, also fell under Una's irrepressible charm. He made a trip to Hollywood in the late 1930s and recorded his adventures there, which he published as part of his autobiography, *Years of the Locust*. He met Una at a function and noted she was the "highlight of the party" and as "amusing in real life as on the screen, with the most charming manners to boot."[1]

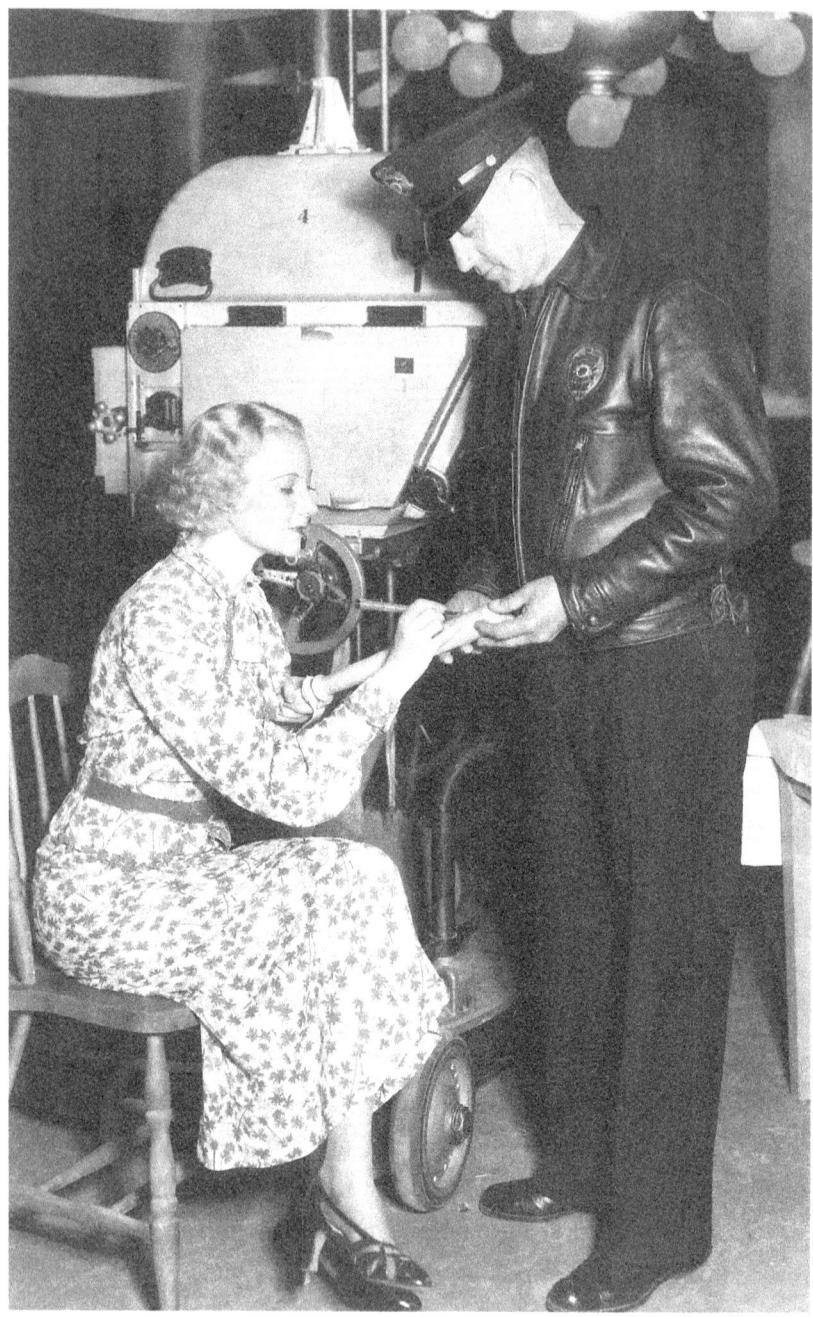

Una takes time to sign an autograph for a fan.

Perhaps not as popular in her own country as in Great Britain, Una nevertheless had her own fair share of devoted followers in the States, some of whom even created fan clubs in her honor, most notably The Una Merkel Club, which was based in Los Angeles. The members of another organization, the Kappa Psi Pharmaceutical fraternity at The Ohio State University, were just as smitten and voted her their favorite actress. They asked for an autographed photo and received one.

Una was always very appreciative of her fans, and they meant the world to her. "My fans have been wonderful. You know, I don't have just the run-of-the-mill fans; several of them are my dear friends. I feel as if I know them as well as I do those who have been around me most of my life."[2] Una's fans often showed their admiration and interest in the form of gifts. One Michigan fan wrote Una every week, always careful to include a copy of *Screen & Radio Weekly* so that Una could see what was written about her and keep up with the latest Hollywood news. A fan once left her a chocolate cake at the studio gate, while another one, this time a theater usher, sent her a collection of pennies that he had collected for six years, some of them dating back to 1859. Still other fans wrote to Una for advice, asking for help with relationship problems, but perhaps Una's most endearing fan was Miss Anna Owens, an elderly lady from Hamilton, Ohio. "I tell her everything, all my joys and sorrows," Una confided. "She is a wonderful help to me in my career. She advises me, counsels me, and encourages me. She has seen every picture I have been in, and when I married, she sent me a perfectly gorgeous dinner set of Spode. Some of my relatives have called on her, and I shall go to see her one of these days."[3] Una kept her word and visited Owens several times over the years and even invited her out to California.

Like most Hollywood actors, Una would sometimes receive the odd fan letter, like the one requesting an autographed photo, only to be followed up a few days later with another that instructed, "Do not send picture. Am moving and decided I do not want it."[4] Una wrote back somewhat testily, "Picture is sent. You'll take it and like it!"[5] On another occasion, a female fan wrote, "I don't care so much about you, but would you send me a picture of your husband? I think he's the best looking man I've ever seen."[6] Una showed the letter around, and Ronnie took some ribbing from their friends. He probably wasn't completely surprised by the lady's interest, though. He bore a striking resemblance to Ronald Colman, and fans sometimes mistook him for the famous actor and asked him for an autograph.

Ronnie, while not that interested in acting or the actual filmmaking process, remained a big film enthusiast and fan of Hollywood celebrities. Una once told the story of how she and Ronnie were invited to Joan Crawford's house for dinner. Once there, Ronnie saw that Crawford had a matchbox that was embossed with her signature. Desperately wanting it as a souvenir, he picked it up and dropped it in his pocket. Una was absolutely mortified when she found out. She sent the matchbox back to Joan the next day, accompanied by a note: "If you've missed anything else, I'll make a formal search of Ronnie's pockets. If I remember correctly, he liked that 16 x 20 framed photograph of you in the den."[7]

Una was not immune to movie-star worship either. Her adoration of Helen Hayes and Lillian Gish has been established, but she also greatly admired Groucho Marx, Roland Young, W. C. Fields, Helen Broderick, and Ted Healy. Greta Garbo also intrigued her, but Una didn't cross paths with her very often on the MGM lot. Una met her only a few times, very briefly, and Una recounted one of these encounters, which occurred when they both were heading toward the same phone booth: "I stepped aside when I saw she had the same objective; I tried to say something, but the words stuck in my throat. Garbo said, 'Go ahead. I'll wait.' So I went into the booth, still dazed. To this day, I don't remember whether I actually called the number I had intended to get!"[8] Reflecting back on Garbo, Una commented that you didn't feel as though you could take any liberties with her, and you felt tentative and self-conscious in her presence. Una also sensed some sadness about her and described her as "a lonely woman."[9]

In the summer of 1937, Una and Ronnie decided the time was right to put their house up for sale, and they were overwhelmed when more than seventy-five people showed up for viewings. Strangely, not one of them made

In 1937, Una and Ronnie decided to put their house up for sale.

an offer. Come to find out, these people weren't house hunters at all, but movie fans hoping to meet Una. Others sought their meetings and autographs with Una more indirectly, like those who came by with cameras and took photos of her ornamental mailbox. When Una went out to investigate, she discovered these fans had already made the rounds at other celebrities' homes, proven by the collection of photos they proudly shared with her.

Carole Lombard and Una in *True Confession*. (Paramount, 1937)

When Una wasn't mingling with fans, she was preparing to work on *True Confession*, a comedy which was filmed in the fall of 1937. Top-billed Carole Lombard plays writer Helen Bartlett, a pathological liar married to Kenneth (Fred MacMurray), an extremely honest and ethical lawyer. Hoping to provide her husband with a case, Helen confesses to a crime she didn't commit and becomes entangled in a murder trial. John Barrymore plays a loony criminologist, while Una rounds out the main characters as Daisy,

Helen's best friend and confidant.

In her ditzy performance, Lombard does prove, as one reviewer put it, that she is the "queen of the new hare-brained comedies."[10] She possesses great comedic timing, inexhaustible energy, and an innate naturalness in front of the camera, as well as no aversion to appearing less than glamorous to fulfill the script's more outlandish requirements. As good as Lombard is, Barrymore is possibly even better, and he nearly walks off with the picture, stealing attention away from his colleagues with his quirky characterization. As for Una, *Variety* qualified her contribution as "excellent."[11] She is given some great dialogue and makes effective use of her non-verbal skills—eye rolling, mouth contortions, and grimaces. Possibly the only misstep in her characterization of Daisy, dictated by the script, comes about when she faints in a scene, a moment of weakness that seems contrived and inconsistent with her character's otherwise robust and resilient personality.

Some of the film was shot at Lake Arrowhead, and while there, Una and Lombard shared a bungalow and struck up a friendship. At first, Una was taken in by Lombard's seeming fragility, and it drew out Una's maternal instinct. However, as time went on, Una realized that Lombard was much stronger than she appeared. Una surmised that people's solicitous concern for Lombard may have come from her selfless and genuine interest in others. "She never spares herself for a moment," Una explained. "She loves to meet people, and she loves to listen to what they have to say. There is no pretense about her. She says what she thinks."[12] Una acknowledged learning a great deal from Lombard, especially her attitude about complaining. "If Carole has anything to complain about, she does it before the picture starts. But once she is set for a job, she allows nothing to interfere. In this way, everyone on the set has a chance to do his own job to the best of his ability."[13]

That's not to say there was no levity during production. After a grueling day filming a water scene, Lombard returned to her bungalow and tried in vain to remove the body makeup on her back. Exasperated, she finally asked Una if she would come over and wash if off. Una obliged, as Lombard chattered away non-stop. Both women started laughing uncontrollably, so much so that Una said that Lombard's back probably didn't get the cleaning it deserved. When Una came back in a little later to say good night, Lombard was sitting up in bed, dressed in a flannel nightgown with a satin bed jacket over it. She was holding a gun, a recent gift from Clark Gable for her birthday, and she was aiming it at different targets, carrying on an imaginary attack.

Director Wesley Ruggles contributed to the fun by pulling all sorts of pranks on Lombard, including replacing the light bulbs in her bathroom with flashbulbs and hiding a rubber spider in her bed sheets. Barrymore generated his own share of guffaws. While filming the trial scene, he kept whispering things in Una's ear, causing her to erupt in laughter, much to Ruggles' dismay. Barrymore complained that he was tired and asked her to poke him when they were ready for his lines. He then proceeded to fall fast asleep. "He had to read his lines from a board," she recalled. "But he read them just as well from a board as most people did without it."[14] Despite or perhaps because of such hijinks, the production ran very smoothly, and at one point the film was five days ahead of schedule.

But the laughter and good cheer gave way to real fear and concern on the morning of October 6, 1937, when Una made her way across the lake in a fast moving boat. The backwash from her vessel was so strong that it caused a man in a nearby skiff to capsize. Not knowing how to swim, he went under the water twice before Una was able to turn the boat around, jump in, and pull him into her boat. She then sped back to Lake Arrowhead village, where someone was waiting to help resuscitate him.

The rest of filming transpired without incident, and when the production concluded at the end of October, Una received an unexpected gift from Lombard—a huge bowl of daisies with a box that contained a gold daisy with a diamond center. The card inside was addressed to Daisy, Una's namesake in the film. Ruggles sent her another gift—a bowl full of Christmas ornaments and several long-stemmed pink roses.

Una Merkel (c. 1938, MGM).

At the end of January 1938, gossipmongers whispered that Una and Ronnie were contemplating divorce, which prompted both of them to issue a staunch public denial. Work didn't offer Una any distraction from the rumors because the studio wasn't sending her any new scripts. Trying to use humor to deflect some of her disappointment, she called a friend to say, "This is Una Merkel, who used to work in pictures."[15]

The ensuing months were no better for her. In February, she auditioned for the role of the ballet dancer in Columbia's *You Can't Take it With You*, but Ann Miller got it. In March, her dog Shanty died after a fall from a staircase. Then, she was passed over for some other parts for which she was briefly considered—Maisie and Dulcy, both of which went to Ann Sothern, and The Wizard of Oz's Glinda the Good Witch, which Billie Burke played so memorably. She even hoped for the part of Melanie in *Gone with the Wind* and tried "paradin' her accent" around Selznick to no avail.[16] But perhaps one of her most crushing disappointments came when she lost the part of Blondie in the eponymous film series. Columbia had almost chosen her and Stuart Erwin for the lead roles, but decided to go with Penny Singleton and Arthur Lake instead.

As the summer of 1938 approached, Una had not worked on a picture for eight months. She did appear on the occasional radio show, but no film roles came her way. She remembered: "I used to wake up in the middle of the night and stew over what was happening to me. I thought maybe I had become the victim of a whispering campaign."[17] Una attributed some of her idleness to an accounting error: "The salary of each player is charged up to the picture in which he's working. If he hasn't worked for two months beforehand, the picture has to absorb that, too. A number of producers on the lot wanted me in their pictures, but they always decided against me because of the heavy charges that had piled up. And every week that I didn't work, the charges got bigger."[18]

Hoping to shake off her growing fear and mounting apprehension, Una decided that if she couldn't change her work situation, she could at least change her appearance. She decided to dye her hair brown because, as she put it, "blondes just seem to be out of style."[19] But her new hair color didn't make her any more marketable at the studio. Una theorized that some of the blame lay in the new screwball comedies that were in vogue at the time: "When I started in this business . . . the leading ladies had to be dignified. You couldn't kick them [or] accidentally throw a pie at 'em . . . that's where I came in, until a change came over pictures, and the leading ladies lost their dignity. The Lombards got kicked, and the Colberts stopped pies, and pretty soon there was so much comedy all over the place that there wasn't any need for little Una anymore. At least there was no need for the dumb, little Una."[20]

Not surprisingly, when Una's contract expired in October 1938, the studio didn't renew it. According to a newspaper report, it was a tearful departure, with many studio employees—hairdressers, makeup artists, electricians, prop boys, and others—all coming to see her off and wish her well. The day she left the studio, Una was despondent. She told one journalist how she numbly climbed into her car and headed for the countryside, driving around aimlessly, not paying attention to much of anything, including her gas gauge. When her car ran out of gas, she had to walk nearly a mile back to the nearest service station. The owner lived on the premises with his wife, who recognized Una and invited her inside to wait as her car was retrieved. "Oh yes, I know you," the woman remarked, "even though you're not in pictures any more. . . . It's too bad you lost your Southern accent. I guess if you had been able to keep it, you'd be going strong yet."[21] Una sat there dumbfounded as the woman continued. "Take those parts you been playing lately. Gosh, in those pictures you are just a girl, no different from a dozen others, but back in those days when you were a nutty little Southern girl, my, I used to laugh my head off at you!"[22] The gas station attendant then returned with Una's car, so she politely excused herself, paid for the gas, and left, muttering to herself, "What a dumbbell I really was to try to make myself over."[23]

After only three days, Una was hired for the new radio show *Texaco Star Theatre*, but only on the condition that she resurrect her Southern accent, which she gladly did. A few months later she was a freelancer and a much less expensive commodity, which landed her back at MGM playing second-lead

Gertie in director S. Sylvan Simon's *Four Girls in White*. This B film chronicles four student nurses as they make their way through three years of training. Simon's fine directing enriches the moderately interesting, albeit sometimes melodramatic plot. While *Film Daily* lamented that Una was "seen much too little for the swell trouper that she is," she does have some fine comedic moments with pal Buddy Ebsen.[24] Dependable character actress Jessie Ralph performs well as head nurse, while lead Florence Rice takes top acting honors with her sensitive portrayal.

(Left to Right) Mary Howard, Florence Rice, Ann Rutherford, and Una in MGM's *Four Girls in White*. (1939)

While Una was making *Four Girls in White*, her father Arno lay ill in the hospital. Not stopping to remove her nurse uniform or makeup, Una left the studio one evening to go directly to the hospital. As she was walking down one of the hospital's corridors, a young doctor walked up and began scolding her: "Better get some of that makeup off your face, or you won't linger long here." Una didn't bother to explain, but politely mumbled, "Yes, sir," and kept on walking.²⁵

In the early part of 1939, tongues started wagging again that Una and Ronnie weren't getting along. This time Una elicited the help of Louella Parsons to set the record straight. The columnist reported that Una was not only angered by the gossip, but she also vehemently denied it. Una announced that she and Ronnie were planning a second honeymoon and were going to fly throughout the southern United States. Una's indignant and pointed response was atypical, and it just underscores how hurtful and painful the gossip must have been for her. It is unclear what prompted such talk of marital discord, but it may have stemmed from Ronnie's spending less and less time at home. His work at the local airplane factory now required him to spend sixteen hours daily on the job in an effort to keep up with the growing demand of foreign orders. Something equally surprising about Una's statement was how she intended to travel—by plane—which must have raised a few eyebrows, particularly those who knew her fear of flying. Nevertheless, Una was true to her word, and she did indeed make her first airplane flight later that year. It was only the first of many more to come.

Una didn't have to wait too long before going back to work. This time Paramount sought her services in its third pairing of Bob Hope and Shirley Ross in *Some Like it Hot*. (The title would eventually be changed to *Rhythm Romance* so as not to confuse it with the successful 1959 Marilyn Monroe film of the same name.) This film has the distinction of being arguably one of Hope's least known films, and he even once described it as the "rock bottom point" in his career.²⁶ The paper-thin plot revolves around Nicky Nelson (Hope), a barker in Atlantic City, who wants to see his protégés—Gene Krupa and his swing band—make the big time. Singer Lily Racquel (Ross) falls for Nicky and wants to help him, but her assistance only brings about more complications.

Una is Flo Saunders, a friend along for the ride, and she does her best to introduce some mirth into the proceedings, but she has little screen time and is essentially superfluous. Krupa and his band emerge as the real stars, and when they are not on screen, interest begins to flag considerably. Hope's wisecracks, Ross's musicality, and Una's cheeriness are not enough to lift this film, but it is redeemed somewhat by a satisfying amount of jitterbugging.

MGM came calling again in the form of producer Sidney Franklin, who specifically asked Una to play sweet Marcia Giles, the faithful maid, in *On Borrowed Time*. Lionel Barrymore plays the lead character, Julian Northrup, a lovable grandfather who traps a personified Death (Cedric Hardwicke) in a tree and won't let him down, hoping to protect his beloved grandson, Pud (Bobs Watson). Una knew the picture was special and said as much to friend Madge Evans at a party. "But," Una continued, "it gives me the strangest feeling. I haven't been able to analyze it."[27] Evans quipped back, "Don't worry. It's probably that you're not used to working in A pictures."[28]

Bobs Watkins, Lionel Barrymore, and Una in *On Borrowed Time*. (MGM, 1939)

Evans was right about *On Borrowed Time*. It was definitely a step up from Una's last film, and it boasted high production values, masterful directing from Harold S. Bucquet, a fine script, and sincere and moving

After MGM failed to renew her contract in 1938, Una became a freelance player. She was invited back to MGM in 1939 for two films. This is one of her last glamour photographs taken at her old studio.

performances by its cast. Una appreciated the role, which gave her a rare opportunity to emote: "Over years of silly parts," she explained, "I seemed to have learned eight to ten tricks of acting that could be turned on and off like a faucet. So when I got into my first heavy scene on this picture, I was doing a Sarah Bernhardt all over the place. I probably hammed it up good."[29]

Watson was a talented child actor, and one of his particular skills was an ability to cry on cue. During some of his heartfelt exchanges with Barrymore, his tears flow freely, and the result is achingly real and moving. "I cried for two days," Una confessed, "but that was easy. Everyone cried, for that matter. Some of those scenes—broke up the whole company. It was so poignant that I could do it all over again—and I will if you don't stop me!"[30]

Around this time, Una's longtime friend and mentor, John Golden, invited her to return to the stage for the summer. She accepted, but as time went on, she began to second guess her decision. She told a reporter that she didn't think she'd have enough rehearsal time to prepare for summer stock. Plus, she hadn't found the right play. Sidney Franklin wanted her for another film, but Una wasn't sure about that either. There were several films she wanted to do, but, as she put it, "I don't dare go ask for them myself. It would be going against custom. So, the only course of action is to suggest that you be mentioned to the right parties as being interested . . . personally, I'd prefer to go in and do my own plugging."[31]

Someone over at Universal heard about Una's plight and thought she'd be perfect as Lily Belle in their next picture. She read the script and wholeheartedly agreed. It was a fateful decision that would offer her one of the most memorable roles of her career.

(ENDNOTES)

[1] Val H. Gielgud, *Years of the Locust* (London: Nicholson & Watson, 1947), 151.

[2] Grace Wilcox, "Miss Charming from Covington," *Milwaukee Journal* (Screen & Radio Weekly Supplement), August 27, 1939, 14.

3. Ibid.

4. Patrick Robertson, *Guinness Movie Facts and Feats* (Enfield: Guinness, 1991), 216.

5. Ibid.

6. Dan Thomas, "In Hollywood: 'Hubby Takes a Bow,'" *Palm Beach Post*, June 27, 1935, 2.

7. Jimmie Fidler, "Fidler in Hollywood," *St. Petersburg Times*, May 14, 1939, 23.

8. Irene Thirer, "Una Merkel Is Contented With Comic Film Roles," *New York Post*, December 31, 1935, 9.

9. Richard Lamparski, *Whatever Became of . . . ?* radio interview with Una Merkel, WBAI, April 7, 1970.

10. Harrison Carroll, "True Confession," *Los Angeles Evening Herald Express*, December 17, 1937.

11. "True Confession," *Variety*, November 24, 1937, 16.

12. Jerry Asher, "Still a Fan," *Silver Screen*, April 1938, 72.

13. Ibid, 73.

14. Leonard Maltin, "FFM Interviews Una Merkel," *Film Fan Monthly*, January 1971, 10.

15. Erskine Johnson, *Los Angeles Examiner*, January 31, 1938.

16. Kyle Crichton, "Something to Fight About," *Collier's Weekly,* April 2, 1938, 58.

17. Marian Rhea, "Una: The Kentucky Bell Ringer," *Radio Mirror*, February 1939, 35.

18. Ibid.

19. "Merkel Tresses Now Light Brown," *Utica New York Observer*, June 2, 1938, 29.

20. Frederick C. Othman, "Una Merkel is Victim of Bookkeeping," *Pittsburgh Post-Gazette*, August 1, 1939, 8.

21. Rhea, "Una: The Kentucky Bell Ringer," 79.

22. Ibid.

23. Ibid.

24. "Four Girls in White," *Film Daily,* January 24, 1939, 6.

25. Hedda Hopper, "Hedda Hopper's Hollywood," *Los Angeles Times,* December 27, 1938, 11.

26 Donald W. McCaffrey, *The Road to Comedy: The Films of Bob Hope* (Westport, CT: Praeger, 2004), 165.

27 Erskine Johnson, "Behind the Makeup," *Los Angeles Examiner,* May 10, 1939.

28 Ibid.

29 Paul Harrison, "Fired by Metro, Una Merkel Wins Fame as Freelancer," *Pittsburgh Press*, June 19, 1939, 6.

30 Ibid.

31 Harry Mines, "Raves and Raps," *Los Angeles Daily News,* July 6, 1939.

Chapter 15
Western Catfight

After her tender performance in *On Borrowed Time*, Una showed considerable mettle and versatility when she signed on to appear in director George Marshall's *Destry Rides Again*, a horse opera that is part comedy, drama, musical, and parody. This film was a departure for Una for several reasons. It was her first western, and the first time since her arrival in Hollywood that her name appeared so low in a cast roster. As ninth-billed Lily Belle Callahan, Una seems to have settled for a role, at least on paper, that was small, unimportant, and perhaps a little unworthy of her. After all, just a few months earlier she had played the second female lead in MGM's *Four Girls in White*, and in her four previous films, she was billed at least fourth or higher.

As Lily Belle, Una shows her husband, Boris (Mischa Auer), who's boss in *Destry Rides Again*. (Universal, 1939)

Una, however, was never one to choose parts based on billing or the number of scenes or lines she had. Instead, she was much more interested in their substance and quality, and she definitely saw something special in the role of Lily Belle, which would allow her to act under director George Marshall's watchful eye and trade barbs with Marlene Dietrich, an actress she had long admired. While these reasons were certainly motivating factors, it is likely that the screenplay's outrageous fight scene between her and Dietrich was the clincher. Una knew this altercation would be one of the film's highlights, and according to Dietrich biographer Donald Spoto, even Marshall and producer Joe Pasternak promised it would make movie history. They were not mistaken. Of all of Una's film roles, Lily Belle is arguably her best known, and it earned her a bit of cinematic immortality.

The setting for *Destry Rides Again* is Bottleneck, a corrupt town controlled by Kent (Brian Donlevy), the resident bad guy who owns the saloon and dance hall. His star attraction is Frenchy (Marlene Dietrich), a sexy chanteuse who is not afraid to use her feminine wiles and seductive singing to draw in customers. Kent hopes to extend his authority outside of town, and with Frenchy's help, he cheats a rancher out of his property and plans to charge ranchers a toll to drive their cattle across it. He then "disposes" of the sheriff and tries to consolidate power by appointing a yes-man in his place—Washington "Wash" Dimsdale (Charles Winninger), the town drunk. Once Washington is sheriff, however, he surprises everyone by swearing off alcohol and taking his post seriously. He decides to clean up the town by hiring a deputy, Tom Destry, Jr. (James Stewart), the son of a legendary lawman. Wash doesn't know that Tom isn't exactly a chip off his father's more fearsome block. Instead, he is a mild-mannered, easygoing pacifist who doesn't believe in carrying a gun. At first, Tom's presence in Bottleneck does little to reassure the town's residents, and he quickly becomes an object of scorn and derision. Undaunted, he eventually proves quite resourceful in tackling many of the challenges facing him, including winning the respect of the townspeople, subduing the bad guys, and taming the wild, unruly Frenchy.

As the leads, Stewart and Dietrich have great chemistry and play off each other perfectly. He plays the folksy, unassuming, down-to-earth deputy with natural aplomb, while she plays her wild, aggressive character to the hilt. She gets into the spirit of her character by rolling her own cigarettes, strutting around in revealing clothing, and crooning three ballads, including "See What the Boys in the Back Room Will Have," which went on to be one of her signature numbers. While most critics appreciated Stewart's portrayal, they seemed more impressed by Dietrich's bravado acting. *Time* magazine, for example, claimed that it was her best performance since arriving in Hollywood.[1] These plaudits helped revive her career, which a few years earlier had floundered after she was branded "box office poison" and Paramount bought out her contract.[2]

Destry Rides Again boasts an impressive array of supporting players who contribute greatly to the film's success. Brian Donlevy supplies most of the film's more dramatic moments. He is very convincing as the villainous Kent, whose disarming smile belies his ruthless nature. As for comedy, much of it falls on the broad (as in humor) and very capable shoulders of Mischa Auer, who plays Russian cowboy Boris, Lily Belle's henpecked second husband. Charles Winninger enjoys some fine moments as the sheriff, while Samuel S. Hinds makes the most of his memorable performance as the town's tobacco-chewing mayor. Irene Hervey, through no fault of her own, is perhaps the weakest link. She invests her portrayal of Janice Tyndall, Tom Destry's possible love interest, with all the sweetness and wholesomeness required, but the part gives her little to do besides look attractive. Perhaps the role she actually wanted was Lily Belle. Years later she confided, "I always wanted to be a Una Merkle [sic] but I never got the parts she played, the light, comedy roles."[3]

Una's Lily Belle could hardly be described as window dressing. She is plain-featured and wears simple, unadorned clothing, but what she lacks in beauty or culture, she makes up for in gumption, heart, and spirit. Beneath her rather unassuming exterior beats the heart of a feisty frontier lady who is hot-tempered, bossy, and not afraid of going after what she thinks is rightfully hers. In many ways, she seems more masculine than Boris, her weak-willed husband, whom she routinely belittles, dominates, and calls a "Russian lummox." If that weren't humiliating enough, she calls him "Callahan," her first husband's surname and even goes so far as to hang a photo of her former spouse over the conjugal bed.

Lily Belle also emasculates her husband through the symbolic use of a gun. As writer Wes D. Gehring points out in his book *Parody as Film Genre*, Lily Belle sometimes resorts to "waving around a large phallic-like shotgun" to maintain control.[4] It doesn't take viewers long to see who really wears the pants in this relationship, and a plot device makes this point even more explicit. In one scene, Boris literally loses his pants to Frenchy in a poker game, and Lily Belle plays the traditionally masculine role of "protector" by coming to his rescue and defending his honor by retrieving them. This scene sets up the much anticipated, inevitable confrontation between Lily Belle and Frenchy, a meeting which degenerates into a physical, all-out brawl.

During the advertising and promotions that surrounded this film, the press seized on the catfight and used it in various ways to draw viewers into theaters. *Life* magazine chose a direct approach, promoting the slugfest in a small feature that included several photos of the women wrestling on the barroom floor and getting soaked from Destry's water bucket. The *Los Angeles Examiner* took a more tongue-in-cheek approach, poking fun of Dietrich's artificial, flamboyant screen image, saying that "the hair-pulling contest with Una Merkel in *Destry Rides Again* should be something. But if Miss Merkel pulls off her [Dietrich's] eyelashes, Dietrich is sunk."[5]

Una and Marlene Dietrich after their knock-down-drag-out fight in *Destry Rides Again*. (Universal, 1939)

This advance publicity worked like a charm, and spectators flocked to theaters to see Dietrich's return and the much ballyhooed fight. Marlene and Una did not disappoint them, never once relying on the stunt doubles hired for the scene. The actual brawl is preceded by a heated exchange. Lily Belle pushes her way through the men in the saloon and bellows at Frenchy, "Hey you! Give me those pants. And from now on, leave my husband alone." Frenchy folds her arms in front of her while a smug grin plays across her face. "I don't want your husband, Mrs. Callahan—all I want is his money—and his pants." Lily Belle answers with, "And how'd you get 'em? By making eyes at him while you cheated, you . . . you, gilded lily, you!" Frenchy leans back seductively and purrs, "But Mrs. Callahan, you know he would rather be cheated by me than married to you." Before Frenchy can bat those fake eyelashes twice, Lily pounces on her, pushing her back onto a table, and the catfight begins.

Just before the cameras began rolling for this scene, Dietrich, who wanted the action to look as realistic as possible, whispered to Una, ". . . kick me, hit me, tear my hair. You can punch me, too—because I am going to punch you!"[6] Una followed her advice. The pivotal fight scene, although just shy of two minutes long, is every bit as exciting as you might expect, with much hair pulling, clawing, punching, kicking, and rolling around on the floor. At one point, the two women fall off the table, and the fighting continues unabated. Lily Belle even tears off one of Frenchy's shoes and begins beating her with it. Tom Destry brings the wrestling match to an end by dousing the women with a bucket of water. *Variety*, impressed with the brawl, opined that "Una Merkel cuts herself a nice slice of attention as Auer's wife, who engages . . . Miss Dietrich in a fight that proves not only the hottest bit of action in the film but the outstanding drag-'em-out item in 90 minutes of superlative rowdyism."[7]

In an interview with Leonard Maltin, Una recalled how the scene was shot: "Mr. Marshall said, 'Once you get started on this, just keep going as long as you can; don't worry, the camera will follow you.' We did the whole thing, and we turned our checks over to the stunt girls! . . . All through the fight scene we were whispering to each other 'Are you all right?' 'Can you finish it?' 'Are you OK?' We did it in one continuous take; I thought they'd never call 'Cut.'"[8]

When Marshall finally did say "cut," crew members greeted Una and Marlene with a hearty round of applause. Una successfully completed the fight scene, but she definitely looked worse for wear. She explained that Marlene's high heeled shoes were partly to blame: "Marlene stepped on my feet with her French heels. The toenails never grew back. She was stronger than me. She was very powerful, and I was very thin. Luckily, I have a remarkable constitution. I was bruised from head to foot when it was over. I looked like an old peach, green with brown spots. And I felt like one, too."[9]

In fact, Una spent a few days at the hospital after the shoot, mainly at the urging of her physician, who was concerned that she might have sustained internal injuries. Despite this ordeal, Una never expressed any anger or bitterness toward Marlene, whom she described as a "wonderful girl."[10] She even found her disarmingly charming and sophisticated. "She has Eve written all over her. Someone should make a picture called *The Garden of Eden* and let Marlene play the part of Eve," Una commented. "The only trouble is that she'd be too clever to eat the apple."[11]

Una was not quite as charitable toward director George Marshall after one particular incident during production. One day while enjoying a day off, she received a call requesting she come in to the studio to film a few scenes. Ever compliant, Una arrived on set to find that the crew was not yet ready for her. She retired to her dressing room and waited to be summoned. She waited and waited, but no word ever came. Disgruntled and tired, Una took a little nap, and she awakened three hours later to find the studio completely dark and deserted. She angrily confronted Marshall about it, and he answered her rather nonchalantly, "Forgot all about you. We decided to hold your scenes over until tomorrow."[12]

Destry Rides Again premiered at the Rivoli Theatre in New York on November 29, 1939, and it opened to rave reviews. *Hollywood Citizen News* critic James Crowe noted that the film was "remarkable in itself as an all-around audience pleaser and box office smash hit. Last night's preview audience . . . was one of the most highly enthusiastic this reporter has ever seen."[13] *Time* magazine was also complimentary, stating that the film would probably be voted best of the year.[14]

Una was certainly buoyed by *Destry*'s considerable success, and riding the crest of her renewed popularity, she signed on for another film, Warner Bros.' *Saturday's Children*. Unfortunately, on December 29, she came down with an acute case of pneumonia and had to be hospitalized. In the meantime, her part was reassigned to Lee Patrick, and Una missed her one and only opportunity to be directed by the legendary Vincent Sherman.

As Una lay in the hospital, unable to join friends as they joyously rang in the 1940s, she never could have imagined that her illness was only the first of many setbacks, disappointments, and hardships that she would face that decade. The coming years would be some of the worst she would ever experience, both professionally and personally, and they would nearly cost her her very life.

(ENDNOTES)

[1] "Destry Rides Again," *Time* magazine, Dec. 18, 1939, 76.

[2] Harry Brandt, "Box Office Poison" ("Dead Cats"), *Independent Film Bulletin*, May 3, 1938.

[3] Nancy Anderson, "Irene Hervey Always Lovely," *Daily News* (Kingsport, TN), Sept. 24, 1974, 7.

[4] Wes D. Gehring, *Parody as Film Genre* (Westport, CT: Greenwood Press, 1999), 72.

[5] Erskine Johnson, "Behind the Makeup," *Los Angeles Examiner,* Sept. 6, 1939.

[6] Maria Riva, *Marlene Dietrich* (New York: Random House, 1992), 494.

[7] "Destry Rides Again," *Variety*, Dec 6, 1939, 14.

[8] Leonard Maltin, FFM Interviews Una Merkel," *Film Fan Monthly,* January 1971, 11.

[9] Roy Pickard, *James Stewart: The Hollywood Years* (London: Hale, 1992), 38.

[10] David Ragan, "Kentucky Charm in Hollywood," *Courier-Journal* (Louisville, KY), January 22, 1950, 23.

[11] Elizabeth Wilson, "Saint or Devil?" *Screenland*, February 1940, 29.

[12] Jimmie Fidler, "Jimmie Fidler in Hollywood," *Los Angeles Times,* Oct. 24, 1939, 16.

[13] James Francis Crow, "Destry Rides Again," *Hollywood Citizen News*, Nov. 29, 1939.

[14] "Destry Rides Again," *Time* magazine, Dec. 18, 1939, 76.

Bob Burns and Una in *Comin' Round the Mountain*. (Paramount, 1940)

Chapter 16
Free Agent

After a few weeks in the hospital, Una was on the mend, and Ronnie celebrated her recovery by taking her to Slapsy Maxie's, a popular Los Angeles nightclub. She didn't resume her film work right away, but she had plenty to keep her busy. She and Ronnie had sold their Hollywood home a few months earlier and moved to Beverly Hills, where they rented a smaller house owned by a physician. Apart from their doorbell, which frequently stuck and had to be released by a pin, their new dwelling boasted a beautiful garden adorned with poinsettias, crepe myrtle, magnolia, and sycamore trees. There, nestled among them, was a single holly tree that Una transplanted from her previous house. She couldn't bear leaving it behind because it had been a gift from her gardener, whose daughter shared her namesake. Una was also the young girl's godmother.

Speaking of her white-painted brick house, Una once claimed that its architect never designed it, but simply "dreamed it one hectic night."[1] It had three suites upstairs—one for Bessie, another for Arno, and the largest for Una and Ronnie. The second floor also had a large deck that was ideal for enjoying the California sun. In fact, it was rumored that one-time tenant director Sidney Franklin cured his arthritis by sunbathing there. Downstairs, Una delighted in the well-stocked library and her "rollerdrome," the spacious living room, with its thirty arches and as many tiny alcoves. Her mother, on the other hand, was enchanted by the white marble fireplace, which she thought was a perfect showcase for her most cherished possessions: two Dresden vases given to her as wedding presents.

Una enjoyed living in Beverly Hills, as did many of her fellow thespians—Robert Taylor and wife Barbara Stanwyck lived right down the street—and she sometimes received their mail by mistake. What she couldn't abide, however, was the large number of neighborhood dogs who were tied up most of the day and barked incessantly. The situation became so bad that Una took matters into her own hands: "I went next door and asked them if their dogs didn't annoy them—and they said they never even heard them. Isn't that something?"[2]

When Una wasn't settling in her new home, she was guest-starring on the radio. At the end of January 1940, she joked around with Charlie on the *Edgar Bergen and Charlie McCarthy Show*. In February, she joined Fanny Brice and Dick Powell on *Good News of 1940*, and the following month she was heard on *Vallee Varieties*. With all her recent radio appearances, it seems fitting that Una would star opposite radio star Bob Burns and six other radio personalities in *Comin' Round the Mountain*, a comedy film about feuding hillbillies, mountain music, and a backwoods election. The silly plot is rife with stereotypical characters and uneven performances, and *Variety* lambasted its poor production values and "shoddy" material.[3] Burns supposedly requested Una to play opposite him, but not even her effervescent charm could salvage this disappointing film, whose brief musical interludes are its most redeeming features.

Some of the picture was filmed at Lake Arrowhead, and the behind-the-scenes action there was sometimes more interesting than what appeared in the finished movie. In an eerie repeat of another near fatal water incident that occurred at the lake three years earlier during the filming of *True Confession*, Una once again saved someone's life. This time it was a five-year-old toddler who fell off a dock just as Una's boat approached. When she got to him, she reached over the side of the boat and grabbed hold of his jacket, holding him aloft until the boat pilot could retrieve him.

Another time, studio workers were startled by horrible screams emanating from a make-shift cabin that had been constructed as a wardrobe and makeup room for the female players. All of a sudden, Una and a half dozen scantily clad women raced out of the cabin, shrieking uncontrollably. When crew members went to the cabin to investigate, they found the reason for all the ruckus: a three-foot king snake coiled up on the dressing room floor.

Fortunately, production wasn't all bad. During the two-week shoot at the lake, Una and Ronnie kept in touch by sending and receiving telegrams and letters. Ronnie was away in New York on business, and he called Una every day. He even timed his return to California to coincide with her arrival back home. From all appearances, the couple were as close as always, putting to rest any hint of a rift in their relationship.

In the summer, it was Una's turn to go to the Big Apple. Early on the morning of July 6, 1940, she participated in the *Lincoln Highway* radio show, a program that the *New York Times* deemed "practically an automatic stop" for personalities visiting the East Coast.[4] Then she was off to the New York World's Fair, where she made a personal appearance as part of the Una Merkel Day that was proclaimed in her honor. She spent almost two more weeks in New York before returning to California.

It wasn't long afterwards that the news broke that William Harris, theater director and producer, hoped to hire Una and Stuart Erwin for a Broadway play that autumn, but it never materialized. Instead, they both signed on to

Stuart Erwin, Baby Sandy (Alexandra Lee Henville), and Una in Universal's *Sandy Gets Her Man.* (1940)

appear in the Universal film *Sandy Gets Her Man*. The eponymous leading lady was a precocious two-year-old, Alexandra Lee Henville, known to the world as Baby Sandy. The pint-sized star was appearing in her fifth film, and it was the first to capitalize on her newly acquired verbal skills. One of her best ones, this film has Sandy playing with tear gas bombs, careening down the street on a fire truck, and awaiting rescue atop a burning building. When not under duress, she spends the city's payroll, celebrates a birthday, and plays matchmaker for her widowed mother (Una).

While some critics carped about the film's weak plot, few could deny Sandy's likability, screen presence, and winning personality. Actress Henville enjoyed "playing games" in front of the camera, and she remains very much the star and monopolizes attention throughout the film. All Una, Erwin, and the rest of the cast can do is simply offer their fine support to the scene-stealing youngster in this funny, lighthearted romp.

A young woman walks into a dining room and perfunctorily greets her mother, sister, and grandmother. She then sits down and breaks down into histrionic sobs, bemoaning how her father was caught leaving a saloon the other day. As if that weren't bad enough, he was also seen smoking a pipe. "I'll starve myself to death!" she exclaims in an exaggerated tone. "That's the easiest way. It's not so difficult to do." Then she looks askance, raises her voice an octave and squeaks out, "I tried it yesterday afternoon." This was Una's first scene in her next film, W. C. Fields' *The Bank Dick*, in which she plays daughter Myrtle to Fields' Egbert Sousé (pronounced the French way "Soo-Zay," as he liked to remind everyone).

While shooting *The Bank Dick*, Una befriended W. C. Fields, who appreciated her kindness during his bout of intoxication on the set. (Universal, 1940)

The film, which Fields also wrote, is a showcase of his many talents, which include sight gags, physical dexterity, verbal banter, and perfect comic delivery. Add to these skills a frenetic plot in which Fields, a misanthropic alcoholic, apprehends a bank robber, conceals his future son-in-law's embezzling, directs a film, and engages in a rip-roaring car chase, and you have all the ingredients for a first-rate comedy that makes for one of Fields' finest cinematic offerings.

Fields was given great autonomy on the set, and it wasn't always easy working with him. One challenge was his penchant for straying from the script. If he thought a scene was too long, he would simply tear off a few pages of the script. He kept Una on her toes, but she didn't mind. She facilitated her task by winning Fields over early in production. On the first day of shooting, he arrived two hours late, clearly intoxicated. The first scene called for Una to go over and kiss him, and when she did, Fields apologized, knowing his breath reeked of alcohol. "Mr. Fields, on you it smells like Chanel No. 5," she reassured him.[5] Moved by her kindness, he replied, "Honey, you're in!"[6] He was wonderful to her for the rest of the filming, even taking time to teach her how to juggle. When asked about him years later, Una said he was a "pretty grand person."[7]

In the fall of 1940, Una got her next role by accident. Paramount, realizing it had struck gold with Hope, Crosby, and Lamour in *Road to Singapore*, concocted another goofy adventure for the trio. This time they would cavort across Africa in *Road to Zanzibar*. Glenda Farrell was originally cast as Lamour's pal, Julia, but she couldn't get out of a stage commitment and was replaced by Minerva Pious, a brunette comedienne from the Fred Allen radio show. However, it was decided that Julia should be a blond to contrast with dark-haired Lamour, so Una, a sandy blond at the time, was called to take over.

In the film, Chuck Reardon (Crosby) is a promoter whose main attraction is his buddy Hubert 'Fearless' Frazier (Hope). The two cross paths with con artists Donna Latour (Lamour) and Julia Quimby (Una), and the foursome face adventure in the form of slave traders, cannibals, fire, wrestling gorillas, rhinos, snakes, and an incongruous orchestra that begins playing out of

Dorothy Lamour and Una in *Road to Zanzibar*. (Paramount, 1941)

nowhere to accompany the players in their musical numbers. There is plenty of tomfoolery to go around to compensate for any holes in the drifting plot. Laughter is the main objective, which the cast members bring forth easily. What wasn't so funny for them was an outbreak of flu that hit the set. The fearless quartet continued to work despite being ill, and Lamour recalled that their respective fevers became the basis for a contest. Each person would take his or her temperature, and whoever had the lowest fever would buy lunch for the others. Hope ended up picking up the tab.

Una may have lost the contest, but she made points with the many autograph seekers who visited the set one day. She was more than happy to sign her name, but she asked her fans for their autograph in return, leaving them dazed and confused. They didn't know that she, too, collected autographs. "I have two hundred and thirty-seven autographs already," she explained, "and I've been doing this only a short time. Those people are as interesting to me as I am to them . . . three bank presidents, several world statesmen, a couple of dozen newspaper men, famous writers, girls on vacation from finishing schools, a genuine cowboy, a couple celebrating their golden wedding anniversary, and many others."[8]

With the arrival of 1941, Una decided she needed to change her look, so she dyed her hair an attractive auburn. In early February, she reported to Universal to begin work on *Double Date*, which was former silent film actor Glenn Tryon's first directing effort. Una is Elsie Kirkland, a noted painter who falls in love for the very first time. The object of her affection is Roger Baldwin (Edmund Lowe), and all seems promising except that Elsie's niece (Peggy Moran) and Roger's son (Rand Brooks) are dead set against the union and do everything in their power to thwart it.

Edmund Lowe and Una in *Double Date*. (Universal, 1941)

Although Tryon was confronted with a rather unoriginal storyline, he was able to infuse some energy and interest in it by the sheer strength of his talented cast. Lowe, known for his elegant and dapper gentlemen, plays against type and is convincing as the unsophisticated, down-to-earth Roger. Moran and Brooks give spirited interpretations of their bratty characters, while Una, according to one reviewer, "equals, if not tops, all her previous combined comedy-romance portrayals and gives Peggy Moran real competition in the glamour line."[9]

What Tryon couldn't control was the inclement weather, which completely stopped production for four days and interrupted work countless other times. One day torrential rains came down so fast that extras were trapped at the back of the Universal lot. Una stayed behind to help them make their way to the entrance, and she was commended for her altruism in a local newspaper.

A few days after completing *Double Date*, Una began work on another Universal picture, *Cracked Nuts*, overseen by Edward Cline, who had directed her in *The Bank Dick* a year earlier. She was paired for the fifth and final time with Stuart Erwin, who plays Lawrence, a yokel who comes to the big city to marry his girlfriend, Sharon (Una), after he wins $5,000 in a contest. When he arrives, he meets up with Boris Kabikoff (Mischa Auer), a swindler who tricks him into investing in a mechanical man, which is really Kabikoff's friend Eddie (Shemp Howard), a blond-obsessed "hyperblondiac," dressed up in a robot suit. It's up to Sharon to help Lawrence sort everything out and recoup his money.

Erwin is very likable as the naive bumpkin, as is Una, who counters his ingenuousness with her gentle dose of worldliness. The role called for her to dye her hair back to light blond, and she looks very striking indeed, with shades of the old MGM Una showing through in her character's sparkling energy and verve. She is attractive and very much an able partner in comic support, leading one critic to remark that she was "one of Hollywood's ace comediennes."[10]

As good as Erwin and Una are, the real star of the film is Ivan the Robot, which was made to look like Auer, complete with mustache and hairpiece.

Una in a glamour shot. (Universal, 1941)

Ivan was also fitted with lights that would flash when he spotted a blond female, and he sometimes emitted flushing noises, suggesting he was capable of bodily functions. As expected, many funny moments are built around this "Frankentin," as one character calls him. In the film, Shemp's character is the one in the robot suit, but the person who actually wore and operated it during filming was former vaudevillian Ernie Stanton. When he would complain about not having enough air in the hot suit, director Cline would glibly tell him to hold his breath. When Stanton grumbled that the heavy, seven-piece metal suit was uncomfortable and causing bruises, Cline jested that he be more careful ... so as not to damage it. Cline's flippant behavior wasn't meant to be dismissive or mean-spirited. He simply liked to joke around with his actors and keep things lighthearted on the set, all of which helped to create a relaxed atmosphere that was more conducive to the comedy and silliness needed for this wacky film.

In April 1941, Ronnie returned from the Southwest, where he had been opening a new plane factory. He and Una went for a little getaway, and Una confided to a reporter that despite Ronnie's workload, he was not too busy to steal away with her every once and awhile. "I'm one girl who's really enjoying her marriage," she continued. "My career fits in very well—keeps me interested. Every woman should have some outside interest from her home to keep her viewpoint fresh—and herself interested."[11]

The summer saw Una back in New York City, where she did a few more radio shows, but she also took time to get reacquainted with old friends. One person she looked up was former MGM buddy Madge Evans, who hadn't made a film for three years. She had married playwright Sidney Kingsley back in 1939, and the couple relocated to the East Coast, where they had been living happily in New Jersey. Una spent three weekends with them, admiring their beautiful 50-acre farm, which included an apple orchard, the trees of which were planted by the previous owner—Una's actor friend Ernest Truex.

When she wasn't working on films or doing radio shows, Una threw herself into helping with the war effort. Earlier in the year, she and Irene Hervey had entertained soldiers at the North Aviation plant in Inglewood,

California, where Ronnie worked. Back East, she participated in a "V for Victory" cruise on the Hudson and finished up the year appearing in a show to benefit the United States and the United Kingdom. Una longed to do more and would eventually get her wish, but it would be in an unexpected locale fraught with considerable risk and peril.

(ENDNOTES)

[1] Betty Boone, "Inside the Stars' Homes," *Screenland*, February 1940, 74.

[2] May Mann, "Una Forgets Inhibitions After Face Slapping Role," *Ogden Standard Examiner*, April 20, 1941, 13.

[3] "Comin' Round the Mountain," *Variety*, August 14, 1940, 14.

[4] Jack Gould, "Expenses, Plus," *New York Times*, May 3, 1942, 10.

[5] Leonard Maltin, "FFM Interviews Una Merkel," *Film Fan Monthly*, January 1971, 11.

[6] Ibid.

[7] Ibid.

[8] "Star Turns Tables on Autograph Fans," *Road to Zanzibar* pressbook (Paramount, 1941), 20.

[9] "Amusements: Majestic Theatre," *Daily Times* (Beaver/Rochester, PA), June 20, 1941, 16.

[10] "Robot Hero of Comedy," *Los Angeles Times*, July 18, 1941, 13.

[11] May Mann, "Una Forgets Inhibitions After Face Slapping Role," 13.

Chapter 17
Entertaining the Troops

After the attack on Pearl Harbor on December 7, 1941, and the United States' subsequent entrance into World War II, Ronnie was working more than ever. Work obliged him to relocate to Dallas, Texas, to serve as assistant to the president of the North American Aviation Corporation, where he took care of everything from statistics to problems on the assembly line. Una told a reporter around this time that she saw her husband "less often these days than if he were in the army!"[1]

Una dealt with Ronnie's absence and her ticking biological clock by reaching out to some of the more than 300,000 Chinese children who were made orphans during their country's ongoing war with Japan, which had broken out in 1937. This cause became more real and personal to Una after she met Bowlum Lee, an adorable two-and-a-half-year-old, who had been adopted by a New York restaurateur. Spurred into action, Una became involved with United China Relief, and she sponsored several orphans and even offered pre-paid "proxy" adoption forms to her friends at Christmas that year, inciting them to spend time with children in need.

After a brief return to California in January 1942, Una was back in New York City the following month to do more radio work. She was staying in her hotel of choice, the luxurious Essex House, this time on the thirty-fifth floor, where she had a commanding view of Central Park and upper Manhattan. The city had grown on her over the years, and now she adored it and its inhabitants, describing them as full of vitality. "I love it like nothing else," she declared and playfully confessed that one of the reasons was the city's choice of girdles, which was superior to what she found back in California.[2]

While Una performed in the occasion radio show, her film career was slowing down. She had two films released in 1942, but they had been completed the year before. In the first, *The Mad Doctor of Market Street*, she snagged top billing playing Margaret Wentworth, "Aunt" to Claire Dodd's Patricia Wentworth. Lionel Atwill, however, took top honors in certain ads and one-sheet movie posters. The film tells the story of a "chemist," Dr. Ralph Benson (Atwill), who flees the law after an experiment in suspended animation goes terribly wrong. He boards an ocean liner bound for the South Seas, but his trip is interrupted when a fire breaks out. He, Margaret, Patricia, and a few others escape aboard a life boat which runs aground on a nearby island. Benson tricks the island natives there into thinking that he's a god and decides to continue his experiments on the rest of the castaways.

Atwill seems to relish his hammy role and gleefully overacts, making the most of his scenes and occasional close-ups. Dodd, Richard Davies, and Nat Pendleton all provide able support. Una's Margaret is a curious character, and the viewer is left wondering what racket she and Patricia are running, especially after she tells the latter, "The next time I have a niece, she's going to be younger than me." Elsewhere, Margaret comes across as a "Dumb Dora" character. At one point she tries to converse with a native who only grunts in return. Mistaking his mode of communication for indigestion, Margaret tells him to be more careful about what he eats.

Another time she absent-mindedly strips down to her undergarments and waves her polka dot dress to attract the attention of a passing plane. She becomes embarrassed by her unclad state when someone asks if she ever did burlesque. One of Margaret's final silly moments comes near the end of the film, when she and the others are trying to escape the island with natives in hot pursuit. She tells her companions that they should wait and wish their pursuers a proper good-bye, a suggestion her friends wisely ignore.

While Una made it look effortless, she explained to Hedda Hopper that playing such silly dames could be taxing, requiring half her energy to believe the characters, and the other half to make them believable to an audience. Nevertheless, the *Hollywood Reporter* rewarded her efforts and singled her out in a review, saying that she was the bright spot in the feature. Reviews of the film, however, were generally not as complimentary. One critic complained that "rarely has anything more ponderous or tasteless come out of the film capitol."[3]

Una's second film of 1942 was *Twin Beds*, an old recycled Broadway farce about newlywed Mike Abbot (George Brent), who just wants to spend some quiet time with Julie (Joan Bennett), his wife. He never gets his wish because Julie's good deeds lead to all sorts of complications, including their small apartment being overrun by two other warring couples. Third-billed Mischa Auer, who plays Russian singer Nicolai Cherupin, steals every scene, and he's particularly effective in one protracted one in which he tries to avoid being caught in Julie's apartment. Una and the rest of the cast rise to the occasion and perform admirably, but they are limited by the hackneyed plot, which the *New York Post* says is "so predictable that suffering without physical pain reaches new and unprecedented levels."[4]

During production, even Una wondered about some of the horseplay characteristic of farcical films like *Twin Beds:* "I've heard that it tickles people to see someone's dignity shattered by being spilled on the derriere or meeting a pie with their chins. But comics aren't *dignified,* and still people laugh."5

Una, it seems, was starting to tire again of all the comedic roles she was offered: "I would like to do something like the wife in *Angel Street.* I believe I could do it. I'd even do it in a road company. But I'd need a lot of study and rehearsal. After Hollywood I'm a bit rusty."6 The role never came her way, so in September 1942, she created a revue of her own and played New York before taking it on the road, hitting the East and West Coast, with a stopover in British Columbia, Canada. She teamed up with vaudeville veteran Frank Fay and screen player Anne Nagel. Una and Fay did a skit about camp life, which, according to *Billboard*, "registered favorably," although the magazine was less enthusiastic about Nagel, whose singing didn't even rate as mediocre.7 Una followed up this tour with other vaudeville shows and personal appearances, performing alongside Jan Murray, Ray Heatherton, Lawrence Welk, and Walter Donohue. A critic for the *Washington Post*, Marjorie Kelly, caught Una's act with Donohue and found it pleasing enough, but she was more captivated by Una's strong stage presence, charisma, and physical attributes. "It is more fun just looking at Miss Merkel, discovering that her hair is really red, and . . . watching her inimitably inane facial expressions . . . than it is listening to what goes on."8

* * *

Warner Bros.' patriotic *This Is the Army* was one of the highest grossing films of 1943. It garnered three Oscar nominations and won one for Best Score. This morale-boosting film consists of seventeen songs by Irving Berlin and a thin plot about a father and son (George Murphy and Ronald Reagan) , who each put on stage shows before they march off to World War I and World War II, respectively. Una plays Rose Dibble, wife to Eddie Dibble (Charles Butterworth). Una's part is little more than a walk-on, but, as she claimed, it still qualified her as Joan Leslie's honorary parent: "In the early part of the picture, I play Charley [sic] Butterworth's wife . . . but after the

Hair and costume test for *This is the Army*. (Warner Bros., 1943)

1917 sequence, I fade out, and I don't know whether I leave him or die in childbirth or just fade into thin air. But then, later on in the picture, Charley has a daughter, and it's Joan Leslie. He hasn't had any other wife, so she must be mine!"⁹ When asked what she remembered about Una during production, Leslie wrote that she regrettably never had any scenes with that "great lady," but considered her a "very fine actress."¹⁰

Harry Lane, Una, and Gwen Kenyon in *Quack Service*. (Columbia, 1943)

In September 1943, *Quack Service* was released. It was the first of two comedy shorts that Una had signed to make with Columbia, a studio whose short subject comedy unit seemed to prize gags, slapstick, and pace over character development, subtlety, and sophisticated plot. In this one, she was paired with Gwen Kenyon, with whom she worked well. The two had great chemistry and made for an attractive duo, prompting one male character, ever mindful of the ongoing war, to say of them: "I thought sugar was rationed."

Throughout *Quack Service*, laughs follow as the flustered women endure one physical gag after another, all in an attempt to serve a subpoena on a wily physician. Una takes the brunt of the pratfalls—falling over spilled moth balls, spinning around a dance floor, hanging outside a window, not to mention an exhausting obstacle course over beds in a hospital. She manages to survive this punishing exertion, eliciting lots of chuckles along the way, but it's obvious that her wincing, groaning, and gasping are all too real. It's all she can do just to keep up with the rigorous physical demands of the scene. Off-screen, exercise never was one of Una's favorite pursuits. "I guess," she said, "that I'm just a spectator at heart—not even that, because I don't care a thing about watching other people! I do like to walk, when there is something to see."[11]

In one funny scene, Una is forced to keep puffing away on a smelly cigar, and the displeasure she registers on screen is priceless. She didn't smoke in real life, so this part gave her a rare opportunity to show just how much she didn't enjoy lighting up. Her father related the story of the first time she had to smoke on-screen. It came along not long after she arrived in Hollywood, and it caused Una much nervousness and consternation. "Daddy, what in the world will I do?"[12] she had asked anxiously. Arno's unorthodox response was, "Listen, baby. I'll get you some cigarettes and help you practice."[13] According to Arno, the more Una practiced, the worse she got. "When I saw that picture," he guffawed, "it was a riot!"[14]

Between films, Una kept busy with personal appearances, helping with the Red Cross, performing at local Army camps, devoting three nights a week to the Hollywood Canteen, and selling war bonds. This last endeavor was particularly important to her and once, while on a visit to San Francisco, she decided she would try a new approach. Dispensing with her Dumb Dora persona, she stood in a department store window and earnestly recited Thomas Paine's famous speech, which began, "These are the times that try men's souls. . . ." One gentleman was so spellbound by the rousing words that he rushed inside to purchase a $50,000 bond. Proud of the result, Una announced that she ought to do it more often.

As much as Una enjoyed selling bonds for her country, she aspired to do more by entertaining troops overseas. In August of 1943, the War Department approved her vital statistics, but didn't indicate where she might be sent. She told a reporter that if she were assigned to Bermuda, she would feel a little guilty because it would sound too much like a vacation. "Naturally, I'll be glad to go anywhere I'm sent. We all just want to go where the entertainment need is greatest."[15]

Una, Harry Parke (Parkyakarkus), and Cobina Wright, Sr. in *Sweethearts of the U.S.A.* (Monogram, 1944)

While Una impatiently waited for her overseas assignment, she tried to focus on her floundering film career. She received few film offers, and her cinematic career was in the doldrums, approaching its nadir. In late August, she began filming *Sweethearts of the U.S.A.*, which gave her a rare opportunity to play the lead role in a film with strong patriotic overtones. This misleadingly named musical comedy was produced by Monogram Pictures, a leading Poverty Row studio known for its westerns and the popular *East Side Kids* and *Bowery Boys* series. Una plays Patsy Wilkins, an inept worker in a defense plant. After a mishap on the job, she dreams that she teams up with Parkyakarkus (Harry Parke), a bungling detective, and together they open a night club, manage a band, and try to catch some criminals on the lam.

This breezy, lighthearted film clocks in at a mere sixty-three minutes and has great potential, but it is marred by a flimsy plot and weak writing. Parkyakarkus "Parky" doles out some humor with his malapropisms and spoonerisms, but his butchering of the English language only goes so far to offset the insipid dramatic sequences. Una is very likable and endearing, and she tries valiantly to make the asinine plot more credible. The often cringeworthy material, though, lets her down. Things do improve considerably during the musical and dance numbers, which fortunately make up the backbone of the picture. Donald Novis, formerly a tenor soloist on the *Fibber McGee and Molly* radio program, and Lillian Cornell, former member of the Chicago Opera Company, provide the redeeming vocals. They make a charming couple and are ably supported by no less than three orchestras, led by Jan Garber, Henry King, and Phil Ohman. Several dance routines nicely complement the musical merriment, especially an enchanting rhumba performed by a talented couple.

On October 6, 1943, Una began work on her second short for Columbia, *To Heir is Human*, in which she is top-billed and teamed with veteran film comic Harry Langdon. The studio was more generous than usual with the budget, which is reflected in the longer running time, better musical score, and overall higher production values. Less care was given, however, to choosing a director, with Harold Godsoe ultimately getting the honors. Although experienced as an assistant director, he had served as principal director only once before, back in 1931, and would never do so again after *To Heir is Human*. The resulting short has Una as a would-be detective enlisted to look for Harry Fenner (Langdon), a missing heir whose family members want him dead so that they can inherit. Slapstick abounds as Una and Harry narrowly escape one deadly mishap after another, but even their combined talent cannot rescue this knockabout, frenetically paced short. Critics were for the most part uniformly unimpressed, and they kvetched about how unfunny it was. Perhaps some of the blame can be placed on director Godsoe's clumsy, unskilled handling, but as *Box Office* opined, the "weak script and unimaginative business" didn't help.[16] Years later Leonard Maltin, famous film historian and critic, interviewed Una, and he asked her about working with Langdon. She shot him a funny look before telling him that she had never made a film with the comic actor. "I was a great admirer of Harry Langdon," she continued, "so I'd certainly remember if I'd ever worked with him."[17] Maltin didn't insist, and Una's reaction suggests just how little of an impression this short made on her.

In early fall of 1943, the Hollywood Victory Committee called Una, asking if she would like to go to the South Pacific, where she would have the distinction of being one of the first female entertainers brought there to perform. Before answering, she was surprised to learn—and glad to be sitting down—that Gary Cooper would be one of her traveling partners. As soon as she heard his name, she immediately accepted and even joked, "When does the plane leave?"[18] She didn't have long to wait. The United Service Organization (USO) brought her, Cooper, actress Phyllis Brooks, and accordion player Andy Arcari to Hollywood, where they were briefed and inoculated. They were then housed in a hotel to await their orders. On October 16, they were asked to make their way to San Francisco to board a B-24A Bomber Liberator. It flew them first to Honolulu, then on to Brisbane, Australia, where they arrived on November 7. After a short rest, the group traveled to northern Australia to perform for General George Marshall; then it was off to New Guinea, where they spent over six weeks.

The group traveled from camp to camp, and their routine was basically the same: a performance early in the day, followed by a visit to a hospital, and another show in the evening. Performances consisted of singing, telling jokes, and acting out skits. One of Una's special moments included singing *Oklahoma*'s "I'm Just a Girl Who Cain't Say No." Cooper would do some of Jack Benny's material, but his most anticipated contribution was his recitation of Lou Gehrig's famous Yankee Stadium speech, which he had done a year

Una entertaining the troops in New Guinea during World War II.
(December 1943)

earlier in his film *The Pride of the Yankees*. The men would listen to it in respectful silence, some of them weeping. He, Una, and the rest of the crew would conclude each show singing the rousing "Pistol Packin' Momma" to thunderous applause.

To say that conditions in New Guinea were harsh is an understatement. Shows took place in open-air theaters, often on the backs of army trucks with their sides dismantled. In other places, boards were hastily thrown together as makeshift stages. Under the arc lights, these performing areas could reach 130 degrees, and the illumination attracted countless insects. "I never saw so many bugs in all my life," Una exclaimed, and she related how a red mist of flying ants once hovered near the stage, blocking out the faces of the audience.[19] Of that occasion, Brooks noted that as soon as she and the others would open their mouths to sing or speak, swarms of ants would rush in, and the next several minutes would be spent blowing and spitting them out.

Torrential rainfall also didn't help matters. During one performance, the troupe played on a platform covered by a tarpaulin. After every number, a few GIs had to take poles and push the tarpaulin up and over the back of the stage to drain off the excess water and mudpacks that threatened to collapse it. Una was amazed to see the enlisted men sitting there in such discomfort for the show, and she was even more surprised to learn from a commanding officer that they had been waiting there six hours, even foregoing lunch, in eager anticipation of the spectacle.

Despite the rain, frequent electrical outages, Spartan living quarters, air-raid alerts, and enemy fire (once less than half a mile away), Una and her fellow performers were committed to bringing a little bit of home, happiness, and joy to their appreciative audiences. They would mingle with the soldiers, talk about home, share anecdotes, sign autographs and short snorter bills, and visit the sick in the hospitals. When possible, the soldiers gave the troupe members notes and objects to carry back to loved ones. Others would ask questions about Eleanor Roosevelt, whom they had seen a year earlier during her South Pacific tour. Cooper would answer them, "We saw her tracks in the sand at one of the islands where we stopped, but we couldn't tell which way they were headed."[20] Stories about the First Lady abounded, and Una wrote to a friend about one she had heard. Apparently Mrs. Roosevelt paid a visit to a hospital and interacted with a desperately ill young boy there, kept alive by feeding tubes and blood plasma. At some point, Mrs. Roosevelt leaned over and kissed him gently, and this gesture had remarkable results—it revived his will to live.

If the servicemen were happy to see the entertainers there, the natives were just as intrigued, especially with Una and Brooks. "On some of the islands they have never seen a white woman, and when we came, they stood around and stared at us and giggled," Una remembered.[21] Some of the children even spied on the two women while they were bathing in a barrel that had been set up in a tent. Every now and then, the women would see a child's hand furtively lift up the tent flap to take a peek at them. Brooks, who had picked up some of the natives' language, would shoo the kids away, saying the equivalent of "Very bad. Very bad." But the children would answer back playfully in their language, "Very good. Very good!"[22]

Perhaps one of the most moving shows occurred a few weeks before Christmas. Brooks wanted to surprise Una for her birthday on December 10, so she begged the mess sergeant to come up with something resembling a cake, even if it was a "bun with a candle stuck in it."[23] The man exceeded all expectations, whipping up an extraordinary cake that fed several hundred. The men sang *Happy Birthday* to Una, and she broke down and cried. In fact, she cried often during the trip, living up to her reputation as the troupe's most sentimental member. Tears would flow when Arcari played popular Christmas carols, and the boys joined in. Other times she would cry just seeing the men sitting together and watching a film projected onto a white fence. Not surprisingly, she became very emotional during her last performance, which happened right before Christmas, but this time, she was not alone. Arcari, Cooper, and Brooks all three succumbed to their emotions and broke down. They exchanged kisses, warm wishes, and expressed how much the trip had meant to them. All of them hoped to come back again to entertain, and Cooper summed up the feelings of the group when he called it "the greatest emotional experience" of a lifetime.[24]

Although Una loved her overseas experience, it had taken an emotional, psychological, and physical toll on her, and she returned home fragile and very changed. She reflected back on what she felt that Christmas eve of 1943: "I came home from three months in New Guinea and found I was too emotionally involved with everything. I'd seen too much. It was like having no skin over your nerves."[25] She kept busy, hoping it would improve her condition. Three days after Christmas she filled in for an ailing Hedy Lamarr on a trip to Utah to greet service men at Ogden Air Service Command. Still sporting yellowish wrists, the side effects of anti-malarial drugs, Una recounted her experience in Australia and New Guinea and spoke passionately about the strikes taking place throughout the United States: "There is no one who has a right to strike while this war is going on, and anyone who does anything to delay this war one day longer, should get down on their knees and ask for forgiveness."²⁶ Una encouraged the crowd to purchase war bonds, and then, choking back emotions, she movingly told them, "If you had seen those boys over there when we said goodbye to get home for Christmas, you'd do anything to get this war over."²⁷

During her visit to the base, Una expressed her desire to return overseas someday to entertain the troops, but her main goal at the moment was to find a good acting role. She had to concede that there'd never be another audience like the GIs. She instinctively turned toward her first love, the theater, and began reading plays, but she turned down any roles offered to her. "I'd find myself wishing it was so bad," she admitted, "so I wouldn't have to take it."²⁸ Her major stumbling block was her fear, made worse by her extensive film experience. Critics, she believed, either heaped generous praise on film actors or came after them with a hatchet.

One person who still had faith in Una's stage abilities was her old pal John Golden. One of his plays, *Three is a Family*, had opened almost a year earlier at New York's Longacre Theater and was still going strong. This farce, written by the successful team of Phoebe and Henry Ephron, told the story of a daughter with a baby who moves back in with her middle-aged parents, forcing them to grapple with everything from pregnancies and domestic squabbles to wartime conditions. Ethel Owen played the acid-tongued spinster sister in the original play, but she was plagued with illness early on. Then Hollywood came knocking, and Owen thought it best to leave. Golden was convinced that with a few modifications the role would be perfect for Una, so he sent the Ephrons over to Hollywood to sound her out. Ever loyal to Golden, Una was delighted at the offer, thinking it would ease her back into the theater. She could star in a successful Broadway play and even come aboard mid-run, avoiding the horrifying prospect of an opening night. Given the green light, the Ephrons began working on changing the character to suit her. The old sister morphed into a younger aunt who was less shrill and cantankerous, but still plenty cynical. In Una's capable hands, the part truly became her own. She stepped into the role unannounced on March 28, 1944, to good reviews, showing that her years in Hollywood had not diminished

Una, William Wadsworth, Katharine Bard, and Robert Burton in John Golden's *Three is a Family.* (1944)

her stage technique, talent, or rapport with live audiences.

Nine days later Una's predecessor's name was still on the painted sign in front of the theater. Confronted with the problem, the sign painter claimed that he didn't have the necessary paint to cover up Owen's name to replace it with Una's. Taking the whole incident in stride, Una said that it didn't matter, but there was another matter she couldn't shrug off so easily. Ronnie had decided to leave her, and he promptly moved out of their Beverly Hills home. Bessie, not wanting to be left alone in the house—Arno's business ventures still kept him abroad—packed up her belongings and made her way to New York City, where she and Una moved the following month into their new permanent residence—a sixteenth-floor apartment in Una's beloved Essex House. A new chapter for Una had begun.

(Endnotes)

1. "Art of Relaxation Is Best Aid In Keeping Young, Says Actress," *Washington Post*, February 14, 1942, 9.

2. John Ferris, "Between Phone Calls, Una Merkel Tells All—Wants One Serious Role," *Milwaukee Journal*, March 10, 1942, 1.

3. William Boehnel, "The Mad Doctor of Market Street," *New York World Telegram*, January 5, 1942.

4. Archer Winsten, "Movie Talk," *New York Post*, May 1, 1942, 47.

5. "Corny Humor," *Twin Bed*s pressbook (Edward Small Productions, 1942), 9.

6. Ferris, "Between Phone Calls, Una Merkel Tells All—Wants One Serious Role," 1.

7. Joe Cohen, "Vaudeville Reviews: State, New York," *Billboard*, September 26, 1942, 16.

8. Marjorie Kelly, "Una Merkel's at Loew's Capitol, With 'Du Barry,'" *Washington Post*, August 7, 1943, 8.

9. Ibid.

10. Joan Leslie, letter to author, July 2009.

11. "Art of Relaxation Is Best Aid In Keeping Young, Says Actress," *Washington Post*, February 14, 1942, 9.

12. "Film Star's Father Never Resents Being Called 'Una Merkel's Papa,'" *Times-Picayune*, December 19, 1946, 23.

13. Ibid.

14. Ibid.

15. Patricia Grady, "Now Is the Time—Appearances Before Servicemen Are Risky, Says Hollywood Star Here for Week's Stay," *Washington Post*, August 8, 1943, 2.

16. "To Heir is Human," *Box Office*, February 19, 1944, 14.

17. Leonard Maltin, "The Harry Langdon Mystique," *Leonard Maltin's Movie Crazy* blog, October 29, 2012, accessed January 23, 2015, http://blogs.indiewire.com/leonardmaltin/the-big-book-of-harry-langdon.

18. "Gary Cooper Arrives in Australia," British Pathé newsreel, 1943, accessed January 17, 2015, http://www.britishpathe.com/video/gary-cooper-arrives-in-australia/.

19. Irving Drutman, "Una Merkel Finds Neither Rain nor Ants Keep GIs From Shows," *New York Herald Tribune*, May 21, 1944.

[20] Joseph P. Lash, *Eleanor and Franklin* (Franklin Center, Pa.: Franklin Library, 1971), 886.

[21] Alice P. West, "Star Aroused by Labor Troubles in Midst of War," *Ogden Standard Examiner*, December 29, 1943, 7.

[22] Fredda Dudley, "South Sea Saga," *Movies*, May 1944, 46.

[23] Ibid.

[24] "Gary Anxious to Repeat His Camp Tour," *Salt Lake Tribune*, January 8, 1944, 14.

[25] Phyllis Battelle, "Una Merkel, Once Top Comedienne, Happy to be Back in Public View," *Corsicana Daily Sun*, February 6, 1958, 4.

[26] Alice P. West, "Star Aroused by Labor Troubles in Midst of War," 7.

[27] Ibid.

[28] Drutman, "Una Merkel Finds Neither Rain nor Ants...." *New York Herald Tribune*, May, 21, 1944.

Chapter 18
Tragedy

Around the time Una was appearing in *Three is a Family*, Forrest Cummings, a sailor in the U.S. Navy, made his way to New York City with shipmate Travis Partain. The two men were in Times Square when they came across two ladies. His friend decided to work his winning smile and charm on the younger one, while Cummings, embarrassed and apologetic, started to chat up the older one. She looked familiar to him, but he couldn't place her. When he asked her about it, she chuckled and asked him if he ever went to the movies. It was then that Una revealed who she was. In his autobiography, Cummings wrote that Una "always came across as plain, but not so. She was attractive, friendly, and very outgoing."[1] He and Partain took Una and her pal to the Latin Quarter for drinks and dinner. "When we left the ladies and were heading back to the ship," Cummings continued, "Travis found a note in his jacket pocket with two $20.00 bills. Una Merkel wrote to me several times while I was in the Pacific, another indication of her warmth and sincerity. It was, indeed, the thrill of a lifetime."[2]

In September 1944, Una left New York to take *Three Is a Family* on a transcontinental tour, starting in Connecticut, then Pennsylvania, before heading westward. She especially enjoyed the audiences on the West Coast, whom she described as "sophisticated," and cited those in Idaho, for example, as getting the humor and jokes that people in New York and more cosmopolitan towns didn't always get.[3] The tour finished up in mid-January 1945 in Canton, Ohio; Una then headed back home for some much needed rest and relaxation.

Una arrived in New York with only the clothes on her back. Her others were packed safely away in trunks, which she had sent ahead of her, but they didn't arrive for several days. In the meantime, she didn't let her limited wardrobe dampen her fun. She went to the Stork Club, and while there, the press asked her to step outside and pose for a photograph with a horse and sleigh. She obliged, but she put her foot down when they asked for a second photo, this time with Ann Sheridan. Pointing to her clothes, she quipped, "In these I'll pose with a horse anytime, but never with a glamorous screen star."[4]

Possibly due to her inadequate clothing, Una contracted a severe cold, which waylaid her for a while. She was still suffering with it on March 4, and that evening she took a few sleeping pills before retiring to bed. She left the bottle, which had only a few pills left in it, on her bedside table and drifted off to sleep. In the early hours of the morning, Bessie got out of bed, found a pencil and scrawled out a barely decipherable note, which she addressed to Bid, her pet name for Arno.[5] She left it on a living room table. She wrote about being ill, her life being worse than death and seeing no other way out: "Be good to her [Una]. She has had so many rotten deals in this world . . . I love you both very much. . . . May God have pity on my soul and forgive me for any wrong I may be doing, but I can't take it any longer. Everything I have, which is not very much, for you and Una. I leave you both forever. God bless you both."[6]

The final resting place of Una's mother, Elizabeth "Bessie" Phares Merkel, in Highland Cemetery, Fort Mitchell, Kentucky.
(Courtesy of author and Therese Duzinkiewicz Baker.)

Bessie then made her way to the kitchen, where she took a razor blade and slashed both wrists. Hoping to spare Una the effects of her next act, she closed the kitchen door and stuffed a large bath towel in the crack beneath it. She then walked over to the gas range and turned on all four burners.

Around 5:00 a.m. on March 5, the night watchman at the Essex House grew suspicious after smelling gas outside of Una's suite. He called the night bell captain, who opened the door to find the entire apartment permeated with gas fumes. Una was discovered first, unconscious in her bed. Seeing the bottle on the nightstand, they thought she may have taken an overdose, so they seized the bottle so that the contents could be analyzed. Bessie was found on the kitchen floor and declared dead as soon as the police arrived.

Nevertheless, an emergency squad worked to revive her for more than an hour. It took half that time to resuscitate Una, who was transferred to an ambulance that sped toward Roosevelt Hospital. On the way there, she slipped unconscious again. Hospital officials contacted Arno in Mexico City to tell him the bad news. Una had only a 50–50 chance of survival. Not long afterwards, doctors managed to revive her, and they upgraded her condition, reporting that she was out of danger. When she was fully alert, Una refused to talk to anyone and was eventually moved to St. Clare's Hospital. Meanwhile, her mother's body was examined and released and sent back to Covington, Kentucky, where a funeral and burial took place a few days later. Bessie was sixty-one years old.

As soon as he heard the tragic news, Arno boarded a plane for New York, but his arrival was delayed by inclement weather. In the meantime, Ronnie received word of what happened and flew in from California. Of all of Una's friends, it was Madge Evans who proved to be the most caring and solicitous. She rushed to Una's side, eager to comfort her ailing friend, but Una was not easily consoled. She and her mother had always been very close, and Una was absolutely devastated by the suicide. Over the next few weeks she lost all her appetite and eventually dropped below one hundred pounds.

During this critical time, Una was not permitted to move from her bed, nor allowed any visitors or phone calls. Each day she was placed in a wheelchair and wheeled down the hall to be weighed. When she gained back sufficient weight and strength, she was released from the hospital, but her troubles were far from over. Una sank deeper and deeper into depression, which led to a relapse in October of that year. This time she had a complete nervous breakdown. Ruminating on this difficult time period, Una said, "People are too apt to dodge facts. It is so much easier to close your eyes, to sidestep, to look at the pleasant side, to think of something else. But when the breakdown came, I realized I couldn't fight it, so I simply gave up. I *had* to. There was nothing else to do."[7]

Arno had her admitted to a small hospital in Glendale, California, to recuperate. The rest and treatment did her good, as did shifting focus off herself and redirecting it towards others—the new babies, the accident cases, operations, and recoveries taking place in the facility. She gradually began to take more and more interest in life and those around her. "It was like being born again," she recalled. "Everything I looked at, every little common daily experience I had was like a beautiful, new adventure."[8]

Family friends who owned a ranch outside of Palm Springs, California, invited her and Arno for a visit, and the two gladly accepted. While there, Una basked in the beautiful surroundings and got acquainted with some of the resident animals. A pack of seven dogs followed her around "like a parade," and at night a desert tom cat would curl up on an adjoining pillow on her bed and run his paws through her hair.[9] This salubrious environment worked wonders for her health, as did Una's fans around the world who offered support in uplifting cards and letters. Over the years her British fans had not forgotten their favorite character actress, and they remained some of her most fervent devotees. They sent her many letters that were full of prayers, best wishes, and in many cases, money. Arno was so concerned about the situation that he asked journalist Louella Parsons to convey a message from him in her column. It read, "We are so grateful, but I wish it could be made clear that Una is not broke. It has worried her to have people think she is without money, and she would like the English fans, particularly, to receive word she is not destitute."[10]

In December of that year, Una and Arno began traveling. Their first stop was New Orleans, the birthplace of her maternal grandmother, Mary Phares (née Mary Elizabeth Alexander). Una took advantage of the visit to do some genealogy work, telling one reporter that she was looking up all the Alexanders in the phone book. Afterwards, father and daughter traveled to Miami, Florida, where they rented a little bungalow for the Christmas holidays. They stayed there for the next several months, and Una kept house, doing the cooking, cleaning, sewing, and all the washing. For the latter, she spurned the washing machine, opting for the old-fashioned method: "I did it in the bathtub—sheets and everything. Wrung them out by twisting them around the faucet.... I even washed my father's seersucker suits, the kind men wear so much down in Florida. At first I had to do the pants over four times because I didn't get the creases right. Poor Father looked as though he were going to jump!"[11]

Next, she and Arno lived aboard a schooner that operated between Wilmington, North Carolina, and the West Indies. As she had done in Miami, Una kept busy, earning her keep as a deckhand. All this hard work was beneficial, helping her to regain her health and confidence. Una also spent this time reflecting and writing long letters to friends in her home town of Covington, possibly hoping to reconnect with those who knew and remembered her mother. None of these letters has surfaced, however, to shed any light on Bessie's illness or the circumstances leading up to her tragic death. Una spoke very little about the incident, except to say that her mother was ill and despondent. She confided that the loss meant so much to her that "the loss of anything or anybody else can't mean very much anymore."[12]

This apathy extended to her career, and at the time, Una didn't care if she worked or not. "It was just as if the bucket had gone down into the well once too often," she explained. "Can you understand? There were bills to be paid, but no gumption to pay them."[13] Friends and loved ones rallied around her and forced her to work again, and as she readily admitted, if it hadn't been for them, she may have retreated back to Covington, idling her time away knitting on the back porch.

Besides her friends, something else motivated Una's comeback. It was the lure of a good part, and Una herself may have planted the seed for it. At the end of 1945, she spoke briefly to the press, effusing about her love of the South and joy of being a native Kentuckian. Quoting a line from J. M. Barrie's play *What Every Woman Knows*, which associated the quality of charm to the bloom of a woman, she observed that the comparison was particularly true of Southern women. It wasn't long afterwards that Una was offered the part of a Southerner in *It's a Joke, Son!*—the first production of newly founded Eagle-Lion Studios.

Kenny Delmar played the leading role of Beauregard Claghorn, a blustery Southerner whose love for his native region is as strong and enduring as his

Kenny Delmar and Una in *It's a Joke, Son!* (Eagle-Lion, 1947)

hatred for the North and all its inhabitants. This Southern gentleman, who continues to buy Confederate Army bonds and won't concede the South's defeat in the American Civil War, eventually gets drawn into the race for senator. His political nemesis turns out to be a very worthy opponent indeed—his wife Magnolia (Una).

It's not surprising that Eagle-Lion wanted to make this film, considering that it already had an established fan base, thanks to Delmar's recurring appearance as the character on Fred Allen's successful radio show. The studio even borrowed Claghorn's best known catchphrase, "It's a Joke, Son!" for the film's title. Claghorn was so popular that Delmar had already played the character on two popular recordings. Even Warner Bros. jumped on the bandwagon, drawing inspiration from the character to create Foghorn Leghorn, its animated rooster. Delmar's Claghorn, despite his bombast and contempt for everything and everyone Northern, resonated with the public, who enjoyed laughing at his excessive behavior and outlandish remarks. Perhaps the audience saw through his rhetoric, realizing that deep down he was essentially a good, decent fellow. His wife, Magnolia, saw to it that he was something else—obedient! With her pragmatic, no-nonsense attitude, she was the perfect foil to her aimless, ineffectual husband.

It's a Joke, Son! was a pleasant experience for Una. She enjoyed returning to moviemaking, and the camaraderie on the set was an extra bonus. Her leading man, Delmar, a certified Northerner, couldn't resist giving her "advice" about how to do a proper Southern accent. Una would protest, reminding him that she was from Kentucky, but Delmar would have none of it, insisting, "I'm from Boston, but I talk like a *real* Democrat."[14] Atmosphere on the set was so congenial that at times it seemed like a family reunion, especially when many of Una's old friends and colleagues flocked over to see her and welcome her back. Fans were no exception. During Visitors' Day at the studio, one film enthusiast marched right over to Una and exclaimed, "Oh, Miss Merkel, I used to play hooky from school just to go see your pictures."[15] Not wanting the whole truth to get in the way of a good comeback, Una shot back, "Indeed. Well, I used to play hooky from school to be *in* those pictures."[16]

With the completion of *It's a Joke, Son!* in the summer of 1946, Una had appeared in seventy-five films (including her shorts and silent films), and her cinematic career stretched back nearly twenty-five years. Consequently, she felt qualified to say what was needed for an extended career in motion pictures, and it certainly wasn't beauty or physical charms: "The actress who can't get by on just physical appeal has to turn to perfecting her acting technique, and as a result, she seems to stay in pictures a lot longer than the average pinup cutie," she announced.[17] Una cited her many films to support her argument and admitted that she never discouraged an ordinary-looking girl from pursuing a film career. "I always tell them, 'When you can't give 'em looks, give 'em laughs.'"[18]

Una and Ronnie weren't doing much laughing a few months later in November. They met to settle property and alimony claims for their impending divorce. In a signed agreement, Ronnie agreed to pay Una twenty-five percent of his gross income for sixty-two months, with a provision that monthly payments would not fall below $172.50, nor exceed $400.[19] Una filed for divorce in Miami the following month, just before flying down to Mexico City to spend Christmas with her father. Una told reporters that the divorce was a result of war-time separation. Ronnie had been away on a lot of foreign missions, and their two-and-a-half-year separation followed. "I certainly never got married believing there might someday be a divorce," she said. "And I'm sure he didn't either. But I don't think people who are married should be away from each other too long. It's awfully easy to work apart that way. We've been married fifteen years, and that's a long time."[20]

(Endnotes)

[1] "Highlights from the Career of a Less than Illustrious Magician," *Magical Past-Times: The On-Line Journal of Magic History*, accessed June 13, 2012, http://web.archive.org/web/20111003045014/http://www.miraclefactory.net/mpt/view.php?id=12&type=articles.

[2] Ibid.

[3] "West Sophisticated, Una Merkel Describes Audience Reactions," *Deseret News,* December 4, 1944, 8.

4. Leonard Lyons, "The Lyons Den," *Pittsburgh Post-Gazette*, January 22, 1945, 19.

5. Some newspapers mistakenly reported the note was addressed to Ronnie Burla.

6. "Miss Merkel Out of Danger, Mother Suicide," *Buffalo Courier-Express,* March 6, 1945, 3.

7. Constance Palmer, "How Una Merkel Won Her Victory," *Screenland,* February 1947, 42.

8. Ibid, 95.

9. "Hollywood Sights and Sounds," *Niagara Falls Gazette*, October 9, 1946, 16.

10. Louella O. Parsons, *Charleston Gazette*, October 30, 1945, 13.

11. Palmer, "How Una Merkel Won Her Victory," 95.

12. Ibid.

13. Phyllis Battelle, "Una Merkel, Once Top Comedienne, Happy to be Back in Public View," *Corsicana Daily Sun,* February 6, 1958, 4.

14. Sara Hamilton, "Comeback," *Photoplay*, April 1947, 135.

15. "Old Home Week," *It's a Joke, Son!* pressbook (Eagle-Lion, 1947), 27.

16. Ibid.

17. "Cheer up, Girls; Laughs Outlast Looks in Films," *Milwaukee Journal* (Green Sheet), September 12, 1946, 1.

18. Ibid.

19. "Una Merkel Files Suit on Back Alimony," *Los Angeles Times*, November 6, 1947, 2.

20. "Una Merkel Sues After 15 Years," *Daytona Beach Morning Journal,* December 4, 1946, 4.

Chapter 19
Phoenix Rising from the Ashes

It's a Joke, Son! was released in January 1947, and while it was mildly successful at the box office, it did not enjoy an international release because it was thought its American humor and political themes wouldn't go over well in foreign markets. Reviews didn't help its chances. *Variety* complained the slapstick was "laid on with a heavy trowel,"[1] while the *Hollywood Reporter* complained the storyline was "chock full of corn."[2] Granted, the film is old-fashioned and absurd in places, but it does have some genuinely funny moments and an undeniable charm. Director Benjamin Stoloff keeps both from waning with good pacing and finely realized characterizations. June

Kenny Delmar and Una in *It's a Joke, Son!* (Eagle-Lion, 1947)

Lockhart is wholesomely beautiful and radiates a lovely innocence and sincerity in her scenes. Una plays dominant wife and mother with confidence and aplomb, and in her best scene, she nimbly dodges and outmaneuvers Claghorn as he tries to steal a kiss. As for Delmar, he deserves considerable kudos for his exuberant performance. He invests his character with such vigor and vitality that he remains dynamic and interesting, if not flamboyant, which is altogether fitting for Claghorn's natural excesses. This bravura performance notwithstanding, Delmar still faces keen competition from two unsuspecting colleagues. The first is a clever dog named Daisy, who wins over the audience with her amazing tricks and stunts. The other is five-year-old Anthony Sydes, who, as winsome Michael, steals a scene in which he accidentally spikes the punch that is served to the Daughters of Dixie.

In March 1947, Una made her first radio appearance since her breakdown. She appeared with Lee Bowman on *Cavalcade of America* in an episode called "The Stirring Blood," which dealt with the RH factor in blood. The show was so well received by physicians and the public for its clear explanations that the actors were asked to reprise their roles for a June broadcast.

This same month also saw Una granted an uncontested divorce from Ronnie. The charge was desertion. This official parting, however, was not without complications because two months later Ronnie lost his job as an executive at North American Aviation. When Una learned the news, she telephoned him and offered to waive alimony until he was gainfully employed again. She reported that he was "grateful" and accepted her offer.[3]

It was in May that Una began work on her second feature for Eagle-Lion Films, *Man from Texas*, starring James Craig and Lynn Bari. This ambitious western contained memorable photography by Jackson J. Rose, fine art direction by Edward L. Ilou, and strong performances from cast members. Craig plays the contradictory El Paso Kid with conviction and vigor, while Lynn Bari, as Kid's long-suffering wife, is gracious, poised, and sympathetic in a limited role. Johnny Johnston was affable enough as Billy Taylor, Kid's faithful sidekick, and he contributed some first-rate vocals. Stalwart character actors Harry Davenport and Sara Allgood round out the cast and provide solid support.

Una plays the Widow Weeks, a put-upon frontier woman who, at the age of fourteen, was traded by her father for a mule and married to a violent, good-for-nothing drunk. He not only got her pregnant nine times in as many years, but he also deserted her and placed a lien on their property. The El Paso Kid takes pity on her, giving her the money she needs and advising her to safeguard the receipt, or "recipe" as she likes to call it.

Una knew a great part when she saw it, and she played it for all it was worth, even chewing up the scenery a bit. Looking very much like Lily Belle from *Destry Rides Again*, her Widow Weeks is just as spunky, but without the cruelty and insensitivity. She evinces real tenderness and vulnerability and is featured in two main scenes, the first more sentimental and poignant, the second more lighthearted, showcasing her character's indomitable spirit and earthy naturalness. Una supplies the funniest moment in the film in the latter scene, in which the town banker (Harry Davenport) tells his deputy to pat her down and forcibly remove the receipt she's concealing, regardless of its location. "I ain't lived alone and helpless for nothing," she spits back at them, "and any man aiming to take my clothes off for a recipe, better not try it in a bank!" She also gets the film's last laugh when, in the film's concluding minute, Billy plants an innocent peck on her cheek, and she whacks him upside the head, squawking, "You're in church, you durn fool!"

Variety felt that Una faltered in the role, but placed the blame on the weak screenplay. The *Hollywood Reporter*, however, was singularly impressed by her "grand job" of acting and described it as the most "conspicuous" in the film.[4] Overall, though, critics were underwhelmed by what they saw, finding fault with the loose, rambling plot, trite dialogue, and occasional dullness. Reflecting back on the film, Lynn Bari thought the original source material, the 1938 Broadway play *The Missouri Legend*, was quite good, but, as she put it, "they put in all this action to liven it up. They ruined it."[5]

In the summer of 1947, Una was back in old, familiar territory, the MGM backlot, to play in *The Bride Goes Wild*. She was Miss Doberly, dutiful secretary to a publisher (Hume Cronyn), who must contend with "Uncle Bump" (Van Johnson), a beloved children's author who actually dislikes kids and has an overweening appetite for alcohol. Match him up with a prim and proper illustrator (June Allyson) and a mischievous orphan (Jackie "Butch" Jenkins), and the conditions are ripe for a successful comedy. Writer Albert Beich hedged his bets by including copious amounts of slapstick, and the cast, Johnson in particular, carry it off with panache and much humor.

Director Norman Taurog had his hands full maintaining order on the set. Allyson and Johnson, already good friends, reportedly clowned around so much that Taurog once had to call off filming for the day. Another time young Jenkins, with whom Taurog had curried favor with bubble gum and toys, could not seem to get through a certain scene without flubbing his lines. When things didn't improve, the director walked over and asked the freckled-faced youngster what was wrong. Jenkins answered that he had been wondering if he could throw a ball as high as the ceiling on another stage on the lot. Taurog halted production and gave the boy permission to go and find out. When the young actor returned, he announced to everyone, "Couldn't do it," and then proceeded to do the scene flawlessly.[6]

As Miss Doberly, Una is a far cry from her previous role as Widow Weeks. She is the epitome of the perfect modern office assistant. Competent, loyal, and resourceful, she keeps her boss's business afloat and running smoothly, and it doesn't hurt that she's attractive with impeccable style and taste. Immaculately groomed and manicured, she cuts a fine figure with her perfect hair, makeup, and fashionable business attire. Aside from some snarky remarks and withering looks, she doesn't have much to do until the end of the film, when she is caught up in an utterly madcap car chase, in which she is nearly decapitated, buried under a carload of hay, and struck by oncoming traffic.

Some reviewers objected to the film's heavy-handed horseplay, seeing shades of the farcical Mack Sennett. One newspaper critic cited the car chase as one example, but also objected to the film's "poverty of invention."[7] Another publication warned that "slapstick will be the barometer of your enjoyment of the picture."[8] These criticisms notwithstanding, this droll film is great family fare, capably served up by the players, and in the case of Jackie "Butch" Jenkins, strengthened by a heartwarming interpretation.

* * *

Just weeks after completing *The Bride Goes Wild*, Una fell ill from an undisclosed ailment. She no longer had a home in Los Angeles, but her residence of choice was the Miramar Hotel in Santa Monica, where she sought refuge to recuperate. She soon discovered, however, that it wasn't quite as idyllic as she had hoped. One evening an American pilot and a group of Swedes threw a party in their room, and it quickly got out of hand. The partyers received angry phone calls about the racket, but they continued their loud celebrating. Fed up, Una threw a peignoir over her informal dress and marched down to the suite, where she rapped on the door. "I decided that if I couldn't stop it, I'd join it," she recalled.[9] Stepping past her greeter to join the revelers inside, she found that her presence instantly quieted the festivities, much to the relief of the other hotel guests. Una stayed until the get-together was over and confessed on her way out that she had actually enjoyed herself.

Something else that helped Una's recovery was the promise of romance in her life. In November, she began seeing Fred Ferris, a sports announcer on the West Coast. The two were spotted together frequently in restaurants and at various social functions, and they even spent Christmas holidays together. It's difficult to know, however, just how romantically involved the two really were. During the nearly three years they were together, Una rarely if ever talked about him to the press, and the two spent as much time apart as they did together, pursuing their respective careers. It is possible that Ferris was simply a dear friend and frequent escort, not unlike John Arledge had been years earlier.

Whatever her relationship with Ferris, Una was still dealing with Ronnie over the sticky question of alimony. After having waived Ronnie's alimony until he could get back on his feet, she learned a few months later that he had gone out and purchased an expensive automobile. She was livid. She sued him for back alimony in the amount of $776.25, and her lawyer went after him aggressively, placing liens on his property and garnishing his wages. The suit languished in the courts for almost two more years before the judge urged the lawyers for both sides to drop the case, which they did.[10]

Una made no films in 1948, but she did sign on that year for a recurring role in the very popular radio show *The Great Gildersleeve*, whose eponymous character was brilliantly played by Harold Peary. She first appeared on February 18 and received co-star billing with him, playing Adeline Fairchild, a Southern cousin to Leila Ransom (Shirley Mitchell), who had once been engaged to Gildersleeve but got cold feet and left him at the altar. During her one-year stint on the show, Adeline moves into her cousin's home, catches Gildy's eye, gets engaged to him, almost adopts an abandoned baby, but never ties the knot with the perennial bachelor. Instead, she turns her attention to opening a millinery business, but closes up shop and leaves town once she discovers that Gildy was actually engaged to her and Cousin Leila at the same time.

Una performed in a total of thirty-one *Gildersleeve* episodes, and the part seemed to be custom-made for her. Taking advantage of the clever writing, she shone in her witty repartee with Peary, always giving a capital performance. She claimed it was a relief to play the calculating Adeline, who wasn't all "frill and froth."[11]

In November 1949, she took a tentative step into television by appearing on the game show *Pantomime Quiz*, in which she played a variation of charades, a game she used to enjoy at her house parties back in the 1930s. Her fellow competitors were Vincent Price, Adele Jergens, and Hans Conried. As novel as the experience was, Una still longed to return to the stage, but her fears always stymied her. She got her chance that fall when she was persuaded to appear in *My Sister Eileen*, a comedy about residents of Greenwich Village. She was the title character's jesting sister. The *Los Angeles Times* was very complimentary, saying she "highlights the provocative affair with her clever wise-cracking style."[12] The play was successful enough to go on tour in the Southwest, and the whole experience was daunting but ultimately therapeutic: "I didn't know whether I could memorize a part when I took the engagement," she said. "I felt just like someone being tossed into the water and told to swim. It was a wonderful experience to know that you were getting your bearings again."[13]

Una was revitalized and full of confidence after her successful run with *Eileen*. If her future in the theater seemed secure, it was less so in Hollywood, where she had been fifth-billed in her last film. She was at a crossroads in her cinematic career. After *The Bride Goes Wild*, she was approached by Cardinal Pictures to appear in their romantic comedy *My Dear Secretary* and was offered her choice of two roles. She passed on both. The first ended up going to young Helen Walker, a svelte blond, while the other went to zaftig Florence Bates, who was sixty years old. While some might cite these disparate roles as proof of casting directors' faith in Una's range and versatility, she had a different explanation, saying, "They don't know what to do with me now."[14] Columbia, however, came to her rescue at the end of 1949, offering her a plum role— the female lead opposite William Bendix in the baseball comedy *Kill the Umpire*. Una knew a good thing when she saw it and accepted it right away, not having to be asked twice.

(ENDNOTES)

[1] "It's a Joke, Son!" *Variety,* January 22, 1947, 17.

[2] "It's a Joke, Son!" *Hollywood Reporter,* January 21, 1947, 3.

[3] "Una Merkel Claims Alimony Arrears," *Los Angeles Times,* March 15, 1949, 2.

[4] "Story's Confusion Hurts BO Chances," *Hollywood Reporter,* March 30, 1948, 3.

[5] Jeff Gordon, *Foxy Lady: The Authorized Biography of Lynn Bari* (Duncan, OK: BearManor Media, 2010), 288.

[6] Leonard Lyons, "The Lyons Den," *New York Post and Home News,* March 2, 1948, 14.

[7] James R. Parish, *Hollywood's Great Love Teams* (New Rochelle, NY: Arlington House Publishers, 1974), 639.

[8] Ibid.

9. Henry W. Clune, "She Joined It," *Democrat Chronicle* (Rochester, NY), September 20, 1947, 13.

10. Una Merkel *vs.* Roland L. Burla, Case no. 535927, Los Angeles Superior Court, decided June 6, 1949.

11. "Una Merkel," *Radio and Television Mirror,* December 1948, 68.

12. Katherine Von Blon, "Una Merkel 'Eileen' Star," *Los Angeles Times*, September 12, 1949, 7.

13. Edwin Schallert, "Merkel Climbs Back," *Los Angeles Times,* July 8, 1951, 7.

14. David Ragan, "Kentucky Charm in Hollywood," *Courier-Journal* (Louisville, KY), January 22, 1950, 22.

Una in Columbia Pictures' *Kill the Umpire*. (1950)

Chapter 20
Mothers, Matrons, and Companions

In January 1950, Una decided to divest herself of the many possessions she had accumulated over the years, and she entrusted the firm of Lewis S. Hart auctioneers to handle the sales. The company touted the auction as its inaugural one of the year, and among the items up for bid were imported chinaware, furniture, sterling crystal, and art objects. Una then set her sights on finding new accommodations, which she found in a seaside cottage between Santa Monica and Malibu.

When journalist David Ragan caught up with her there, she was in good spirits, telling him that she had never felt better in her life. Her dad was a topic of conversation: "My father is the most marvelous person in the world," she began. "He has the humor and disposition of a high-powered salesman, which he is. But he long ago gave up selling tangible things."[1] She went on to explain that he lived in Mexico, where he is "trying to sell the country back to the natives! He believes in the pot of gold at the end of the rainbow, and so do I!"[2] Knowing that the interview was destined for the readers of the *Louisville* (Kentucky) *Courier*, Una mentioned some of her childhood friends by name and spoke briefly about her early days in Kentucky. Then, in what must have been regarded as incredibly trusting, even back in the more innocent 1950s, she gave Ragan permission to do the unthinkable—print her home address in the article, along with an invitation for Kentuckians to drop by and pay her a visit!

In May 1950, *Kill the Umpire* was released to lukewarm fanfare. William Bendix is Bill Johnson, a former baseball player whose obsession with the game costs him numerous jobs until he accepts his father-in-law's suggestion to become an umpire. Una plays his enduring wife and gets ample opportunity to vent her frustrations through an occasional tirade, reprimand, and when all else fails, a book hurled at her husband's head.

A. H. Weiler of the *New York Times* was only moderately impressed and seemed most preoccupied with making baseball-related puns in his review, commenting that the film "connects with only a few before going down swinging," and later describing the supporting cast as "in there pitching," in what was "strictly minor league stuff."[3] These remarks notwithstanding, the film makes for a rollicking good time, full of funny slapstick, clever writing, an impressive, hair-raising car chase, and fine performances by the lead actors. Perfectly cast as Bill Johnson, Bendix was a good-natured lug who has his share of faults, but an equal amount of Everyman appeal. He handles the story's demanding comedy with consummate skill, generating many knockabout laughs in the process. Una is convincing as his irritated helpmate, and she gets a few good lines; the best one, in response to "What's for dinner?" was her caustic "Boiled catcher's mitt!"

Gloria Henry, who would go on to play Alice Mitchell in the hit television show *Dennis the Menace*, played Una's and Bendix's eldest daughter. Her acting assignment required her to do little more than look beautiful and swoon over her boyfriend (Jeff Richards), but the film let her mingle with coworkers. "Una Merkel became a very good friend of mine," she remembered. "We palled around; I'd pick her up since she didn't like to drive. But, after my first child was born, she sent a beautiful gift for Jeffrey, and I never heard from her again. She thought I should stay home with the kid instead of gallivanting around with her."[4]

* * *

Twentieth Century-Fox had high hopes for *My Blue Heaven* when it appeared in the fall of 1950. More than a year before filming began, Darryl Zanuck had written a memo to producer Sol Siegel saying the film might become one of the most important of the year, possibly even better than two of Betty Grable's previous films, *Mother Wore Tights* and *When My Baby Smiles at Me*, which had gone on to be the studio's top-grossing films for 1947 and 1948, respectively.[5] He was wrong, at least in terms of box office receipts, although it was the studio's third highest grossing film in 1950 behind *Wabash Avenue* and *All About Eve*. Although it wasn't as financially successful as expected, *My Blue Heaven* still has much to recommend it— intriguing musical numbers, lavish production values, beautiful photography, and effective performances all around. Capitalizing on their team of Dan Dailey and Grable a third time, 20th Century-Fox showcased them in this poignant story of married performers who desperately want to have children but face many obstacles. Una plays a kindhearted lady at an adoption agency. She is sympathetic to the couple's plight and thinks they'd make suitable parents, but she must convince her austere supervisor, who is skeptical of entertainers who adopt.

Hers was not a large role, but Una played it deftly, capturing a delicate balance between disciplined professional lady and solicitous human being, portraying both sides of her character with notable grace and poise. She barely registered a mention in reviews, which mostly panned the film. *New York Times* critic Bosley Crowther found it the "gooiest and guckiest musical film from Twentieth Century-Fox in years,"[6] while the *Chicago Tribune* felt the writers couldn't decide what type of film they were creating, so they combined too many different elements and emotional registers, making it "indigestible."[7] Mitzi Gaynor, however, appearing in her first full-featured film, did stand out, with *Variety* saying she possessed a "pert and saucy face and the kind of figure boys don't forget; she's long on terping and vocalizing."[8]

Una had returned to the stage that summer in La Jolla, a coastal town just outside of San Diego. She appeared in Tennessee Williams' *Summer and Smoke* at the La Jolla Playhouse, a theater founded three years earlier by Dorothy McGuire, Mel Ferrer, and Gregory Peck. She was Mrs. Winemiller, the mentally unstable mother of a spinster daughter (McGuire) who pines away for a handsome medical student (John Ireland). The play was a rousing success, and the troupe took it on a fourteen-week tour of the West and Southwest, to very favorable reviews. Una's performance was particularly well received, and typical were the laudatory remarks from Edwin Schallert of the *Los Angeles Times*, who observed that she "sustained the air of complete madness most successfully, in a portrayal that is a large departure for her."[9] Una gave most of the credit to the talented McGuire: "Dorothy was such a help in building up my confidence. She is so earnest and sincere that you are bound to put your whole heart into working with her."[10]

If Una had an easy time with the critics, she found life on the road more problematic. In Colorado, she fractured a toe while stepping out of a clawfoot tub. A quick-witted amateur medico in the cast fashioned her a makeshift splint, saving her from hobbling around on crutches. Despite this mishap, Una and the crew had a great time. "Please tell folks," Una urged a reporter, "life on the road is easier than it was way back when. Hotels are better, meals are better, people are just lovely."[11] The players also had the advantage of performing to full houses, where audiences were hungry for good dramas and received them warmly.

In November 1950, Una's final film of 1950 was released, Columbia's *Emergency Wedding*. It was a remake of the studio's *You Belong to Me* (1941), which had Barbara Stanwyck and Henry Fonda in the leading roles. This version had Larry Parks as Peter Kirk, a rich playboy who meets and marries Dr. Helen Hunt (Barbara Hale) after a whirlwind romance. Their conjugal bliss is short-lived, however, when Kirk's incessant jealousy and lack of ambition threaten to derail their relationship.

The leads do an admirable job of injecting some energy and buoyancy into this feature. Parks has good timing and a light comedic touch, while Hale coaxes some nuance and depth from the prosaic storyline. Jim Backus and Una compete for the honor of most valuable supporting player. Backus stands out as Park's blabbering drunk friend, and Una takes advantage of every on-screen moment as a faithful nurse. Walter Winchell wrote that Una's scene-stealing performance was the "neatest bit of larceny since Brink's."[12]

In an interview given during the filming of *Emergency Wedding*, Una proclaimed that stealing scenes and "hamming" have their place and can liven up a scene. She also couldn't help taking a little dig at the new acting style that Marlon Brando and others were ushering into Hollywood. "I think people are apt to get tired of hearing a lot of speech-making from the screen and welcome a little old-style scene-stealing," she said.[13] "I can't help showing what I feel on my face, though. It just wouldn't be possible for me to act the new way—mumbling lines with my eyes half-closed and a deadpan expression. When I feel like yelling, I yell!"[14] Una also had a word to say about Hollywood's obsession with female voluptuousness, especially the undue interest shown to actresses whose claim to fame were their heaving and over-endowed breasts: "These days an actress either has to have a bust or *be* a bust," she sighed.[15]

Throughout her brief appearances in *Emergency Wedding*, Una uses a full array of verbal and non-verbal language to garner attention, but in one scene, she has a special trick up her sleeve. She and Hale try to calm an angry Parks, who has burst into Hale's medical office. Una casually walks over and picks up a heavy figurine off Hale's desk and hides it behind her back, ostensibly to conk Parks with it if he gets too out of control. Viewers watch her carefully, transfixed, wondering what she'll do next, and in so doing, they look away from the main players. Una's gambit has been successful, and it was done with considerable deftness and finesse.

Although the film boasts first-rate acting, diverting scenes, and some cleverly written dialogue, it doesn't quite coalesce into a satisfactory whole. Perhaps it's the implausibility of the leading couple falling in love so quickly or the too facile ending, but the film just misses the mark, giving credence to the *New York Times*' assessment that it is simply not what "the doctor ordered."[16]

It was back to MGM for *Rich, Young and Pretty*, released in the summer of 1951. She replaced Marjorie Main who had other commitments. The story, written by Sidney Sheldon and Dorothy Cooper, is about a young Texas woman (Jane Powell) who travels to Paris with her father (Wendell Corey). While there, she falls in love with a French man (Vic Damone) and reunites with her French mother (Danielle Darrieux), whom she thought was dead. While some reviewers criticized the hackneyed plot, they were mostly indulgent with this frothy confection, which was easy on the eyes and ears. The *New York Times* was complimentary of the performers except one, Vic Damone, who was described as "stiff and callow."[17] Another adjective might have been "petrified." Sheldon was on the set, and he recalled a timorous Damone asking veteran director Norman Taurog for a drink of water before a take. The gruff director yelled back "No!" and continued to shoot.[18]

Damone wasn't the only one in the cast who had difficulties. Powell was pregnant and battling morning sickness. At one point, MGM had to send a car to pick her up because she couldn't stand, much less drive to the studio. Darrieux posed a difficult type of problem, although she may not have seen it that way, when the wardrobe and hair departments discovered shocks of hair under her arms during routine costume fittings.

While Darrieux was having something removed, Una was putting something on—eyeglasses. She decided to wear them to make her look older, and along with her more mature look, she took on a protective, motherly demeanor for her portrayal of Glynnie, the companion/housekeeper of the

Costume test for *Rich, Young and Pretty*. (MGM, 1951)

family. While most reviews failed to mention her, the *Washington Post* noted her reliability in supplying humor, calling her an "old standby, always good for a single laugh."[19] One of her funniest moments occurs when a telephone operator calls, telling her in French that London (Londres) is calling. Misunderstanding, Glynnie thinks the woman is asking her about laundry, and she responds that she doesn't need any. One scholar goes so far as to posit that Glynnie's ignorance of French served another purpose—making her character more appealing to "provincial American viewers who were suspect of anything foreign."[20] While this assertion may be true, it takes nothing away from Glynnie's memorable moments, including one in which she's hit by a door while hiding behind it, trying to overhear a private conversation. "Watch where you're going," she cries out unapologetically. "I'm eavesdropping."

In her next picture, Una was reunited with director George Marshall, with whom she hadn't worked since *Destry Rides Again*. This time around it was in the zany screwball comedy *A Millionaire for Christy*, the plot of which has legal secretary Christabel "Christy" Sloan (Eleanor Parker) notifying Peter Ulysses, a radio show host (Fred MacMurray), that he has won $2 million. Pal Patsy (Una), a cynical and wisecracking co-worker, sees a gold-digging possibility, but Christy is horrified by the suggestion: "What are you trying to do to my principles?" she asks. "They're all I have left." Patsy answers her coolly, "Put 'em in moth balls," and that is just what Christy does, pursuing Peter and getting involved in one hilarious complication after another.

Parker's husband was the producer of the film, and it was he who suggested she do the part, hoping it would be a change of pace from her more serious, dramatic roles. He was right, and Parker said that making the film was the "happiest, most wonderful time" she had had up to that point in her career.[21] Her enjoyment is reflected in her lively performance, which is enhanced by the high-energy plot, high production values, snappy dialogue, and ever dependable theatrics of MacMurray and Richard Carlson, the latter given a rare opportunity to show his comedic flair.

Una's part is brief, but consequential and bears many of the hallmarks of her beloved 1930's characterizations—wit, sass, and vitality. She is a master of little bits of stage business that greatly flesh out her portrayal. Take, for instance, the effortless way she leans back in her chair and props her feet up on a desk during her pivotal conversation, which tell us much about her character's confident insouciance. For good measure, she takes it even further, adding a subtle slapstick element, attempting to rest her elbows on a table, but missing badly. This is classic Una Merkel, and she demonstrates that her comedic skills are as finely tuned as ever.

Una headed right back to 20th Century-Fox to complete *Golden Girl*, a film starring Mitzi Gaynor as Lotta Crabtree, a real-life American entertainer who was popular during the 19th century. The film showcases fanciful period costumes, attractive outdoor footage, and of course Gaynor's fine singing and dancing. Critics were very impressed by Gaynor's overall talent, but some were more reticent about the film's overly long sequences and occasional sentimentality.

Harry Carter, Una, and Mitzi Gaynor in 20th Century-Fox's *Golden Girl*. (1951)

As Mary Ann, Lotta's protective mother, Una fared very well with the critics. The *Hollywood Reporter* thought she was "splendid" and "looking lovely,"[22] while *Daily Variety* observed that she was "up to her old tricks of scene-stealing."[23] Her performance rings true and probably owes much of its authenticity to the rapport she establishes with Gaynor. Even Gaynor's mother noticed this special connection during filming, prompting her to remark at the time that Una "looks as though she loves Mitzi as I do."[24] Una was certainly fond of her young colleague and admired her boundless energy and theatrical acumen: "She has so much exuberance and pep and so much common sense," she told a *Los Angeles Times* critic.[25]

Years later, Gaynor spoke about the film to Robert Osborne, host for Turner Classic Movies, and she recalled that Una was "lovely," but didn't seem to have much time for the rest of the cast. "She was going through something strange and wondrous," Gaynor added rather cryptically, "but she can do that if she wanted to."[26]

While Una was filming *Golden Girl*, another director on the 20th Century-Fox lot, Walter Lang, asked to see her. He was getting ready to start filming *With a Song in My Heart*, the biopic of singer/actress Jane Froman, portrayed by Susan Hayward. He wanted Una to play the role of Sister Marie. Una agreed, despite having to squeeze it into her schedule while working on *Golden Girl*. "I had always wanted to play a nun. It was a small part, but I loved it," she confided.[27] She had only two scenes, but the second one gave her a chance to shine. She enters Hayward's hospital room to watch a rehearsal of a number in an upcoming show. Hayward's husband is there, and not thinking about how unseemly it might be, he asks Una to join in as a chorus girl. She tries halfheartedly to great humorous effect before being relieved of her embarrassing assignment. Dressed in a nun's habit, Una's range of movement is restricted, but her expressive eyes and non-verbal gestures more than compensate and effectively communicate her nervous awkwardness.

In the summer of 1951, Una went back to the La Jolla summer playhouse to play the female lead opposite Philip Ober in William Inge's psychological play *Come Back, Little Sheba*. It was a challenging part for her, and she took it on with great trepidation, admitting that she was "petrified" at the thought of playing the Shirley Booth role, which the actress had done so magnificently on Broadway.[28] Despite her fears, Una performed exceptionally, with the *Los Angeles Times* praising hers and Ober's work as an "acting triumph."[29]

The play was so successful that Una was asked to reprise her role several months later in Phoenix, Arizona. Meanwhile, Paramount heard about her success at La Jolla and asked for a favor. The studio was preparing a film adaptation of *Sheba*, and while there wasn't a part for her (Shirley Booth was already cast), they needed someone familiar with Booth's role to come out and do tests with Burt Lancaster. Booth couldn't do it because she was otherwise engaged. Una obliged and worked with him for five days. He was very grateful and made a point of not forgetting her selfless act.

Una then set off for Phoenix, where she arrived in mid-winter. She faced problems almost as soon as she arrived. First, she discovered the play would have to be delayed because her leading man was committed to another play and couldn't make rehearsals. Second, she had to endure brutally cold weather in a winter that ended up being one of the worst in fifty-two years. When Una finally returned to Los Angeles on March 2, 1952, she was exhausted and suffering from influenza. She arrived to an empty house—her father was still in Mexico—so she called for a doctor to come over. He did so, and when he left, she reportedly was feeling better. Just to be safe, though, a nurse was summoned to check on her periodically. That evening Una telephoned a few friends, and they were concerned enough to pay her a visit the following day. When they arrived, Una's nurse was there to greet them. She described how she had discovered Una unconscious earlier that day, apparently from an overdose of sleeping pills. Una had been rushed to St. John's Hospital in Santa Monica, where officials set about contacting Arno, who promptly collapsed upon hearing the news. Meanwhile, reporters clamored for more information about Una's prognosis. Her doctor released a statement saying that she was in critical condition, and it was unclear whether she would survive.

(Endnotes)

1. David Ragan, "Kentucky Charm in Hollywood," *Courier-Journal* (Louisville, KY), January 22, 1950, 22.

2. Ibid.

3. A. H. Weiler, "William Bendex Calls Balls and Strikes in 'Kill the Umpire' at the Rivoli Theatre," *New York Times,* May 29, 1950, 10.

4. Michael Fitzgerald, "Gloria Henry: From B Films to Sitcoms," *Classic Images*, February 2006, 76.

5. Darryl F. Zanuck, memo to Sol Siegel (May 27, 1949), Twentieth Century-Fox Collection, University of Southern California (USC), *My Blue Heaven* (Folder 1/4). Siegel was also optimistic about the production. See the Twentieth Century-Fox Records of the Legal Department and the Twentieth Century-Fox Produced Scripts Collection at the UCLA Arts (Special Collections Library).

6. Bosley Crowther, "Betty Grable, Dan Dailey Bring Video to Films in 'My Blue Heaven' at the Roxy," *New York Times,* September 16, 1950, 11.

7. Mae Tinee, "A Good Cast Is Lost in This Film Musical: 'My Blue Heaven,'" *Chicago Tribune*, August 18, 1950, 7.

8. Herb Golden, "My Blue Heaven," *Variety*, August 23, 1950, 8.

9. Edwin Schallert, "'Summer and Smoke' Brilliant Stage Event," *Los Angeles Times,* October 24, 1950, 9.

10. Edwin Schallert, "Merkel Climbs Back," *Los Angeles Time*s, July 8, 1951, 7.

11. Jack Goodman, "Western Triumph: La Jolla Company Runs Successful Tour Presenting 'Summer and Smoke,'" *New York Times*, October 29, 1950, 99.

12. Walter Winchell, "Walter Winchell . . . In New York: Broadway Spotlight," *Washington Post,* November 15, 1950, 17.

13. Patricia Clary, *Oxnard Press Courier*, May 3, 1950, 8.

14. Ibid.

15. Mike Connolly, "Hollywood Report," *Modern Screen*, April 1953, 23.

16. A. H. Weiler, "'Emergency Wedding' at Palace," *New York Times*, December 22, 1950, 19.

17. A. H. Weiler, "Jane Powell and Vic Damone in 'Rich, Young, and Pretty' Film Fare at Capitol," *New York Times*, July 26, 1951, 17.

18. Sidney Sheldon, *The Other Side of Me* (New York: Warner Books, 2005), 216.

19. "'Rich, Young, Pretty' Offers Frothy, Colorful Performance," *Washington Post*, August 30, 1951, 10.

20. Alisia G. Chase, "An American Heroine in Paris: Hollywood and Women in the City of Light in the 1950s" (PhD diss., University of Minnesota, 2002), 91.

21. Gene Handsaker, "Star Recalls 10 Years of Screen Roles," *Salt Lake Tribune*, Oct. 24, 1951, 41.

22. "Golden Girl," *Hollywood Reporter*, November 1, 1951, 4.

23. "Golden Girl," *Daily Variety*, November 1, 1951, 3.

24. Brand, Harry, "Vital Statistics on 'Golden Girl,'" Production file for *Golden Girl* (20th Century-Fox, 1951), Academy of Motion Picture Arts and Sciences, 6.

25. Schallert, "Merkel Climbs Back," 7.

26. Mitzi Gaynor, "TCM Salute to Mitzi Gaynor 5 of 5 Golden Girl (Intro)," YouTube Video, 4:54, posted May 31, 2014, https://www.youtube.com/watch?v=1GFVXcL2-ow.

27. Leonard Maltin, "FFM Interviews Una Merkel," *Film Fan Monthly*, January 1971, 8.

28. Schallert, "Merkel Climbs Back," 7.

29. "Una Merkel and Ober Score Hits in 'Sheba,'" *Los Angeles Times*, August 3, 1951, 16.

One of Una's costume tests for *The Merry Widow*. (MGM, 1952)

Chapter 21
Pressing On

After two days, Una was out of danger, but she didn't leave the hospital until almost a week later on March 10, 1952. Some newspapers made a point of mentioning that Una's overdose took place almost seven years to the day after her mother's suicide, intimating some kind of connection between the two. Others suggested that Una's actions may have been caused by some disappointment over her career. When Una heard all this speculation, she became distraught and tried to set the record straight. "Nothing was further from the truth," she said in one column. "It was all a terrible mistake. I was ill but not despondent."[1] Hedda Hopper's column reported that the overdose was definitely not premeditated, and Una was sorry for all the commotion the incident had caused. "I was unaware that the disease [influenza] set up certain toxic conditions that made sleeping pills more dangerous than usual," Una explained. "But I've had my lesson. From now on, if suffering from insomnia, I intend to lie in bed, eat peanut butter and crackers, and read my mysteries. People have been so kind to me since the accident; I don't want them to think they have misplaced confidence in me."[2]

Una's many fans and friends began reaching out to her with love and concern. The studios sent bouquets of flowers, along with messages of cheer and encouragement. Letters came pouring in from around the world, including service men in Korea and even ex-GIs who had seen Una in the South Pacific during World War II. In all, Una received almost five hundred letters, and she tearfully told a reporter how the outpouring of support had been wonderful, yet very emotional for her: "The incident proved to me that something good always comes out of the bad things that happen to us."[3]

While it is still unclear whether Una actually tried to take her own life, there is no doubt that Lana Turner, who played the lead in Una's next film, did attempt suicide just before filming began. Distraught over two miscarriages and a recent separation from her third husband, Turner swallowed pills and slashed her left wrist. MGM tried to cover up the attempt by saying she fell through a glass shower door, but her telltale scar revealed otherwise. Fortunately, as the ultra-rich title character in *The Merry Widow*, Turner was able to conceal her wrist with expensive furs, bracelets, and gloves, not to mention an estimated $150,000 worth of other accoutrements. She was the embodiment of feminine grace, poise, and elegance and a perfect complement to Fernando Lamas' masculine persona. The film was well received. *Newsweek*'s review was typical, characterizing the production as a "first-class *Merry Widow* and a fine tribute to the last grand master of the Viennese Waltz."[4]

James Frasher, who later became Lillian Gish's long-time manager, was at the studio during the production, visiting his friend Thomas Gomez. He met Una, and during their conversation, she spoke about Turner, saying, "Have to be careful I don't slip and call her Jeanette."[5] Una was of course referring to Jeanette MacDonald, with whom she appeared in Ernst Lubitsch's feature

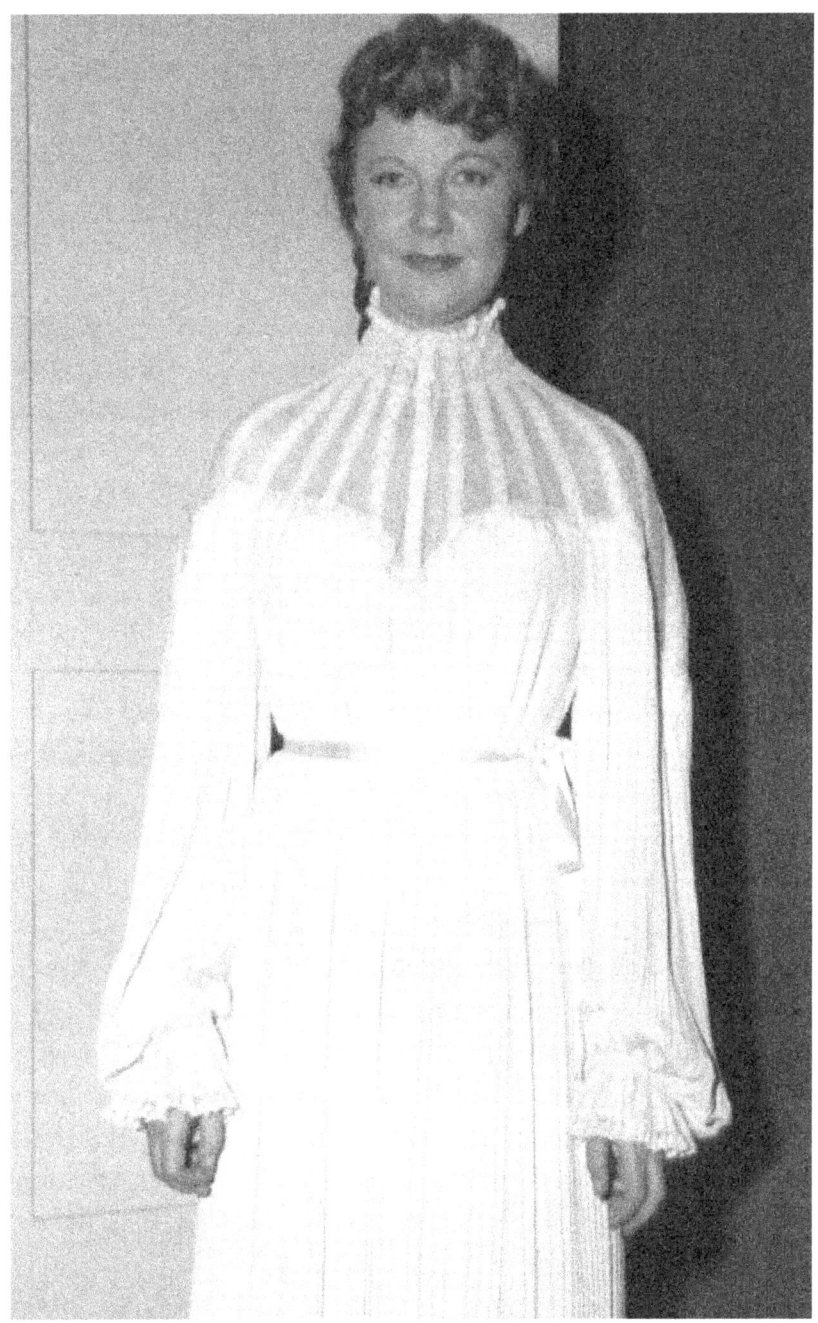
Another costume test for *The Merry Widow*. (MGM, 1952)

back in 1934. Of that illustrious cast, Una was the only main player to appear in the later Technicolor version. This second time around she was Turner's companion, Kitty, who masquerades as her wealthy friend to test whether Lamas is looking for love or monetary gain. Benefitting from the glamour treatment, Una looked particularly lovely and acquitted herself admirably in the lighthearted role. When comparing her parts in the two films, she thought Kitty was the better one.

In September 1952, Una appeared alongside Charles Boyer in "My Wife Geraldine," the premiere episode of *Four Star Playhouse*, a television anthology series that starred four different movie stars—Charles Boyer, David Niven, Ida Lupino, and Dick Powell—in a fixed rotation. The story has bachelor Boyer wanting a very coveted job, but applicants must be married. Therefore, he decides to invent a wife for himself. When he can't produce her, people get suspicious and think foul play must be involved. Una plays it straight as his infatuated landlord, who wishes she could snag her handsome tenant for herself. Reviews were laudatory, complimenting Boyer on his portrayal, as well as Una and a few others for their sound support. The show's professional photography, skillful directing, and well-crafted script were also commended.

A few months later Una followed up with another televised performance. This time she supported Edmund Gwenn in "Guardian of the Clock," a Schlitz Playhouse production that saw him fired from his job for being too old, and the revenge he exacts by turning back time. While one trade journal extolled Una's "excellent characterization," it also found the production sluggish, marred by too much narration and too little action.[6]

Una was cast as Debbie Reynolds' mother in MGM's *I Love Melvin*, which starred Donald O'Connor as the eponymous character, a lowly photographer's assistant who falls in love with Judy (Reynolds), a chorus girl. The two get to know each other during multiple photo shoots, and Melvin, hoping to impress Judy and win her over, promises to get her on the cover of *Look* magazine. When he can't deliver on his idle boast, the couple's love is put to the test.

This musical comedy was conceived by MGM to recapture some of the charisma that Reynolds and O'Connor exuded in *Singing in the Rain*, but it is formulaic and predictable. It still has, however, some delightful scenes and serves as a veritable showcase for its stars' multifaceted talents. The songs are catchy and well-suited to the actors' voices and enhance Robert Alton's original dance sequences. The most memorable one is a football ballet in which Reynolds, covered in brown suede and lacing, plays a football and is tossed, kicked, and fumbled around in an amazing gridiron choreography. O'Connor shows off his considerable skill in several pleasing routines, including one on roller skates and another in a murder pantomime, in which he enacts all the parts.

While the singing and dancing take center stage in this film, the acting remains solid. The leads are dynamic and endearing, showing perceptive feeling in their interpretation. Adorable Noreen Corcoran, who plays Reynolds' articulate little sister, is an inveterate scene-stealer and possesses poise and intelligence well beyond her years. Una and Allyn Joslyn add sincerity to the proceedings with their uncontrived naturalness.

Richard Anderson is good in a thankless role. Sensible, level-headed, and restrained in his scenes, he is an ideal, romantic rival to O'Connor. This was his second film with Una—he had been in *Rich, Young, and Pretty* (1951)—and when asked about her, he remembered that she "was fun, knew her lines and was always on time . . . a talented actress and great to be around."[7]

Una wouldn't have another film release for the rest of 1953. Instead, she devoted herself to television and the stage. Her first television show that year was an adaptation of the famous short story "The Monkey's Paw," in which a mysterious talisman grants its owners three wishes. Although somewhat ponderous in places, the story is redeemed by its heavy suspense, fear-inducing atmosphere, and fine theatrics. Una was singled out for her compelling performance as the anguished mother, with *Daily Variety* noting that the story gives her an opportunity for "serious acting, and she projects this new facet with convincing style."[8]

Interviewed that summer, Una spoke about television, admitting that it was a "godsend" for actors, although she personally found it disconcerting to perform before cameras and a live audience at the same time.[9] She marveled at television's fast production schedule, which often culminated in a program being ready to air within five days. She knew that television was not just a passing fad and was prescient about the new medium's potential: "I don't know how it can be worked out," she began, "but perhaps the day will come when people with TV sets will pay a small fee to have good shows in their home."[10]

In July, Una went to Hartford, Connecticut, to see her aunt, whom she hadn't visited for five years. While there, the elderly lady broke her hip, and Una stayed on to take care of her. With her proximity to New York City, Una was available when a casting call went out for the play *The Remarkable Mr. Pennypacker*. Although it was a comedy, Una was cast in a straight role as the maiden aunt. The story concerns the title character (Burgess Meredith), a bigamist who lives with his unsuspecting wife (Martha Scott) and children in Wilmington, Delaware, all the while maintaining a complete second family in nearby Philadelphia.

Martha Scott was a talented, much acclaimed actress, but if she felt slighted, she could be demanding. She shared equal billing with Meredith but thought director Alan Schneider favored her male co-star by placing him center stage more often than she was. She also became upset over the amount of time that Una spent with the children onstage, complaining to her manager that Una held them three times as much as she did. When Schneider heard these complaints, he lost his temper and angrily told Scott's manager that "Una Merkel really loves those kids, and they love her. Martha hates them. All she does is worry about whether they're blocking her, or messing up her dress. And they know it."[11]

If things were stormy behind the scenes, it didn't adversely affect the show. On the contrary, critics hailed it as a hit, with the *New York Times* raving that it was an "uproarious show" that was "drenched in laughter."[12] The *Chicago Tribune* found it "excellent fun," and the public agreed.[13] The play ran for over 220 performances, closing in the summer of 1954.

Early in the run, a journalist met with Una backstage for an interview, and Una was in good spirits, relating how she was often recognized in public: "Truck drivers call out to me, 'Hello, Una!'" she said. "Today a man driving a big beer truck offered me a ride to the theater. On New Year's Day, my father and I were walking along the street and a man called out, 'Happy New Year, Una!' That makes me feel so good. It's not so good when they aren't sure who I am. On one day I was mistaken for Lillian Gish, Nydia Westman, ZaSu Pitts, and Glenda Farrell."[14]

Una also confided that someone else had called her recently—her ex-husband, Ronnie. He had remarried, but the marriage had not lasted. He and Una had recently reconciled and were seeing each other again, with Ronnie planning to visit her in New York. "We're better friends than when we were married," she claimed.[15] But this renewed relationship did not endure. That same year Ronnie moved to Hawaii to start a new business, and he stayed there. He eventually married again, and this union lasted until his death in 1991.

As it often happened in interviews, the conversation turned to Una's Southern accent. In a surprising remark that contradicted much of what she had said over the years, Una stated that she didn't think she had a Southern accent, nor did she even consider herself Southern! She explained that her hometown of Covington, Kentucky, was practically the Midwest.

No matter how she defined her birthplace, Una soon got the chance to see her beloved Kentucky again. Burt Lancaster, who was preparing to direct his first film, *The Gabriel Horn* (later renamed *The Kentuckian,*) had remembered Una's kindness to him years earlier when he was testing for *Come Back, Little Sheba*. He decided to return the favor by offering her the role of Sophie Wakefield, sister-in-law to his Eli Wakefield, a frontiersman who wants to leave his native Kentucky with his son (Donald MacDonald) to start a new life in Texas.

Filming began in the Bluegrass State in the summer of 1954, and it wasn't all smooth sailing. First, Macdonald became ill and briefly held up production. Then, some of the more than four hundred twenty-five animals in the shoot became uncooperative. During one scene, a mule got spooked by a

Donald MacDonald (back to camera), Una, John McIntire, Burt Lancaster, and Dianne Foster (United Artists, 1955)

reflector and bolted, tossing extras around and causing much havoc. Another scene called for Wakefield's trusty canine companion, Faro, to fight a local dog and thrash him soundly. The only problem was that the Kentucky dog was much more combative and defeated the more docile, Hollywood-trained dog every time. The crew eventually had to take drastic measures and tape the more aggressive dog's jaws shut to ensure Faro's victory. Finally, there was an unfortunate handcuffing incident. A publicist believed he could drum up some free press by persuading a teenager to handcuff himself to actress Diana Lynn, who played a schoolmarm in the film. The adolescent played along and was summarily charged with breach of peace, let out on bail, and then fined $25 (which the publicist paid). In addition to these setbacks and distractions, Lancaster discovered that directing was much more difficult than anticipated. He was forthcoming about his challenges, saying, "I had no one to help me. I just struggled through on my own."[16]

Fortunately, there were some happy moments during filming. The cast and crew enjoyed the hospitality of the locals, many of whom were starstruck by the celebrities in their midst. One motel owner in London, Kentucky, no doubt inspired by Grauman's Chinese Theater, had cast members leave their footprints and autographs in wet cement slabs that he displayed in front of his establishment. (Una signed her name, but didn't leave any footprints.) Kentucky Governor Lawrence W. Wetherby honored the cast and principal crew by commissioning them as Kentucky Colonels. There was also the good old-fashioned Southern cuisine, which everyone enjoyed, particularly Lancaster, who noted that everything was so much like home that even the "silverware should have been homemade."[17] Finally, the crew was able to celebrate the nuptials of female lead Dianne Foster, who married her fiancé in Owensboro, Kentucky, near the end of the shoot.

Una's return to Kentucky was greeted with little fanfare, with no major interviews or featured articles about her appearing in the local papers. If she had been asked to describe her character of Sophie Wakefield, she may not have had many positive things to say because it certainly wasn't one of her most endearing roles. Her Sophie spends most of her time fussing at Faro for lounging on her furniture, although in one scene she does loosen up enough to sing and dance a little. Overall, her part was inconsequential and did not offer any challenges or memorable moments, much less advance her career. Nevertheless, Una did seem to enjoy her sojourn back to her home state. On the last day of her stay, a photographer from the *Owensboro Messenger* snapped a photo of her smiling broadly, and it graced the front page. The caption read she was preparing to return to Hollywood, where she would soon celebrate twenty-five years on the screen. It added that she planned to continue working, as she put it, "until they catch up with me."[18] According to the by-line, the photo was taken just after Una had blown a good-bye kiss to the city and the wonderful people she met there during her three-week stay.

Television viewers next saw Una in "A Miracle in the Rain," an episode in Ben Hecht's *Tales of the City*, a summer replacement for *Four Star Playhouse*. The story revolves around Ruth, (Phyllis Thaxter), a New York secretary who lives with her frail mother (Una). While taking shelter from a rainstorm, Ruth meets Art, (William Prince), a Southern GI, and the two fall in love before he goes off to war. He is killed in action, and Ruth sinks into a physical decline until she is saved by a miraculous event. Hecht had originally published a novella of this tearjerker in 1948. This adaptation of the story was the third one to be televised, and it would be adapted and released again three years later as a motion picture. CBS spared no expense on the budget for this series. It had excellent production values, and top actors were hired, including Madeleine Carroll, Ann Rutherford, Barry Nelson, and others. Hecht's material, however, suffered when it was condensed down to half-hour segments, and it was not helped by his decision to avoid any type of hard-hitting material, such as bloodshed and violence. As a result, the episodes suffered, as *TV Guide* complained, "from too much sweetness and light."[19]

Una returned to Hollywood to play in a televised Christmas show called "Two Little Minks" on the series *Studio One in Hollywood*. This poignant, uplifting story focuses on a man (Frank McHugh) who, thinking he will inherit money after the imminent death of his rich, old uncle, goes out and spends his last dime to purchase a mink coat for his wife (Una). The only problem is that his uncle isn't ready to die yet. As the female lead, Una had a part worthy of her considerable talent in this modern-day parable, which was touted in papers as "charming" and "excellently cast."[20]

The Kentuckian was released in the summer of 1955, and critics enthused about the Kentucky landscape, which was beautifully rendered by Technicolor and Cinemascope. They also praised the poetic dialogue, and Lancaster's attention to detail. However, the general consensus was the plot could have been tighter, with more action and fewer incidental elements. *Variety* saw Lancaster's performance as "too self-conscious,"[21] while the *New York Times* judged Walter Matthau's screen debut as woefully overacted and right out of the "old tent-show school."[22] Nevertheless, the film was invited to be shown at the Venice Film Festival, where it was nominated for a Golden Lion Award, but lost out to Carl Theodor Dreyer's *Ordet* (*The Word*).

A few months later Una appeared as a congenial busybody in an episode of *Kraft Theatre* called "Trucks Welcome." Rita Gam starred as the wife of a truck driver (James Gregory) whose frequent absences put their marriage in jeopardy. The *New York Times* thought Una and Gregory contributed fine performances, but was less taken with Gam, who had tried to dress down and forego mascara to play the part, but still came across as too beautiful to be credible.

At the end of November 1955, Una learned that she had been signed to appear in a play based on Eudora Welty's novella *The Ponder Heart*. She didn't know it then, but this role would be the most important one of her stage career, propelling her into that exclusive pantheon of actors who are recognized as the best in their field and worthy of the highest accolades their profession can bestow.

(Endnotes)

[1] Bob Thomas, "Life Looks Fine to Una Merkel," *Owosso-Argus Press*, July 23, 1952, 16.

[2] Hedda Hopper (staff), "Looking at Hollywood," *Los Angeles Times,* March 15, 1952, 3.

[3] Thomas, "Life Looks Fine to Una Merkel," 16.

[4] *Newsweek*, October 13, 1952.

[5] James Frasher conversation with author, August 30, 2012.

[6] "Guardian of the Clock," *Daily Variety*, January 26, 1953.

[7] Richard Anderson, note to author, June 28, 2013.

[8] "The Monkey's Paw," *Daily Variety,* April 8, 1953.

[9] Erika Einsle, "Una Merkel Sees Cinemascope Answer to Three-Dimension Movies," *Hartford Courant*, July 16, 1953, 6.

[10] Ibid.

[11] Alan Schneider, *Entrances: An American Director's Journey* (New York: Viking, 1986), 175.

[12] Brooks Atkinson, "Liam O'Brien's 'Remarkable Mr. Pennypacker,' a Family Comedy at the Coronet," *New York Times*, December 31, 1953, 11.

[13] John Chapman, "Two Dramas Are Diverting Stage Fare," *Chicago Tribune*, January 10, 1954, 13.

14. Rhea Talley "Una Merkel's No Southern Gal, Y'all," *Courier-Journal* (Louisville, KY), January 10, 1954, 4.

15. Ibid.

16. Kate Buford, *Burt Lancaster: An American Life* (Cambridge, MA: Da Capo Press, 2001), 141.

17. "Mrs. M.A. Bell Enjoyed Cooking For Lancaster," *Sentinel-Echo* (London, KY), September 16, 1954, 1.

18. "Returns to Hollywood" (photo caption), *Owensboro Messenger*, October 7, 1954, 1.

19. "Tales of the City," *TV Guide*, August 28, 1953, 20.

20. "Today's Television Programs," *Long Island Star-Journal*, December 20, 1954, 25.

21. "The Kentuckian," *Variety*, July 13, 1955, 6.

22. Bosley Crowther, "Lancaster as 'Kentuckian,'" *New York Times*, September 2, 1955, 13.

Chapter 22
Tony Award

The Ponder Heart opened in Broadway's Music Box Theater on February 16, 1956, and it ran for 149 performances. It recounts the story of Daniel Ponder (David Wayne), who has inherited his family's fortune, but doles it out selflessly to practically everyone he meets, much to the dismay of his niece, Edna Earle (Una). Ponder soon has more pressing difficulties than his shrinking inheritance: he is accused of killing his simple-minded, teenage wife (Sarah Marshall).

Although Welty's novella had won over critics, this play, adapted by Joseph Fields and Jerome Chodorov, met with mixed reviews. The *New York Herald Tribune* was complimentary, as was the *New York Post*, which went so

Playbill for *The Ponder Heart*. (1956)

far as to call the play "one of the funniest and most engaging of the season's comedies."[1] The *Daily Mirror* disagreed, calling it a "frail" vehicle,[2] while other reviewers seized on the play's slight, predictable plot. The critics did agree, however, on the acting, which earned high praise and admiration. Wayne and Una, in particular, received their fair share of plaudits. Brooks Atkinson of the *New York Times* enthused that they were the two actors "whose taste and daintiness give the comedy its distinctiveness and keep it on the level of a comedy of rural manners."[3] In another article, he raved that Una was "ideal" as Edna and her participation in the play was inspired casting.[4]

Una was very impressed with David Wayne. She described him as one of the finest actors around, so good, in fact, that they didn't know what to do with him. In another interview, she imagined that her castmates must have thought her a "wet smack" because she seldom went to parties, preferring to stay home and read instead.[5] But Sarah Marshall, one of the youngest members of the cast, thought very highly of Una and shared some very poignant memories of her with this author:

> Una and I shared a dressing room at the New York Theatre. This was unheard of for a star of Una's magnitude. But I do not recall her commenting on the arrangement. (The other star, David Wayne, came to his senses early in the run, and we moved to separate dressing rooms, and he took "ours.")
>
> Opening night, I believe, our wonderful author Eudora Welty came unannounced to the theater. She sat in the audience long after the show had finished—an usher asked if she needed help—Miss Welty explained that she had written the book the play was based on and, as she had enjoyed our performance so much, [asked,] 'Do you think I could go backstage. . . ?' She was ushered back, and we were all thrilled to meet her. I remember Una and Miss Welty talking quietly, and I thought 'There isn't an ego between them.' They were just two lovely, talented women enjoying each other.

> I remember also Una's devotion to her father. He was such a quiet, gentle man and would come very often and sit in Una's dressing room . . . Her character, Edna Earle in *The Ponder Heart*, had a line about my character Bonnie Dee: 'Looks like she could sit all day and try to figure out how the tail of the C got through the L in the Coca-Cola sign.' What a line and how beautifully she said it.[6]

Just a few weeks into the run, Una learned that her interpretation of Edna Earle had earned her a Tony nomination for Distinguished Supporting or Featured Dramatic Actress. It was the first time in the history of the award that nominees were announced ahead of time. The award ceremony, televised for the very first time, took place in New York City's Plaza Hotel on April 1, 1956. Jack Carter was Master of Ceremonies, and Helen Hayes was a presenter. Una won the award in her category, beating out Diane Cilento, Anne Jackson, and Elaine Stritch. Incredulous at having won, Una said that it was due to her friends, intimating that they had perhaps lobbied on her behalf. During the ceremony, she watched actress Faye Emerson receive a kiss from musician Skitch Henderson and joked, "I would have been willing to settle for that."[7]

The same month the Tony Awards were given out, *The Kettles in the Ozarks* was released. Like the other films in the Ma and Pa Kettle series, this one had its requisite amount of silliness and slapstick elements. It was also the first not to have Percy Kilbride as Pa Kettle. The veteran actor had retired just before production began. Una signed on to do the film, but after reading the final script, she regretted her decision. She went to her agent and exclaimed, "Can't you get me out of this? It's awful!"[8] Audiences and most critics agreed, and it was a box office disappointment. In this outing, Ma (Marjorie Main) and her thirteen "young'uns" travel to the Ozarks to visit her brother-in-law, Uncle Sedge (Arthur Hunnicutt), who's remarkably similar to his brother in character and disposition, except he won't marry, despite being engaged to spinster Bedelia Baines (Una) for the past twenty years. Bedelia, with Ma's help, tries to get him to change his mind and settle down.

Arthur Hunnicutt marries Una as Marjorie Main, Paul Wexler (holding Bible), Richard Deacon, and Pat Goldin look on in *The Kettles in the Ozarks*. (Universal, 1956)

Despite her reservations about the film, Una was positive about the future and told reporters that she was entering a new phase in her career. "My health is great," she continued, "and I have a feeling of great expectancy since escaping all those giddy comedy roles I played for so many years."[9] Even though playing Bedelia didn't enhance her career, Una did concede that the film actually turned out better than she had anticipated. She liked working with Marjorie Main, whom she thought was friendly and one of the few top-ranking comediennes allowed to show some good sense in comic portrayals.

The Ponder Heart ended its run in June of 1956, but Una's fans saw her again that August when she appeared in a pilot for a new television show called *Calling Terry Conway*. Ann Sheridan starred as the title character who worked in a luxurious Las Vegas hotel as head of public relations. The episode had been filmed nearly two years earlier, but it had run into problems when sponsors worried about their association with a show that was even loosely connected with the gambling industry. After the first episode of the show aired, NBC summarily dropped it.

That summer Una was called back to California to work on RKO's *Bundle of Joy*, but her return to Hollywood almost had tragic consequences when Arno was struck by a car as he attempted to cross Hollywood Boulevard. He was rushed to a nearby hospital, where X-rays were taken, but released not long afterwards when results showed no broken bones or serious injuries.

Bundle of Joy was a musical remake of *Bachelor Mother* (1939), which had starred Ginger Rogers and David Niven. The new version cast Debbie Reynolds as Polly Parrish, a department store worker who finds a baby outside an orphanage and is mistaken for its mother. Una was Mrs. Dugan, a brusque landlady with an understanding heart, who advises Polly and agrees to babysit occasionally. Reynolds' real-life husband, Eddie Fisher, played her love interest, and the studio did everything to ease his initiation into film work. Eminent musician Hugo Winterhalter was brought in to lead the 65-piece orchestra. Fisher sang a few songs, including "Lullaby in Blue," a touching duet with Reynolds, who had her hands full trying to coach him through his scenes and smooth over his mistakes and inexperience. As she later revealed, he took his anger, insecurities, and wounded pride out on her, resulting in a lot of fighting. More stress came from director Norman Taurog's weak direction and frequent memory lapses, the latter causing him to repeat instructions. All these problems notwithstanding, the film turned out to be a satisfying Technicolor comedy that boasted lively dance sequences, memorable music numbers, and stellar support from Una, Adolphe Menjou, Tommy Noonan, and Nita Talbot. Critics were underwhelmed, but filmgoers didn't care. They came out in droves to see Reynolds and Fisher, one of America's sweetheart couples at the time, and this fan support helped make the film one of RKO's biggest hits of the year.

Una stayed in Hollywood to work on *The Girl Most Likely*, a musical remake of another Ginger Rogers film, *Tom, Dick, and Harry* (1941). Jane Powell, having just left MGM, was awarded the title role of Dodie, a flighty young woman who is in a dilemma after accepting marriage proposals from three suitors. Although the plot is uninspired, it is greatly enhanced by several elements, including the ebullient Kaye Ballard as Powell's best friend, the fine music, Powell's accomplished singing, and the extraordinary dance numbers, which were choreographed by Gower Champion. One of his most memorable dance sequences was "Balboa," which had Powell, Cliff Robertson, and some forty other dancers splashing, leaping, and cavorting around in over a foot of water, forming coordinated patterns at a fast, kinetic pace. One critic at the time called it "one of the most exciting ensemble performances ever seen in a film musical," and time has not dulled its exhilarating dynamism and visual appeal.[10]

(left to right) Kelly Brown, Kaye Ballard, Frank Cady, Tommy Noonan, Judy Nugent, Una, Jane Powell, Keith Andes, and Chris Essay in *The Girl Most Likely*. (Universal, 1958)

In the film, Una plays Powell's doting mother, whose main preoccupation is helping her daughter get married. Like the rest of cast and the filmgoing public, she is left speculating who the lucky bachelor will be. At one point, she even asks her daughter point blank, "Which one?" This routine question was not intrinsically funny, but it prompted such giggles from Powell during production that filming had to be stopped for ten minutes. "I can't help it," Powell explained to director Mitchell Leisen. "Una looked at me so severely it felt like the 'evil eye' on me."[11] The scene was started again, and at exactly the same place, laughter broke out again. This time Una was to blame. Leisen called for a five minute "laugh halt," after which the scene was tried again and completed successfully.

Powell had fun making the film and admitted it was the only one in her post-MGM career that she enjoyed doing. Her friendship and respect for Una made the experience all the more pleasurable. In a letter written at the time, Powell confirmed how much she had learned from her colleague, whom she described as a wonderful actress: "Una has helped me understand the intricacies of comedy," she wrote, "because she has been so unstinting in her advice and help."[12]

It was not all fun and laughter on the set, though. The signs of RKO's imminent breakup were clearly visible, and the cast watched as sound stages closed one by one. Not long after the final scenes of *The Girl Most Likely* were shot in January of 1957, all productions on the lot ceased, and the studio was sold to Desilu later that year. The film sat idle a year before being released by Universal, which didn't do much to promote it. When it finally did appear, it went virtually unnoticed, drawing only a lukewarm response from critics. The real losers, however, were moviegoers, who missed out on a cheery, entertaining musical.

After filming was completed, Una rented an apartment on West Fifty-Seventh Street in New York City. She told the Hollywood press: "All of my furniture is still here, and I think I'll just leave it here. I'd like to do some television and a New York legitimate production, but naturally I hope to be in Hollywood often for picture work."[13]

At the end of January 1957, Una appeared in an episode of *Playhouse 90* entitled "The Greer Case," and it was one of her most critically acclaimed television appearances of the decade. The story, taken from a real case in the New York court system, revolves around a rich matron (Anita Louise) who bequeaths an inheritance to her illegitimate son, whom she abandoned many years earlier. Melvyn Douglas is the man who claims to be the son, and Una, his loving wife. The *New York Times* thought the story a bit detail-laden, but still very interesting and enhanced by an all-star cast. Douglas, Louise, and Edmund Gwenn were cited for their authentic, affecting portrayals, along with Una, whose acting was deemed "warm and human."[14] Another New York newspaper, equally impressed with Una and Douglas, stated they were "marvelously warm and restrained."[15]

A few months later Una followed up this success with another television appearance, this time on *The Red Skelton Show*. In the episode "Freddie and the Happy Helper," she played a rich, compassionate lady who wants to help Freddie (Skelton) and his hobo friends. She gives them her house and is nearly destitute after a spending spree, which includes planting flowers in the Mojave Desert to make it look less barren, giving sweaters to homeless dogs, distributing milk to cats, and providing area birds with new birdbaths. Eventually Freddie and his friends come to her rescue and help her regain her home and fortune.

Una was on more familiar ground in *The Fuzzy Pink Nightgown*, which found her playing Bertha, a retired entertainer who is the personal assistant and good friend to popular film star Laurel Stevens (Jane Russell), who mysteriously disappears on her way to a movie premiere. Bertha's worst fears are confirmed when she learns that her boss has been kidnapped and held for ransom. Despite the limitations of its script, the film has its diverting moments, and Russell is delightful, fulfilling her acting duties with considerable panache. Una's Bertha has a few good moments. One example is her opening scene, during which she sashays confidently into the room, armed with Laurel's missing eyebrow pencil, which she is using to complete a crossword puzzle. She hands a girdle to Laurel, who rejects it, saying she can't wear such a thing to a film premiere. Nonplussed, Bertha taps her playfully on the bottom and says, "They're *your* hips, kid." In another memorable line, Bertha aptly describes her strong-willed friend: "Beneath that iron glove of yours is nothing but a little old iron fist!" For the rest of the film, Bertha's primary objective is to notify the police about her friend's disappearance, even at the risk of bodily harm, which she sustains when knocked unconscious by a hefty phone dropped on her head.

As for the alluring nightgown mentioned in the title, it proves to be a letdown. Russell wears it briefly, but the film's black and white cinematography never allows it to be seen and appreciated to full effect, much like her beautiful gowns and blond hair (she wore a blond wig for the film). Russell admitted that color, or the lack thereof, was a point of contention between her and director Norman Taurog. She had wanted the film to be a noir-like thriller, whereas he had imagined a Technicolor comedy. Both were ultimately disappointed by the end product, as were many critics and the public.

In August, the La Jolla Playhouse invited Una back to appear as the female lead in *Career*, a play chronicling the vicissitudes of an actor (Don Taylor) from the Great Depression onwards. Una played his understanding agent with what one Los Angeles critic called "high efficiency," in a play that was hailed as one of the best of that season.[16] One of Una's youngest colleagues in the play was a senior at the University of Southern California and an apprentice at La Jolla Playhouse that summer. His name was Paul Comi, and he wowed critics with his small part as a drunken soldier, which led to his being signed by 20th Century-Fox. Of the mostly British cast, Una stood out, and Comi remembered her fondly, characterizing her as "a very kind and helpful person."[17]

In the late summer of 1957, CBS cast Una in "The Secret of the Red Room," an episode of its *Climax!* series. This very melodramatic adaptation of a story by Mary Loos relates how a dying writer (Michael Rennie) suddenly makes a miraculous recovery and even starts becoming younger when placed in the mysterious room of the title, which was located in the mansion of a young friend (Anna Maria Alberghetti). *Variety*'s Dave Kaufman savaged this overwrought drama, criticizing everything from Paul Nickell's ineffective direction and the implausible plot, to the overacting cast, all of which led him to call it an "unhappy hour" of television.[18]

CBS' "Aladdin," which was a part of *The Dupont Show of the Month*, aired in February of 1958. Cole Porter supplied the score, his only effort for television, and Sal Mineo played the title role, with Una as his mother. Writer S. J. Perelman kept most of the best known elements of the story in the ninety-minute show, including Aladdin's magic lamp and genie (Geoffrey Holder), the beautiful princess (Anna Maria Alberghetti), nefarious musician (Cyril Ritchard), and emperor (Basil Rathbone). While the show was still in production, Una was interviewed and spoke frankly about how she felt being back in the public eye. "I wouldn't say *radiant*," she began, "but *happy*. And grateful that so many people remember me."[19]

Una's fans hadn't forgotten her, but "Aladdin" didn't give them a great performance to savor or appreciate, which was unfortunate considering its high production values, pageantry, and fine cast. Una's part called for her to do some singing and dancing, which she did competently, but little else. Saddled with a puerile script, she compensated by overacting, at one point even dramatically placing her forearm on her forehead in fear and surprise, a histrionic gesture right out of melodramatic theater or early silent film. The result is unintentionally funny but consistent with the rest of the goofy antics. When discussing the role, Una did not speak of its limitations or her interpretation but was more preoccupied by her physical appearance, specifically the makeup used to embody her Asian character: "I hope they don't give me slanty eyes," she reported. "I have enough trouble seeing with my eyes wide open, and if they narrow them down to slits, I might as well play my part in braille."[20] Una was surprisingly silent about the large, unattractive—and very fake-looking—black wig that she would wear throughout, which only served to undermine her credibility even more.

Despite its shortcomings, "Aladdin" does occasionally show some magic and charm. Porter's score contains some fine songs, most notably his heavenly "I Adore You," which the bewitching Alberghetti sings so beautifully. Mineo enlivens some of the story's duller moments with his particular brand of virility, and Ritchards proves most effective at channeling what *Variety* called his "stylized buffoonery" to create a memorable villain.[21]

Una followed up "Aladdin" by appearing on another CBS show that summer—*The United States Steel Hour*—in an episode called "Flint and

Fire," in which she supported leads Robert Culp and Gloria Vanderbilt, a young couple whose hopes of marrying were thwarted by stubborn pride and preconceived notions. With its finely written dialogue and first-rate performances, the drama rose above its sentimental moments to win the praise of critics, who were especially impressed by Vanderbilt's emotionally-charged performance in a very demanding role. The successful on-screen chemistry between her and Culp, however, was hard won. Culp had been upset about not receiving top billing, so he retaliated by sleepwalking through rehearsals. A few newspapers reported that Vanderbilt had become so exasperated that she resorted to kicking him in the shins to elicit some kind of reaction, but all that changed once producers acquiesced to his demands. Suddenly Culp came to life and gave his customary fine performance.

Una's last film of the 1950s found her back at MGM in *The Mating Game*. She was Ma Larkin to Paul Douglas' Pop Larkin, the owners of a Maryland farm and parents of a brood of children, the eldest the very attractive Mariette (Debbie Reynolds). When a reporter asked Douglas about the subject of the film, the actor naughtily replied that it was about springtime and lovemaking, more specifically farm animals wanting to make love, his daughter wanting to marry and make love, but most of all, he and his wife wanting to make love.

Douglas is right insofar as the film is inspired by its title, with its fecund environment and frequent sexual innuendoes, but there's a bit more to the story than that. Pop Larkin, it seems, has never once paid taxes, so the IRS sends Lorenzo Charlton (Tony Randall), a no-nonsense tax agent, to investigate. Hilarity ensues when the family tries to get Lorenzo to loosen up, and while doing so, he falls in love with Mariette.

This was Reynolds' first film after her much publicized split from Eddie Fisher, and the stress had taken a physical toll on her. She weighed a mere ninety pounds, and Director George Marshall kept milk shakes on hand to give her a boost. Besides her slimmer frame, though, Reynolds showed little outward signs of inner turmoil. She was a true professional, putting on a brave face, rolling up her sleeves, and immersing herself in her role, which had her jumping from a two-story hayloft, riding bareback on a boar, horse jumping,

Una Merkel and Paul Douglas in *The Mating Game*. (MGM, 1959)

and driving at breakneck speed. She did it all while putting on a gamesome performance, much to the delight and admiration of her colleagues. The film was well received, with Reynolds and Randall getting most of the kudos. Douglas and Una contribute their share of laughs, and one critic, who was particularly impressed by Una, described hers as a "four-star performance."[22]

The Mating Game was the third and last film that Una and Reynolds made together, and the second time that Una played Reynolds' mother. As she had done with Jean Harlow years earlier, Una used to sit and talk at length with Reynolds during breaks. One of their conversations must have alluded to an unfortunate mishap that occurred while they were filming a spirited scuffle. During the melee, Una was wielding a shovel, and she accidentally hit Reynolds in the face with it, causing her mouth to swell. Horrified by what she had done, Una was very apologetic, but the young actress took the incident in stride, harboring no ill will. She even gave Una a gold locket on a bracelet, inscribed, "To My Other Mother." Years later, Reynolds wrote that of all her movie mothers, Una was "the sweetest and most loving of all," and the two remained close after filming concluded, exchanging letters for years.[23]

In early December 1958, just a few weeks after she completed work on *The Mating Game*, Una began rehearsals for *Listen to the Mocking Bird*, adapted and directed by Edward Chodorov. The play centers around three elderly ladies (Una, Eva Le Gallienne, and Billie Burke), residents in an English boardinghouse, who are suspected of murdering their landlady. The play was plagued with problems from the very start. First, Burke had a hearing impairment and difficulty memorizing her lines. She had to be equipped with an earpiece and fed her lines, which particularly annoyed Le Gallienne, who railed against her co-star in her diary: "Burke was impossible," she wrote. "She made a shambles of the drunk scene. Una & I were quite upset by it all. I've never had to put up with this kind of thing & it's only by God's Grace I've been able to keep calm."[24] Second, the weather was problematic during parts of the tour, ranging from brutally cold temperatures in Boston to storms so severe in Cleveland that the city was declared a disaster area. Third, critics generally had mixed feelings about the play, complimenting the acting, but not the play itself. Finally, as if things couldn't get any worse, a fire swept through the theater in Washington, D.C., destroying all the sets and effectively bringing the show to a close. All these challenges notwithstanding, Una liked the play and wrote to a friend afterwards that it was just starting to get good when the fire occurred.

Una was back treading the boards in July 1959. She traveled to Pennsylvania for a stint at the Bucks County Playhouse, nicknamed by some as America's most famous summer theater. The play was *Cradle and All*, and she was the female lead, a middle-aged woman who discovers that she is pregnant, much to her husband's and grown daughter's chagrin. Rounding out the cast was a young Dick Van Dyke, playing in one of his first important stage roles. Una's role proved to be challenging on several different levels, and she wrote to a friend, detailing all her difficulties:

> One more performance and I am out of this nightmare. In all my 40 years in the theatre and screen, I never was faced with so many long speeches and different situations. We had two weeks rehearsal, and we just played two weeks. This I must say, the audiences loved it and howled at each performance—but it needs much rewriting. Fortunately, we have a lovely company and crew—our director and author, too, are fine men—BUT, BROTHER—I HAVE HAD IT. I think this will be my last play. I am going back to California. My father is failing so very rapidly, and I fear [he] must go into the hospital for a kidney-bladder operation—at his age, 77 years—it's not too easy to take, and he is all I have.[25]

Nevertheless, Una didn't return to California right away. She stayed on the East Coast to appear in the last theatrical role of her career, which was all the sweeter because it was on Broadway. The role was Essie, wife to newspaper editor Nat Miller (Walter Pidgeon) in *Take Me Along*, a musical adaptation of Eugene O'Neill's *Ah, Wilderness!*, a nostalgic look at an American family in the early 20th century. Ruth Warrick had originally been cast in the role, but producer David Merrick thought she was too young. Robert Morse played the couple's lovesick teenage son, while Jackie Gleason was the carefree, often tipsy Uncle Sid, who pursued schoolmarm Lily (Eileen Herlie). Una and the rest of the supporting cast received favorable notices, but critics seemed to save most of their praise for Gleason, whose bouncy exuberance stole the show. His presence, at least during one performance, also saved the show from almost certain disaster.

Playbill for *Take Me Along*. (1959)

Valerie Harper, who went on to television fame as Rhoda, played a minor role in the production, and she recalled the time when a disturbed man stood atop the railing in front of his opera box and threatened to jump to the stage below. When Gleason realized what was happening, he stopped the orchestra and raised a hand in the man's direction, commanding him to stay put. Theater security was able to arrive in time to pull the distraught individual off the edge.

Harper had fond memories of Gleason and genuinely liked him, something she had in common with Una, who told a reporter that she had never seen a company get along so well, and Gleason was one of the reasons: "Jackie is an angel," she effused. "At Christmas he gave everyone in the company a present—the chorus, the crew, the orchestra—he didn't miss a soul. His room looked like a department store."[26] But this wasn't Gleason's only act of kindness and generosity. When Una decided to leave the show almost a year into its run, Gleason held the curtain for fifteen minutes after her last performance in order to announce her departure to the audience. He then offered her a gift from him and the rest of the cast: a solid gold bracelet embossed with symbols related to her character in the show. "When the curtain finally came down, and I turned to thank Jackie for his kind words," Una explained, "a whole flock of waiters came onstage pushing tables loaded with food and champagne. Jackie had arranged for Sardi's to cater a surprise party for me—and we all had a ball until four in the morning."[27]

When asked about Una, Robert Morse remembered being close to her as was the rest of the cast, and he described her as "delightful."[28] He wrote that he didn't recollect anything else memorable and made no reference to the rumor that Walter Winchell had circulated at the time that hinted at some sort of romance between Una and Morse. (Allegedly, they were caught smooching behind the stage.) Incidentally, when this juicy tidbit hit the newspapers, Una called up Winchell and laughed at his gullibility. "I didn't know I was a femme fatale!" she quipped.[29]

But one thing that Morse did mention was trying to avoid Gleason during the play's run, although it's unclear whether this remark was a lighthearted reference to the enmity between his and Gleason's onstage characters or something more personal. What is clear is that others connected with the play had less than positive memories and interactions with Gleason. While Walter Pidgeon mentioned some happy times with the cast during rehearsals, he also noted that Gleason had "a very low boredom threshold and started interpolating his routines. Audiences loved that kind of stuff, and we could have run forever, but Jackie finally left out of sheer boredom."[30] Producer Merrick, who made no attempt to hide his negative feelings, objected to Gleason's extravagant spending and lackadaisical attitude off stage, and newspapers regularly printed their ongoing quarrels.

Director Peter Glenville, a charismatic, genteel Englishman, helped to mitigate some of the tension. He was born into a theatrical family and claimed to come from a line of Irish vaudevillians, which may have given him more sensitivity and insight into Gleason and his way of working. Glenville's formidable presence, along with his fine directing abilities, drew out the best from his performers, and he would eventually make it to Hollywood, where he would have a distinguished career as a film director. While there, he and Una would cross paths again, and their second meeting would leave an indelible impact on her film career and legacy.

(ENDNOTES)

[1] Review of *The Ponder Heart, New York Post,* February 2, 1956.

[2] Review of *The Ponder Heart*, *Daily Mirror*, February 17, 1956.

[3] Brooks Atkinson, "Comedy of Rural Manners: Music Box Welcomes 'The Ponder Heart,'" *New York Times,* February 17, 1956, 14.

[4] Brooks Atkinson, "'Ponder Heart'—David Wayne is Ideal in Southern Comedy," *New York Times*, February 26, 1956, 1.

[5] Joan Hanauer "Actress Fears They'll Realize She Likes Job," *Anderson Herald* (Anderson, IN), June 17, 1956, 36.

[6] Sarah Marshall, letter to author, June 25, 2012.

[7] Earl Wilson, "Earl Wilson's Broadway: The Midnight Earl," *Sarasota Herald-Tribune*, April 5, 1956, 22.

[8] Leonard Maltin, "FFM Interviews Una Merkel," *Film Fan Monthly*, January 1971, 14.

[9] Erskine Johnson, "Flicker Flashes from Filmland," *Southeast Missourian*, June 9, 1955, 4.

[10] James Powers, "'Girl Most Likely,' Breezy," *Hollywood Reporter,* December 17, 1957, 3.

11. Harold Heffernan, "Giggles on Set Help Break Work Tension," *Herald Statesman* (Yonkers, NY), October 19, 1956, 5.

12. Jane Powell, letter to Ed Martin, Universal Collection, University of Southern California (USC), *The Girl Most Likely,* Box 460, Folder 131.

13. Nervin Houser, "The Girl Most Likely," *RKO Radio Studio Handbook of Publicity Data*, September 18, 1956, Universal Collection (USC), Box 435.

14. Jack Gould, "'Greer Case' by Peck Acted on Channel 2," *New York Times,* February 1, 1957, 34.

15. Walter Hawver, "CBS Scores Success with 2 Major Plays," *Knickerbocker News* (Albany, NY), February 1, 1957, 12.

16. Edwin Schallert, "Fine Cast Does Right by 'Career,'" *Los Angeles Times,* August 8, 1957, 9.

17. Paul Comi, letter to author, June 2012.

18. Review of "The Secret of the Red Room," *Daily Variety*, September 16, 1957.

19. Phyllis Battelle, "Una Merkel, Once Top Comedienne, Happy to be Back in Public View," *Corsicana Daily Sun*, February 6, 1958, 4.

20. Steven Scheuer, "TV Keynotes: Una Merkel Loses Track of Films," *Herald Statesman* (Yonkers, NY), February 21, 1958, 44.

21. Review of "Aladdin," *Variety*, February 26, 1958.

22. Arlene Jackson, "'The Mating Game' Packs Laugh Wallop at Proctor's," *Schenectady Gazette*, May 30, 1959, 8.

23. Debbie Reynolds, forward to *Mom in the Movies: The Iconic Screen Mothers You Love (and a Few You Love to Hate)*, by Richard Corliss (New York: Simon and Schuster, 2014), x.

24. Helen Sheehy, *Eva Le Gallienne: A Biography* (New York: Knopf, 1996), 353.

25. Una Merkel, letter to Jon Essex, August 8, 1959, Author's collection.

26. Ward Morehouse, "Una Merkel Little Changed by the Years," *Toledo Blade*, February 14, 1960, 2.

27. Eleanor Corrigan, "TV's Butter & Egg Man," *Los Angeles Times,* October 9, 1960, 4.

28. Robert Morse, note to author, June 2013.

29. Walter Winchell, "This and That," *Buffalo Courier-Express*, May 31, 1960, 12.

30. James E. Bawden, "Walter Pidgeon: Team Player," *Films of the Golden Age*, Winter 2008–2009, 30.

Chapter 23
Mrs. Winemiller, Disney, and Television

On February 8, 1960, during her run in *Take Me Along*, Una was honored with a star on the Hollywood Walk of Fame. It was a bright moment in a time period eclipsed by her father's deteriorating health. By June, Arno's medical problems had worsened to the point that he needed surgery, and he wanted his doctor in California to perform the procedure. Una decided she would leave her show and accompany him to the West Coast. On the day of her final New York performance, she read in the newspaper that Peter Glenville would also be leaving soon for California to direct the film version of *Summer and Smoke*. By coincidence, she saw him that evening at Sardi's, where she and her father were dining. She contemplated going over and asking him to consider her for the part of Mrs. Winemiller, the part she had played on stage nearly a decade earlier, but decided against it and left. Having second thoughts, she returned. "Usually people didn't think of me in connection with anything that could be halfway dramatic, at least not in pictures," Una recalled. "I had done two or three things at La Jolla that gave me the idea that I could do something different. In fact, I had deliberately done the plays at La Jolla to get into a different range."[1] After she explained all this to Glenville, he said he would keep her in mind. Not long after arriving in Hollywood, she also met with Hal Wallis to discuss the role, but he wasn't too convinced that she was right for it. She persisted, nevertheless, and wrote a letter to him and Glenville, reiterating her interest and even stating she'd be willing to make a screen test if necessary, something she hadn't done for years. They took her up on her offer, and she won the part, passing the test with flying colors.

Work on *Summer and Smoke* would begin later in the year, but in the meantime, Una was offered other jobs. One of the first to come her way was the role of Martha Roosevelt in NBC's *Our American Heritage* series, which she declined, preferring to appear in her first Disney film, *The Parent Trap*, an adaptation of a German novel about identical twin sisters whose parents divorce when the girls are still babies. Separated and raised by one of their parents on different coasts of the United States, the twins—Sharon and Susan—don't even know about each other, but meet by chance at a summer camp. They decide to switch places in an attempt to reconcile their parents. Hayley Mills played both girls, with Maureen O'Hara and Brian Keith as Maggie and Mitch, respectively, the estranged parents. Joanna Barnes played Vicky, Mitch's jealous fiancé, while Una was Mitch's lovable housekeeper, Verbena, the first to suspect what is going on and whose mantra, "I'm not saying a word. I mind my own business," was often repeated, but never heeded.

While Una's role of Verbena wasn't a large one, she made it memorable. In the commentary track for *The Parent Trap* DVD, Hayley Mills describes to director David Swift what made Verbena so appealing: "She was just perfect . . . motherly, sweet . . . and the right age . . . the right influence in the house.

Maureen O'Hara, Una, and Brian Keith in *The Parent Trap*.
(© Walt Disney Productions, 1961)

There's no kind of feeling that perhaps Mitch might have been attracted to [her] . . . not that she wasn't attractive, it's just that she was in the motherly kind of mode."[2] Mills never refers to Una personally in the commentary, only her character of Verbena, but Una was more forthcoming about her young colleague in a newspaper interview granted around the time of the film's release. She freely disclosed her admiration for Mills, especially her ardent professionalism: "She takes her work seriously. She is never demanding and always ready to laugh—the most relaxed actress I have ever known."[3]

Like Mills, Una also made a favorable impression on several of her castmates, as their recollections can attest. Joanna Barnes, who had only limited contact with her, recalled that she was "very soft-spoken and extremely gracious."[4] Someone who got to know her much better was Susan Henning, the twelve-year-old girl who played the other twin—seen from behind, the side, or in three-quarter shots—in certain scenes that required Hayley to interact with her twin sister. Henning (whose married name is Schutte) shared with this writer what she remembered about Una, who, in her opinion, was brilliantly cast:

> In addition to her coloring, gentle face, and soft, round features, Una had a warm, nurturing voice and gentle demeanor that made you feel comfortable. She was cuddly, friendly, and had hugs for you. She made the film better and personified what you think of as the ideal grandmother figure. As far as professionalism, she was always prepared, prompt, and knew her lines, and her timing was perfect. She exuded joy, happiness, and confidence, and I really believe she had the spiritual gift of uplifting others.[5]

If Verbena was kind, loving, and maternal, Una's next film character—Mrs. Winemiller—was the polar opposite, defined by her cold, calculating, and neurotic demeanor. As filming on *Summer and Smoke* began in December of 1960, Una began to develop the character, an elderly lady who lives in the American South in the early part of the 20th century. While director Peter Glenville was there to offer assistance, she relied heavily on the advice she had gleaned a decade earlier from James Neilson, her director at La Jolla. "Remember," he had told her. "You're married to a very strict minister, and you were very young when you were married. He brought you up as if you were under glass."[6]

Using this explanation, Una fleshed out what she considered an ill-defined character, although the script does reveal some clues about this demented lady. When her daughter, Alma (Geraldine Page), was just an adolescent, Mrs. Winemiller apparently suffered a nervous breakdown and regressed into a spoiled, infantile kleptomaniac, who is subject to fits and tantrums when she doesn't get her way. Mrs. Winemiller's mind, although shrouded behind a childish exterior, still has moments of lucidity. She seems to have an uncanny perceptiveness about Alma, whom she sometimes taunts in stinging, yet truthful barbs: "Alma's in love. Alma's in love," she screams. Another one of her favorite refrains is "Spy! Spy!" and it accurately describes Alma's clandestine behavior toward John Buchanan, Jr. (Laurence Harvey), the handsome young doctor next door.

Una as Mrs. Winemiller in *Summer and Smoke*. (Paramount, 1961)

Although Mrs. Winemiller has several important scenes in the film, perhaps her most compelling one is her heated exchange with Alma. The latter, provoked into a retaliatory barrage of threats and reproaches, accuses her mother of stealing away her youth and being malicious and self-indulgent. Mrs. Winemiller reacts to the scolding in a complex, nuanced way, demonstrating Una's superb acting and artistry. Throughout the scene, a panoply of emotions plays across her face, ranging from fear and surprise to confusion and pain. Then, in a flash, her jaw and eyes harden, and her rebellious spirit resurges. She denies Alma's accusations and refuses to listen further. She cries out plaintively, "I am kind; I am kind!" Alma is unmoved and continues her recriminations, but they have an unexpected effect. Instead of whipping her mother into submission, they almost seem to feed her mounting aggression and resolve. "You *do* spy on him," Mrs. Winemiller shrieks back and rises imperiously from her chair. She then pushes Alma out of the way and walks toward her menacingly. The two women begin fighting over a stolen hat but are stopped when Mr. Winemiller intercedes. He berates his wife and commands her to go upstairs. She obeys, walking like a slump-shouldered beast of burden, slow and heavy laden with the weight of what she's just done. As writer Nancy S. Kinney so discerningly points out, Mrs. Winemiller "represents a less strong version of Alma who broke down under the strain of excessive piety and repression. She is the specter of what Alma might become."[7]

During lulls on the *Summer and Smoke* set, Una busied herself looking through freighter folders and brochures, planning for a long sea cruise she wanted to take with her father. "I owe Dad a holiday in particular," she explained. "He was holed up in a New York apartment a whole year while I was busy rehearsing and playing in *Take Me Along* on Broadway with Jackie Gleason. Now he's with me in an apartment here in Hollywood waiting again...."[8]

When her role was completed, Una composed a letter to Hal Wallis, thanking him for letting her play Mrs. Winemiller. "It was an experience I shall treasure for many reasons," she wrote. "It is a part and a story that I love as you must know, and there was so much kindness, consideration, and help from every department at Paramount."⁹ She and Arno then embarked on a much needed vacation, and upon their return, they moved from their Hollywood Boulevard apartment to a home in Palm Desert, where they could enjoy a respite from noise and smog.

Aside from an episode of NBC's *Here's Hollywood*, which aired in May, Una didn't work in 1961. She eagerly awaited the release of *Summer and Smoke* and wanted to attend the November premiere in California, but the customary invitation and free tickets never came. She was very hurt by the slight and contacted her friend Jerry Asher, who contacted Paramount on her behalf. He learned that the studio had indeed invited Una, but the invitation and tickets were sent to her former address. Paramount then contacted Una's talent agency, William Morris, about it, and officials there mistakenly reported that she was in New York. They never got back to the studio with Una's new address. After the premiere in California, Hal Wallis heard what happened, and he wrote to Una to express his regret over the whole incident. He also took the occasion to praise her "beautiful job on the picture," which he noted had been duly hailed by both the public and the press.¹⁰

Variety was one such publication, opining that Una "cuts herself a memorable cameo."¹¹ The *Los Angeles Times* concurred, noting she was "notably good."¹² Members of the Academy of Motion Pictures Arts and Sciences were equally impressed and nominated her for an Oscar for Best Actress in a Supporting Role. One of Hal Wallis' associates, Paul Nathan, called her to share the good news. When she was told, Una began laughing, thinking it couldn't be true. When the reality of the situation sank in, her thoughts turned to her wardrobe and what she might wear for the award ceremony. She had no formal evening wear, so she went out and bought a champagne brocade gown with matching jacket.

She wasn't the only cast member to be recognized by the Academy. Geraldine Page earned an Oscar nomination as Best Actress, and Rita Moreno, who played one of Laurence Harvey's sultry love interests in the film, was also nominated—not for her appearance in *Summer and Smoke*—

but as Best Supporting Actress in *West Side Story*. Finally, *Summer and Smoke* garnered two other nominations, one for Best Art Direction-Set Decoration and the other for Best Music.

Una was one of the sentimental favorites to win. Paramount ran a good campaign on her behalf, but the bookmakers, managers of Loew's Theatres, put her odds of winning at only 10–1. She attended the ceremony on April 9, 1962, with her father by her side. They sat right behind Moreno and George Chakiris and listened as Rock Hudson announced that Moreno won in her category. The latter's acceptance speech was the succinct: "I can't believe it!" Years later, when asked about not winning, Una said that she hadn't minded losing. "I was so happy with the nomination—that pleased me to no end. I'm still tickled to death with it."[13] As for Moreno's winning performance, Una admitted to never seeing it, but commented that she felt the Oscars should have two categories, one for comedies/dramas and the other for musicals, because the people in the musicals win so often. If Una was rather nonchalant about her loss, the studio heads at Paramount were probably less indifferent and very disappointed to see that *Summer and Smoke* didn't take home a single statuette.

The following month Una's attention was diverted from acting to politics. Richard Nixon was the Republican candidate running against Democratic incumbent governor Pat Brown in the California gubernatorial race. Una and Arno, staunch Republicans, were energized after seeing one of Nixon's campaign telethons on television. Una felt moved to pen him a letter, expressing her support: "From the first day in public office, Father and I have been 'Win With Nixon' advocates, and today that feeling is truer and deeper than ever."[14] She went on to say that in the hearts of both Republicans and Democrats there was a need for him to be governor, and she offered her services to his cause. The letter was accompanied by two checks, totaling $20.

Una proved not to be remiss in her civic and spiritual duties either. Learning about the plight of homeless cats in New York City that were left frozen, starving, or injured by the city's urban renewal efforts, she decided to help. She joined entertainers Orson Bean and Jack Carter, and American

Major League Baseball shortstop Phil Rizzuto as sponsors of the Save a Cat League. She also sent money to her Methodist church back in Covington, Kentucky, and a flagstone in front of the entrance there has her name on it, a record of her financial support over the years.

* * *

It wasn't long before Una was thinking about acting again. "I'll go wherever there's a good acting part awaiting me," she said. "Fortunately, I'm financially independent, and I can pick and choose what I want. One of the joys of reaching a character woman's age is the opportunity of playing wonderful character roles."[15] One such role came along in the summer of 1962 when she began working on her second Disney film, *Summer Magic*. She played the churlish Mariah Popham, who doesn't believe in rainbows or silver linings: "I like to believe in a cloud that's a first-class cloud, thick and black clean through," her character announces curtly. "I always expect the worst and ain't ever been disappointed." She is the perfect foil to her eternally hopeful husband, Osh (Burl Ives), a kindhearted postmaster of a small rural town, who welcomes a displaced Bostonian widow (Dorothy McGuire) and her three children—played by Hayley Mills, Eddie Hodges, and Jimmy Mathers—and helps them get settled into their new surroundings.

Summer Magic, a musical remake of RKO's *Mother Carey's Chickens* (1938), showcases the musical talent of several cast members, Ives and Eddie Hodges in particular. The latter, who was only fifteen years old during filming, was perfectly cast as Hayley's brother, Gilly. Portraying an aspiring composer, he was given several scenes to demonstrate his musical prowess and did so very effectively. He shared with this author his memories of working with Una:

> I can tell you that she was very easy to be around, and that was a good thing for a young performer. She was very relaxed and got on well with everyone—cast and crew. She was an experienced

Una, Burl Ives, and Peter Brown in *Summer Magic*.
(© Walt Disney Productions, 1963)

actor, so there was no question that she would do her job well. And that she did. . . .

The thing I most remember about Una is that she was so serene. She always had that enigmatic, 'Mona Lisa' kind of smile on her face. She was an actor's actor, a trouper. You just knew that when she walked onto the set—she was ready to work. She knew camera angles, lighting, and movement like the back of her hand. Her comedic timing was impeccable. She worked so well with Burl Ives.
Her character avoided involvement with other characters, and she did that perfectly in front of her camera. Behind the camera, she was warm, friendly, and fun to be around. She was an actor you would always want to work with again. So many actors are difficult—this makes for a stressful day on a set. Una made working enjoyable. I especially liked the way she treated young performers as equals.[16]

(c. 1963) As she approached sixty, Una was as attractive and hardworking as ever.

After completing *Summer Magic*, Una took a break from the cinema to devote herself to television. In the fall of 1962, she played a housekeeper who aspires to marry off her gold-digging daughter on an episode of *The Real McCoys*. Over a year later, television audiences were treated to two more appearances: first on *The Bill Dana Show*, where she was a clever card shark who organized a floating poker party; the second, an episode of *Burke's Law* ("Who Killed Cynthia Royal?") found her playing a rich apartment owner whose missing Siamese cat was thought to be connected to the murder of a tenant.

When she wasn't working, Una was getting acclimated to a simple life at home. She told reporters, "I had almost forgotten how enjoyable it is to plan and prepare simple meals, to test new recipes, and to dine quietly at home with close family or friends."[17] She and her father, whom she described at the time as a "young and lively 81," decided that they wanted to maintain a second residence back in Hollywood.[18] Therefore, they took much of their furniture and prized possessions—including many of Una's mother's old cookbooks, kitchen utensils, linens, and dishes—out of storage to refurnish their apartment.

* * *

In the early part of 1964, ABC introduced a new television show called *Destry*, a comedy Western based on the film *Destry Rides Again*. The series starred John Gavin, who played gun-shy Tom Destry's son, Harrison, a man wrongly imprisoned for robbery, but now free and roaming the West in search of the men who framed him. The series ran for thirteen episodes, and the third one, "Law and Order Day," begins with Harrison narrating his encounter with the "most treacherous, sneaky, untrustworthy, two-faced critter who ever bankrupted a municipality."[19] As viewers find out, this infamous thief is an old, frail-looking, grey-haired lady named Granny Farrell, superbly incarnated by Una, the guest star of the week.

While it is uncertain whether she was chosen for the part in *Destry* because of her memorable role in the 1939 film, Una's selection as Granny was very fitting and turned out to be a brilliant bit of casting. She threw herself into this meaty role with gusto and explored various subtleties of the character, using her innocent countenance, expressive eyes, and disarming accent to create a believable character who was very likable despite some serious moral shortcomings.

The role of Granny not only demanded some distinctive characterization, but also some rigorous physical exertion. One scene called for Una to wield an umbrella and use it in a spirited fight against some of her cohorts in crime. Director John Florea, concerned for her safety, asked if she would like a stunt double. She declined, and thinking back on her film role in *Destry Rides Again*, replied, "I didn't use one 25 years ago. Why should I start now?"[20]

Una followed up her delightful performance in *Destry* with Disney's *A Tiger Walks*, the tale of a young lady (Pamela Franklin) and her efforts to save an escaped four-hundred-pound Bengal tiger from her sheriff dad (Brian Keith) and the fearful townspeople who prefer killing it to taking it alive. Una plays the town's hard-nosed, penny-pinching hotel owner who has no compunction about telling disruptive visitors to leave, eavesdropping on the sheriff's operations, or gouging guests for their meager accommodations. Although only on-screen a few minutes, Una creates a memorable character and makes every scene count. She even throws in a recurring inside joke for good measure, humming the famous Disney tune "Zip-A-Dee-Doo-Dah" in nearly all of her scenes.

This was Una's third and final Disney film, and over the course of the years, she had become friends with Walt Disney. They sent each other letters and cards on special occasions, and she was even invited as one of his special guests for a railroad-type party at his home, where he proudly displayed and rode a miniature train he had built there. When asked about what Disney was like at the studio, she remembered his wandering onto the set all the time, knowing exactly what was going on. "I liked him very much—admired him," she said.[21]

Again, Una turned to television when she wasn't doing films. First, she appeared on *The Cara Williams Show* as a lady who, because of a clerical error, has been classified as a piece of office equipment and spends her days knitting paper clips and counting passersby in Williams' company. Next came two more guest spots on *Burke's Law*, both in 1965. The first one had her playing against type as a wrestling aficionado. She and four other suspects are thought to have slain a professional wrestler with a poisoned dart during a match. For the second, she was an annoying lonely hearts club hostess who may have known something about the death of an eminent physician and his missing wife. Una's interpretation of the latter role was particularly well received, with one newspaper citing hers as the best cameo performance of the episode.

In the spring of 1966, Una was back at her old studio MGM for the last cinematic role of her career, *Spinout*, which happened to be Elvis Presley's twenty-second movie. Like many of his previous ones, this film was formulaic, but it offered up some pleasant moments despite a hackneyed plot, which one critic derided was "so thin you could inhale it."[22] Elvis' Mike McCoy is a personable, down-to-earth singer who belts out nine songs, dances and cavorts with a bevy of beautiful gals, finds himself pursued by three of them—Shelley Fabares, Diane McBain, and Deborah Walley—and ends up driving a juiced-up Duesenberg in a race. He is ably supported in a few brief scenes by Cecil Kellaway and Una, who play a rich couple whom Presley flatters and cajoles into taking a vacation so that he can take temporary possession of their house.

Una was interviewed on set and was quoted as saying that she no longer wanted to work too hard. She spoke about her father's good health and vigor, saying, "He's like a boy, except for his arthritis."[23] Arno's health, however, soon took a turn for the worse. He and Una went to Florida for the summer, and the day after they arrived, Una had to rush him to the hospital, where he stayed for four months. "He had about everything done to him. All the operations you could think of," she recalled. "Nobody but the doctor and myself thought he'd pull through."[24] To make matters worse, when they finally made it back to California, Una broke out in a bad case of shingles.

Una didn't work for over a year, content to stay home with her father. When asked why she didn't do more television, Una conceded that television was difficult and explained that while she wouldn't mind doing a certain number of episodes, she didn't want to do a whole series. One assignment she did accept was that of Aunt Alta in "Home to Judgment," a 1968 episode of the television show *I Spy*. This role would be the final one of her long, illustrious career. Robert Culp wrote the script and stated it was one of his and co-star Bill Cosby's favorites. The plot had Kelly (Culp) and Alexander (Cosby) hiding out on the farm of Kelly's aunt and uncle (Will Geer), where they are all terrorized by some very persistent assassins. Culp based the characters of Aunt Alta and Uncle Harry on his own grandparents, and he originally wanted Beulah Bondi and Walter Brennan for the parts, but they were unavailable. When casting director Mike Fenton brought in Una and Geer, Culp was disappointed, especially with Una, whom he thought was one "hell of a reach" for the part.[25] He quickly changed his mind, though, when he saw how movingly she portrayed her character: "Miss Merkel's sweetness in the character of Alta enveloped everybody. Her innocence in the face of horror was deeply touching. The sight of her watching helplessly as Kelly makes a series of homemade bombs on her kitchen table brings tears to my eyes even today."[26]

It is difficult to refute Culp's assessment of Una's characterization. It is a very demanding role, and she plays it brilliantly, using her visceral interpretation to create an immediacy that is both hauntingly real and unsettling. Drawing upon her rich reserves of emotion, and with her eyes often brimming with tears, she convincingly conveys pain and terror, all while maintaining a long, sustained level of fear. This is no simple feat, but Una accomplishes it memorably, relying on her considerable talent, sensitivity, and years of experience and training. The result is nothing less than spellbinding, and it makes for a compelling end to an extraordinary career.

(ENDNOTES)

1. Leonard Maltin, "FFM Interviews Una Merkel," *Film Fan Monthly,* January 1971, 12–13.

2. Hayley Mills, commentary, *The Parent Trap* (DVD, Vault Disney Collection), Walt Disney Video, 2002.

3. Liza Wilson, "Hayley," *Pittsburgh Post-Gazette* (American Weekly supplement), June 25, 1961, 7.

4. Joanna Barnes, letter to author, June 26, 2012.

5. Susan Henning-Schutte, telephone interview with author, August 9, 2013.

6. Ray Neilson, radio interview with Una Merkel, Ray Neilson Celebrity Interviews Collection, University of Central Arkansas Archives, Sept. 1979.

7. Nancy S. Kinney, "Summer and Smoke," In vol. 5 of *Magill's Survey of Cinema: English Language Films,* second series, ed. Frank N. Magill (Englewood Cliffs, NJ.: Salem Press, 1981), 2343.

8. *Los Angeles Mirror,* January 6, 1961.

9. Una Merkel, letter to Hal Wallis, February 1, 1961, Hal Wallis Papers, Academy of Motion Picture Arts and Sciences.

10. Hal Wallis, letter to Una Merkel, November 29, 1961, Hal Wallis Papers, Academy of Motion Picture Arts and Sciences.

11. "Summer and Smoke," *Variety,* September 6, 1961.

12. Philip K. Scheuer, "Bitter Irony, Passion, and a Grim Jest," *Los Angeles Times,* November 12, 1961, 3.

13. Richard Lamparski, *Whatever Became of. . . ?* radio interview with Una Merkel, WBAI, April 7, 1970.

14. Una Merkel, Box 510, Series 320, Richard Nixon Pre-Presidential Materials (Laguna Niguel). Richard Nixon Presidential Library and Museum, Yorba Linda, California. National Archives and Records Administration. Letter to Richard M. Nixon. May 30, 1962. Nixon Pre-Presidential Papers.

15. Studio Biography of Una Merkel, production file for *Summer and Smoke* (Paramount, 1961), Academy of Motion Picture Arts and Sciences.

16. Eddie Hodges, letter to author, June 18, 2013.

17. Freida Zylstra, "Una's Happy to Be Cooking Again," *Chicago Tribune,* July 1, 1963, 12.

18. Ibid.

19. *Destry: The Complete Series*, "Law and Order Day," DVD, directed by John Florea (Eugene, OR: Timeless Media Group, 2011).

20. "Una Merkel is 'Fighter' Again," *Buffalo Courier Express*, February 16, 1964, 24.

21. Maltin, "FFM Interviews Una Merkel," 14.

22. "Herb Kelly, "Movie Review: 'Spinout,'" *Miami News*, December 1, 1966, 5.

23. Dick Kleiner, "'Spinout,' A Film of Many Meanings," *McKinney Courier Gazette*, May 12, 1966, 4.

24. Lamparski, radio interview with Una Merkel, April 7, 1970.

25. Robert Culp, commentary, "Home to Judgment," *I Spy* (DVD), Image Entertainment, 2008.

26. Ibid.

Chapter 24
Back Home to Kentucky

Near the end of the 1960s, Una and her father were spending more and more time outside of Hollywood. They had moved from their second home in Palm Desert to one in nearby Palm Springs. Una wrote to her pal Jackie Gleason in February of 1969 to thank him for his Christmas gift—an unusual watch—and to share the news that they wanted to move back to Hollywood. Arno's health was failing again, and they hoped the doctors there might be more helpful. "We haven't been too happy in this house and neighborhood," Una confessed. "It's been quite lonely."[1] They ended up moving into a very modern apartment in the Hancock Park area of Los Angeles. Una decorated it with antiques that Arno had collected during his travels around the world.

In the summer of 1969, author and radio personality Richard Lamparski went to California to interview celebrities for his radio show *Whatever Became of. . . ?* Una was among those at the top of his list, and he had no problem finding her: her name and address were still listed in the phone book. During the interview, he asked her what type of part she'd still like to do, and she answered: ". . . a good part, and I don't mean by that a big part. I feel the English theater has the answer to performances because sometimes even the biggest stars play smaller parts. It's the part . . . the essence of the part itself that counts."[2]

As much as she would have liked a good part, Una felt fortunate that she didn't have to work. She could take it easy. Thinking back on all the years she performed, she told Lamparski, "You feel like you have a little time coming to you."[3] Besides, she felt she ended her career on a high note: "I kind of tied it up in blue ribbon,"[4] she told another interviewer.

Now that she was no longer working, Una could devote her free time to taking care of Arno, whose health and happiness were her main preoccupations. He passed away at the end of 1969, two days before Christmas. He was eighty-seven years old. He was taken back to Fort Mitchell, Kentucky, a little town outside of Covington, where he was buried beside his beloved Bessie in Highland Cemetery. Una went there for the burial and avowed to one of her friends that the next time she came back, it would be for her own funeral.

*   *   *

Visitors who traveled to Covington, Kentucky, in the early 1970s would have found an overcrowded car dealership located on the corner of Fourth and Greenup Streets, right beside an unpretentious brick dwelling with a wide front porch. Some people thought this old house was an eyesore, having long outlived its usefulness, so they welcomed seeing bulldozers raze it to the ground in the fall of 1972. Others were more sentimental about it and couldn't help but feel a pang of sadness at its demolition. To them, it was a local attraction: Una Merkel's birthplace some seventy years earlier.

Although it is not known what Una thought about the destruction of her birthplace, she most certainly heard about it from her friends in Covington, with whom she corresponded regularly. One of them was astounded at Una's "genuine thirst for news from Covington,"[5] while another confirmed that Una had "kept her contacts" and "always had a soft spot in her heart for Covington."[6] The special feelings that Una felt for Covington actually extended beyond the city limits to the state as a whole, as evidenced in a letter she addressed to a fan in the 1970s: "I guess we Kentuckians are hard to keep down—that's my home state—I'm still awfully proud of it."[7]

As fond as she was of Kentucky, Una preferred to stay in her adopted California, where she had no financial worries, thanks to the bequest of a generous aunt. "I didn't even know she had a cent, but I never cease to be grateful to her."[8] Una's apartment had a beautiful balcony, where she could sit and listen as chimes rang out twice daily at a nearby Methodist church. The rest of her time was usually spent catching up on her sleep, reading, and answering fan mail. Her best friend and nearby neighbor, Virginia Mollenhauer, witnessed her receiving letters from all over the world: "She'd get the mail, and if there was a manila envelope in it, she'd say, 'Oh, another fan.'"[9]

Una's last years weren't all carefree and leisurely. She had to contend with the usual complaints of old age, including bouts of arthritis, failing eyesight, and broken bones. Richard Lamparski, who visited her from time to time, recalled that she was sometimes embarrassed for him to come over. She had gained so much weight and suffered from swollen legs that made walking difficult without a cane. She eventually hired people to do chores around the apartment and assist her with errands. At one point she admitted to Lamparski that she could hardly do anything for herself.

"She was quite lonely," Lamparski remembered. "There was a sadness to her."[10] He urged her to telephone him whenever she wanted, but she hesitated, saying, "I hate to call you. I'll bother you."[11] Sometimes she did call, though, and Lamparski made a point of phoning her on special occasions like Valentine's Day and Christmas Eve.

During one of his visits, Lamparski looked around Una's apartment and noticed that she didn't display her Tony Award. However, he did see a stunning piece of cobalt blue crystal glass tucked away on a distant bookshelf. He pointed to it and said, "Do you mind me saying this? It needs the light, Una. No one sees it, and it is so pretty....You need to put it out."[12] Without saying a word, Una went over, dusted it off, and put it in a bag as a gift for him. Embarrassed by what had happened, Lamparski tried to refuse it, but Una insisted he take it. She told him that her father had been an importer and brought it back from a trip to Czechoslovakia.

Another time Una got out an album filled with movie stills. She and Lamparski were looking through them, and they stumbled across a few of her from the 1930s, when she was a fetching blond. She looked at them and admitted, "I really was kinda cute. I wish I'd known that then. I always thought I came over as a hick."[13]

Lamparski usually profiled celebrities in his book series one time, but he featured Una (and some others) multiple times because she was so popular with fans and readers. "She was a doll," Lamparski said, "and almost egoless, which is very strange for an actress."[14] He recalled that when he took photos of her to include in his books, she didn't even bother to put on makeup.

When writer Jess Hoaglin caught up with Una in 1975, she maintained: "I am really leading such a quiet life at this time there is very little to report. I'm sure your readers would not be interested in hearing all about my various hospital visits due to eye trouble and a broken arm, but I am happy to report that I'm feeling fine...."[15]

Just a few years later Una was not as cheerful. Her mobility was further hindered by pain in her legs, which had become progressively worse. "I had four pinched nerves on the sciatica nerve, and it was not funny. I even had people say, 'Don't let anybody—I don't care how good they are—touch your spine.' Well, I finally decided I had to make the decision. I couldn't go on the rest of my life with my leg giving me more and more pain all the time. I was like a prisoner in this apartment . . . so I had the operation."[16] The procedure was, as Una called it, a "miracle," and it gave her a new lease on life.[17] A reporter found her to be as "zippy as ever, a lovely, cordial, ever youthful woman," and when the topic of age came up, Una exclaimed, "I'm 75, but I don't feel like it!"[18]

Reconnecting with some of her old Hollywood friends added to Una's newly found happiness. Eleanor Powell called Una one day and suggested they go to a theater that ran vintage films. Una agreed, and the two had a wonderful time watching themselves in *Broadway Melody of 1936*. Nevertheless, this outing was unusual for Una, who had little interaction with her former peers. Some of this was due to Una's modest, self-effacing nature, and her tendency to keep a respectful distance from her more famous colleagues. Once, when recounting her time at MGM, she surprisingly said that she actually "knew very few people at the studio."[19] Likewise, she divulged that when working with Spencer Tracy and Clark Gable, she could never call them by their first names. She always used the deferential "Mister" because, as she explained it, "When you're working with great artists whom you respect so much, you have to be formal."[20] Una may have been reluctant to be too familiar with certain colleagues, but she had the innate gift of getting along with practically everyone, allowing her to make the incredible statement at the end of her career: "I don't remember in all those years ever being with unpleasant people."[21]

Una was reunited with some of her former co-workers during public appearances in the late seventies and early eighties. In May of 1979, Una was feted when the National Film Society honored her and seven others with an American Screen Classic Award at their annual awards dinner. She put in a final appearance that year at an opening-night party to kick off a film retrospective dedicated to vintage MGM films. In March of 1980, she joined Charlton Heston, Alfred Hitchcock, Fred MacMurray, Beulah Bondi, and many others to celebrate the life and work of Jimmy Stewart in a televised tribute show.

Although Una enjoyed mingling with her former cohorts, she was just as content to admire them vicariously through performances. She saw Buddy Ebsen one evening on a television award show and felt like applauding. "It

Una Merkel and Henry Brandon at the National Film Society convention, May 1979. *(Courtesy of photographer Alan Light)*

made me feel just wonderful," she told a reporter, "because Buddy and the older stars were the best things in the show."[22] She would get to see her old studio friends one more time on the silver screen during her last outing before she died. She dressed to the nines and went to a local movie theater to watch a film that was still dear to her heart—*42nd Street*.

Early on January 2, 1986, Una called her best friend, Virginia Mollenhauer, complaining of a stomach ache. "Oh, honey. I don't feel very well," she murmured.[23] Later that evening she died. The official cause of death was cardiac arrest, a complication of atherosclerotic heart disease (plaque buildup in artery walls) and arteriosclerosis (hardening of the arteries). Una had turned eighty-two years old just a few weeks earlier.

On January 9, Una's body was flown back to Kentucky and was taken immediately for interment in Highland Cemetery, where she would be buried next to her parents, who were not far from her maternal grandparents. Friends from across the country called the funeral home in Covington to offer their condolences, including Harry Morgan and Jackie Gleason. Neither was able to make the trip, but Gleason's secretary issued a statement: "He loved Una. They've exchanged Christmas cards and correspondence over the years. He really admired and loved her."[24] Gleason sent a blanket of fifty red carnations with accompanying baby's breath, his trademark, to cover the blue-steel casket. His flowers were the only ones that Una received.

Una Merkel's Gravestone
(Courtesy of author and Therese Duzinkiewicz Baker.)

There was no service planned, nor were any mourners expected, but three did come to pay their respects. The first was Rev. Ted Nicholas, pastor of the First United Methodist Church, where Una attended as a child. He came at the request of his congregation. No prayers were said, but he gave a brief eulogy, in which he described Una as someone who "brought joy and cheer to many."[25] Una's childhood friend, Clyde Day, insisted on attending. "I wanted to come . . . My cousin corresponded with her regularly. My cousin is now dead, but (Ms. Merkel) used to send money to my cousin to put flowers on her parents' grave."[26] The final mourner was Vera Webster, a long-time friend whose mother-in-law from her first marriage was best friends with Una's mother, Bessie. Webster remembered how much Una adored her parents and added that she was "very witty . . . a special person, very loving."[27]

An example of Una's legendary wit was recounted in a brief piece that appeared in a Kentucky publication not long after her death. The story goes that once during her heyday at MGM in the 1930s, a studio photographer took her back in the film galleries with the hopes of getting some cheesecake photos of her. "Do you mind if I take some pictures of you in the nude?" he asked. Una looked at him calmly and replied, "If you take better pictures with your clothes off, it's OK with me."[28]

* * *

Two years after Una's death, writer and fan Warder Harrison went to visit her grave and was grieved and appalled to see that she had been buried in an unmarked grave. As specified in Una's will, her remaining assets and possessions had been doled out to distant relatives, friends, and charitable organizations, and once that was done, there simply hadn't been enough left to get her a marker. Harrison went into the main office of the cemetery and set up a "Una Merkel Memorial Fund" to rectify this omission. He then wrote to twenty-five of Una's co-stars, solicited donations, and placed an ad in a popular movie magazine at the time, *Hollywood Studio Magazine*, to collect more money. Harrison received $120, which he sent to the cemetery. Local efforts then collected another $325, which was sufficient to purchase Una's headstone and put it in place.

In the spring of 1991, Una received another accolade. A historical marker dedicated to her was unveiled in Goebel Park in Covington. The marker recognizes her Tony Award and Academy Award nomination, as well as her prolific career in motion pictures. It was a well-deserved honor, but marred somewhat by a mistake on the plaque that states that Una was in sixty-six films, whereas she actually appeared in almost one hundred.

Historic marker honoring Una Merkel in Goebel Park, Covington, Kentucky
(Courtesy of the author and Therese Duzinkiewicz Baker.)

More recently, interest in Una continues unabated on television, the Internet, and social media. The cable channel Turner Classic Movies, for example, has paid special tribute to her a number of times by airing a whole day of her films on her birthday. She continues to be featured on a multitude of websites, blogs, and online forums. Finally, she has an increasing presence on Facebook, Pinterest, and other social media outlets, showing that her popularity is far from waning, but on the rise.

Una would probably wonder why she still inspires so much interest today, and there are no easy answers. Is it due to her sassy wit, prodigious talent, and Southern charm? Her folksy, down-to-earth persona? Perhaps her inspiring perseverance in the face of adversity, or her humble, gracious attitude toward life's vicissitudes? Maybe it's the way she was able to draw forth a chuckle, laugh, or tear—her ability to touch and move people in a truthful, meaningful way. Whatever the reasons for her enduring popularity, one thing remains certain: there will never be another Una Merkel. With her passing, the world lost a unique performer, but more importantly, an incredibly loving, caring, and decent human being.

Fortunately, much of Una's film, television, and radio output still survives and can be easily accessed, two factors that bode well for the legacy of her oeuvre. Her work has the potential to thrill, delight, and amaze fans for generations to come, and every time they see one of her performances, a little bit of Una will live on. It's a comforting thought, and one that probably would have pleased her. You can almost hear her whisper in that lilting Southern drawl of hers, "It's awfully nice to be remembered."[29]

(c. 1935) Una Merkel—Gone but not forgotten. (MGM)

(ENDNOTES)

[1] Peggy Kreimer and Monica Dias, "Home Grown Movie Star Comes Home Last Time," *Kentucky Post*, January 8, 1986, 3.

[2] Richard Lamparski, *Whatever Became of...?* radio interview with Una Merkel, WBAI, April 7, 1970.

[3] Ibid.

[4] Ray Neilson, radio interview with Una Merkel, Ray Neilson Celebrity Interviews Collection, University of Central Arkansas Archives, June 1978.

[5] Chester F. Geaslen, "Film Star's Birthplace Demolished in Covington," *Cincinnati Enquirer*, October 15, 1972, 4.

[6] Peggy Kreimer and Monica Dias, "Home Grown Movie Star Comes Home Last Time," *Kentucky Post;* January 8, 1986, 3.

[7] Una Merkel, letter to Gene Hunt, February 7, 1979, author's collection.

[8] Nancy Anderson, "Una was Numero Dos," *Reading Eagle* (PA), September 15, 1978, 9.

[9] Una Merkel biographical folder, Kenton County Public Library, Covington, Kentucky.

[10] Lamparski, phone interview with author, January 5, 2008.

[11] Ibid.

[12] Ibid.

[13] Lamparski, *Whatever Became of...?* 8th Series, (New York: Crown, 1982), 209.

[14] Lamparski, phone interview with author, January 5, 2008.

[15] Jess L. Hoaglin, *Wherever is...? The Stars of Yesteryear* (Los Angeles: J. L.H, 1981), 40.

[16] Ray Neilson, radio interview with Una Merkel, June 1978.

[17] Ibid.

[18] Anderson, "Una was Numero Dos," 8.

[19] Ibid.

[20] Ibid, 9.

[21] Lamparski, *Whatever Became of...?* (Eight Series), 209.

[22] Anderson, "Una was Numero Dos," 9.

23. Una Merkel Biographical folder; Kenton Co. Public Library, Covington, Kentucky.

24. Jim Calhoun, "Three Mourners Cry For Covington's Comic Actress," *Cincinnati Enquirer*, January 10, 1986, 1.

25. Ibid.

26. Ibid.

27. Ibid.

28. "Chatter," *Courier Journal Magazine* (Louisville, KY), February 23, 1986, 13.

29. Lamparski, radio interview with Una Merkel, April 7, 1970.

Una Merkel (c. 1937, MGM)

APPENDIX
Una Merkel and Jazz Babies (1928)

In the late 1920s, Cine-Arts Productions, Inc. was a Hollywood-based company that specialized exclusively in creating 16mm films in a wide variety of genres for amateur markets and home library use. In 1928, they released *Jazz Babies*, a mischievous stag film about several women in a finishing school who make wagers about whether they can catch grapes in their mouths. Those who aren't successful lose the bet and their pajama tops!

Some viewers who have seen *Jazz Babies* think they recognize Una as one of the featured brunettes in the short. They assume that Una must have had dark hair when she was younger and lightened it later in her career. In one sense, they are correct. Una's naturally blond hair did darken as she got older.

In the late 1920s, however, Una lightened her hair to regain her original blond tresses, and newspaper accounts and photographs confirm this change.

The hair issue aside, this author concedes that the woman in *Jazz Babies* does bear a resemblance to Una, both physically and in some of her body language—one arm placed akimbo—a pose that Una sometimes adopted for dramatic effect, but this author is not convinced it is Una for several reasons. First, there's the question of time and opportunity. In 1928, Una appeared almost daily on Broadway in a long run of *Coquette* that lasted until September of that year. Then she immediately left to take the play on tour around the country for another ten months. When did she have time that year to travel to Hollywood to appear in this short?

Second, why would she have done it? Una definitely didn't need the work. Her stage career was on the upswing, and at the time, she could already boast two Broadway shows and several off-Broadway productions to her credit. As for money, Una had worked in the theater since 1924, and with her long-term contract with producer John Golden, she had a regular income. Besides, she didn't need much money. She lived with her parents and never had to worry about being financially independent.

Third, why would a woman who had such obvious self-esteem issues—she called herself a "wallflower"[1] and one of those "unfortunate souls born with an inferiority complex"[2]—feel the need to disrobe and expose her breasts in this cheap production? Was it an attempt to overcome her ongoing fears, insecurities, and inhibitions? Did she want to live vicariously as someone else to escape her own reality? Perhaps, but it doesn't seem probable for someone who once said that "we should know when we are acting and when we are not—else, we would lose track of ourselves altogether."[3]

When all these factors are taken into consideration, it seems highly unlikely that the mysterious lady in *Jazz Babies* is Una Merkel, but rather someone who looks a great deal like her. However, the jury is still out, and until further evidence is uncovered, nothing can be said conclusively. The identity of the dark-haired lady remains obscure, like many of Hollywood's other unsolved mysteries.

(Endnotes)

1. Una Merkel, "Wallflowers Can Bloom," *Cosmopolitan*, June 1942, 28.

2. Barrett Kiesling, "Una Merkel is 'Surprise Girl' of Movie Colony," *Pittsburgh Press*, July 30, 1937, 12.

3. Ibid.

Credits

UNA MERKEL ON STAGE

The Big Show (Music by Raymond Hubbell, book by R.H. Burnside, lyrics by John Golden); Hippodrome Theatre, New York. August 31, 1916–May 05, 1917. Charles Dillingham (producer); staged by R.H. Burnside; choreographed by Ivan Clustine and Mariette Lorette. Cast: Ellen Dallerup, George Hermann, Annette Kellerman, Haru Onuki, Pavlova, Hilda Ruckerts, Katie Schmidt, Six Brown Brothers, Toto, Alexander Volinine, and many others, including Una Merkel (chorus girl).*

Note: Pavlova danced an abbreviated version of Tchaikovsky's "Sleeping Beauty," but was replaced after opening night by swimming star Annette Kellerman.

*Una most likely performed opening night, but left the show soon afterwards to return to school in Covington, KY.

Montmartre (by Pierre Frondaie, translated by Benjamin Glazer); Belmont Theatre, New York. February 13, 1922–May 1, 1922. The Players' Assembly (producer); staged by Clarke Silvernail. Cast: Frank Doane, Mabel Frenyear, Winifred Harris, Arthur Hohl, Mae Hopkins, Brandon Hurst, Galina Kopernak, Helen Lowell, Una Merkel* (cigarette girl), Clarke Silvernail, Helen Ware

*Una's participation in this play cannot be substantiated. In studio biographies and several of her obituaries, it was reported that she appeared in this production, but credits indicate that her supposed role was played by "Alta Mearkle."

Two By Two (by John Turner and Eugenie Woodward); Selwyn Theatre, New York. February 23, 1925–March 7, 1925. Jessie Trimble, Inc. (producer); Cast: Minette Buddecke, Lawrence D'Orsay, Frank Fayne, Beatrice Herford, Howard Lindsay, Lucille Lortell, Una Merkel (Marriage License Bureau worker), Charlotte Walker.

The Poor Nut (by J.C. Nugent and Elliott Nugent); Henry Miller Theatre, New York. April 27, 1925–May 1, 1925. Patterson McNutt (producer), staged by Howard Lindsay. Cast: Percy Helton, Cornelius Keefe, Wright Kramer, Norma Lee, Una Merkel (spectator in stands), Joseph Mitchell, Elliott Nugent, Florence Shirley, John Webster,

Pigs (by Anne Morrison and Patterson McNutt); Little Theatre, New York. September 1, 1924–June 1, 1925. John Golden (producer); staged by Frank Craven. Cast: Philip Barrison, May Buckley, Alan Bunce, Wallace Ford, Maude Granger, Rosemary Hilton,* James Kearney, Frederic Malcolm, George Henry Trader, Nydia Westman

*Una was the understudy for Ms. Hilton in the role of Lenore Hastings and replaced her in late spring 1925.

Pigs, Stage Tour: September 1, 1925–February 1927. John Golden (producer), Frank Craven (director); Cast: Gertrude Augarde, Philip Barrison, May Buckley, Wallace Ford, Una Merkel (Mildred Cushing), Elaine Temple, George Henry Trader, Emerson Treacy

*Two Girls Wante*d (by Gladys B. Unger); Little Theatre, New York; September 9, 1926–October 1926; John Golden Theatre, New York; November 1, 1926–June 1927*. John Golden (producer), staged by Winchell Smith; Cast: Charlotte Denniston, May Duryea, William Hanley, John Humphrey, Charles Laite, James C. Lane, Grace Menken, Frank Monroe, Mary Philips, Herbert Saunders, Beverly Sitgreaves, Nydia Westman
*Una only appeared in the play for two weeks in March 1927, replacing Nydia Westman, who played Marianna Miller.

The Gossipy Sex (by Lawrence Grattan); Mansfield Theatre, New York. April 19, 1927–May 7, 1927. John Golden (producer), staged by Sam Forrest; Cast: Philip Barrison, Joan Carvel, John Cherry, Eva Condon, Harry Forsman, Norval Keedwell, Florence Mason, Grace Menken, Una Merkel (Anna Sterling), Lynne Overman, Thomas W. Ross, George Spelvin, Ralph Theodore, Helen Weir.

Vaudeville Tour (Northeast and Midwest of USA); Summer 1927; Lynne Overman, Una Merkel, E. J. Blunkall

Coquette (by George Abbott and Ann Preston); Maxine Elliott's Theatre, New York. November 8, 1927–September 15, 1928. Jed Harris and Lee Shubert (producers), George Abbott (director); Cast: Frederick Burton, Elliot [Eliot] Cabot, Frank Dae, Helen Hayes, Andrew J. Lawlor, Jr., Una Merkel

(Betty Lee Reynolds), Abbie Mitchell, Gaylord Pendleton, G. Albert Smith, Phyllis Tyler, Charles Waldron.

Coquette, Stage Tour: October 1928–July 20, 1929. Cast: Frederick Burton, Frank Clayton, Helen Hayes, Andrew J. Lawlor, Jr., Una Merkel (Betty Lee Reynolds), Carmen Miller, Abbie Mitchell, Gaylord Pendleton, Bryant Sells, G. Albert Smith, Charles Waldron.

Salt Water (by Daniel Jarrett); John Golden Theatre, New York. November 26, 1929–February 1, 1930*. John Golden (producer); Cast: Robert Burton, Claude Cooper, Frank Craven, William Edmunds, Edythe Elliott, Alan Goode, James C. Lane, Henry Lawrence, Una Merkel (Marion Potter)
*Una left the production in January 1930.

Vaudeville Tour and Special Appearances:
New York, New England, West Coast, Midwest, and British Columbia, Canada (September 1942–September 1943); Una appeared with a number of different artists and performers on the circuit, including the Barry Sisters, Betty Brewer, Bonnie Baker, Ann Corio, Dolly Dawn, Enrica & Novello (dance team), Frank Fay, Clarence Gaskill, Ray Heatherton and band, Betty Kean, John Kirby and orchestra, Johnny Long and band, Jan Murray, Anne Nagel, Eddie Parks, Lawrence Welk.

Three is a Family (by Phoebe & Henry Ephron); Longacre Theatre, New York. March 1944–September 1944; on tour through January 1945. Henry Ephron (director); Cast: Una Merkel (Irma Dalrymple), Robert Burton, Ruth Weston, William Wadsworth.

My Sister Eileen (by Joseph A. Fields and Jerome Chodorov); New Horizons Theater, Pacific Palisades, CA. September 7–25, 1949. Frederick Berest (director); Cast: Una Merkel (Ruth Sherwood), Louise Arthur, Lynwood Howe, Peter Graves.

The Sombrero Playhouse, Phoenix, AZ. February 14–19, 1950. Cast: Una Merkel (Ruth Sherwood), Kay Buckley, Vince Barnett

Summer and Smoke (by Tennessee Williams); La Jolla Playhouse, La Jolla, CA. July 18–23, 1950; August–October 1950 tour. James Neilson (director); Cast: Dorothy McGuire, John Ireland, Una Merkel (Mrs. Winemiller)

Come Back, Little Sheba (by William Inge); La Jolla Playhouse, La Jolla, CA. July 31–August 5, 1951. James Neilson (director); Cast: Una Merkel (Lola), Philip Ober, Marion Marshall.
The Sombrero Playhouse, Phoenix, AZ. February 19–26, 1952. Paul Guilfoyle (director); Cast: Una Merkel (Lola), John O'Connor, and Ann Chatin.

The Remarkable Mr. Pennypacker (by Liam O›Brien) Coronet Theatre, New York. December 30, 1953–July 10, 1954. Alan Schneider (director); Cast: Burgess Meredith, Martha Scott, Thomas Chalmers, Una Merkel (Aunt Jane), Glenn Anders, Phyllis Love, Michael Wager.

The Ponder Heart (by Joseph A. Fields and Jerome Chodorov, based on a novella by Eudora Welty); Music Box Theatre, New York. February 16, 1956–June 23, 1956. The Playwrights' Company: Maxwell Anderson, S. N. Behrman, Elmer Rice, Robert E. Sherwood, Sidney Howard (producers); Robert Douglas (director); Cast: David Wayne, Will Geer, Juanita Hall, Don Hanmer, Sarah Marshall, Una Merkel (Edna Earle Ponder).

Career (by James Lee); La Jolla Playhouse, La Jolla, CA. August 6–18, 1957. Andrew McCullough (director); Cast: Don Taylor, Una Merkel (Shirley Drake), Ray Danton, Maggie Hayes, Bethel Leslie, Ralph Neff, Jules Davis, Paul Comi.

Listen to the Mocking Bird (by Edward Chodorov); Tour of Boston, Cleveland, and Washington, D.C. (December 27, 1958–January 29, 1959). The

Playwrights' Company: Maxwell Anderson, Robert Anderson, Elmer Rice, Robert E. Sherwood, Roger L. Stevens and John F. Wharton (producers); Edward Chodorov (director); Cast: Eva Le Gallienne, Billie Burke, and Una Merkel (Faith Borrow)

Cradle and All (by Sumner Arthur Long); Bucks County Playhouse, New Hope, PA. July 27–Aug 9, 1959. Henry Denker (director); Cast: Loring Smith, Una Merkel (Edith Lambert), Dick Van Dyke, Sally Kemp.

Take Me Along (by Joseph Stein, Robert Russell, text; Bob Merrill, music & lyrics) Shubert Theatre, New York. October 22, 1959–December 17, 1960*. David Merrick (Producer); Peter Glenville (director); Cast: Jackie Gleason, Eileen Herlie, Walter Pidgeon, Una Merkel (Essie Miller, Nat's wife), Robert Morse, Nicole Barth, Alvin Beam, Valerie Harper.
*Una left the production in June 1960 and was replaced by Doris Dalton.

UNA MERKEL ON FILM

Love's Old Sweet Song (1923)
(Short film)
Norca Pictures Productions. Directed by J. Searle Dawley. Screenplay by Augustus Bertilla (story) and Jacques Byrne. Produced by Lee De Forest. Cinematography by Freeman H. Owens. Music by J.L. Molloy.
Cast: Louis Wolheim (The Wanderer), Helen Weir (Eunice), Donald Gallaher (Charlie), Helen Lowell (Mother), Baby Margaret Brown (Babs), Ernest Hilliard (Power), Una Merkel.

For Woman's Favor (1924)
(Film had one sequence filmed in Prizma colors.)
Lund Productions, distributed by Lee-Bradford Productions. Directed by Oscar Lund. Story adapted from "The Falcon" by Giovanni Boccaccio.

Cinematography by Marcel Le Picard and Robert Olsson.

Cast: Seena Owen (June Paige), Elliott Dexter (Howard Fiske), Wilton Lackaye (Bracken), Irma Harrison (The Lamb), Henry Hull (The Fool/The Lover), Paul McAllister (The Wolf), Arthur Donaldson (The Brother), *Una Merkel (undetermined role).

* A *New York Times* article, "The Other Girl in *Coquette*," (December 25, 1927), p. 4, reported that Una had appeared in the color sequence, but her appearance cannot be confirmed.

The Fifth Horseman (1924)
E. M. MacMahon Productions. Directed by E. M. McMahon. Screenplay by E. M. McMahon. Produced by E. M McMahon.
Cast: Cornelius Keefe (John Franklin), Una Merkel (Dorothy), Joseph Depew (Sonny), Charles Brook (Tom Mather), Alice May (Jane Mather), Leslie Stowe (Colonel Woodson), Horace Haine (Red Hogan), William Black (Bill Gorman), Al Stewart (Buck Daniels), Louis Reinhard (Pete Orloff), Philip Van Loan (St. John the Divine), Gregory Blackton (The Fifth Horseman).

Abraham Lincoln (1930)
D. W. Griffith Productions/Feature Productions, Inc., distributed by United Artists. Directed by D. W. Griffith. Screenplay by John W. Considine Jr. (story), Stephen Vincent Benet and Gerrit Lloyd. Produced by D. W. Griffith and Joseph M. Schenck. Cinematography by Karl Struss. Music by Hugo Riesenfeld. Edited by James Smith. Set Decoration by William Cameron Menzies. Sound by Harold Witt. Costume Design by Walter J. Israel.
Cast: William L. Thorne (Tom Lincoln), Lucille La Verne (Mid-Wife), Helen Freeman (Nancy Hanks Lincoln), Otto Hoffman (Offut), Walter Huston (Abraham Lincoln), Edgar Dearing (Armstrong), Una Merkel (Ann Rutledge), Russell Simpson (Lincoln's Employer), Charles Crockett (Sheriff), Kay Hammond (Mary Todd Lincoln), Helen Ware (Mrs. Edwards), E. Alyn Warren (Stephen A. Douglas/General Grant), Jason Robards, Sr. (Herndon),

Gordon Thorpe (Tad Lincoln), Ian Keith (John Wilkes Booth), Hobart Bosworth (General Lee), Henry B. Walthall (Colonel Marshall).

The Eyes of the World (1930)
Inspiration Pictures, Inc., distributed by United Artists. Directed by Henry King. Screenplay by Brewster Morse and Clarke Silvernail, from the novel *The Eyes of the World* by Harold Bell Wright. Produced by Henry King and Sol Lesser. Cinematography by John P. Fulton and Ray June. Edited by Lloyd Nosler. Sound by Ernest Rovere.
Cast: Eulalie Jensen (Mrs. Rutledge), Hugh Huntley (James Rutledge), Myra Hubert (Myra), Florence Roberts (The Maid), Una Merkel (Sybil), Nance O'Neil (Myra), John Holland (Aaron King), Fern Andra (Mrs. Taine), Frederick Burt (Conrad La Grange), Brandon Hurst (Mr. Taine), William Jeffrey (Bryan Oakley).

The Bat Whispers (1930)
Joseph M. Schenck Productions for Art Cinema Corp., distributed by United Artists. Directed by Roland West. Screenplay by Roland West, from the play *The Bat* by Mary Roberts Rinehart and Avery Hopwood. Produced by Joseph M. Schenck. Cinematography by Ray June and Robert H. Planck. Edited by Hal C. Kern and James Smith. Set Decoration by Paul Crawley. Sound by Oscar Lagerstrom.
Cast: Chester Morris (Detective Anderson/The Bat), Una Merkel (Dale Van Gorder), Chance Ward (Police Lieutenant), Richard Tucker (Mr. Bell), Wilson Benge (Butler), DeWitt Jennings (Police Captain), Sidney D'Albrook (Police Sergeant), S. E. Jennings (Man in Black Mask), Grayce Hampton (Cornelia Van Gorder), Maude Eburne (Lizzie Allen), Spencer Charters (Caretaker), William Bakewell (Brook), Gustav von Seyffertitz (Dr. Venrees), Hugh Huntley (Richard Fleming), Charles Dow Clark (Detective Jones), Ben Bard (The Unknown).

The Command Performance (1931)
(Although the article "The" is often omitted from the title in many print and online sources, it should be included as part of the title.)
Also known as *He's a Prince* (Title used in re-issue prints.)
James Cruze Productions, Inc., distributed by Tiffany Productions. Directed by Walter Lang. Screenplay by Maude Fulton and Gordon Rigby, from the play *The Command Performance* by C. Stafford Dickens. Produced by Samuel Zierler. Cinematography by Charles Schoenbaum.
Cast: Neil Hamilton (Prince Alexis and Peter Fedor), Una Merkel (Princess Katerina), Helen Ware (Queen Elinor of Sherblandt), Albert Gran (King Nicholas of Kordovia), Lawrence Grant (Count Vellenburg), Thelma Todd (Lydia), Vera Lewis (Queen Elizabeth of Kordovia), Mischa Auer (Duke Charles of Votrav), Burr McIntosh (Masoch), Wilhelm von Brincken (Capt. Boyer), Murdock MacQuarrie (Blondel).

Don't Bet on Women (1931)
Also known as *All Women are Bad*
Fox Film Corporation. Also known as *Don't Bet on Women*. Directed by William K. Howard. Screenplay by Leon Gordon, Lynn Starling, and William Anthony McGuire (story). Produced by William Fox and John W. Considine Jr. Cinematography by Lucien N. Andriot. Edited by Harold D. Schuster. Art direction by Duncan Cramer. Sound by Albert Protzman. Costume Design by Sophie Wachner.
Cast: Edmund Lowe (Roger Fallon), Jeanette MacDonald (Jeanne Drake), Roland Young (Herbert Drake), J. M. Kerrigan (Chipley Duff), Una Merkel (Tallulah Hope), Helene Millard (Doris Brent).

Six Cylinder Love (1931)
Fox Film Corporation. Directed by Thornton Freeland (Assistant Director, Sam Wurtzel). Screenplay by William Conselman and Norman Houston, from the play *Six-Cylinder Love* by William Anthony McGuire. Produced by William Fox and John W. Considine Jr. Cinematography by Ernest Palmer.

Edited by J. Edwin Robbins. Art Direction by Duncan Cramer. Sound by Albert Protzman. Costume design by Sophie Wachner.

Cast: Spencer Tracy (Donroy), Sidney Fox (Marilyn Sterling), Edward Everett Horton (Monty Winston), Lorin Raker (Gilbert Sterling), William Collier Sr. (Richard Burton), Una Merkel (Margaret Rogers), Bert Roach (Harold Rogers), Ruth Warren (Mrs. Burton), William Holden (Stapleton), El Brendel (Axel).

The Maltese Falcon (1931)

Warner Bros. Pictures, Inc. Directed by Roy Del Ruth (Assistant Directors Eddie Sowders and William Cannon). Screenplay by Maude Fulton, Brown Holmes, Lucien Hubbard, from the novel *The Maltese Falcon* by Dashiell Hammett. Cinematography by William Rees. Music by Leo F. Forbstein. Edited by George Marks. Art direction by Robert Haas. Sound by George Groves and Elmer Hagland. Costume design by Earl Luick.

Cast: Bebe Daniels (Ruth Wonderly), Ricardo Cortez (Sam Spade), Dudley Digges (Caspar Gutman), Una Merkel (Effie), Robert Elliott (Dundy), Thelma Todd (Iva Archer), Otto Matieson (Joel "Joe" Cairo), Walter Long (Miles Archer), Dwight Frye (Wilmer Cook), J. Farrell MacDonald (Tom Polhause).

Daddy Long Legs (1931)

Fox Film Corporation. Directed by Alfred Santell (Assistant Director, Marty Santell). Screenplay by Sonya Levien and S.N. Behrman, from the play *Daddy Long-Legs* by Jean Webster. Produced by Sol M. Wurtzel. Cinematography by Lucien Andriot. Edited by Ralph Dietrich. Art direction by William Darling. Music by Hugo Friedhofer. Sound by Joseph E. Aiken and W.D. Flick.

Cast: Janet Gaynor (Judy Abbott), Warner Baxter (Jervis Pendleton), Una Merkel (Sally McBride), John Arledge (Jimmy McBride), Claude Gillingwater (Riggs), Effie Ellsler (Mrs. Semple), Kendall McComas (Freddie Perkins), Kathlyn Williams (Mrs. Pendleton), Elizabeth Patterson (Mrs. Lippett), Louise Closser Hale (Miss Pritchard), Sheila Mannors

(Gloria Pendleton), Edwin Maxwell (Wykoff), Martha Lee Sparks (Katie).

The Bargain (1931)
First Nationals Pictures, distributed by Warner Bros. Directed by Robert Milton. Screenplay by Robert Presnell, from the play *You and I* by Philip Barry. Cinematography by Sol Polito. Edited by Jack Rawlins. Art direction by John Hughes. Music by David Mendoza.
Cast: Lewis Stone (Maitland White), Evalyn Knapp (Veronica Daune), Charles Butterworth (Geoffrey Nichols), Doris Kenyon (Nancy White), John Darrow (Roderick White), Oscar Apfel (G.T. Warren), Una Merkel (Etta), Nella Walker (The Patroness).

Wicked (1931)
Fox Film Corporation. Directed by Allan Dwan (Assistant Director, Jack Boland). Screenplay by Gordon Rigby, Con Conrad, Adela Rogers St. John, Kenyon Nicholson, and Kathryn Scola. Produced by John W. Considine Jr. Cinematography by Peverell Marley. Music by Carli Elinor and R. H. Bassett. Edited by Jack Dennis. Art direction by Robert Haas. Sound by George Leverett.
Cast: Elissa Landi (Margot Rande), Victor McLaglen (Scott Burrows), Una Merkel (June), Irene Rich (Mrs. Luther), Alan Dinehart (Blake), Theodore von Eltz (Tony Rande), Oscar Apfel (Judge Edwin Luther), Mae Busch (Arlene), Ruth Donnelly (Fanny), Eileen Percy (Stella), Joseph W. Reilly, Blanche Payson (Matron), Kathleen Kerrigan (Miss Peck), Blanche Friderici (Mrs. Johnson), Lucille Williams (Prisoner), Alice Lake (Prisoner), William Pawley (Policeman), G. Pat Collins (Policeman), Jack Grey (Policeman), Clarence Wilson (Juryman).

The Secret Witness (1931)
Also known as *Terror by Night*, *Penthouse Murder*
Famous Attractions, distributed by Columbia Pictures Corporation. Directed by Thornton Freeland. Screenplay by Samuel Spewack, from the novel

Murder in the Gilded Cage by Samuel Spewack. Produced by J.G. Bachmann. Cinematography by Robert Planck. Edited by Louis Sackin. Sound by Corson Jowett.

Cast: Una Merkel (Lois Martin), William Collier Jr. (Arthur "Casey" Jones), ZaSu Pitts (Bella), Purnell Pratt (Police Captain McGowan), Ralf Harolde (Lewis Leroy), Clyde Cook (Larson), June Clyde (Tess), Nat Pendleton (Gunner), Clarence Muse (Jeff).

Private Lives (1931)

Metro-Goldwyn-Mayer Corporation. Directed by Sidney Franklin (Assistant Director, Harry Bucquet). Screenplay by Hans Kraly, Richard Schayer, and Claudine West, from the play *Private* Lives by Noel Coward. Produced by Irving Thalberg. Cinematography by Ray Binger. Edited by Conrad A. Nervig. Art direction by Cedric Gibbons. Recording director, Douglas Shearer. Sound mixer, Fred R. Morgan. Music by William Axt. Costume design by Adrian.

Cast: Norma Shearer (Amanda Prynne), Robert Montgomery (Elyot Chase), Reginald Denny (Victor Prynne), Una Merkel (Sibyl Chase), Jean Hersholt (Oscar), George Davis (Bell hop).

She Wanted a Millonaire (1932)

Fox Film Corporation. Directed by John Blystone (Assistant Director, Jasper Blystone). Screenplay by William Anthony McGuire, William Collier, Sr. (dialogue), Sonya Levien, Frank Dolan, Winfield R. Sheehan, Sally Frank, Dudley Nichols, Hugh Strange, and Imogene Stanley. Produced by John W. Considine, Jr. and William Fox. Cinematography by John Seitz. Edited by Louis Loeffler and Ralph Dixon. Art direction by Gordon Wiles. Sound by E. Clayton Ward and Albert Protzman. Costume design by Dolly Tree.

Cast: Joan Bennett (Jane Miller), Spencer Tracy (William Kelley), Una Merkel (Mary Taylor), James Kirkwood (Roger Norton), Dorothy Peterson (Mrs. Miller), Douglas Cosgrove (Mr. Miller), Donald Dillaway (Humphrey), Tetsu Komai (Charlie), Constantine Romanoff (Monk).

The Impatient Maiden (1932)
Universal Pictures. Directed by James Whale. Screenplay by Richard Schayer and Winifred Dunn, from the novel *The Impatient Maiden* by Donald Henderson Clarke. Produced by Carl Laemmle, Carl Laemmle Jr., and E.M. Asher. Cinematography by Arthur Edeson. Edited by Clarence Kolster and Maurice Pivar. Art direction by Charles D. Hall. Sound by C. Roy Hunter and William Hedgcock.
Cast: Lew Ayres (Myron Brown), Mae Clarke (Ruth Robbins), Una Merkel (Betty Merrick), Andy Devine (Clarence Howe), John Halliday (Albert Hartman), Oscar Apfel (Dr. Wilco), Ethel Griffies (Nurse Lovett), Helen Jerome Eddy (Mrs. Gillman), Bert Roach (Mr. Gillman), Cecil Cunningham (Mrs. Rosy), Lorin Raker (Mr. Rosy), Blanche Payson (Mrs. Thomas), Arthur Hoyt (Mr. Thomas).

Man Wanted (1932)
Warner Bros. Pictures, Inc. Directed by William Dieterle. Screenplay by Robert Lord and Charles Kenyon. Produced by Hal B. Wallis. Cinematography by Gregg Toland. Music by Bernhard Kaun and Leo F. Forbstein. Edited by James Gibbon. Sound by Oliver Garretson. Costume design by Earl Luick.
Cast: Kay Francis (Lois Ames), David Manners (Tom Sheridan), Una Merkel (Ruth Holman), Andy Devine (Andy Doyle), Kenneth Thomson (Fred), Claire Dodd (Ann Le Maire), Elizabeth Patterson (Miss Harper), Edward Van Sloan (Manager), Robert Greig (Harper), Junior Coghlan (youngster in store).

Huddle (1932)
Metro-Goldwyn-Mayer Corporation. Directed by Sam Wood (Assistant Director, John Waters). Screenplay by Walton Hall Smith, C. Gardner Sullivan, Robert Lee Johnson, and Arthur S. Hyman, from the novel *Huddle!* by Francis Wallace. Produced by Sam Wood. Cinematography by Harold Wenstrom. Edited by Hugh Wynn. Art direction by Cedric Gibbons. Recording director, Douglas Shearer. Sound by Charles Wallace. Costume

design by Adrian.

Cast: Ramon Novarro (Tony Amatto), Madge Evans (Rosalie Stone), Una Merkel (Thelma), Ralph Graves (Coach Malcolm Gale), John Arledge (Jim "Pidge" Pidgeon), Frank Albertson (Larry Wilson), Kane Richmond (Tom Stone), Martha Sleeper (Barbara Winston), Henry Armetta (Mr. Amatto), Ferike Boros (Mrs. Amatto), Rockliffe Fellowes (Mr. Stone), Joe Sawyer (Slater).

Red-Headed Woman (1932)
Metro-Goldwyn-Mayer Corporation. Directed by Jack Conway (Assistant Director, Charles Dorian). Screenplay by Anita Loos, from the novel *Red-Headed Woman* by Katharine Brush. Produced by Albert Lewin. Cinematography by Harold Rosson. Music by Raymond B. Egan and Richard A. Whiting. Edited by Blanche Sewell. Art direction by Cedric Gibbons. Recording director, Douglas Shearer. Sound by James Brock. Costume design by Adrian.

Cast: Jean Harlow (Lil "Red" Andrews Legendre), Chester Morris (Bill Legendre, Jr.) Lewis Stone (William Legendre, Sr.), Leila Hyams (Irene Legendre), Una Merkel (Sally), Henry Stephenson (Charles B. Gaerste), May Robson (Aunt Jane), Charles Boyer (Albert), Harvey Clark (Uncle Fred).

They Call It Sin (1932)
First National Pictures, Inc., distributed by Warner Bros. Pictures, Inc. Directed by Thornton Freeland. Screenplay by Lillie Hayward and Howard J. Green, from the novel *They Call it Sin* by Alberta Stedman Eagan. Produced by Hal B. Wallis. Cinematography by James Van Trees. Music by Leo F. Forbstein. Edited by James Gibbon. Art Direction by Jack Okey. Costume design by Orry-Kelly.

Cast: Loretta Young (Marion Cullen), George Brent (Dr. Tony Travers), Una Merkel (Dixie Dare), David Manners (Jimmy Decker), Helen Vinson (Enid Hollister), Louis Calhern (Ford Humphries), Joseph Cawthorn (Mr.

Hollister), Nella Walker (Mrs. Hollister), Elizabeth Patterson (Mrs. Cullen), Erville Alderson (Mr. Timothy Cullen).

Men Are Such Fools (1932)
Jefferson Pictures Corporation, distributed by RKO Radio Pictures. Directed by William Nigh (Assistant Directors Bernard McEveety and Samuel Schnitzer). Screenplay by Thomas Lloyd Lennon, Viola Brothers Shore, and Ethel Doherty. Produced by Joseph I. Schnitzer and Samuel Zierler. Cinematography by Charles Schoenbaum. Music by Mischa Bakaleinikoff. Edited by Viola Lawrence. Art direction by Edward C. Jewell. Sound by Lambert Day and Lodge Cunningham.
Cast: Leo Carrillo (Antonio "Tony" Mello), Vivienne Osborne (Lilli Arno), Una Merkel (Molly), Tom Moore (Tom Hyland), Joseph Cawthorn (Werner), Earle Fox (Joe Darrow), J. Farrell MacDonald (Randolph), Paul Hurst (Stiles), Albert Conti (Spinelli), Paul Porcasi (Klepak), Eddie Nugent (Eddie Martin), Lester Lee (Giuseppe).

Whistling in the Dark (1933)
Metro-Goldwyn-Mayer Corporation. Directed by Elliott Nugent (Co-Director, Charles Reisner; Assistant Director, Errol Taggart). Screenplay by Elliott Nugent, from the play *Whistling in the Dark* by Laurence Gross and Edward Childs Carpenter, as presented by Alexander McKaig. Cinematography by Norbert Brodine. Edited by Ben Lewis. Art direction by Cedric Gibbons. Music by William Axt. Recording director, Douglas Shearer. Sound mixer, James Brock.
Cast: Ernest Truex (Wallace Porter), Una Merkel (Toby Van Buren), Edward Arnold (Jake Dillon), John Miljan (Charlie Shaw), C. Henry Gordon (Ricco Lombardo), Johnny Hines (Slim Scanlon), Joseph Cawthorn (Otto Barfuss), Nat Pendleton (Joe Salvatore), Tenen Holtz (Herman Lefkowitz), Marcelle Corday (Hilda).

The Secret of Madame Blanche (1933)
Metro-Goldwyn-Mayer Corporation. Directed by Charles Brabin (Assistant Director, Robert Golden). Screenplay by Frances Goodrich and Albert Hackett, from the play *The Lady* by Martin Brown. Cinematography by Merritt B. Gerstad. Music by Dr. William Axt. Edited by Blanche Sewell. Art direction by Cedric Gibbons. Recording director, Douglas Shearer. Sound mixer, Paul Neal. Costume design by Adrian.
Cast: Irene Dunne (Sally Sanders St. John, later known as Madame Blanche), Lionel Atwill (Aubrey St. John), Phillips Holmes (Leonard St. John), Una Merkel (Ella), Douglas Walton (Leonard St. John, Junior), C. Henry Gordon (State's attorney), Jean Parker (Eloise Duval), Mitchell Lewis (Duval).

Clear All Wires! (1933)
Metro-Goldwyn-Mayer Corporation. Directed by George Hill (Assistant Director, Joseph M. Newman). Screenplay by Bella Spewack, Samuel Spewack, and Delmer Daves, from the play *Clear All Wires!* by Bella and Samuel Spewack. Produced by George W. Hill. Cinematography by Norbert Brodine. Edited by Hugh Wynn. Art direction by Cedric Gibbons. Music by William Axt. Recording director, Douglas Shearer. Sound mixers, Fred R. Morgan and Robert Shirley.
Cast: Lee Tracy (Buckley Joyce Thomas), Benita Hume (Kate Nelson), Una Merkel (Dolly Winslow), James Gleason (Lefty Williams), Alan Edwards (Pettingwaite), Eugene Sigaloff (Prince Alexander Tomofsky), Ari Kutai (Kostya), C. Henry Gordon (Commissar), Lya Lys (Eugenie Smirnova), John Bleifer (Sozanoff), Lawrence Grant (MacKenzie), Guy Usher (J. H. Stevens), Mischa Auer (Arab leader).

42nd Street (1933)
Warner Bros. Pictures, Inc. Directed by Lloyd Bacon (Assistant Director, Gordon Hollingshead). Screenplay by Rian James and James Seymour, from the novel *42nd Street* by Bradford Ropes. Produced by Darryl Zanuck and Hal B. Wallis. Cinematography by Sol Polito. Music by Leo F. Forbstein

(conductor), Al Dubin and Harry Warren (words and music). Edited by Frank Ware and Thomas Pratt. Art direction by Jack Okey. Sound by Nathan Levinson and Dolph Thomas. Costume design by Orry-Kelly.
Cast: Warner Baxter (Julian Marsh), Bebe Daniels (Dorothy Brock), George Brent (Pat Denning), Ruby Keeler (Peggy Sawyer), Guy Kibbee (Abner Dillon), Una Merkel (Loraine Lolly Fleming), Ginger Rogers (Ann "Anytime Annie" Lowell), Ned Sparks (Thomas Barry), Dick Powell (Billy Lawler), Allen Jenkins (MacElroy), Edward J. Nugent (Terry Neil), Robert McWade (Jones), George E. Stone (Andy Lee), Clarence Nordstrom (Leading man), Henry B. Walthall (The Actor), Toby Wing (Showgirl in "Young and Healthy" number), Louise Beavers (Pansy, maid).

Reunion in Vienna (1933)
Metro-Goldwyn-Mayer Corporation. Directed by Sidney Franklin (Assistant Director, Hugh Boswell). Screenplay by Ernest Vajda and Claudine West, from the play *Reunion in Vienna* by Robert E. Sherwood. Cinematography by George Folsey. Music by Dr. William Axt. Edited by Blanche Sewell. Art direction by Cedric Gibbons. Recording director, Douglas Shearer. Sound mixer, Paul Neal. Costume design by Adrian.
Cast: John Barrymore (Archduke Rudolf Maximilian von Hapsburg), Diana Wynyard (Elena Krug), Frank Morgan (Dr. Anton Krug), Henry Travers (Father Krug), May Robson (Frau Lucher), Eduardo Ciannelli (Poffy), Una Merkel (Ilse Hinrich), Bodil Rosing (Kathie), Bela Loblov (Musician), Morris Nussbaum (Musician), Nella Walker (Countess Von Stainz), Herbert Evans (Count Von Stainz).

Midnight Mary (1933)
Metro-Goldwyn-Mayer Corporation. Directed by William Wellman (Assistant Director, Dolph Zimmer). Screenplay by Gene Markey, Kathryn Scola, and Anita Loos. Produced by Lucien Hubbard. Cinematography by James Van Trees. Music by William Axt. Edited by William S. Gray. Art direction by Stan Rogers. Recording director, Douglas Shearer. Sound mixer,

James Brock. Costume design by Adrian.

Cast: Loretta Young (Mary Martin), Ricardo Cortez (Leo Darcy), Franchot Tone (Tom Mannering, Jr.), Andy Devine (Sam Travers), Una Merkel (Bunny), Frank Conroy (District Attorney), Warren Hymer (Angelo), Ivan Simpson (Tindle), Harold Huber (Puggy), Sandy Roth (Blimp), Martha Sleeper (Barbara Mannering), Charley Grapewin (Clerk), Halliwell Hobbes (Churchill), Robert Emmett O'Connor (Cop), Reginald Barlow (Judge at Mary's murder trial), Louise Beavers (Anna, Mary's maid).

Her First Mate (1933)

Universal Pictures Corporation. Directed by William Wyler. Screenplay by Earle Snell, Clarence Marks, and H. M. Walker, from the play *Salt Water* by Frank Craven, John Golden, and Daniel Jarrett. Produced by Carl Laemmle and Carl Laemmle Jr. Cinematography by George Robinson. Edited by Ted Kent. Art direction by Stanley Fleischer.

Cast: Slim Summerville (John Horner), ZaSu Pitts (Mary Horner), Una Merkel (Hattie Horner), Warren Hymer (Percival Todd), Berton Churchill (Harvey Davis), George Marion (Sam Bowen), Henry Armetta (Nick Socrates), Jocelyn Lee (The red-head).

Broadway to Hollywood (1933)

Metro-Goldwyn-Mayer Corporation. Directed by Willard Mack (Assistant Director John Waters). Screenplay by Willard Mack, Edgar Allan Woolf, Robert E. Hopkins (dialogue). Produced by Harry Rapf. Cinematography by William Daniels and Norbert Brodine. Music by William Axt. Edited by William S. Gray and Ben Lewis. Art direction by Stan(wood) Rogers. Recording director, Douglas Shearer.

Cast: Alice Brady (Lulu Hackett), Frank Morgan (Ted Hackett), Jackie Cooper (Ted Hackett, Jr., as a child), Russell Hardie (Ted Hackett, Jr.), Madge Evans (Anne Ainsley), Mickey Rooney (Ted Hackett III, as a child), Eddie Quillan (Ted Hackett III), Jimmy Durante (Jimmy), Fay Templeton, May Robson (Actress), The Albertina Rasch Dancers, Una Merkel (audience member, uncredited).

Beauty for Sale (1933)

Metro-Goldwyn-Mayer Corporation. Directed by Richard Boleslawski [also spelled Boleslavsky], (Assistant Director, Al Shenberg). Screenplay by Zelda Sears and Eve Greene, from the novel *Beauty* by Faith Baldwin. Produced by Lucien Hubbard. Cinematography by James Howe. Edited by Blanche Sewell. Art direction by Alexander Toluboff. Recording director, Douglas Shearer. Sound mixer, Anstruther MacDonald. Costume design by Adrian.

Cast: Madge Evans (Letty Lawson), Alice Brady (Mrs. Henrietta Sherwood), Otto Kruger (Sherwood), Una Merkel (Carol Merrick), May Robson (Mrs. Merrick), Phillips Holmes (Burt Barton), Eddie Nugent (Bill Merrick), Hedda Hopper (Madame Sonia Barton), Florine McKinney (Jane), Isabel Jewell (Hortense), Louise Carter (Mrs. Lawson), John Roche (Robert Abbott), Charley Grapewin (Freddy Gordon).

Menu (1933)

Metro-Goldwyn-Mayer Corporation. Directed by Nick Grinde. Screenplay by Thorne Smith. Produced by Pete Smith. Music by William Axt.

Cast: Pete Smith (Narrator), Luis Alberni (The Master Chef), Una Merkel (Mrs. Omsk), Franklin Pangborn (John Xavier Omsk).

Bombshell (1933)

Metro-Goldwyn-Mayer Corporation. Directed by Victor Fleming (Assistant Director, Robert Lee). Screenplay by John Lee Mahin and Jules Furthman, from the play *Bombshell* by Caroline Francke and Mack Crane. Produced by Hunt Stromberg. Cinematography by Harold Rosson and Chester Lyons. Edited by Margaret Booth. Art direction by Merrill Pye. Recording director, Douglas Shearer. Sound mixer, William Steinkamp. Costume design by Adrian.

Cast: Jean Harlow (Lola Burns), Lee Tracy ([E. J.] Space Hanlon), Frank Morgan (Pops Burns), Franchot Tone (Gifford Middleton), Pat O'Brien (Jim Brogan), Una Merkel (Mac), Ted Healy (Junior Burns), Ivan Lebedeff (Marquis Hugo di Binelli di Pisa), Isabel Jewell (A girl friend), Louise

Beavers (Loretta), Leonard Carey (Winters), Mary Forbes (Mrs. Middleton), C. Aubrey Smith (Mrs. Middleton). June Brewster (Alice Cole).

Day of Reckoning (1933)
Metro-Goldwyn-Mayer Corporation. Directed by Charles Brabin. Screenplay by Zelda Sears, Eve Greene, from the novel by Morris Lavine. Produced by Lucien Hubbard. Cinematography by Ted Tetzlaff. Edited by Adrienne Fazan. Art direction by Eddie Imazu. Music by William Axt. Recording director, Douglas Shearer.
Cast: Richard Dix (John Day), Madge Evans (Dorothy Day), Conway Tearle (George Hollins), Una Merkel (Mamie), Stuart Erwin (Jerry), George "Spanky" McFarland (Johnny Day), Isabel Jewell (Kate Lovett), James Bell (Slim), Raymond Hatton (Hart), Paul Hurst (Harry), John Larkin (Abraham), Wilfred Lucas (Guard), Samuel S. Hinds (O'Farrell).

The Women in His Life (1933)
Metro-Goldwyn-Mayer Corporation. Directed by George B. Seitz (Assistant Director Robert Golden). Screenplay by F. Hugh Herbert. Produced by Lucien Hubbard. Cinematography by Ray June. Edited by Conrad A. Nervig. Art direction by Eddie Imazu. Music by William Axt. Recording director, Douglas Shearer. Costume design by Adrian.
Cast: Otto Kruger (Kent "Barry" Barringer), Una Merkel (Simmons), Ben Lyon (Roger McKane), Isabel Jewell (Catherine Watson), Roscoe Karns (Lester), Irene Hervey (Doris Worthing), C. Henry Gordon (Tony Perez), Samuel S. Hinds (Thomas J. Worthing), Irene Franklin (Mrs. Florence Steele), Muriel Evans (Molly), Raymond Hatton (Curly), Jean Howard (Information girl), Paul Hurst (Paul).

This Side of Heaven (1934)
Metro-Goldwyn-Mayer Corp. Directed by William K. Howard (Assistant Director, Horace Hough). Screenplay by Edgar Allan Woolf, Florence Ryerson, Zelda Sears and Eve Greene, from the novel *It Happened One Day*

by Marjorie Bartholomew Paradis. Produced by John W. Considine Jr. and William K. Howard. Cinematography by Hal Rosson. Music by William Axt. Edited by Frank Hull. Art direction by Fredric Hope. Recording director, Douglas Shearer.

Cast: Lionel Barrymore (Martin Turner), Fay Bainter (Francene Turner), Mae Clarke (Jane Turner), Tom Brown (Seth Turner), Una Merkel (Birdie), Mary Carlisle (Peggy Turner), Onslow Stevens (Walter Hamilton), Henry Wadsworth (Hal Jennings), Eddie Nugent (Vance Patterson), C. Henry Gordon (William Barnes), Dickie Moore (Freddie).

Screen Snapshots, "Series 13, no. 5" (1934)
(This is a short from a series that shows film stars and celebrities at work and play.) Columbia Pictures Corp. Directed by Ralph Staub. Produced by Harriet Parsons.

Cast: Larry Fine, Ted Healy, Jack Holt, Curly Howard, Moe Howard, Chico Marx, Una Merkel (herself), Harriet Parsons (Narrator).

Murder in the Private Car (1934)
Metro-Goldwyn-Mayer Corp. Directed by Harry Beaumont (Assistant Directors, Harry Sharrock and Earl Taggert). Screenplay by Ralph Spence, Edgar Allan Woolf, Al Boasberg, and Harvey Thew, from the play *The Rear Car* by Edward E. Rose. Produced by Lucien Hubbard. Cinematography by James Van Trees and Leonard Smith. Edited by William S. Gray. Art direction by Cedric Gibbons. Music by William Axt. Recording director, Douglas Shearer. Sound mixer, Charles Wallace.

Cast: Charlie Ruggles (Godfrey D. Scott), Una Merkel (Georgia Latham), Mary Carlisle (Ruth Raymond, later known as Ruth Carson), Russell Hardie (John Blake), Porter Hall (Alden Murray), Willard Robertson (Hanks alias of Elwood Carson), Berton Churchill (Luke Carson), Cliff Thompson (Allen), Fred "Snowflake" Toones (Titus).

Paris Interlude (1934)

Metro-Goldwyn-Mayer Corp. Directed by Edwin L. Marin (Assistant Director, Lesley Selander). Screenplay by Wells Root, from the play *All Good Americans* by S.J. and Laura Perelman. Produced by Lucien Hubbard. Cinematography by Milton Krasner. Music by William Axt and Paul Marquardt. Edited by Conrad A. Nervig. Art direction by Cedric Gibbons. Recording director, Douglas Shearer. Costume design by Adrian.

Cast: Madge Evans (Julie Bell), Otto Kruger (Sam Colt), Robert Young (Pat Wells), Una Merkel (Cassie), Ted Healy (Jimmy), Louise Henry (Mary Louise Porter), Edward Brophy (Ham), George Meeker (Rex Fleming), Bert Roach (Noble), Richard Tucker (Stevens).

The Cat's-Paw (1934)

Harold Lloyd Corporation, distributed by Fox Film Corp. Directed by Sam Taylor and Harold Lloyd (Assistant Directors, Walter Mayo and Edmond F. Bernoudy). Screenplay by Sam Taylor and Clyde Bruckman, from the novel *The Cat's-Paw* by Clarence Budington Kelland. Produced by Harold Lloyd. Cinematography by Walter Lundin. Music by Alfred Newman. Edited by Bernard Burton. Art direction by Harry Oliver. Sound mixer, William Fox. Costume design by Peg O'Neil and Miss Anderson.

Cast: Harold Lloyd (Ezekiel Cobb), Una Merkel (Petunia "Pet" Pratt), George Barbier (Jake Mayo), Nat Pendleton (Strozzi), Grace Bradley (Dolores Dace), Alan Dinehart (Mayor Ed Morgan), Grant Mitchell ("Silk Hat" McGee), E. Alyn Warren ["Fred"] Warren (Tien Wang), Warren Hymer ("Spike" Slattery), J. Farrell MacDonald (Pat Shigley), James Donlan (Red the reporter), Edwin Maxwell (District Attorney Neal), Frank Sheridan (Police Commissioner Dan Moriarty), Fuzzy Knight (stuttering gangster), Vincent [Vince] Barnett (Wilks).

Bulldog Drummond Strikes Back (1934)

20th Century Pictures, Inc., distributed by United Artists. Directed by Roy Del Ruth (Assistant Director William J. Scully). Screenplay by Nunnally

Johnson and Henry Lehrman, from the novel *Bulldog Drummond Strikes Back* by H.C. "Sapper" McNeile. Produced by Darryl F. Zanuck, William Goetz, and Raymond Griffith. Cinematography by J. Peverell Marley. Music by Alfred Newman. Edited by Allen McNeil. Art direction by Richard Day. Costume Design by Gwen Wakeling.

Cast: Ronald Colman (Captain Hugh "Bulldog" Drummond), Loretta Young (Lola Field), Charles Butterworth (Algy), Warner Oland (Prince Achmed), Una Merkel (Gwen), C. Aubrey Smith (Inspector Neilsen), Arthur Hohl (Dr. Owen Sothern), George Regas (Singh), Ethel Griffies (Mrs. Field), Mischa Auer (Hassan), Douglas Gerrard (Parker), Halliwell Hobbes (Bobby), Vernon Steele (Man at wedding).

Have a Heart (1934)
Metro-Goldwyn-Mayer Corp. Directed by David Butler (Assistant Director, Ad Schaumer). Screenplay by Buddy G. DeSylva, David Butler, Florence Ryerson, and Edgar Allan Woolf. Produced by John W. Considine Jr. Cinematography by James Wong Howe. Edited by Ben Lewis. Art direction by Cedric Gibbons. Music by R. H. Bassett and Jack Virgil. Recording director, Douglas Shearer. Costume design by Adrian.

Cast: Jean Parker (Sally Moore), James Dunn (Jimmie Flaherty), Una Merkel (Joan), Stuart Erwin (Gus), Willard Robertson (Mr. Schauber), Samuel S. Hinds (Dr. Spear), Paul Page (Joe Lacy), Muriel Evans (Helen), Kate Price (Mrs. Kelly), Pepi Sinoff (Mrs. Abrahams).

The Merry Widow (1934)
Metro-Goldwyn-Mayer Corp. Directed by Ernst Lubitsch (Assistant Directors, Joseph Newman and Joe Lefert). Screenplay by Ernest Vajda, Samson Raphaelson, Ernst Lubitsch, and Lorenz Hart, from the operetta *Die lustige Witwe* by Leo Stein, Victor Leon, and Franz Lehar. Produced by Irving G. Thalberg and Ernst Lubitsch. Cinematography by Oliver T. Marsh. Music by Franz Lehar; lyrics by Lorenz Hart, Richard Rodgers, and Gus Kahn. Edited by Frances Marsh. Art direction by Cedric Gibbons.

Recording director, Douglas Shearer. Sound mixers, James K. Brock and Mike McLaughlin. Costume design by Ali Hubert and Adrian.
Cast: Maurice Chevalier (Count Danilo), Jeanette MacDonald (Sonia also known as Fifi), Edward Everett Horton (Ambassador Popoff), Una Merkel (Queen Dolores), George Barbier (King Achmed II), Minna Gombell (Marcelle), Ruth Channing (Lulu), Sterling Holloway (Orderly Mishka), Donald Meek (Valet), Herman Bing (Zizipoff).

Evelyn Prentice (1934)
Metro-Goldwyn-Mayer Corp. Directed by William K. Howard (Assistant Director, Horace Hough). Screenplay by Lenore Coffee and Howard Emmett Rogers, from the novel *Evelyn Prentice* by W. E. Woodward. Produced by John W. Considine Jr. Cinematography by Charles G. Clarke. Music by Oscar Radin, William Axt, and Herbert Stothart. Edited by Frank Hull. Art direction by Cedric Gibbons, Edwin B. Willis, and A. Arnold Gillespie. Recording director, Douglas Shearer. Costume design by Dolly Tree.
Cast: William Powell (John Prentice), Myrna Loy (Evelyn Prentice), Una Merkel (Amy Drexel), Rosalind Russell (Mrs. Nancy Harrison), Isabel Jewell (Judith Wilson), Harvey Stephens (Lawrence Kennard), Edward Brophy (Eddie Delaney), Henry Wadsworth (Chester White), Cora Sue Collins (Dorothy Prentice), Frank Conroy (District Attorney Farley), Jessie Ralph (Mrs. Blake).

Biography of a Bachelor Girl (1935)
Metro-Goldwyn-Mayer Corp. Directed by Edward H. Griffith. Screenplay by Anita Loos and Horace Jackson, from the play *Biography* by S. N. Behrman. Produced by Edward H. Griffith and Irving G. Thalberg. Cinematography by James Wong Howe. Music by Herbert Stothart. Edited by William S. Gray. Art direction by Cedric Gibbons. Recording director, Douglas Shearer. Costume design by Adrian.
Cast: Ann Harding (Marion Forsythe), Robert Montgomery (Richard Kurt), Edward Everett Horton (Leander Nolan), Edward Arnold (Feydak),

Una Merkel (Slade), Charles Richman (Kinnicott), Greta Meyer (Minnie), Willard Robertson (Grigsby, process server), Donald Meek (Mr. Irish).

The Night Is Young (1935)
Metro-Goldwyn-Mayer Corp. Directed by Dudley Murphy. Screenplay by Edgar Allan Woolf, Franz Schulz; libretto by Oscar Hammerstein II, from the story by Vicki Baum. Produced by Harry Rapf. Cinematography by James Wong Howe. Music by Sigmund Romberg, Oscar Hammerstein II (librettist), Herbert Stothart (orchestra director), Oscar Radin (conductor). Edited by Conrad A. Nervig. Art direction by Cedric Gibbons. Recording director, Douglas Shearer. Costume design by Dolly Tree.
Cast: Ramon Novarro (Paul Gustave), Evelyn Laye (Lisl Gluck), Charles Butterworth (Willy Fitch), Una Merkel (Fanni), Edward Everett Horton (Szereny), Donald Cook (Toni), Henry Stephenson (Emperor Franz Josef), Rosalind Russell (Countess Zarika Rafay), Herman Bing (Nepomuk), Mitzi (the horse).

One New York Night (1935)
Metro-Goldwyn-Mayer Corp. Directed by Jack Conway. Screenplay by Frank Davis, from the play *Order Please* by Edward Childs Carpenter and Walter C. Hackett. Produced by Bernard H. Hyman. Cinematography by Oliver T. Marsh. Edited by Tom Held. Art direction by Cedric Gibbons. Recording director, Douglas Shearer. Costume design by Dolly Tree.
Cast: Franchot Tone (Foxhall Ridgeway), Una Merkel (Phoebe), Conrad Nagel (Kent), Harvey Stephens (Collis), Steffi Duna (Countess Louise Broussiloff), Charles Starrett (George Sheridan) Louise Henry (Ermine), Tom Dugan (Selby), Harold Huber (Blake), Henry Kolker (Arthur Carlisle).

Baby Face Harrington (1935)
Metro-Goldwyn-Mayer Corp. Directed by Raoul Walsh (Assistant Director, Horace Hough). Screenplay by Nunnally Johnson, Edwin H. Knopf, Charles Lederer, and Barry Trivers, from the play *Something to Brag About* by Edgar

Selwyn and William LeBaron. Produced by Edgar Selwyn. Cinematography by Oliver T. Marsh. Edited by William S. Gray. Art direction by Cedric Gibbons. Recording director, Douglas Shearer.

Cast: Charles Butterworth (Willie), Una Merkel (Millicent), Harvey Stephens (Ronald Lawford), Eugene Pallette (Uncle Henry), Nat Pendleton (Rocky Bannister), Ruth Selwyn (Dorothy), Donald Meek (Skinner), Dorothy Libaire (Edith), Edward Nugent (Albert), Robert Livingston (George), Stanley Fields (Mullens), Raymond Brown (McGuire), Wade Boteler (Glynn), Bradley Page (Dave), Richard Carle (Judge Forbes), G. Pat Collins (Hank), Claude Gillingwater (Colton).

Murder in the Fleet (1935)

Metro-Goldwyn-Mayer Corp. Directed by Edward Sedgwick (Assistant Director, Al Shenberg). Screenplay by Frank Wead, Joe Sherman, and James Gleason, from a story by Edward Sedgwick. Produced by Lucien Hubbard. Cinematography by Milton Krasner. Edited by Conrad A. Nervig. Art direction by Cedric Gibbons. Music by Paul Marquardt. Recording director, Douglas Shearer.

Cast: Robert Taylor (Lieutenant Tom Randolph), Jean Parker (Betty Lansing), Ted Healy (Mac O'Neill), Una Merkel (Toots Timmons), Nat Pendleton (Spud Burke), Jean Hersholt (Victor Hanson), Arthur Byron (Capt. Winslow), Frank Shields (Lieutenant Arnold), Donald Cook (Lieutenant Commander David Tucker).

Broadway Melody of 1936 (1935)

Metro-Goldwyn-Mayer Corp. Directed by Roy Del Ruth (Assistant Director, William Scully). Screenplay by Jack McGowan, Sid Silvers, Edwin Burke, Joseph L. Mankiewicz; Harry Conn (additional dialogue), from a story by Moss Hart. Produced by John W. Considine, Jr. Cinematography by Charles Rosher. Music by Alfred Newman (musical director), Nacio Herb Brown and Arthur Freed (music and lyrics), Roger Edens (arranger), Edward B. Powell (orchestrator). Dance numbers by Dave Gould. Edited by Blanche Sewell. Art direction by Cedric Gibbons. Recording director, Douglas Shearer. Costume design by Adrian.

Cast: Jack Benny (Bert Keeler), Eleanor Powell (Irene Foster, also known as Mlle. La Belle Arlette), Robert Taylor (Bob Gordon), Una Merkel (Kitty Corbett), Sid Silvers (Snoop), Buddy Ebsen (Ted Burke), June Knight (Lillian Brent), Vilma Ebsen (Sally Burke), Nick Long, Jr. (Basil), Robert Wildhack (The snorer), Paul Harvey (Managing editor), Frances Langford (Herself), Harry Stockwell (Himself).

It's in the Air (1935)
Metro-Goldwyn-Mayer Corp. Directed by Charles F. Reisner (Assistant Director, Sandy Roth). Screenplay by Byron Morgan, Lew Lipton, Herman J. Mankiewicz, and Harry Conn. Produced by Harry Rapf and E. J. Mannix. Cinematography by Charles Schoenbaum. Music by William Axt. Edited by William S. Gray. Art direction by Cedric Gibbons. Recording director, Douglas Shearer. Costume design by Dolly Tree.

Cast: Jack Benny (Calvin Churchill), Ted Healy ("Clip" McGurk), Una Merkel (Alice Churchill), Nat Pendleton (Henry Potke), Mary Carlisle (Grace Gridley), Grant Mitchell (W. R. Gridley), Harvey Stephens (Sidney Kendall), Charles Trowbridge (Alfred Drake), Johnny Arthur (Jones), Al Shean (Mr. Johnson), Purnell B. Pratt (Horace McNab), Phillips Smalley (Mr. Winterby), Howard Hickman (Ruby), Larry Wheat (Tubbs), Richard Kipling (Mr. Platt).

Riffraff (1936)
Metro-Goldwyn-Mayer Corp. Directed by J. Walter Ruben (Assistant Director, Dolph Zimmer). Screenplay by Frances Marion, H. W. Hanemann, Anita Loos, John Lee Mahin, Carey Wilson, and George S. Kaufman. Produced by Irving G. Thalberg and David Lewis. Cinematography by Ray June. Music by Edward Ward. Edited by Frank Sullivan. Art direction by Cedric Gibbons. Recording director, Douglas Shearer. Costume design by Dolly Tree.

Cast: Jean Harlow (Hattie Muller), Spencer Tracy (Dutch Muller), Una Merkel (Lil), Joseph Calleia (Nick Lewis), Victor Kilian ("Flytrap"), Mickey Rooney (Jimmy), J. Farrell MacDonald ("Brains" McCall), Roger Imhof ("Pops"), Juanita Quigley (Rosie), Paul Hurst (Belcher), Vince Barnett (Lew), Dorothy Appleby (Gertie), Judith Wood (Mable), Arthur Housman ("Ratsy"), Wade Boteler (Bert), Joe Phillips (Al), William Newell (Pete), Al Hill ("Speed"), Helen Flint (Sadie).

Speed (1936)
Metro-Goldwyn-Mayer Corp. Directed by Edwin L. Marin (Assistant Director, Harry H. Poppe). Screenplay by Michael Fessier, from a story by Milton Krims, and Lawrence Bachmann. Produced by Lucien Hubbard. Cinematography by Lester White. Edited by Ben Lewis and Harry Poppe. Art direction by Cedric Gibbons. Music by Edward Ward. Recording director, Douglas Shearer. Costume design by Dolly Tree.
Cast: James Stewart (Terry Martin), Wendy Barrie (Jane Emery, also known as Jane Mitchell), Una Merkel (Josephine "Jo" Sanderson), Weldon Heyburn (Frank Lawson), Ted Healy (Clarence Maxmillian "Gadget" Haggerty), Ralph Morgan (Mr. Dean), Patricia Wilder (Fanny Lane).

We Went to College (1936)
Metro-Goldwyn-Mayer Corp. Directed by Joseph Santley (Assistant Director, Horace Hough). Screenplay by Richard Maibaum, Maurice Rapf, from a story by George Oppenheimer, and Finley Peter Dunne, Jr. Produced by Harry Rapf. Cinematography by Lester White. Music by William Axt; Wayne Allen and Paul Marquardt (orchestrators). Edited by James E. Newcom. Art direction by Fredric Hope. Recording director, Douglas Shearer. Costume design by Dolly Tree.
Cast: Charles Butterworth (Glenn Harvey), Walter Abel (Phil Talbot), Hugh Herbert (Professor Ellery Standish), Una Merkel (Susan Standish), Edith Atwater (Nina Talbot), Walter Catlett (Senator Budger), Charles Trowbridge (President Tomlin), Tom Ricketts ("Pop").

Born to Dance (1936)
Metro-Goldwyn-Mayer Corp. Directed by Roy Del Ruth (Assistant Director, William Scully). Screenplay by Jack McGowan and Sid Silvers, from a story by Jack McGowan, Sid Silvers and B.G. DeSylva. Produced by Jack Cummings. Cinematography by Ray June. Music by Alfred Newman (music director), Cole Porter (words and music), Leo Arnaud (choral arrangements), Roger Edens (musical arrangements), Edward B. Powell (orchestrator). Dance ensembles by Dave Gould. Edited by Blanche Sewell. Art direction by Cedric Gibbons. Recording director, Douglas Shearer. Sound mixer, William Steinkamp. Costume design by Adrian.
Cast: Eleanor Powell (Nora Paige), James Stewart (Ted Barker), Virginia Bruce (Lucy James), Una Merkel (Jenny Saks), Sid Silvers ("Gunny" Saks), Frances Langford ("Peppy" Turner), Raymond Walburn (Captain Percival Dingby), Alan Dinehart (James McKay), Buddy Ebsen ("Mush" Tracy), Juanita Quigley (Sally Saks), Georges and Jalna (themselves), Reginald Gardiner (Policeman), Barnett Parker (Floorwalker). The Foursome: J. Marshall Smith, L. Dwight Snyder, Ray (also known as Jay) Johnson, and Del Porter.

Don't Tell the Wife (1937)
RKO Radio Pictures, Inc. Directed by Christy Cabanne. Screenplay by Nat Perrin, from the play *Once Over Lightly* by George Holland. Produced by Samuel J. Briskin and Robert Sisk. Cinematography by Harry Wild. Edited by Jack Hively. Art direction by Van Nest Polglase. Recording director, John E. Tribby. Costume design by Renié.
Cast: Guy Kibbee (Malcolm J. "Dinky" Winthrop), Una Merkel (Nancy Dorsey), Lynne Overman (Steven Dorsey), Thurston Hall (Major Manning), Guinn Williams (Lazarus Hubert Gregory "Cupid" Dougal), Frank M. Thomas (Inspector Mallory), William Demarest (Larry Tucker), Lucille Ball (Ann "Annie" Howell), Harry Tyler (Mike Callahan), George Irving (Warden), Bradley Page (Hagar), Si (also known as Cy) Jenks (Sam Taylor).

Good Old Soak (1937)

Metro-Goldwyn-Mayer Corp. Directed by J. Walter Ruben (Assistant Director, Walter Strohm). Screenplay by A.E. Thomas, from the play *The Old Soak* by Don Marquis. Produced by Harry Rapf. Cinematography by Clyde De Vinna. Music by Edward Ward. Edited by Frank Sullivan. Art direction by Cedric Gibbons. Recording director, Douglas Shearer. Costume design by Dolly Tree.

Cast: Wallace Beery (Clem Hawley), Una Merkel (Nellie), Eric Linden (Clemmie Hawley), Judith Barrett (Ina Heath), Betty Furness (Lucy Hawley), Ted Healy (Al Simmons), Janet Beecher (Matilda Hawley), George Sidney (Kennedy), Robert McWade (Webster Parsons), James Bush (Tom Ogden), Margaret Hamilton (Minnie).

Saratoga (1937)

Metro-Goldwyn-Mayer Corp. Directed by Jack Conway (Assistant Directors, Tom Andre and James Dugan). Screenplay by Anita Loos, Robert Hopkins, James Kevin McGuinness, Maurine Dallas Watkins, from a story by Anita Loos, Robert Hopkins. Produced by Bernard H. Hyman and John Emerson. Cinematography by Ray June. Music by Edward Ward and Walter Donaldson; lyrics by Chet Forrest and Bob Wright; Paul Marquardt (orchestrator). Edited by Elmo Veron. Art direction by Cedric Gibbons. Recording director, Douglas Shearer. Costume design by Dolly Tree.

Cast: Clark Gable (Duke Bradley), Jean Harlow (Carol Clayton), Lionel Barrymore (Grandpa Clayton), Walter Pidgeon (Hartley Madison), Frank Morgan (Jesse Kiffmeyer), Una Merkel (Fritzi Kiffmeyer), Cliff Edwards (Tip O'Brien), George Zucco (Dr. Harmsworth Bierd), Jonathan Hale (Frank Clayton), Hattie McDaniel (Rosetta), Frankie Darro (Dixie Gordon), Henry Stone (Hand-Riding Hurley).

Checkers (1937)

Twentieth Century Fox Film Corp. Directed by H. Bruce Humberstone (Assistant Director, J. Gordon Cooper). Screenplay by Lynn Root, Frank

Fenton, Robert Chapin, and Karen DeWolf, from a story by Lynn Root and Frank Fenton. Produced by Sol M. Wurtzel and John Stone. Cinematography by Daniel B. Clark. Music by Samuel Kaylin. Edited by Jack Murray. Art direction by Bernard Herzbrun and Chester Gore. Sound by E. Clayton Ward and William H. Anderson. Costume design by Helen A. Myron.

Cast: Jane Withers (Checkers [Judy]), Stuart Erwin (Edgar Connell), Una Merkel (Mamie Appleby), Marvin Stephens (Jimmy Somers), Andrew Tombes (Tobias Williams), June Carlson (Sarah Williams), Minor Watson (Dr. Smith), John Harrington (Mr. George F. Green), Spencer Charters (Zeb), Francis Ford (Daniel Snodgrass).

True Confessions (1937)
Paramount Pictures, Inc. Directed by Wesley Ruggles (Assistant Director, Arthur Jacobson). Screenplay by Claude Binyon, from the play *Mon crime* by Louis Verneuil and Georges Berr. Produced by Adolph Zukor, Albert Lewin, and William LeBaron. Cinematography by Ted Tetzlaff. Music by Boris Morros. Edited by Paul Weatherwax. Art direction by Hans Dreier and Robert Usher. Sound by Earl Hayman and Don Johnson. Costume design by Travis Banton.

Cast: Carole Lombard (Helen Bartlett), Fred MacMurray (Kenneth Bartlett), John Barrymore (Charley Jasper), Una Merkel (Daisy McClure), Porter Hall (Prosecutor), Edgar Kennedy (Darsey), Lynne Overman (Bartender), Irving Bacon (The coroner), Fritz Feld (Krayler's butler), Richard Carle (Judge), John T. Murray (Otto Krayler), Tom Dugan (Typewriter man), Garry Owen (Tony Krauch), Toby Wing (Suzanne Baggart), Hattie McDaniel (Ella), Eleanor Fisher (Reporter).

"Hollywood Goes to Town" (1938) (Short documentary)
Metro-Goldwyn-Mayer Corp. Directed by Herman Hoffman. Music by David Snell.

Cast: Frank Whitbeck (Narrator), Don Wilson, Judy Garland, Freddie Bartholomew, Una Merkel (herself, arriving alone at movie premiere of *Marie*

Antoinette), Fernand Gravey, John Barrymore, Elaine Barrie, Florence Rice, Adrian, Norma Shearer, Tyrone Power, Spencer Tracy, Fanny Brice, Pete Smith, Robert Young, James Stewart, Jeanette MacDonald, Helen Hayes, and many others.

Four Girls in White (1939)
Metro-Goldwyn-Mayer Corp. Directed by S. Sylvan Simon (Assistant Director, Sandy Roth). Screenplay by Dorothy Yost, from a story by Nathalie Bucknall, and Endre Bohem. Produced by Nat Levine. Cinematography by Leonard Smith. Edited by George Boemler. Art direction by Cedric Gibbons. Music by William Axt and Franz Waxman. Recording director, Douglas Shearer. Costume design by Dolly Tree.
Cast: Florence Rice (Norma Page), Una Merkel (Gertie Robbins), Ann Rutherford (Patricia Page), Mary Howard (Mary Forbes), Alan Marshal (Dr. Stephen Melford), Kent Taylor (Robert Maitland), Buddy Ebsen (Express), Jessie Ralph (Miss Tobias), Sara Haden (Miss Bennett), Phillip Terry (Dr. Sidney), Tom Neal (Dr. Phillips).

Some Like It Hot (1939)
Also Known as *Rhythm Romance*
Paramount Pictures, Inc. Directed by George Archainbaud. Screenplay by Lewis R. Foster and Wilkie C. Mahoney, from the play *The Great Magoo* by Ben Hecht and Gene Fowler. Produced by William LeBaron and William C. Thomas. Cinematography by Karl Struss. Music by Arthur Franklin. Edited by Edward Dmytryk. Art direction by Hans Dreier and A. Earl Hedrick. Sound by George Dutton and Walter Oberst.
Cast: Bob Hope (Nicky Nelson), Shirley Ross (Lily Racquel), Una Merkel (Flo Saunders), Gene Krupa (Gene Krupa), Rufe Davis (Stoney), Bernard Nedell (Stephen Hanratty), Frank Sully (Sailor Burke), Bernadene Hayes (Miss Marble), Richard Denning (Mr. Weems), Clarence H. Wilson (Mr. Ives), Dudley Dickerson (Sam), Harry Barris (Harry piano player), Wayne "Tiny" Whitt (Bass fiddler), J. Scott Smart (Joe).

On Borrowed Time (1939)
Metro-Goldwyn-Mayer Corp. Directed by Harold S. Bucquet (Assistant Director, Marvin Stuart). Screenplay by Alice D.G. Miller, Frank O'Neill, and Claudine West, from the play *On Borrowed Time* by Paul Osborn, from the novel of the same name by Lawrence Edward Watkin. Produced by Sidney Franklin. Cinematography by Joseph Ruttenberg. Music by Franz Waxman; Paul Marquardt and Leonid Raab (orchestrators). Edited by George Boemler. Art direction by Cedric Gibbons. Recording director, Douglas Shearer. Costume design by Dolly Tree.
Cast: Lionel Barrymore (Julian Northrup, Gramps), Sir Cedric Hardwicke (Mr. Brink), Beulah Bondi (Nellie, Granny), Una Merkel (Marcia Giles), Bobs Watson (Pud Northrup), Nat Pendleton (Mr. Grimes), Henry Travers (Dr. Evans), Grant Mitchell (Mr. Ben Pilbeam), Eily Malyon (Demetria Riffle), James Burke (Sheriff Burlingame), Charles Waldron (Reverend Murdock), Ian Wolfe (Charles Wentworth), Phillip Terry (Bill Lowry), Truman Bradley (Dr. James Northrup).

Destry Rides Again (1939)
Universal Pictures Co. Directed by George Marshall (Assistant Director, Vernon Keays). Screenplay by Felix Jackson, Gertrude Purcell, and Henry Myers, from the novel *Destry Rides Again* by Max Brand. Produced by Joe Pasternak and Islin Auster. Cinematography by Hal Mohr. Music by Charles Previn (musical director) and Frank Skinner; Friedrich Hollaender (music); Frank Loesser (lyrics). Edited by Milton Carruth. Art direction by Jack Otterson. Sound by Bernard B. Brown and Robert Pritchard. Costume design by Vera West.
Cast: Marlene Dietrich (Frenchy), James Stewart (Thomas J. Destry Jr.), Mischa Auer (Boris Callahan), Charles Winninger (Washington Dimsdale), Brian Donlevy (Kent), Allen Jenkins (Gyp Watson), Warren Hymer (Bugs Watson), Irene Hervey (Janice Tyndall), Una Merkel (Lily Belle Callahan), Billy Gilbert (Loupgerou), Samuel S. Hinds (Judge Hiram J. Slade), Jack Carson (Jack Tyndall), Tom Fadden (Lem Claggett), Virginia Brissac (Sophie

Claggett), Edmund MacDonald (Rockwell), Lillian Yarbo (Clara), Joe King (Sheriff Keogh), Dickie Jones (Claggett boy), Ann Todd (Claggett girl).

Comin' Round the Mountain (1940)
Paramount Pictures, Inc. Directed by George Archainbaud (Assistant Director, Russell Mathews). Screenplay by Lewis R. Foster, Maxwell Shane, and Duke Atteberry, from story by Lewis R. Foster, Maxwell Shane, and Duke Atteberry. Produced by William C. Thomas. Cinematography by William Mellor. Edited by Stuart Gilmore. Art direction by Hans Dreier and A. Earl Hedrick. Music by Gil Grau, John Leipold, and Frank Loesser. Sound by George Dutton and Gene Garvin.
Cast: Bob Burns (Jed Blower), Una Merkel (Belinda Watters), Jerry Colonna (Argyle Phifft), Don Wilson (Mr. Wilson), Pat Barrett (Uncle Ezra Watters), Harold Peary (Mayor Throckmorton P. Gildersleeve), Bill Thompson (Barney Smoot), Richard Carle (Lester Smoot), Marjorie Bauersfeld (Ma Beagle [Mirandy]), William Demarest (Gutsy Mann), Cliff Arquette (Droopy Beagle), Luke Cosgrave (Uncle Ditto), Leona Roberts (Aunt Polly Watters), Zeffie Tilbury (Granny Stokes).

Sandy Gets Her Man (1940)
Universal Pictures Co. Directed by Otis Garrett and Paul Girard [Gerard] Smith (Assistant Director, Vernon Keays). Screenplay by Sy Bartlett and Jane Storm. Produced by Burt Kelly and Ken Goldsmith. Cinematography by Elwood Bredell. Music by H.J. Salter and Charles Previn. Edited by Philip Cahn. Art direction by Jack Otterson. Music by Hans J. Salter and Charles Previn. Sound by Bernard B. Brown and William Hedgcock. Costume design by Vera West.
Cast: Baby Sandy (Sandy), Stuart Erwin (Bill), Una Merkel (Nan), Edgar Kennedy (Fire Chief Galvin), William Frawley (Police Chief O'Hara), Edward Brophy (Junior), Wally Vernon (Bagshaw), Jack Carson (Tom), William Davidson (Councilman Clark), John Sheehan (Justice), Isabel Randolph (Justice's wife).

The Bank Dick (1940)
Universal Pictures Co. Directed by Edward Cline and Ralph Ceder (Assistant Directors, Fred Frank and Edward Montagne). Screenplay by Mahatma Kane Jeeves (pseudonym for W. C. Fields) and Richard Carroll. Produced by Cliff Work and Jack J. Gross. Cinematography by Milton Krasner. Music by Frank Skinner, Charles Previn, Heinz Roemheld. Edited by Arthur Hilton. Art direction by Jack Otterson. Sound by Bernard B. Brown and William Hedgcock. Costume design by Vera West.
Cast: W. C. Fields (Egbert Sousé), Cora Witherspoon (Agatha Sousé), Una Merkel (Myrtle Sousé), Evelyn Del Rio (Elsie May Adele Brunch Sousé), Jessie Ralph (Mrs. Hermisillo Brunch), Franklin Pangborn (J. Pinkerton Snoopington), Shemp Howard (Joe Guelpe), Richard Purcell (Mackley Q. Greene), Grady Sutton (Og Oggilby), Russell Hicks (J. Frothingham Waterbury), Pierre Watkin (Mr. Skinner), Al Hill (Filthy McNasty), George Moran (Cozy Cochran), Bill Wolfe (Otis), Jack Norton (A. Pismo Clam).

Double Date (1941)
Universal Pictures Company, Inc. Directed by Glenn Tryon (Assistant Director, Edwin Tyler). Screenplay by Scott Darling, Erna Lazarus, and Agnes Christine Johnston. Produced by Joseph G. Sanford. Cinematography by John Boyle. Music by Charles Previn and H.J. Salter. Edited by Otto Ludwig. Art direction by Jack Otterson. Sound by Bernard B. Brown and Jess Moulin. Costume design by Vera West.
Cast: Edmund Lowe (Roger Baldwin), Una Merkel (Aunt Elsie Kirkland), Peggy Moran (Penelope Penny Kirkland), Rand Brooks (Jerry Baldwin), Tommy Kelly (Hodges), Hattie Noel (Lilac), Eddy Waller (Truck driver), William Ruhl (Motorcycle cop), Sam Flint (Doctor), Pat O'Malley (Policeman), Joey Ray (Orchestra leader), Charles Smith (Bud), Nell O'Day (Mary), Janet Warren [also known as Elaine Morey] (Girl), Andrew Tombes (Judge Perkins), Joe [Jack] Downing (burglar), George Chandler (attendant), Frank Sully (Hank).

Road to Zanzibar (1941)
Paramount Pictures, Inc. Directed by Victor Schertzinger (Assistant Director, Hal Walker). Screenplay by Frank Butler, Don Hartman, and Sy Bartlett. Produced by William LeBaron and Paul Jones. Cinematography by Ted Tetzlaff. Music by Victor Young and Arthur Franklin. Edited by Alma Macrorie. Art direction by Hans Dreier and Robert Usher. Sound by Earl Hayman and Don Johnson. Costume design by Edith Head.
Cast: Bing Crosby (Chuck Reardon), Bob Hope (Fearless Hubert Frazier), Dorothy Lamour (Donna Latour), Una Merkel (Julia Quimby), Eric Blore (Charles Kimble), Douglass Dumbrille (Slave trader), Lionel Royce (Monsieur Lebec), Buck Woods (Thonga), Leigh Whipper (Scarface), Ernest Whitman (Whiteface), Noble Johnson (Chief), Joan Marsh (Dimples), Luis Alberni (Proprietor, native booth), Robert Middlemass (Police inspector).

Cracked Nuts (1941)
Universal Pictures Company, Inc. Directed by Edward Cline (Assistant Director, Fred Frank). Screenplay by Erna Lazarus and W. Scott Darling. Produced by Joseph G. Sanford. Cinematography by Charles Van Enger. Music by H.J. Salter and Charles Previn. Edited by Milton Carruth. Art direction by Jack Otterson. Sound by Bernard B. Brown and Jess Moulin. Costume design by Vera West.
Cast: Stuart Erwin (Lawrence Trent), Una Merkel (Sharon Knight), Mischa Auer (Boris Kabikoff), William Frawley (James Mitchell), Shemp Howard (Eddie), Astrid Allwyn (Ethel Mitchell), Mantan Moreland (Burgess), Hattie Noel (Chloe), Francis Pierlot (Mayor Wilfred Smun), Will Wright (Mr. Sylvanus Boogle), Emmett Vogan (McAneny), Tom Hanlon (Radio announcer Mr. Dixon), Pat O'Malley (1st officer).

The Mad Doctor of Market Street (1942)
Universal Pictures Company, Inc. Directed by Joseph H. Lewis (Assistant Director, Melville Shyer). Screenplay by Al Martin. Produced by Paul Malvern. Cinematography by Jerome Ash. Music by H.J. Salter. Edited by

Ralph Dixon. Art direction by Jack Otterson. Sound by Bernard B. Brown and Jess Moulin. Costume design by Vera West.
Cast: Una Merkel (Aunt Margaret Wentworth), Lionel Atwill (Dr. Ralph Benson, also known as Graham), Nat Pendleton (Red Hogan), Claire Dodd (Patricia Wentworth), Anne Nagel (Mrs. William R.B. Saunders), Hardie Albright (William R.B. Saunders), Richard Davies (Jim), John Eldredge (Dwight), Ray Mala (Barab), Noble Johnson (Elan), Rosina Galli (Tanao), Al Kikume (Kalo), Milton Kibbee (Hadley), Byron Shores (Crandall), Tani Marsh (Tahitian dancer).

Twin Beds (1942)
Edward Small Productions, Inc., distributed by United Artists. Directed by Tim Whelan (Assistant Director, Rollie Asher). Screenplay by Curtis Kenyon, Kenneth Earl, and E. Edwin Moran, from the play *Twin Beds* by Margaret Mayo and Salisbury Field. Produced by Edward Small and Stanley Logan. Cinematography by Hal Mohr. Music by Dimitri Tiomkin. Edited by Grant Whytock and Francis D. Lyon. Art direction by John Ducasse Schulze. Sound by Earl Sitar. Costume design by Irene and René Hubert.
Cast: George Brent (Mike Abbott), Joan Bennett (Julie Abbott), Mischa Auer (Nicolai Cherupin), Una Merkel (Lydia), Glenda Farrell (Sonya Cherupin), Ernest Truex (Larky), Margaret Hamilton (Norah), Charles Coleman (Butler), Charles Arnt (Manager).

This is the Army (1943)
Warner Bros. Pictures, Inc. Directed by Michael Curtiz (Assistant Directors, Frank Heath and Jack Sullivan). Screenplay by Casey Robinson, Capt. Claude Binyon, Philip G. Epstein, and Julius J. Epstein, from the play *This is the Army* by Irving Berlin. Produced by Jack L. Warner and Hal B. Wallis. Cinematography by Bert Glennon and Sol Polito. Music by Ray Heindorf, Leo F. Forbstein, and Irving Berlin. Edited by George Amy. Art direction by John Hughes and John Koenig. Sound by C.A. Riggs. Costume design by Orry-Kelly and Leon Robicheau.

Cast: George Murphy (Jerry Jones), Joan Leslie (Eileen Dibble), George Tobias (Maxie Twardofsky), Alan Hale (Sergeant McGee), Charles Butterworth (Eddie Dibble), Dolores Costello (Mrs. Davidson), Una Merkel (Rose Dibble), Stanley Ridges (Major John B. Davidson), Rosemary DeCamp (Ethel), Ruth Donnelly (Mrs. O'Brien), Dorothy Peterson (Mrs. Nelson), Frances Langford (Café singer), Gertrude Niesen (Singer), Kate Smith (Herself), Ronald Reagan (Johnny Jones).

"Quack Service" (1943)
(Short film)
Columbia Pictures Corporation. Directed by Harry Edwards.
Cast: Una Merkel (Daffy), Gwen Kenyon (Dizzy), Stanley Brown (Doctor), Monte Collins (Dr. Brown), Vernon Dent (Mr. Summers), Dudley Dickerson (orderly), Bud Jamison (process server), Blanche Payson (Psychiatric Attendant), 'Snub' Pollard (drunk), Al Thompson (waiter).

"To Heir is Human" (1944)
(Short film)
Columbia Pictures Corporation. Directed by Harold Godsoe. Screenplay by Monte Collins and Elwood Ullman. Produced by Hugh McCollum. Cinematography by George Meehan. Edited by Paul Borofsky. Art direction by Charles Clague.
Cast: Una Merkel (Una), Harry Langdon (Harry Fenner), Christine McIntyre (Velma, Harry's Kissing Cousin), Eddie Gribbon (Bobo), Lew Kelly (A. Raven Sparrow), Vernon Dent (Board Chairman), John Tyrrell (Dr. I. M. Calm).

Sweethearts of the U.S.A. (1944)
Monogram Pictures. Directed by Lewis D. Collins (Assistant Director, William Nolte). Screenplay by Arthur St. Claire, Richard Long, Jane Keith, Sherman Lowe, and Mary Sheldon. Produced by Trem Carr, Lester Cutler, and George M. Merrick. Cinematography by Ira Morgan. Music by Rudy

Schrager and David Chudnow. Edited by George Adams, Stephen Csillag, and George M. Merrick. Art direction by Paul Palmentola. Sound by Corson Jowett. Costume design by Kay West.
Cast: Una Merkel (Patsy Wilkins), Harry Parke [also known as Parkyakarkus] (Parky), Donald Novis (Don Clark), Lillian Cornell (Helen Grant), Teala Loring [also known as Judith Gibson] (Loretta Carver), Joel Friend (Bill Craige), Cobina Wright, Sr. (Mrs. Josephine Carver), Georgann Smith (Juanita Hogan), Marion Martin (Ghost of Josephine), Ralph Sanford (Gilhooley), Vince Barnett (Clipper, third robber), Joe Devlin (Boss, first robber), Jack Baxley (Chief of Police, Sly Slocum), Joseph Kirk (Ghost of Napoleon), Edmund Cobb (Ghost of Captain Kidd), Forrest Taylor (Deacon, second robber).

It's a Joke, Son! (1947)
Bryan Foy Productions, distributed by Eagle-Lion Films, Inc. Directed by Ben Stoloff (Assistant Director, Robert Stillman). Screenplay by Robert Kent and Paul Gerard [Girard] Smith. Produced by Aubrey Schenck. Cinematography by Clyde De Vinna. Music by Alvin Levin. Edited by Norman Colbert. Art direction by Edward C. Jewell. Sound by Frank McWhorter. Costume design by Oleg Cassini.
Cast: Kenny Delmar (Senator Beauregard Claghorn), Una Merkel (Magnolia Claghorn), June Lockhart (Mary Lou Claghorn), Kenneth Farrell (Jeff Davis), Douglass Dumbrille (Dan Healey), Jimmy Conlin (Senator Leeds), Matt Willis (Ace), Ralph Sanford (Knifey), Daisy a dog, (Herself), Vera Lewis (Hortense), Margaret McWade (Whipple sister), Ida Moore (Whipple sister), Anthony Sydes (William).

The Bride Goes Wild (1948)
Metro-Goldwyn-Mayer Corp. Directed by Norman Taurog (Assistant Director, Sid Sidman). Screenplay by Albert Beich. Produced by William H. Wright. Cinematography by Ray June and Sidney Wagner. Music by Rudolph G. Kopp. Edited by George Boemler. Art direction by Cedric Gibbons and

Harry McAfee. Recording director, Douglas Shearer. Costume design by Helen Rose.

Cast: Van Johnson (Greg Rawlings also known as "Uncle Bumps"), June Allyson (Martha Terryton), Jackie "Butch" Jenkins (Danny), Hume Cronyn (John McGrath), Una Merkel (Miss Doberly), Arlene Dahl (Tillie Smith), Richard Derr (Bruce Kope Johnson), Lloyd Corrigan ("Pop"), Elisabeth Risdon (Mrs. Carruthers), Clara Blandick (Aunt Pewtie), Kathleen Howard (Aunt Susan).

Man from Texas (1948)

Eagle-Lion Films, Inc. Directed by Leigh Jason (Assistant Director, Howard W. Koch). Screenplay by Joseph Fields and Jerome Chodorov, from the play *Missouri Legend* by Elizabeth B. Ginty. Produced by Joseph Fields. Cinematography by Jackson J. Rose. Music by Earl Robinson. Edited by Alfred De Gaetano and Norman Colbert. Art direction by Edward L. Ilou. Recording director, Leon Becker. Sound mixer, Percy J. Townsend. Costume design by France Ehren.

Cast: James Craig (Tobias Simms, also known as The El Paso Kid and Toby Heath), Lynn Bari (Zee), Johnnie Johnston (Billy Taylor), Una Merkel (Widow Weeks), Wally Ford (Jed), Harry Davenport (Pop Hickey), Sara Allgood (Aunt Belle), Victor [Vic] Cutler (Charlie Jackson), Reed Hadley (Marshal Gregg).

Kill the Umpire (1950)

Columbia Pictures Corp. Directed by Lloyd Bacon (Assistant Directors, Wilbur McGaugh and Carter DeHaven). Screenplay by Frank Tashlin. Produced by John Beck. Cinematography by Charles Lawton Jr. Music by Heinz Roemheld and Morris Stoloff. Edited by Charles Nelson. Art direction by Perry Smith. Sound by Lambert Day. Costume design by Jean Louis.

Cast: William Bendix (Bill Johnson), Una Merkel (Betty Johnson), Ray Collins (Jonah Evans), Gloria Henry (Lucy), Richard Taylor (Bob Landon),

Connie Marshall (Susan), William Frawley (Jimmy O'Brien), Tom D'Andrea (Roscoe Snooker).

My Blue Heaven (1950)
Twentieth Century-Fox Films Corp. Directed by Henry Koster (Assistant Director, Ad Schaumer). Screenplay by Lamar Trotti and Claude Binyon. Produced by Darryl F. Zanuck and Sol C. Siegel. Cinematography by Arthur E. Arling. Music by Alfred Newman (musical director), Ken Darby (vocal director), Earle Hagen (orchestrator). Edited by James B. Clark. Art direction by Lyle Wheeler and Joseph C. Wright. Sound by Arthur von Kirbach and Harry M. Leonard. Costume design by Charles Le Maire.
Cast: Betty Grable (Kitty Moran), Dan Dailey (Jack Moran), David Wayne (Walter Pringle), Jane Wyatt (Janet Pringle), Mitzi Gaynor (Gloria Adams), Una Merkel (Miss Irma Gilbert), Don Hicks (Young man), Louise Beavers (Selma), Laura Pierpont (Mrs. Johnston).

Emergency Wedding (1950)
Columbia Pictures Corp. Directed by Edward Buzzell (Assistant Director, Earl Bellamy). Screenplay by Nat Perrin and Claude Binyon. Produced by Nat Perrin. Cinematography by Burnett Guffey. Music by Morris Stoloff and Werner R. Heymann. Edited by Al Clark. Art direction by Carl Anderson. Sound by Lambert Day. Costume design by Jean Louis.
Cast: Larry Parks (Peter Judson Kirk, Jr.), Barbara Hale (Dr. Helen Hunt), Willard Parker (Vandemer), Una Merkel (Emma), Alan Reed (Tony), Eduard Franz (Dr. Heimer), Irving Bacon (Filbert), Don Beddoe (Forbish), Jim Backus (Ed Hamley).

Rich, Young and Pretty (1951)
Metro-Goldwyn-Mayer Corp. Directed by Norman Taurog (Assistant Director, Jack Greenwood). Screenplay by Dorothy Cooper and Sidney Sheldon. Produced by Joe Pasternak. Cinematography by Robert Planck. Music by David Rose (musical director/composer), Nicholas Brodszky

(music), Sammy Cahn (lyrics). Edited by Gene Ruggiero. Art direction by Cedric Gibbons and Arthur Lonergan. Sound by Douglas Shearer. Costume design by Helen Rose.
Cast: Jane Powell (Elizabeth Rogers), Danielle Darrieux (Marie Devarone), Wendell Corey (Jim Stauton Rogers), Vic Damone (Andre Milan), Fernando Lamas (Paul Sarnac), Marcel Dalio (Claude Duval), Una Merkel (Glynnie), Richard Anderson (Bob Lennart), Jean Murat (Monsieur Henri Milan), Duci de Kerekjarto (Gypsy leader), Hans Conried (Jean, Maitre D'), George and Katrin Tatar (Hungarian dancers), Monique Chantal (Maid), Four Freshmen (Singing Quartette).

A Millionaire for Christy (1951)
Thor Productions, Inc., distributed by Twentieth Century-Fox Film Corporation. Directed by George Marshall (Assistant Director, Ralph Black). Screenplay by Ken Englund. and Robert Harari. Produced by Bert E. Friedlob. Cinematography by Harry Stradling. Music by Victor Young and David Chudnow. Art direction by Boris Leven. Sound by Frank Webster and Stan Cooley. Costume design by Joe King, Ann Peck, and Elois Jenssen.
Cast: Fred MacMurray (Peter Ulysses Lockwood), Eleanor Parker (Christabel "Christy" Sloane), Richard Carlson (Dr. Roland Cook), Una Merkel (Patsy Clifford), Chris-Pin Martin (Manolo), Douglass Dumbrille (J.C. Thompson), Kay Buckley (June Chandler), Raymond Greenleaf (Benjamin Chandler), Nestor Paiva (Mr. Rapello).

Golden Girl (1951)
Twentieth Century-Fox Film Corp. Directed by Lloyd Bacon (Assistant Directors, Joe Rickerts and Ad Schaumer). Screenplay by Walter Bullock, Charles O'Neal, and Gladys Lehman. Produced by George Jessel. Cinematography by Charles G. Clarke. Music by Alfred Newman and Cyril J. Mockridge. Art direction by Lyle Wheeler and Leland Fuller. Sound by Alfred Bruzlin and Roger Heman. Costume design by Charles Le Maire.
Cast: Mitzi Gaynor (Lotta Crabtree), Dale Robertson (Tom Richmond),

Dennis Day (Mart Taylor), James Barton (John Crabtree), Una Merkel (Mary Ann Crabtree), Raymond Walburn (Cornelius), Gene Sheldon (Sam Jordan), Carmen D'Antonio (Lola Montez).

With a Song in My Heart (1952)
Twentieth Century-Fox Film Corp. Directed by Walter Lang (Assistant Director, Hal Klein). Screenplay by Lamar Trotti. Produced by Lamar Trotti and Darryl F. Zanuck. Cinematography by Leon Shamroy. Music by Alfred Newman (musical director), Ken Darby (vocal director), Leo Robin and Harold Arlen (composers). Art direction by Lyle Wheeler and Joseph C. Wright. Sound by Arthur von Kirbach and Roger Heman. Costume design by Charles Le Maire.
Cast: Susan Hayward (Jane Froman), Rory Calhoun (John Burn), David Wayne (Don Ross), Thelma Ritter (Clancy), Robert Wagner (Paratrooper), Helen Westcott (Jennifer March), Una Merkel (Sister Marie), Richard Allan (Dancer), Max Showalter (Harry Guild).

The Merry Widow (1952)
Metro-Goldwyn-Mayer Corp. Directed by Curtis Bernhardt (Assistant Director, Reggie Callow). Screenplay by Sonya Levien and William Ludwig, from the operetta *Die lustige Witwe* by Franz Lehar, Victor Leon, and Leo Stein. Produced by Joe Pasternak. Cinematography by Robert Surtees. Music by Jay Blackton. Art direction by Cedric Gibbons and Paul Groesse. Sound by Douglas Shearer. Costume design by Helen Rose and Gile Steele.
Cast: Lana Turner ("The Merry Widow" Crystal Radek), Fernando Lamas (Count Danilo), Una Merkel (Kitty Riley), Richard Haydn (Baron Popoff), Thomas Gomez (King of Marshovia), John Abbott (Marshovian ambassador), Marcel Dalio (Police sergeant), King Donovan (Nitki), Robert Coote (Marquis De Crillon), Sujata Rubener (Gypsy girl), Lisa Ferraday (Marcella), Shepard Menken (Kunjany), Ludwig Stossel (Major Domo).

I Love Melvin (1953)

Metro-Goldwyn-Mayer Corp. Directed by Don Weis (Assistant Director, Marvin Stuart). Screenplay by George Wells. Produced by George Wells. Cinematography by Harold Rosson. Music by George Stoll, Skip Martin, Mack Gordon & Josef Myrow (composers), Robert Van Eps (orchestrator). Art direction by Cedric Gibbons, Jack Martin Smith, and Eddie Imazu. Sound by Douglas Shearer. Costume design by Helen Rose.

Cast: Donald O'Connor (Melvin Hoover), Debbie Reynolds (Judy LeRoy), Una Merkel (Mom Schneider), Richard Anderson (Harry Flack), Allyn Joslyn (Frank Pop Schneider), Les Tremayne (Mr. Henneman), Noreen Corcoran (Clarabelle Schneider), Jim Backus (Mergo), Barbara Ruick (Studio guide), Robert Taylor (Guest star).

The Kentuckian (1955)

Hecht-Lancaster Productions/James Productions Inc., distributed by United Artists. Directed by Burt Lancaster (Assistant Directors, Richard Maybery and Nate Slott). Screenplay by A.B. Guthrie Jr., from the novel *The Gabriel Horn* by Felix Holt. Produced by Harold Hecht. Cinematography by Ernest Laszlo. Music by Bernard Hermann. Production design by Ted (Edward S.) Haworth. Sound by John Kean, Paul Schmutz Sr., and Wayne Fury. Costume design by Norma, Esther Krebbs, and Carl Walker.

Cast: Burt Lancaster (Big Eli Wakefield), Dianne Foster (Hannah Bolen), Diana Lynn (Susie Spann), John McIntire (Zack Wakefield), Una Merkel (Sophie Wakefield), John Carradine (Zybee Fletcher), John Litel (Pleasant Tuesday Babson), Rhys Williams (Constable), Edward Norris (Roulette dealer), Walter Matthau (Stan Bodine), Donald MacDonald (Little Eli Wakefield).

The Kettles in the Ozarks (1956)

Universal-International Pictures Co., Inc. Directed by Charles Lamont (Assistant Director, Joseph E. Kenny). Screenplay by Kay Lenard, based on characters from the novel *The Egg and I* by Betty MacDonald. Produced by Richard Wilson. Cinematography by George Robinson. Art direction by Alexander Golitzen and Alfred Sweeney. Music by Joseph Gershenson. Sound by Leslie I. Carey, Robert Pritchard, David Janssen. Costume design by Jay A. Morley Jr.

Cast: Marjorie Main (Ma Kettle), Arthur Hunnicutt (Sedge Kettle), Una Merkel (Miss Bedelia Baines), Ted de Corsia (Professor), Olive Sturgess (Nancy Kettle), David O'Brien (Conductor), Richard Eyer (Billy Kettle), Cheryl Callaway (Susie Kettle), Joe Sawyer (Bancroft Baines), Sid Tomack (Benny), Louis DaPron (Mountaineer), Harry Hines (Joe), Jim Hayward (Jack Dexter), Richard Deacon (Big Trout), Pat Goldin (Small Fry), George Arglen (Freddie), Eddie Pagett (Sammy), Pat Morrow (Sally), Bonnie Franklin (Betty), Elvia Allman (Meek man's wife), Sarah Padden (Miz Tinware), Paul Wexler (Reverend Martin).

Calling Terry Conway (1956)
Television movie—see entry under "Una Merkel on Television."

Bundle of Joy (1956)
RKO Radio Pictures, Inc. Directed by Norman Taurog (Assistant Director, Emmett Emerson). Screenplay by Norman Krasna, Robert Carson, and Arthur Sheekman. Produced by Edmund Grainger. Cinematography by William Snyder. Art direction by Albert S. D'Agostino and Walter Holscher. Music by Walter Scharf and Hugo Winterhalter. Sound by Jean Speak and Terry Kellum. Costume design by Howard Shoup.

Cast: Eddie Fisher (Dan Merlin), Debbie Reynolds (Polly Parrish), Adolphe Menjou (John B. Merlin), Tommy Noonan (Freddie Miller), Nita Talbot (Mary Hawkins), Una Merkel (Mrs. Dugan), Melville Cooper (Adams), Bill Goodwin (Mr. Creely), Howard McNear (Mr. Appleby), Robert H. Harris (Mr. Hargraves), Mary Treen (Matron), Edward S. Brophy (Dance contest judge), Gil Stratton (Mike Clancy), Scott Douglas (Bill Rand).

The Fuzzy Pink Nightgown (1957)
Russ-Field Productions, distributed by United Artists. Directed by Norman Taurog (Assistant Director, Stanley H. Goldsmith). Screenplay by Richard Alan Simmons, from the novel *The Fuzzy Pink Nightgown* by Sylvia Tate. Produced by Robert Waterfield. Cinematography by Joseph LaShelle. Art direction by Serge Krizman. Sound by Fred Lau. Costume design by Billy Travilla, Oscar Rodriguez, and Evelyn Carruth.
Cast: Jane Russell (Laurel Stevens), Kenan Wynn (Dandy), Ralph Meeker (Mike Valla), Fred Clark (Sgt. Ed McBride), Una Merkel (Bertha), Robert Harris (Barney Baylies), Benay Venuta (Daisy Parker), Bob Kelley (Television announcer), Dick Haynes (Disk jockey), John Truax (Flack), Milton Frome (Lt. Dempsey), Adolphe Menjou (Arthur Martin).

The Girl Most Likely (1958)
Stanley Rubin Productions, intended for release by RKO Radio Pictures but distributed by Universal Pictures. Directed by Mitchell Leisen (Assistant Director, Richard Moder). Screenplay by Devery Freeman and Paul Jarrico. Produced by Stanley Rubin and William Dozier. Cinematography by Robert Planck. Art direction by Albert S. D'Agostino and George W. Davis. Music by Nelson Riddle and Richard Pribor. Edited by Harry Marker and Dean Harrison. Sound by Frank Webster and Terry Kellum. Costume design by Renie.
Cast: Jane Powell (Dodie), Cliff Robertson (Pete), Keith Andes (Neil Patterson, Jr.), Kaye Ballard (Marge), Tommy Noonan (Buzz), Una Merkel (Mom), Kelly Brown (Sam Kelsey), Judy Nugent (Pauline), Frank Cady (Pop), Nacho Galindo (Mexican photographer), Chris Essay (Steward).

The Mating Game (1959)
Metro-Goldwyn-Mayer Corp. Directed by George Marshall (Assistant Director, Al Jennings). Screenplay by William Roberts, from the novel *The Darling Buds of May* by H.E. Bates. Produced by Philip Barry Jr. Cinematography by Robert Bronner. Art direction by William A. Horning

and Malcolm Brown. Music by Jeff Alexander. Edited by John McSweeney Jr. Recording supervisor, Franklin Milton. Costume design by Helen Rose.

Cast: Debbie Reynolds (Mariette Larkin), Tony Randall (Lorenzo Charlton), Paul Douglas (Sidney Pop Larkin), Fred Clark (Oliver Kelsey), Una Merkel (Ma Larkin), Philip Ober (Wendell Burnshaw), Philip Coolidge (Rev. Osgood), Charles Lane (Inspector General Bigelow), Trevor Bardette (Chief Guthrie), Bill Smith (Barney), Addison Powell (David DeGroot), Rickey Murray (Lee Larkin), Donald Losby (Grant Larkin), Cheryl Bailey (Victoria Larkin), Caryl Bailey (Susan Larkin).

The Parent Trap (1961)

Walt Disney Productions, distributed by Buena Vista Distribution Co. Directed by David Swift (Assistant Director, Ivan Volkman). Screenplay by David Swift, from the novel *Das doppelte Lottchen* by Erich Kästner. Produced by Walt Disney and George Golitzen. Cinematography by Lucien Ballard. Art direction by Carroll Clark and Robert Clatworthy. Music by Paul Smith, Franklyn Marks (orchestrator), Richard M. Sherman and Robert B. Sherman (songs). Edited by Philip W. Anderson. Sound by Robert O. Cook, Dean Thomas, and Evelyn Kennedy. Costume design by Bill Thomas, Chuck Keehne, and Gertrude Casey.

Cast: Hayley Mills (Sharon McKendrick/Susan Evers), Maureen O'Hara (Maggie McKendrick), Brian Keith (Mitch Evers), Charlie Ruggles (Charles McKendrick), Una Merkel (Verbena), Leo G. Carroll (Reverend Mosby), Joanna Barnes (Vicky Robinson), Cathleen Nesbitt (Louise McKendrick), Ruth McDevitt (Miss Inch), Crahan Denton (Hecky), Linda Watkins (Edna Robinson), Nancy Kulp (Miss Grunecker), Frank De Vol (Mr. Eaglewood).

Summer and Smoke (1961)

Hal Wallis Productions, distributed by Paramount Pictures. Directed by Peter Glenville (Assistant Directors, Mickey Moore and James Rosenberger). Screenplay by James Poe and Meade Roberts, from the play *Summer and Smoke* by Tennessee Williams. Produced by Hal B. Wallis and Paul Nathan.

Cinematography by Charles Lang Jr. Art direction by Hal Pereira and Walter Tyler. Music by Elmer Bernstein. Edited by Warren Low. Sound by Phil Mitchell and Charles Grenzbach. Costume design by Edith Head.
Cast: Laurence Harvey (John Buchanan), Geraldine Page (Alma Winemiller), Rita Moreno (Rose Zacharias), Una Merkel (Mrs. Winemiller), John McIntire (Dr. Buchanan), Thomas Gomez (Papa Zacharias), Pamela Tiffin (Nellie Ewell), Malcolm Atterbury (Reverend Winemiller), Lee Patrick (Mrs. Ewell), Casey Adams [Max Showalter] (Roger Doremus), Earl Holliman (Archie Kramer).

Summer Magic (1963)
Walt Disney Productions, distributed by Buena Vista Distribution Co. Directed by James Neilson (Assistant Director, Austen Jewell). Screenplay by Sally Benson, from the novel *Mother Carey's Chickens* by Kate Douglas Wiggin. Produced by Walt Disney and Ron Miller. Cinematography by William Snyder. Music by Buddy Baker, Richard M. Sherman and Robert B. Sherman (songs), Camarata (vocal supervisor). Edited by Robert Stafford. Sound by Robert O. Cook, Dean Thomas, and Evelyn Kennedy. Costume design by Bill Thomas, Chuck Keehne, and Gertrude Casey.
Cast: Hayley Mills (Nancy Carey), Burl Ives (Osh Popham), Dorothy McGuire (Margaret Carey), Deborah Walley (Cousin Julia), Eddie Hodges (Gilly Carey), Jimmy Mathers (Peter Carey), Michael J. Pollard (Digby Popham), Wendy Turner (Lallie Joy Popham), Una Merkel (Maria Popham), Peter Brown (Tom Hamilton), James Stacy (Charles Bryant), O. Z. Whitehead (Mr. Perkins), Harry Holcombe (Henry Lord), Jan Stine (Mr. Perkins' son), Hilda Plowright (Mary).

A Tiger Walks (1964)
Walt Disney Productions, distributed by Buena Vista Distribution Co. Directed by Norman Tokar (Assistant Director, John C. Chulay). Screenplay by Lowell S. Hawley, from the novel *A Tiger Walks* by Ian Niall. Produced by Walt Disney, Bill Anderson, and Ron Miller. Cinematography by William

Snyder. Music by Buddy Baker and Bob Brunner. Edited by Grant K. Smith. Sound by Robert O. Cook and Evelyn Kennedy. Costume design by Chuck Keehne and Gertrude Casey.

Cast: Brian Keith (Sheriff Pete Williams), Vera Miles (Dorothy Williams), Pamela Franklin (Julie Williams), Sabu (Ram Singh), Edward Andrews (Governor Robbins), Una Merkel (Mrs. Watkins), Peter Brown (Vern Goodman), Kevin Corcoran (Tom Hadley), Frank McHugh (Bill Watkins), Arthur Hunnicutt (Mr. Lewis), Merry Anders (Betty Collins), Jack Albertson (Sam Grant), Connie Gilchrist (Mrs. Lewis), Theodore Marcuse (Josef Pietz), Frank Aletter (Joe Riley), Rajah (Himself, a Bengal tiger).

Spinout (1966)

Euterpe, Inc., distributed by Metro-Goldwyn-Mayer. Directed by Norman Taurog (Assistant Directors Claude Binyon Jr., Donald Verk, and James Westman). Screenplay by Theodore J. Flicker and George Kirgo. Produced by Joe Pasternak and Hank Moonjean. Cinematography by Daniel L. Fapp. Art direction by George W. Davis and Edward Carfagno. Music by George Stoll and Robert Van Eps. Edited by Rita Roland and Frank Urioste. Recording supervisor, Frank Milton. Sound mixer, Larry Jost. Costume design by Lambert Marks and Margo Weintz.

Cast: Elvis Presley (Mike McCoy), Shelley Fabares (Cynthia Foxhugh), Diane McBain (Diana St. Clair), Deborah Walley (Les), Dodie Marshall (Susan), Jack Mullaney (Curly), Will Hutchins (Lieut. Tracy Richards), Warren Berlinger (Philip Short), Jimmy Hawkins (Larry), Carl Betz (Howard Foxhugh), Cecil Kellaway (Bernard Ranley), Una Merkel (Violet Ranley), Frederic [also spelled Frederick] Worlock (Blodgett), Dave Barry (Harry).

UNA MERKEL ON RADIO

Edwin Schallert interview (March 14, 1934); Cast: Madge Evans and Una Merkel.

Edwin Schallert interview (March 21, 1934); Cast: Paul Muni and Una Merkel.

Fleischmann's Yeast Hour (December 19, 1935), "Church Mouse." Cast: Una Merkel, Conrad Nagel, Joe Cook.

Movie Club (December 27, 1935); Cast: Una Merkel.

Al Jolson's Revue (February 29, 1936); Cast: Elissa Landi, Una Merkel, Mary Taylor, Maxine Lewis.

Dorsey Orchestra (May 7, 1936), "Bing Crosby Songs." Cast: Bob Burns, Toscha Seidel, George Raft, Una Merkel.

Hollywood Hotel (November 13, 1936), "Scene from *Born to Dance*." Cast: Dick Powell, Eleanor Powell, Una Merkel, James Stewart.

Good News of 1938 (March 31, 1938); Cast: Lionel Barrymore, Maureen O'Sullivan, Jack Conway, Gilbert Russell, Fanny Brice, Una Merkel, Frank Morgan, Connie Boswell, Louis B. Mayer, Robert Taylor.

Good News of 1938 (April 28, 1938); Cast: Max Baer, Fanny Brice, Maureen O'Sullivan, Una Merkel, and others.

Good News of 1938 (May 5, 1938); Cast: Robert Young, Meredith Willson and His Orchestra, Ted Pearson, Judy Garland, Frank Morgan, Fanny Brice, Hanley Stafford, Clark Gable, Florence Rice, Cedric Wilson, Una Merkel.

Good News of 1938 (May 26, 1938); Cast: Douglas McPhail, Fanny Brice, Gus Kahn, Hanley Stafford, Meredith Willson and His Orchestra, Robert Montgomery, Robert Young, Ted Pearson, Una Merkel, Verna Felton, Virginia Bruce.

Texaco Star Theatre (October 5, 1938). Note: "Theatre" is sometimes spelled "Theater" in advertisements. Cast: Adolphe Menjou, Bette Davis, Charles Ruggles, Una Merkel, Jane Froman, Kenny Baker, Ned Sparks, Max Reinhardt, David Broekman's orchestra.

Texaco Star Theatre (October 12, 1938); Cast: Adolphe Menjou, Una Merkel, Charles Ruggles, Jane Froman, Kenny Baker, Ned Sparks, Max Reinhardt, John Barrymore, Elaine Barrie, Noah Berry.

Texaco Star Theatre (October 19, 1938) ; Cast: Adolphe Menjou, Una Merkel, Charles Ruggles, Jane Froman, Kenny Baker, Ned Sparks, Max Reinhardt, Miriam Hopkins.

Texaco Star Theatre (October 26, 1938); Cast: Adolphe Menjou, Una Merkel, Charles Ruggles, Jane Froman, Ned Sparks, Kenny Baker, Max Reinhardt, and Verree Teasdale.

Texaco Star Theatre (November 2, 1938); Cast: John Barrymore, Kenny Baker, Una Merkel, Adolphe Menjou, Charles Ruggles, Max Reinhardt, Lurene Tuttle, J. Scott Smart, Ned Sparks, David Broekman and His Orchestra.

Texaco Star Theatre (November 9, 1938); Cast: John Barrymore, Una Merkel, Charles Ruggles, Ned Sparks, Kenny Baker, Jane Froman, Max Reinhardt, Billy Halop, Leo Gorcey, Bobby Jordan, Paula Winslowe.

Texaco Star Theatre (November 16, 1938); Cast: John Barrymore, Fay Bainter, Ned Sparks, Jane Froman, Una Merkel, Charles Ruggles, John Arledge, Max Reinhardt, Ray Erlenborn.

Texaco Star Theatre (November 23, 1938); Cast: John Barrymore, Paula Winslowe, Francia White, Spring Byington, June Carlson, George Ernest,

Thornton Wilder Charles Ruggles, Una Merkel, Kenny Baker, Ned Sparks, Jane Froman, Ray Erlenborn.

Texaco Star Theatre (November 30, 1938); Cast: John Barrymore, Herbert Marshall, Andrea Leeds Kenny Baker, Una Merkel, Charles Ruggles, Ned Sparks, Jane Froman, Max Reinhardt.

Texaco Star Theatre (December 7, 1938); Cast: John Barrymore, Una Merkel, Ned Sparks, Charles Ruggles, Jane Froman, Frank Parker, Paula Winslowe, Elaine Barrie.

Texaco Star Theatre (December 14, 1938); Cast: John Barrymore, Olivia de Havilland, Nana Bryant, Una Merkel, Kenny Baker, Jane Froman, Charles Ruggles, Ned Sparks, .

Texaco Star Theatre (December 21, 1938); Cast: John Barrymore, Frances Dee, Adolphe Menjou, Una Merkel, Ned Sparks, Charles Ruggles, Jane Froman, Kenny Baker.

Texaco Star Theatre (December 28, 1938); Cast: John Barrymore, Mary Astor, True Boardman, Kenny Baker, Una Merkel, Jane Froman, Charles Ruggles, Ned Sparks.

Variety Show (December 14, 1939); Cast: Efrem Zimbalist, Jack Holt, Una Merkel, Bing Crosby, Bob Burns.

The Edgar Bergen and Charlie McCarthy Show (January 28, 1940); Cast: Charles McCarthy, Edgar Bergen, Lansing Hatfield, Una Merkel, Mortimer Snerd.

Lux Radio Theatre (February 26, 1940), "Swing High, Swing Low." Cast: Rudy Vallee, Virginia Bruce, Cecil B. DeMille, Corrine Miller, Edward Marr,

Josephine MacLean, Martha Wentworth, Melville Ruick, Roscoe Karns, Una Merkel, Bill Wright, Enrico Ricardi, Marlene Schools, Lois Collier, James Eagles, Julie Bannon.

Good News of 1940 (February 29, 1940); Cast: Fanny Brice, Dick Powell, Una Merkel, Connie Boswell.

Vallee Varieties (March 14, 1940); Cast: Rudy Vallee (Julius Caesar), Una Merkel (Calpurnia), Arthur Q. Bryan (Marc Antony).

Lincoln Highway (July 6, 1940), "Love on America's Greatest Road." Cast: Una Merkel.

Bob Hope Variety (March 25, 1941); Cast: Bob Hope, Jerry Colonna, Una Merkel.

Kate Smith Variety (March 28, 1941); Cast: Dorothy Lamour, Bob Hope, Abbott and Costello, Una Merkel.

Listen America (August 1, 1941); Cast: Paul V. McNutt (master of ceremonies), Dr. Morris Fishbein (guest scientist), Una Merkel (the "voice of the people"), Walter Slezak.

Your Happy Birthday (August 1, 1941); Cast: Una Merkel.

Lincoln Highway (August 2, 1941), "Betsy Barnes." Cast: Una Merkel, John McIntire, Lawson Zerbe, Minerva Pious, Kenny Delmar, James Van Dyke, Carleton Young, Alan Devitt.

Johnny Presents (October 21, 1941), "Nancy Bacon Reporting." Cast: Una Merkel.

Johnny Presents (November 4, 1941), "Nancy Bacon Reporting." Cast: Una Merkel.

Johnny Presents (November 11, 1941), "Nancy Bacon Reporting." Cast: Una Merkel.

Johnny Presents (November 18, 1941), "Nancy Bacon Reporting." Cast: Una Merkel.

Johnny Presents (November 25, 1941), "Nancy Bacon Reporting." Cast: Una Merkel.

Johnny Presents (December 2, 1941), "Nancy Bacon Reporting." Cast: Una Merkel.

Johnny Presents (December 9, 1941), "Nancy Bacon Reporting." Cast: Una Merkel.

Johnny Presents (December 16, 1941), "Nancy Bacon Reporting." Cast: Una Merkel.

Johnny Presents (December 23, 1941), "Nancy Bacon Reporting." Cast: Una Merkel.

Johnny Presents (December 30, 1941), "Nancy Bacon Reporting." Cast: Una Merkel.

Johnny Presents (January 6, 1942), "Nancy Bacon Reporting." Cast: Una Merkel.

Ray Block Orchestra (January 13, 1942); Cast: Una Merkel.

Johnny Presents (January 20, 1942), "Susan Bright, Detective." Cast: Una Merkel.

Johnny Presents (January 27, 1942), "Susan Bright, Detective." Cast: Una Merkel.

Bob Burns Variety Show (March 24, 1942); Cast: Bob Burns, Ginny Simms, Billy Artist's orchestra, Una Merkel.

The Great Gildersleeve (May 10, 1942); Cast: Earle Ross, Harold Peary, Jim Bannon, Lillian Randolph, Lurene Tuttle, Una Merkel, Walter Tetley.

Stage Door Canteen (September 17, 1942); Cast: Bert Lytell, Una Merkel, Andrews Sisters, Frank Fay.

Double or Nothing (September 18, 1942); Cast: Walter Compton, Frank Forest, Nat Brusiloff, Una Merkel, Roberto Hernandez, Julio Garzon.

Armstrong Theater of Today (October 24, 1942); Cast: Una Merkel.

Lux Radio Theater (February 1, 1943), "The Showoff." Cast: Hal Peary, Una Merkel, Beulah Bondi.

Hollywood (August 3, 1943); Cast: Paula Stone, Una Merkel.
Stage Door Canteen (August 12, 1943); Cast: Mary Martin, Una Merkel, Bert Lytell, Jack Smith.

Swingshift Frolic (April 14, 1944); Cast: Una Merkel (guest judge).

Louis Sobel Program (May 8, 1944); Cast: Una Merkel (guest).

Showtime (May 15, 1944); Cast: Una Merkel, Johnny Morgan, and others.

Stars Over Hollywood (October 7, 1944), "Career Women." Cast: Una Merkel.

Atlantic Spotlight (February 17, 1945); Cast: Vic Oliver, Una Merkel.

Hollywood Theater (January 10, 1947), "Marriage of Inconvenience." Cast: Una Merkel.

Cavalcade of America (March 10, 1947), "The Stirring Blood." Cast: Lee Bowman and Una Merkel.

Cavalcade of America (June 2, 1947), Reprise of "The Stirring Blood." Cast: Lee Bowman and Una Merkel.

The Great Gildersleeve (February 18, 1948), "Adeline Fairchild Arrives." Cast: Harold Peary, Una Merkel, John Wald, Louise Erickson, Walter Tetley, Earle Ross, Lillian Randolph, Richard LeGrand, Arthur Q. Bryan.

The Great Gildersleeve (February 25, 1948), "Treats Birdie with Kindness." Cast: Harold Peary, Una Merkel, John Wald, Louise Erickson, Walter Tetley, Earle Ross, Lillian Randolph, Richard LeGrand.

The Great Gildersleeve (March 10, 1948, "Considers Virtues of Marriage." Cast:

Harold Peary, Una Merkel, John Wald, Louise Erickson, Walter Tetley, Earle Ross, Lillian Randolph, Richard LeGrand, Arthur Q. Bryan, Ken Christy.

The Great Gildersleeve (March 17, 1948), "Worried about Duel." Cast: Harold Peary, Una Merkel, John Wald, Louise Erickson, Walter Tetley, Earle Ross, Lillian Randolph, Richard LeGrand, Gloria Holliday, Arthur Q. Bryan.

The Great Gildersleeve (March 24, 1948), "Jolly Boys Invaded." Cast: Harold

Peary, Una Merkel, John Wald, Louise Erickson, Walter Tetley, Earle Ross, Lillian Randolph, Richard LeGrand, Arthur Q. Bryan, Ken Christy.

The Great Gildersleeve (March 31, 1948), "Marjorie Loves French Teacher." Cast: Harold Peary, Una Merkel, John Wald, Louise Erickson, Walter Tetley, Earle Ross, Lillian Randolph, Richard LeGrand, Ben Alexander.

The Great Gildersleeve (April 7, 1948), "Baseball Field." Harold Peary, Una Merkel, John Wald, Louise Erickson, Walter Tetley, Earle Ross, Lillian Randolph, Richard LeGrand, Arthur Q. Bryan, Tommy Bernard, Stan Farrar.

The Great Gildersleeve (April 21, 1948), "Pretends Adeline is Secretary." Cast: Harold Peary, Una Merkel, John Wald, Louise Erickson, Walter Tetley, Earle Ross, Lillian Randolph, Richard LeGrand, Stan Farrar, Arthur Q. Bryan.

The Great Gildersleeve (April 28, 1948), "Kitchenware Salesman." Cast: Harold Peary, Una Merkel, John Wald, Louise Erickson, Walter Tetley, Earle Ross, Lillian Randolph, Richard LeGrand, Arthur Q. Bryan, John McIntire.

The Great Gildersleeve (May 5, 1948), "Fishing with Leroy." Cast: Harold Peary, Una Merkel, John Wald, Louise Erickson, Walter Tetley, Earle Ross, Lillian Randolph, Richard LeGrand, Arthur Q. Bryan, Ken Christy.

The Great Gildersleeve (May 12, 1948), "Malingers at Home." Cast: Harold Peary, Una Merkel, John Wald, Louise Erickson, Walter Tetley, Earle Ross, Lillian Randolph, Richard LeGrand, Arthur Q. Bryan, Ken Christy, Tommy Bernard.

The Great Gildersleeve (May 19, 1948), "Green Thumb Club." Cast: Harold Peary, Una Merkel, John Wald, Louise Erickson, Walter Tetley, Earle Ross, Lillian Randolph, Richard LeGrand, Arthur Q. Bryan, Gloria Holliday, Eleanor Audley.

The Great Gildersleeve (June 2, 1948), "Fired." Cast: Harold Peary, Una Merkel, John Wald, Louise Erickson, Walter Tetley, Earle Ross, Lillian Randolph, Richard LeGrand, Arthur Q. Bryan, Ken Christy, Gloria Holliday, Stan Farrar.

The Great Gildersleeve (September 8, 1948), "Mystery Baby." Cast: Harold Peary, Una Merkel, John Wald, Mary Lee Robb, Walter Tetley, Earle Ross, Lillian Randolph, Richard LeGrand, Ken Christy.

The Great Gildersleeve (September 15, 1948), "Sitting with Baby." Cast: Harold Peary, Una Merkel, John Wald, Mary Lee Robb, Walter Tetley, Earle Ross, Lillian Randolph, Richard LeGrand.

The Great Gildersleeve (September 29, 1948), "Naming the Baby." Cast: Harold Peary, Una Merkel, John Wald, Mary Lee Robb, Walter Tetley, Earle Ross, Lillian Randolph, Richard LeGrand, Arthur Q. Bryan, Ken Christy, Gloria Holliday.

Family Theatre (September 30, 1948), "Gramps." Cast: Irene Dunne, Victor Moore, Una Merkel, Henry Blair, Virginia Gregg, Michael Hayes, Tony La Frano (announcer), Norman Field.

The Great Gildersleeve (October 6, 1948), "Welfare Investigator." Cast: Harold Peary, Una Merkel, John Wald, Mary Lee Robb, Walter Tetley, Earle Ross, Lillian Randolph, Richard LeGrand, Arthur Q. Bryan, Gloria Holliday, Eleanor Audley.

The Great Gildersleeve (October 13, 1948), "Aunt Hattie Visits Again." Cast: Harold Peary, Una Merkel, John Wald, Mary Lee Robb, Walter Tetley, Earle Ross, Lillian Randolph, Richard LeGrand.

The Great Gildersleeve (October 27, 1948), "Proposes to Adeline." Cast:

Harold Peary, Una Merkel, John Wald, Mary Lee Robb, Walter Tetley, Earle Ross, Lillian Randolph, Richard LeGrand, Gale Gordon, Tommy Bernard.

The Great Gildersleeve (November 3, 1948), "Announcing Engagement." Cast: Harold Peary, Una Merkel, John Wald, Mary Lee Robb, Walter Tetley, Earle Ross, Lillian Randolph, Richard LeGrand, Arthur Q. Bryan, Ken Christy.

The Great Gildersleeve (November 10, 1948), "Engaged to Two Women." Cast: Harold Peary, Una Merkel, John Wald, Mary Lee Robb, Walter Tetley, Earle Ross, Lillian Randolph, Shirley Mitchell, Richard LeGrand, Arthur Q. Bryan, Gloria Holliday.

The Great Gildersleeve (November 17, 1948), "Breaking One Engagement." Cast: Harold Peary, Una Merkel, John Wald, Mary Lee Robb, Walter Tetley, Earle Ross, Lillian Randolph, Shirley Mitchell, Richard LeGrand, Hal March.

The Great Gildersleeve (November 24, 1948), "Helicopter Ride." Cast: Harold Peary, Una Merkel, John Wald, Mary Lee Robb, Walter Tetley, Earle Ross, Lillian Randolph, Richard LeGrand, Stan Farrar.

The Great Gildersleeve (December 8, 1948), "Disappearing Gifts." Cast: Harold Peary, Una Merkel, John Wald, Mary Lee Robb, Walter Tetley, Earle Ross, Lillian Randolph, Richard LeGrand, Ken Christy.

The Great Gildersleeve (December 15, 1948), "Cutting Back on Gifts." Cast: Harold Peary, Una Merkel, John Wald, Mary Lee Robb, Walter Tetley, Earle Ross, Lillian Randolph, Richard LeGrand, Arthur Q. Bryan.

The Great Gildersleeve (December 22, 1948), "Family Christmas." Cast: Harold Peary, Una Merkel, John Wald, Mary Lee Robb, Walter Tetley, Earle Ross, Lillian Randolph, Richard LeGrand, Arthur Q. Bryan, Ken Christy.

The Great Gildersleeve (December 29, 1948), "Wedding Imminent." Cast: Harold Peary, Una Merkel, John Wald, Mary Lee Robb, Walter Tetley, Earle Ross, Lillian Randolph, Richard LeGrand, Arthur Q. Bryan, Ken Christy.

The Great Gildersleeve (January 19, 1949), "Leroy's Toothache." Cast: Harold Peary, Una Merkel, John Wald, Mary Lee Robb, Walter Tetley, Earle Ross, Lillian Randolph, Richard LeGrand, Gloria Holliday.

The Great Gildersleeve (February 2, 1949), "Hat Shop Proposed." Cast: Harold Peary, Una Merkel, John Wald, Mary Lee Robb, Walter Tetley, Earle Ross, Lillian Randolph, Richard LeGrand, Gale Gordon, Arthur Q. Bryan.

The Great Gildersleeve (February 9, 1949), "Hat Shop Opening." Cast: Harold Peary, Una Merkel, John Wald, Mary Lee Robb, Walter Tetley, Earle Ross, Lillian Randolph, Richard LeGrand, Arthur Q. Bryan, Eleanor Audley.

The Great Gildersleeve (February 16, 1949), "Leila May Close Shop." Cast: Harold Peary, Una Merkel, John Wald, Mary Lee Robb, Walter Tetley, Earle Ross, Lillian Randolph, Shirley Mitchell, Richard LeGrand.

Stars Over Hollywood (April 30, 1949), "Sweet Adeline." Cast: Una Merkel.

Stars Over Hollywood (December 10, 1949), "They Always Come Back." Cast: Una Merkel.

Family Theater (June 24, 1953), "The Daughter-in-Law." Cast: Audrey Dalton and Una Merkel.

Family Theater (December 1, 1954), "Summer Replacement." Cast: Desi Arnaz, Una Merkel, Marvin Miller.

Make Up Your Mind (March 29, 1956); Cast: Una Merkel.

UNA MERKEL ON TELEVISION

Pantomime Quiz (CBS, November 8, 1949); Cast:, Vincent Price, Frank DeVol, Hans Conried, Gail Robbins, Adele Jergens, Bob Waterfield, Una Merkel, Glenn Langan.

Four Star Playhouse (CBS, September 25, 1952), "My Wife Geraldine." Directed by Robert Florey. Cast: Charles Boyer (Mr. Graham), Porter Hall (J.R. Martin), Una Merkel (Rose Barton), Noreen Nash (Salesgirl), Jim Hayward (Mr. Blake), Don Dillaway (Mr. Peters), Barbara Woodell (Neighbor), William Boyett (Interne).

Schlitz Playhouse (CBS, January 23, 1953), "Guardian of the Clock." Directed by Roy Kellino. Cast: Hugh Beaumont, Edmund Gwenn (Himself – Narrator), Bill McLean, Una Merkel, John Monaghan, Judy Osborne, Frank J. Scannell, Ludwig Stössel (Clockman), Ben Welden, Roland Winters.

Your Jeweler's Showcase (CBS, April 7, 1953), "The Monkey's Paw." Directed by Douglas Heyes and Sheldon Leonard. Cast: Walter Kingsford, Nolan Leary, Una Merkel, Ford Rainey, Edward Ryan, Rhys Williams.

Willys Theatre Presenting Ben Hecht's Tales of the City (CBS, August 20, 1953), "Miracle in the Rain." Directed by Robert Stevens. Cast: Ben Hecht (Narrator), Mildred Dunnock, Una Merkel, William Prince, Phyllis Thaxter.

Studio One in Hollywood (CBS, December 20, 1954), "Two Little Minks." Directed by Paul Nickell. Cast: Betty Furness (Herself, Commercial Spokeswoman), Walter Hampden (Uncle Silas), Frank McHugh (Nobby Bishop), Una Merkel (Parsis McHugh).

Kraft Theatre (NBC, October 12, 1955), "Trucks Welcome." Cast: Rita Gam, James Gregory, Joe Maross, Una Merkel.

The 10th Annual Tony Awards (DuMont, April 1, 1956); Cast: Jack Carter (Himself, Host); numerous guests, including Una Merkel (Herself, Winner: Best Featured Actress in a Play).

Calling Terry Conway (NBC, July 3, 1956). Cast: Ann Sheridan (Terry Conway), Una Merkel (Pearl McGrath), Philip Ober (Stan).

Playhouse 90 (CBS, January 31, 1957), "The Greer Case." Cast: Richard Joy (Himself, Announcer), Melvyn Douglas (Howard Hoagland), Zsa Zsa Gabor (Erika Segnitz), Edmund Gwenn (Jack Baldwin), Phillip Reed (Francis Wells), Jane Darwell (Annie Jackson), Una Merkel (Louise Hoagland), Raymond Burr (Lester Friedman), Anita Louise (Mabel Seymour Greer), Alan Marshal (Raymond Armbruster).

The Red Skelton Show (CBS, May 7, 1957), "Freddie and the Happy Helper." Directed by Seymour Berns. Cast: David Rose and His Orchestra (Themselves), Art Gilmore (Announcer), Una Merkel (Mrs. Van Wyck), Red Skelton (Freddie the Freeloader).

Climax! (CBS, September 12, 1957), "The Secret of the Red Room." Cast: Anna Maria Alberghetti (Kate), Judith Evelyn (Nurse Helm), Arthur Franz (Franco), Robert H. Harris, Una Merkel (Maud), Michael Rennie (Lorenzo).

The DuPont Show of the Month (CBS, February 21, 1958), "Aladdin." (Also known as "Cole Porter's 'Aladdin.'" Directed by Ralph Nelson. Cast: Dennis King (Astrologer), Anna Maria Alberghetti (Princess), Alec Clarke (Prime Minister), George Hall (Chamberlain), Geoffrey Holder (Genie), Una Merkel (Aladdin's Mother), Sal Mineo (Aladdin), Howard Morris (Wu Fang), Basil Rathbone (Emperor), Cyril Ritchard (Sui-Janel), Akim Tamiroff (Undetermined role).

The United States Steel Hour (CBS, July 16, 1958), "Flint and Fire." Cast: Robert Culp, Gloria Vanderbilt, Una Merkel.

Here's Hollywood (NBC, May 31, 1961). Cast: Richard Crenna (Himself), Una Merkel (Herself).

The Real McCoys (CBS, November 18, 1962), "The New Housekeeper." Cast: Walter Brennan (Grandpa Amos McCoy), Richard Crenna (Luke McCoy), Tony Martinez (Pepino), Abigail Shelton (Mary Gaylord), Una Merkel (Mrs. Gaylord)

The 34th Annual Academy Awards (ABC, April 9, 1962); Directed by Richard Dunlap. Cast: Bob Hope (Himself – host); numerous guests, including Una Merkel (Herself – Nominee: Best Actress in a Supporting Role).

The Bill Dana Show (NBC, December 1, 1963), "The Poker Game." Cast: Arthur Batanides (Augie), Lewis Charles (Ace), Bill Dana (Jose Jimenez), Joel Fluellen, Jonathan Harris (Mr. Phillips), Bern Hoffman (Fastie), Bill Idelson (Babcock), Ray Kellogg, Una Merkel (Mrs. Hatten), Amzie Strickland (Mrs. Phillips), Fredd Wayne (Cliff).

Burke's Law (ABC, December 13, 1963), "Who Killed Cynthia Royal?" Directed by Charles F. Haas. Cast: Gene Barry (Capt. Amos Burke), Gary Conway (Det. Tim Tilson), Regis Toomey (Det. Les Hart), Leon Lontoc (Henry), Frankie Avalon (Max), Macdonald Carey (Ben Gardner), Stubby Kaye (Joey Carson), Marilyn Maxwell (Eudora Carey), Una Merkel (Miss Samantha Cartier), Kathleen Nolan (Maura), Erika Peters (Miss Miles), Peter Leeds (Lt. Martin), Christine Williams (chorus girl), Jack Reitzen (workman), Beverly Reed (first ad-lib girl).

Destry (ABC, February 28, 1964), "Law and Order Day." Directed by John Florea. Cast: John Gavin (Harrison Destry), Una Merkel (Granny Farrell),

Jerome Cowan (H.B. Grubbs), Elisha Cook Jr. (Leech), Ben Gage (The Sheriff), Warren J. Kemmerling (Badger), Ken Drake (The Deputy), Ken Mayer (The Conductor), Charlotte Knight (The Landlady), Norman Leavitt (The Wayback Bartender), Dan White (Stableman).

The Cara Williams Show (CBS, October 21, 1964), "Amelia Hofstetter, Please Go Home." Cast: Cara Williams (Cara Bridges/Wilton), Frank Aletter (Frank Bridges), Jack Sheldon (Fletcher Kincaid), Jeanne Arnold (Mary Hammilmeyer), Una Merkel (Amelia Hofstetter), Paul Reed (Damon Burkhardt).

Burke's Law (ABC, January 6, 1965), "Who Killed the Strangler?" Directed by Sam Freedle. Cast: Gene Barry (Capt. Amos Burke), Gary Conway (Det. Tim Tilson), Regis Toomey (Det. Les Hart), Leon Lontoc (Henry), Frankie Avalon (Ralph Hirt), Jeanne Crain (Lorraine Turner), Annette Funicello (Anna Najensky), Una Merkel (Mrs. Thomas Barrett), Robert Middleton (Ezekiel Kindworth aka 'Rocky Mountain'), Quinn O'Hara (Sally Lou), Margaret Muse (Madame Tamrovia), Michael Fox (Coroner George McLeod), Sharyn Hillyer (Rosie Belle), Michelle Breeze (Cora Lee), Joy Harmon (Barbara Sue).

Burke's Law (ABC, April 14, 1965), "Who Killed the Rabbit's Husband?" Directed by Jerry Hopper. Cast: Gene Barry (Capt. Amos Burke), Gary Conway (Det. Tim Tilson), Regis Toomey (Det. Les Hart), Gloria Grahame (Doris Landers), Leon Lontoc (Henry), John Ireland (Bullock), Una Merkel (Clara Lovelace), Sal Mineo (Lew Dixon), Paul Richards (Lennie 'Leonardo' Krull), Francine York (Francesca), Joanne Ludden (Gina Landers Holt), Lou Krugman (Art Sanders), Stafford Repp (Cody the Bartender), Bill McLean (Concessionaire), Phil Arnold (Barney Halsey).

I Spy (NBC, January 8, 1968), "Home to Judgment." Directed by Richard C. Sarafian. Cast: Robert Culp (Kelly Robinson), Bill Cosby (Alexander

Scott), Will Geer (Uncle Harry), Una Merkel (Aunt Alta), Robert Sampson (Cowboy), Robert Donner (Mailman), Walter Coy (Sheriff Homer), Michael Preece (Phantom #2), Allen Pinson (Phantom #1), Gene LeBell (Man).

The American Film Institute Salute to James Stewart (CBS, March 16, 1980). Produced by George Stevens, Jr. Cast: James Stewart (Himself, Honoree); numerous guests, including Una Merkel (Herself).

Selected Bibliography

Bakewell, William. *Hollywood be Thy Name*. Metuchen, N.J.: Scarecrow Press, 1991.

Balio, Tino. *United Artists: The Company Built by the Stars*. Madison: University of Wisconsin Press, 1976.

———. *United Artists: The Company That Changed the Film Industry*. Madison: University of Wisconsin Press. 1987.

Basinger, Jeanine. *A Woman's View: How Hollywood Spoke to Women, 1930–1960*. New York: Knopf, 1993.

Baxter, John. *Hollywood in the Thirties.* New York: A.S. Barnes, 1968.

Bergan, Ronald. *The United Artists Story.* Crown Publishers, Inc. 1986.

Bogdanovich, Peter. *Allan Dwan: The Last Pioneer*. New York: Praeger, 1971.

Buford, Kate. *Burt Lancaster: An American Life*. Cambridge, MA: Da Capo Press, 2001.

Butler, David and Irene K. Atkins. *David Butler*. Metuchen, NJ: Scarecrow Press, 1993.

Cahn, William. *Harold Lloyd's World of Comedy*. New York: Sloan and Pearce, 1964.

Chase, Alisia G. *An American Heroine in Paris: Hollywood and Women in the City of Light in the 1950s*. PhD diss., University of Minnesota, 2002.

Corliss, Richard. *Mom in the Movies: The Iconic Screen Mothers You Love (and a Few You Love to Hate)*. New York: Simon and Schuster, 2014.

Crane, Cheryl and Cindy De La Hoz. *LANA: The Memories, the Myths, the Movies*. Philadelphia: Running Press, 2008.

Dalrymple, Jean. September Child: *The Story of Jean Dalrymple*. New York: Dodd, Mead & Company, 1963.

Dooley, Roger B. *From Scarface to Scarlett: American Films in the 1930s*. San Diego: Harcourt Brace Jovanovich, Publishers. 1981.

Ellenberger, Allan R. *Ramon Novarro: A Biography of the Silent Film Idol, 1899–1968*. Jefferson, NC: McFarland, 2009.

Eyman, Scott. *Ernst Lubitsch: Laughter in Paradise*. Baltimore: The Johns Hopkins University Press, 2000.

Finler, Joel W., and Bennett Finler. *The Hollywood Story*. New York: Crown Publishers, 1988.

Fitzgerald, Michael. *Universal Pictures: A Panoramic History in Words, Pictures, and Filmographies*. New Rochelle, NY: Arlington House Publishers. 1977.

Gehring, Wes D. *Parody as Film Genre*. Westport, CT: Greenwood Press, 1999.

Gielgud, Val H. *Years of the Locust*. London: Nicholas and Watson, 1947.

Golden, Eve. *Platinum Girl: The Life and Legends of Jean Harlow.* New York: Abbeville Press, 1991.

Gordon, Jeff. *Foxy Lady: The Authorized Biography of Lynn Bari.* Duncan, OK: BearManor Media, 2010.

Hamann, G.D. *Una Merkel in the 1930's.* Hollywood: Filming Today Press, 2006.

Hark, Ina Rae. *American Cinema of the 1930s: Themes and Variations.* New Brunswick: Rutgers University Press, 2007.

Harper, Valerie. *I, Rhoda.* New York: Gallery Books, 2013.

Harter, Chuck and Michael J. Hayde. *Little Elf: A Celebration of Harry Langdon.* Duncan, OK: BearManor Media, 2012.

Hemming, Roy. *The Melody Lingers On: The Great Songwriters and Their Movie Musicals.* New York: Newmarket Press, 1986.

Herman, Jan. *A Talent for Trouble: The Life of Hollywood's Most Acclaimed Director, William Wyler.* New York: Da Capo Press, 1997.

Hoaglin, Jess L. *Wherever is…? The Stars of Yesteryear.* Los Angeles: J. L.H, 1981.

Jewell, Richard B. and Vernon Harbin. *The RKO Story.* New York: Arlington House, 1982.

Kobal, John. *Gotta Sing, Gotta Dance: A Pictorial History of Film Musicals.* New York: Hamlyn, 1971.

Lamparski, Richard. *Whatever Became of...?* 8th series. New York: Crown, 1982.

Lash, Joseph P. *Eleanor and Franklin.* Franklin Center, PA: Franklin Library, 1971.

Lloyd, Annette D'Agostino. *Harold Lloyd: Magic in a Pair of Horn-Rimmed Glasses.* Albany, GA: BearManor Media, 2009.

Magill, Frank N., ed. *Magill's Survey of Cinema: English Language Films.* Englewood Cliffs, NJ: Salem Press, 1981.

McCaffrey, Donald W. *The Road to Comedy: The Films of Bob Hope.* Westport, CT: Praeger, 2004.

Moonjean, Hank. *Bring in the Peacocks: Memoirs of a Hollywood Producer.* Bloomington, IN: BearManor Media, 2004.

Parish, James R. *The Hollywood Beauties.* New Rochelle, NY: Arlington House Publishers, 1978.

———. *Hollywood's Great Love Teams.* New Rochelle, N.Y.: Arlington House Publishers, 1974.

Parish, James R. and Ronald L. Bowers. *The MGM Stock Company: The Golden Era.* New Rochelle, N.Y: Arlington House Publishers, 1974.

Pickard, Roy. *James Stewart: The Hollywood Years.* London: Hale, 1992.

Pitts, Michael R. *Poverty Row Studios, 1929–1940: An Illustrated History of 53 Independent Film Companies, with a Filmography for each.* Jefferson, NC: McFarland, 1997.

Powell, Jane. *The Girl Next Door, and How She Grew.* New York: Morrow, 1988.

Reynolds, Debbie. *Debbie—My Life.* New York: Pocket Books, 1988.

———. Forward to *Mom in the Movies: The Iconic Screen Mothers You Love (and a Few You Love to Hate)*, by Richard Corliss, ix–xiv. New York: Simon and Schuster, 2014.

Riva, Maria. *Marlene Dietrich.* New York: Random House, 1992.

Robertson, Patrick. *Guinness Book of Movie Facts and Feats.* Enfield: Guinness, 1991.

Schneider, Alan. *Entrances: An American Director's Journey.* New York: Viking, 1986.

Sennett, Ted. *Hollywood Musicals.* New York: Harry N. Abrams, 1981.

Sheehy, Helen. *Eva Le Gallienne: A Biography*. New York: Knopf, 1996.

Sheldon, Sidney. *The Other Side of Me*. New York: Warner Books, 2005.

Slide, Anthony. *The American Film Industry: A Historical Dictionary*. New York: Limelight Editions, 1990.

Soares, André. *Beyond Paradise: The Life of Ramon Novarro*. Jackson, MS: University Press of Mississippi, 2010.

Solomon, Aubrey. *The Fox Film Corporation, 1915-1935: A History and Filmography*. Jefferson, NC: McFarland, 2011.

Spoto, Donald. *Blue Angel: The Life of Marlene Dietrich*. New York: Copper Square Press, 2000.

Sragow, Michael. *Victor Fleming: An American Movie Master*. New York: Pantheon Books, 2008.

Stenn, David. *Bombshell: The Life and Death of Jean Harlow*. Raleigh, NC: Lightning Bug Press, 2000.

Swindell, Larry. *Spencer Tracy: A Biography*. Cleveland, OH: New American Library, 1969.

Thomas, Tony and Aubrey Solomon. *The Films of 20th Century-Fox: A Pictorial History*. Secaucus, NJ: Citadel Press, 1985.

Thompson, Frank T. *William A. Wellman*. Metuchen, NJ: Scarecrow Press, 1983.

Tranberg, Charles. *Walt Disney & Recollections of the Disney Studios: 1955–1980*. Albany, GA: BearManor Media, 2012.

Turk, Edward B. *Hollywood Diva: A Biography of Jeanette MacDonald*. Berkeley: University of California Press, 1998.

Tuska, Jon. *The Detective in Hollywood*. Garden City, NY: Doubleday, 1978.

Vance, Jeffrey and Suzanne Lloyd. *Harold Lloyd: Master Comedian*. New York: Harry N. Abrams, 2002.

Vieira, Mark A. *Irving Thalberg: Boy Wonder to Producer Prince.* Berkeley: University of California Press, 2010.

———. *Sin in Soft Focus: Pre-Code Hollywood.* New York: Harry N. Abrams, 1999.

Vineberg, Steve. *High Comedy in American Movies: Class and Humor from the 1920s to the Present.* Lanham, MD: Rowman & Littlefield, 2005.

Wagenknecht, Edward and Anthony Slide. *The Films of D. W. Griffith.* New York: Crown Publishers, 1975.

Index

*Numbers in **bold** indicate photographs*

42nd Street **100**, 100-102, 104, 155, 346, 274-275

Abbott, George 24, 361
Abel, Walter 177, 178, 386
Abraham Lincoln xiv, 25-26, 28, 32-35, **33**, 39, 44, 365-366
Academy Awards xv, 98, 118, 329-330, 348, 421
Adrian 66, 370, 372, 374, 375, 376, 377, 378, 380, 381, 382, 385, 387, 390
Ah, Wilderness! 317
"Aladdin" 312-313, 420
Alberghetti, Anna Maria 312, 313, 420
Alberni, Luis 118, 377, 394
All About Eve 279
All Women are Bad see *Don't Bet on Women*
Allen, Fred 232, 264
Allgood, Sara 270, 398

Allyson, June 271, 398
Alton, Robert 295
Alviene School of Dramatic Art 12
"American Film Institute Salute to James Stewart, The" 423
Anderson, Richard 295, 400, 402
Andes, Keith **309**, 404
Arcari, Andy 248, 251
Arledge, John 55-57, **57**, 59, 80, 123, 272, 368, 372, 409
Armida 81
Asher, Jerry 329
Atkinson, Brooks 305
Atwater, Edith 177, 386
Atwill, Lionel 97, 240, 374, 395
Auer, Mischa **218**, 220, 222, 235, 241, 367, 374, 381, 391, 394, 395
Ayres, Lew 69, 371

Baby Face Harrington 146-147, 383-384
Baby Sandy **230**, 230, 392
Bachelor Mother 308
Backus, Jim 281, 399, 402
Bacon, Lloyd 101, 374, 398, 400
Bainter, Fay 124, 379, 409
Bakewell, William 41, 366
Ballard, Kaye 309, **309**, 404
Bank Dick, The 231-232, **231**, 235, 393
Barbier, George 132, **154**, 155, 380, 382
Bard, Ben **41**, 366
Bard, Katharine **253**
Bargain, The 49, **51**, 52, 369
Bari, Lynn 269, 270, 398
Barnes, Joanna 324, 325, 405
Barrie, J. M. 262
Barrie, Wendy 175, 386
Barrymore, John 16, 104, 204, 205, 206, 375, 389, 390, 409, 410
Barrymore, Lionel 124, 212, **212**, 214, 379, 388, 391, 408
Basinger, Jeanine 75
Bat Whispers, The 40-42, **41**, 60, 366
Bates, Florence 274
Baxter, Warner 55, 100, 101, 368, 375
Bean, Orson 330
Beauty for Sale 110-113, **112**, 377
Beery, Wallace **180**, 181, 388
Beich, Albert 271, 397
Belmont Theatre 17, 360
Bendix, William 274, 278, 279, 398
Bennett, Joan 59, 73, 241, 370, 395
Benny, Jack 81, 159, 160-161, **161**, **162**, 163, 248, 385

Bergen, Edgar 228, 410
Berkeley, Busby 101, 102
Berlin, Irving 242, 395, 407
Bernhardt, Sarah 69, 214
Big Show, The 10, 359
Bill Dana Show, The 334, 421
Biography of a Bachelor Girl 138-139, 382
Blondell, Joan 100
Blunkall, E. J. 22, 361
Bombshell **119**, 119-120, 377
Bondi, Beulah 337, 345, 391, 413
Booth, Margaret 120, 377
Booth, Shirley 287
Born to Dance **165**, 165-171, **167**, **168**, 194, 197, 387, 408
Bow, Clara 119-120
Bowman, Lee 269, 414
Boyer, Charles 294, 372, 419
Brabin, Charles 98, 123, 374, 378
Brady, Alice 111, 113, 376, 377
Brando, Marlon 281
Brandon, Henry **346**
Breen, Joseph 135
Brennan, Walter 337, 421
Brent, George 95, 241, 372, 375, 395
Brice, Fanny 228, 390, 408, 411
Bride Goes Wild, The 270-272, 274, 397-398
Broadway Melody of 1936 158-160, **159**, 161, 165, 166, 345, 384-385
Broadway to Hollywood 117, 376
Broderick, Helen 202
Broken Blossoms 11-12
Brook, Charles 18, 365
Brooks, Phyllis 248, 249, 250-251
Brooks, Rand 234, 235, 393
Brown, Kelly **309**, 404
Brown, Nacio Herb 159, 384
Brown, Peter **332**, 406, 407
Brown, Tom 124, 379
Bruce, Virginia 166, 168, 387, 408, 410
Bucquet, Harold S. 212, 370, 391
Bulldog Drummond Strikes Back 134-135, **135**, 380-381
Bundle of Joy 308, 403
Burke, Billie 208, 316, 364
Burke's Law 334, 336, 421, 422
Burla, Ronald 58-59, 67, 69, **70**, 71-73, **72**, 76, 81, 84, 86, 87, 133-134, 146, 149-152, 163, 169, 178, 202, **203**, 208, 211, 227, 228, 229, 237, 238, 239, 253, 260, 265, 266, 269, 272-273, 297
Burns, Bob **225**, 228, 392, 408, 410, 413

Burton, Robert **253**, 362
Butler, David 137, 381
Butterworth, Charles 49, 134, **135**, 135, 146, 147, 157-158, **158**, 242, 244, 369, 381, 383, 384, 386, 396

Cabanne, Christy 179, 180, 387
Cabot, Elliot 24, 361
Cady, Frank **309**, 404
Calhern, Louis 93, 95, 372
Calleia, Joseph 188, 189, 386
Calling Terry Conway 307-308, 420
Campbell, Malcolm 175
Cara Williams Show, The 336, 422
Cardinal Pictures 274
Career 312, 363
Carlisle, Mary 65, 124, 141, 142-143, 379, 385
Carlson, Richard 284, 400
Carpenter, Edward Charles 143, 373, 383
Carrillo, Leo 85, 373
Carroll, Earl 16
Carroll, Madeleine 300
Carter, Harry **285**
Carter, Jack 306, 330, 420
Carter, Mrs. Leslie 69
Cat's-Paw, The 131-134, **132**, 380
Cavalcade of America 269, 414
Chakiris, George 330
Champion, Gower 309
Chatterton, Ruth 55
Checkers 194-195, **195**, **196**, 388-389
Chevalier, Maurice **154**, 155, 382
Chodorov, Edward 316, 363, 364
Chodorov, Jerome 303, 362, 363, 398
Christian Endeavor Society 16
Cilento, Diana 306
Cine-Arts Productions, Inc. 355
Clark, Charles Dow **41**, 366
Clarke, Charles G. 48, 382, 400
Clarke, Mae 69, 124, 371, 379
Clear All Wires! 98-99, 374
Climax! 312, 420
Cline, Edward 235, 237, 393, 394
Cody, Lew 81
Colbert, Claudette 25, 209
Colman, Ronald 134, 202, 381
Come Back, Little Sheba xv, 286-287, 297, 363
Comi, Paul 312, 363

Comin' Round the Mountain **225**, 228-229, 392
Command Performance, The 42-44, **43**, 367
Conried, Hans 273, 400, 419
Considine, Jr., John W. 24-25, 28, 34, 44, 58, 365, 367, 369, 370, 379, 381, 382, 384
Conway, Jack 84, 146, 192, 372, 383, 398, 408
Cooper, Dorothy 282, 399
Cooper, Gary 86, 248, 248-249, 250, 251
Coquette xiv, 22-27, 44, 356, 361-362, 365
Corcoran, Noreen 295, 402
Corey, Wendell 282, 400
Cornell, Lillian 247, 397
Cortez, Ricardo 52, 53-54, **53**, 107, 108, 368, 376
Cosby, Bill 337, 422
Coward, Noel 62, 65, 67, 370
Cracked Nuts 235, 237, 394
Cradle and All 317, 364
Craig, James 269, 398
Craven, Frank 27, 360, 361, 362, 376
Crawford, Joan xiv, 202
Cronyn, Hume 271, 398
Crosby, Bing 168, 232, 394, 408, 410
Crowe, James 223-224
Crowther, Bosley 280
Culp, Robert 314, 337, 421, 422
Cummings, Forrest 257-258
Daddy Long Legs 55-56, **56**, 368-369
Dalrymple, Jean 27, 362
Damone, Vic 282, 400
Dangerous Female see *Maltese Falcon, The*
Daniels, Bebe 52-53, **100**, 100, 101, 368, 375
Darrieux, Danielle 282, 400
Darrow, John 49, 369
Davenport, Harry 270, 398
Davies, Richard 240, 395
Davis, Bette xiv, 16, 80, 409
Day of Reckoning 120-123, **121**, 124, 378
Day, Clyde **7**, 8, 347-348
Day, Virginia 8
De Forest, Lee 17, 25, 364
Deacon, Richard **307**, 403
Dees, Mary 193
Delmar, Kenny 262, **263**, 264, **268**, 269, 397, 411
Dempster, Carol 17, 18, 34
Denny, Reginald 65, 67, 370
Destry 334-335, 421-422
Destry Rides Again 217-224, **218**, **221**, 270, 284, 334, 335, 391-392
Devine, Andy **68**, 69, 71, 75, 107, 123, 371, 376

DeVoe, Daisy 119-120
Dietrich, Marlene 218-223, **221**, 391
Disney, Walt 324, 331, 335, 405, 406
Dix, Richard 120, 122, 378
Dodd, Claire 240, 371, 395
Donlevy, Brian 218, 219, 391
Donohue, Walter 242
Don't Bet on Women 44, 47-49, **50**, 367
Don't Tell the Wife 179-180, 387
Double Date 234-235, **234**, 393
Douglas, Melvyn 311, 420
Douglas, Paul 314, **315**, 315, 405
Dressler, Marie 110
Dreyer, Carl Theodor 300
Dubin, Al 101, 375
Duna, Steffi 143, 383
Dunn, James 136, 381
Dunne, Irene 97, 98, 374, 416
DuPont Show of the Month, The 312-313, 420
Dvorak, Geraldine 193
Dwan, Allan 58, 369
Dyer, Peter John 34

Eagle-Lion 262, 264, 269, 397, 398
Ebsen, Buddy 159-160, 166, 210, 345-346, 385, 387, 390
Ebsen, Vilma 159, 385
Eburne, Maude 40, 42, 366
Edens, Roger 168, 169, 384, 387
Edgar Bergen and Charlie McCarthy Show, The 228, 410
Elliott, Edythe 27, 362
Emergency Wedding 281-282, 399
Emerson, Faye 306
Ephron, Henry 252, 362
Ephron, Phoebe 252, 362
Ernst, Richard Pretlow 82
Erwin, Stuart **121**, 122-123, 136, **136**, 194-195, **196**, 208, 229-230, **230**, 235, 378, 381, 389, 392, 394
Essay, Chris **309**, 404
Essex House (New York City) 240, 253, 259
Evans, Madge **74**, 80-81, 111, **112**, 120, 122, 125, 127, 163, 186, 212, 237, 260, 372, 376, 377, 378, 380, 407
Evelyn Prentice 137-138, 139, 382
Eyes of the World, The **36**, **37**, 38-39, 366

Fabares, Shelley 336, 407
Fairy and The Imp, The 8
Farrell, Glenda 101, 232, 297, 395

Fay, Frank 242, 362, 413
Fenton, Mike 337
Ferrer, Mel 280
Ferris, Fred 272
Fidler, Jimmie 169
Fields, Joseph 303, 362, 363, 398
Fields, W. C. 202, 231-232, **231**, 393
Fifth Horseman, The 18-19, 365
First Methodist Episcopal Church see First United Methodist Church
First United Methodist Church **5**, 8, 347,
Fisher, Eddie 308, 314, 403
"Flint and Fire" 421
Florea, John 335, 421
Fonda, Henry 281
Fontanne, Lynn 104
Ford, Wallace 21, 360, 361, 398
Foster, Dianne **298**, 299, 402
Four Girls in White 210, **210**, 217, 390
Four Star Playhouse 294, 299-300, 419
Fox, Sidney 54, 368
Francis, Kay 75, 100, 371
Franklin, Pamela 335, 407
Franklin, Sidney 104, 212, 214, 228, 370, 375, 391
Frasher, James 292
"Freddie and the Happy Helper" 311, 420
Freed, Arthur 159, 384
Freeland, Thornton 54, 367, 369, 372
Froman, Jane 286, 401, 409, 410
Fuzzy Pink Nightgown, The 311-312, 404

Gable, Clark xiv, 189, **190**, 190, 193, 206, 345, 388, 408
Gabriel Horn, The see *Kentuckian, The*
Galsworthy, John 151
Gam, Rita 301, 419
Garber, Jan 247
Garbo, Greta 183, 202
Gavin, John 334, 421
Gaynor, Janet 55, **56**, 163, 368
Gaynor, Mitzi 280, 285, **285**, 286, 399, 400
Geer, Will 337, 363, 423
Gehrig, Lou 248-249
Gehring, Wes D. 220
Gielgud, John 199
Gielgud, Val 199
Girl Most Likely, The 308-310, **309**, 404
Girls' Annex High School 11
Gish, Lillian xiv, 11-12, 13, 14, 32, 34, 49, 60, 165, 202, 292, 297

Gleason, Jackie 317, 318-320, 328, 341, 347, 364
Glenville, Peter 320, 323, 324, 326, 364, 405
Godsoe, Harold 247-248, 396
Goebel Park 348, **349**
Golden Girl 285-286, **285**, 400-401
Golden, Eve 84
Golden, John 20, 27, 28, 31-32, 214, 252, 356, 359, 360, 361, 362, 376
Goldin, Pat **307**, 403
Gomez, Thomas 292, 401, 406
Good News of 1940 228, 411
Good Old Soak **180**, 180-181, **182**, 183, 190, 388
Goode, Alan 27, 362
Gossipy Sex, The 21-22, **22**, 179, 361
Gran, Albert **43**, 44, 367
Great Gildersleeve, The 273, 413-418
"Greer Case, The" 310-311, 420
Gregory, James 301, 419
Griffith, David Llewelyn Wark (D. W.) xiv, 11-12, 17, 25-26, 28, 34-35, 365
"Guardian of the Clock" 294, 419
Gwenn, Edmund 294, 311, 419, 420

Hale, Barbara 281, 399
Hall, Mordaunt 39, 101, 124
Hall, Radclyffe 60
Hall, Thurston 180, 387
Hamilton Grange Reformed Church 16
Hamilton, Neil 17, 18, 42, **43**, 44, 367
Hamlet 16
Hammett, Dashiell 52, 53, 368
Hampton, Grayce 40, 42, 366
Hanks, Nancy 82, 365
Hardie, Russell 141, 376, 379
Harding, Ann 138, 139, 382
Hardwicke, Cedric 212, 391
Harlow, Jean xiv, **82**, 83, 84, **119**, 119, 120, 123, 169, 185-189, **186**, 192-193, 316, 372, 377, 386, 388
Harper, Mary Ann **121**, 123
Harper, Valerie 318, 319, 364
Harris, Jed 22, 24, 27, 361
Harris, Jr., William 229
Harrison, Warder 348
Harvey, Laurence 326, 329, 406
Have a Heart 135-137, **136**, **137**, 381
Hayes, Helen xiv, 22, 23, 24, 26, 27, 86-87, 123, 165, 183, 202, 306, 361, 362, 390
Hayward, Susan 286, 401
He's a Prince see *Command Performance, The*
Healy, Ted 119, 125, 148, 160, 161, 181, 202, 377, 379, 380, 384, 385, 386, 388

Heatherton, Ray 242, 362
Hecht, Ben 163, 299, 300, 390, 419
Henderson, Skitch 306
Henning-Schutte, Susan 325-326
Henry, Gloria 279, 398
Henville, Alexandra Lee see Baby Sandy
Her First Mate 104, 105-107, **106**, **107**, 376
Herbert, Hugh 177, 386
Here's Hollywood 329, 421
Herlie, Eileen 317, 364
Hersholt, Jean 81, 370, 384
Hervey, Irene 123, 220, 237-238, 378, 391
Heston, Charlton 345
Heyburn, Weldon 175, 386
Hilliard, Ernest 17, 364
Hilton, Rosemary 20, 360, 361
Hinds, Samuel S. 220, 378, 381, 391
Hitchcock, Alfred 345
Hoaglin, Jess 344
Hodges, Eddie 331-332, 406
Holder, Geoffrey 313, 420
Holland, John **37**, 366
Hollywood Canteen 245
Hollywood Victory Committee 248
Holmes High School (Covington, KY) 10, 11
Holmes, Phillips 97, 111, 374, 377
"Home to Judgment" (see *I Spy*) 337, 422-423
Hope, Bob xiv, 211, 232, 233, 390, 394, 411, 421
Hopper, Hedda 241, 291-292, 377
"Horse With the Dreamy Eyes, The" (song) 192
Horton, Edward Everett 54, 138, 139, 155, 157-158, 368, 382, 383
Howard, Leslie 177
Howard, Mary **210**, 390
Howard, Shemp 235, 237, 393, 394
Howard, William K. 47, 367, 378, 379, 382
Howe, James Wong 136, 381, 382, 383
Huddle 80, 371-372
Hudson, Rochelle 67
Hudson, Rock 330
Humberstone, H. Bruce 195, 388
Hume, Benita 99, 374
Hunnicutt, Arthur 306, **307**, 403, 407
Huntley, Hugh **37**, 366
Huston, John 52
Huston, Walter 32-33, **33**, 34, 365
Hymer, Warren 105, 106-107, 109, 376, 380, 391

I Love Melvin 294-295, 402
I Spy 337, 422-423
Ilou, Edward L. 269, 398
Impatient Maiden, The **68**, 69, 71, 371
Inge, William 286, 363
International Federation of Catholic Alumnae 138
Ireland, John 280, 363, 422
It's a Joke, Son! 262-264, **263**, 265, 267, **268**, 269, 397
It's in the Air 160-163, **161**, **162**, 385
Ives, Burl 331, **332**, 332, 406

Jackson, Anne 306
Jazz Babies 355-356
Jenkins, Jackie "Butch" 271, 272, 398
Jergens, Adele 271, 272, 398
Jewell, Isabel 123, 137-138, 142, 377, 378, 382
Johnson, Van 271, 398
Johnston, Johnny 269, 398
Jordan, Dick 31, 57, 58, 59, 67, 149, 150-151
Joslyn, Allyn 295, 402
June, Ray 42, 366, 378, 385, 387, 388, 397

Karns, Roscoe 123, 378, 411
Kaufman, Dave 312
Keefe, Cornelius 18, 360, 365
Keeler, Ruby 100, 101, 102, 375
Keith, Brian 324, **325**, 335, 405, 407
Kellaway, Cecil 336, 407
Kelly, Marjorie 242
Kennedy, Edgar 175, 389, 392
Kentuckian, The 297-299, **298**, 300, 402
Kenyon, Doris 49, 369
Kenyon, Gwen **244**, 244, 396
Kerrigan, J. M. **50**, 367
Kettles in the Ozarks, The 306-307, **307**, 402-403
Kibbee, Guy 179, 180, 375, 387
Kilbride, Percy 306
Kill the Umpire 274, **276**, 278-279, 398-399
King, Henry 38, 366
Kingsley, Sidney 237
Kinney, Nancy S. 328
Kirkwood, James 59, 370
Knight, June 160, 385
Kobal, John 102
Kraft Theatre 301, 419
Kruger, Otto 111, 123, 125, 127, 377, 378, 380

Krupa, Gene 211, 390
Ku Klux Klan 19

La Jolla Playhouse 280, 312, 363
Lake, Arthur 208
Lamarr, Hedy 251
Lamas, Fernando 292, 294, 400, 401
Lamour, Dorothy 232, **233**, 233, 394, 411
Lamparski, Richard xiv, 342, 343-344
Lancaster, Burt 287, 297, **298**, 298, 299, 300, 402
Landi, Elissa 58, 369, 408
Lane, Harry **244**
Lane, Marjorie 168
Lang, Walter 42, 286, 367, 401
Langdon, Harry 247, 248, 396
Langford, Frances 159, 167, 168, 169, 385, 387, 396
"Law and Order Day" 334, 421-422
Lawlor, Jr., Andrew 24, **25**, 27, 28-29, 39-40, 42, 44-45, 47, 361, 362
Lawrence, Gertrude 65
Laye, Evelyn 157, **158**, 383
Le Gallienne, Eva 316, 364
Lee Bradford Corporation 16
Lee, Bowlum 240
Lehar, Franz 155, 381, 401
Leisen, Mitchell 310, 404
LeRoy, Mervyn 100-101
Leslie, Joan 242, 244, 396
Lewis, Vera **43**, 367, 397
Lincoln Highway Radio Show, The 229
Lindbergh, Charles 125
Listen to the Mocking Bird 316, 363-364
Lloyd, Harold 131-134, **132**, 380
Lockhart, June 269, 397
Lombard, Carole xiv, **204**, 204-206, 209, 389
Long, Jr., Nick **159**, 385
Loos, Anita 83, 372, 375, 382, 385, 388
Louise, Anita 310, 311, 420
Love's Old Sweet Song xiv, 17, 364
Lowe, Edmund 47, 234, **234**, 235, 367, 393
Lowell, Helen 17, 360, 364
Loy, Myrna xiv, 137, 382
Lubitsch, Ernst 155, 156, 157, 292-293, 381
Lunt, Alfred 104
Lupino, Ida 294
Lyman, Abe 81
Lynn, Diana 298, 402

MacArthur, Charles 27, 87
MacDonald, Donald 297, **298**, 402
MacDonald, Jeanette 48, 79, 155, 157, 292, 367, 382, 390
Macfadden, Bernarr 18
MacMurray, Fred 204, 284, 345, 389, 400
Mad Doctor of Market Street, The 240-241, 394-395
Main, Marjorie 282, 306, **307**, 307, 403
Maltese Falcon, The 52-54, **53**, 368
Maltin, Leonard 222, 248
Man from Texas 269-270, 398
Man Wanted 75, 80, 371
Manners, David 75, 93, 95, 107, 371, 372
Manners, Dorothy 192
Marin, Edwin L. 125, 175, 380, 386
Marsh, Mae 18,
Marshall, George (Director) 217, 218, 222, 223, 284, 314, 391, 400, 404
Marshall, George C. (General) 248
Marshall, Sarah 303, 305-306, 363
Marx, Groucho 202
Mathers, Jimmy 331, 406
Mating Game, The 314-316, **315**, 404-405
Matthau, Walter 300, 402
Mayer, Louis B. 84-85, 408
McBain, Diane 336, 407
McCarthy, Charlie 228, 410
McFarland, George "Spanky" **121**, 122, 123, 378
McGowan, John "Jack" 166, 384, 387
McGuire, Dorothy 280, 331, 363, 406
McHugh, Frank 300, 407, 419
McIntire, John **298**, 402, 406, 411, 415
McKinney, Florine 111, **112**, 377
McMahon, E. M. 18, 365
Men Are Such Fools 85-86, **86**, 373
Menjou, Adolphe 308, 403, 404, 409, 410
Menu 117-118, 377
Meredith, Burgess 296, 363
Merkel, Arno 1, **2**, 2, 3, 4, 6, 11, 12, 16, 28, 67, **70**, 71, 163, 187, 189, 190, 210, 228, 245, 253, 258, 260, 261, 262, 287, 308, 323, 329, 330, 336, 341, 342
Merkel, Elizabeth "Bessie" 2, **2**, 3, 4, 7, 8, **70**, 71, **115**, 163, 164, 228, 253, 258-260, **259**, 262, 342, 348
Merkel, Carl 11
Merkel, Una
  Academy Award nomination of, xv, 329, 330, 348
  accent of, 8, 20, 55, 79-80, 105, 111, 179,
    195, 208, 209, 264, 297, 335
  birth of, xiii, 2-3
  childhood and youth of, 4-13, 15-16

death and burial of, 346-348
desire to have children of, 151, 239-240
education of, 7, 10, 11, 12, 16
elocution, dance, and acting lessons of, 8, 10, 12, 16
entertaining troops, See World War II work of
experience as model, 18
films of, See (titles of individual films)
friendships of, See (individual's name)
health of, 7, 69, 193-194, 224, 227, 233, 258, 260-261,
    272, 280, 287, 291-292, 307, 336, 343, 344-345
hobbies of, xv, 7-8, 118, 123, 151, 165, 187, 343
insecurities of, xiii, 15, 54, 59, 87, 133-134, 164-165,
    187, 252, 274, 286-287, 356
lawsuit associated with, 272-273
marriage of, 72, 72-73, 76, 79, 149-152, 163, 208, 211,
    237, 239, 253, 265, 269, 272-273
musical ability of, 8-10, 168
name, meaning and pronunciation of, 3-4
nervous breakdown of, 260-261
physical appearance of, xiii-xiv, 7-8, 10, 11-12,
    38-39, 95, 188, 192, 208-209, 232, 235, 242,
    257, 265, 286, 294, 326, 343, 344, 355-356
political views of, 251-252, 330
popularity of, 8, 169, 199, 201, 209, 261, 264, 292,
    343, 349-350
possible overdose of, 287, 291-292
professionalism of, xiv, 143, 146, 295, 326, 331-332
radio work of, See (titles of individual shows)
relationship with parents, 4, 149, 151, 187, 348
religiosity and spirituality of, 7, 8, 11, 16, 331,
    343, 347
salary-related issues of, 27, 28, 60, 62, 84-85, 208
stag film, unlikely participation of, See Appendix
stage fright of, 8, 24, 164-165
star on Hollywood Walk of Fame of, 323
television work of, See (titles of individual shows)
temperament of, 6
theater work of, See (titles of individual plays)
theatrical training of, 8, 12, 16
Tony Award win of, xv, 306, 348,
vaudeville tours of, xiv, 22, 242
views on acting, 32, 265, 281
wit of, 10, 258, 281, 319, 348
World War II work of, 237-238, 245-246,
    248-252, 249, 292
writings of, xv, xvi, 17, 18, 31, 32, 69, 87, 99, 151

Merrick, David 317, 320, 364
Merry Widow, The (1934) 155-157, 292, 294, 381-382
Merry Widow, The (1952) **290**, 292, **293**, 294, 401
Midnight Mary 107-110, **110**, 375-376
Miller, Ann 208
Millionaire for Christy, A 284-285, 400
Mills, Hayley 324-325, 331, 405, 406
Milton, Robert 52, 369
Mineo, Sal 313, 420, 422
"Miracle in the Rain" 299-300, 419
Mitchell, Shirley 273, 417, 418
Mollenhauer, Virginia 343, 346
"Monkey's Paw, The" 295, 419
Montgomery, Robert **61**, 65, 66, 67, 98, 138, 139, 370, 382, 408
Montmartre 17, 360
Moran, Peggy 234, 235, 393
Moreno, Rita xv, 329, 330, 406
Morgan, Frank 104, 105, 119, 189, **190**, 193, 375, 376, 377, 388, 408
Morgan, Harry 347
Morin, Relman 97
Morris, Chester 25, 41, 42, 83, 366, 372
Morse, Robert 317, 319, 364
Mother Carey's Chickens 331, 406
Mother Wore Tights 279
Murder in the Fleet 147-148, **148**, 384
Murder in the Private Car 141-143, **142**, 379
Murphy, George 242, 396
Murray, Jan 242, 362
My Blue Heaven 279-280, 399
My Dear Secretary 274
My Sister Eileen 273-274, 362-363
"My Wife Geraldine" 294, 419
Myrow, Josef 402

Nagel, Anne 242, 362, 395
Nagel, Conrad 164, 383, 408
Nathan, Paul 329, 405
Neilson, James 326, 363, 406
Nelson, Barry 300
Nicholas, Ted 347
Nickell, Paul 312, 419
Night is Young, The 157-158, **158**, 383
Niven, David 294, 308
Nixon, Richard 330
Noonan, Tommy 308, **309**, 403, 404
Nordstrom, Clarence 102, 375
Novarro, Ramon 80, 123-124, 157, 372, 383

Novis, Donald 247, 397
Nugent, Elliott 20, 88, 90, 360, 373
Nugent, Judy **309**, 404

O'Connor, Donald 294, 295, 402
O'Hara, Maureen 324, **325**, 405
O'Neil, Nance **37**, 366
O'Neill, Eugene 317
O'Sullivan, Maureen 113, 408
Ober, Philip 286, 287, 363, 405, 420
Ohman, Phil 247
Oland, Warner 134, 381
On Borrowed Time 212, **212**, 214, 217, 391
One New York Night 143, **144**, **145**, 146, 383
Ordet (The Word) 300
Osborne, Robert 286
Osborne, Vivienne 85, 373
Our American Heritage 324
Overman, Lynne 21, 22, 179, 180, 361, 387, 389
Owen, Ethel 252, 253
Owens, Anna 201

Page, Geraldine 326, 329, 406
Paine, Thomas 245
Pangborn, Franklin 117, 118, 377, 393
Pantomime Quiz 273, 419
Parent Trap, The 324-326, **325**, 405
Paris Interlude 125, **126**, 127, 380
Parke, Harry **246**, 247, 397
Parker, Eleanor 284, 400
Parker, Jean 136, **136**, 374, 381, 384
Parks, Larry 281, 399
Parsons, Louella 79-80, 97, 211, 261
Partain, Travis 257-258
Pasternak, Joe 218, 391, 399, 401, 407
Patrick, Lee 224, 406
Peary, Harold 273, 392, 413-418
Peck, Gregory 280
Pendleton, Nat **88**, **148**, 148, 160, 161, 240, 370, 373, 380, 384, 385, 391, 395
Penthouse Murder see *Secret Witness, The*
Perelman, S. J. 313, 380
Personal Property 178-179
Phares, Elizabeth see Merkel, Elizabeth "Bessie"
Phares, John Alexander 4
Phares, Mary Elizabeth Alexander (Una's Grandmother) 3, 4, 11, 12, 261
Phonofilm 17
Pickford, Mary 25, 55

Pidgeon, Walter 189, 317, 319-320, 364, 388
Pigs 20-21, 31, 360-361
Pine Grove Pavilion 15
Pious, Minerva 232, 411
Pitts, ZaSu 60, 105, 107, 124, 297, 370, 376
Planck, Robert H. 42, 366, 370, 399, 404
Playhouse 90 310-311, 420
Ponder Heart, The xv, 301, 303-306, **304**, 307, 363
Poor Nut, The 20, 360
Porter, Cole 168, 312-313, 387, 420
Powell, Dick **100**, 102, 228, 294, 375, 408, 411
Powell, Eleanor xiv, 158, 160, 166, **168**, 168, 169, 345, 385, 387, 408
Powell, Jane 282, 308, 309-310, **309**, 400, 404
Powell, William 137, 382
Power, Helen Emma Reaume 8
Power, Patia see Power, Helen Emma Reaume
Power, Tyrone 8, 390
Presley, Elvis 336, 407
Price, Vincent 273, 419
Pride of the Yankees, The 249
Prince, William 300, 419
Private Lives **61**, 62, 65-67, 98, 104, 370

Quack Service **244**, 244-245, 396
Quigley, Juanita 165, 386, 387

Rabwin, Marcella 187
Ragan, David 277-278
Raker, Lorin 54, 368, 371
Ralph, Jessie 210, 382, 390, 393
Randall, Tony 314, 315, 405
Rathbone, Basil 313, 420
Reagan, Ronald 242, 396
Real McCoys, The 334, 421
Red Skelton Show, The 311, 420
Red-Headed Woman **82**, 83-84, 372
Remarkable Mr. Pennypacker, The xv, 296, 363
Rennie, Michael 312, 420
Reunion in Vienna **103**, 104-105, 375
Reynolds, Debbie 294, 295, 308, 314-316, 402, 403, 405
Rhythm Romance see *Some Like it Hot*
Rice, Florence 210, **210**, 390, 408
Rich, Young, and Pretty 282-284, **283**, 295, 399-400
Riffraff **186**, 188-189, 385-386
Ritchard, Cyril 313, 420
Rizzuto, Phil 331
Road to Zanzibar 232-233, **233**, 394

Robertson, Cliff 309, 404
Robson, May 104, 186, 372, 375, 376, 377
Rogers, Ginger 100-101, 102, 160, 308, 375
Roosevelt, Eleanor 250
Rose, Jackson J. 269, 398
Rosenblatt, Freda 106
Ross, Shirley 211, 212, 390
Ruggles, Charles 141, **142**, 142, 379, 405, 409, 410
Ruggles, Wesley 206, 389
Ruhl, Arthur 26
Ruskin, Harry 185
Russell, Jane 311, 312, 404
Russell, Rosalind 157, 382, 383
Ruth, Roy Del 160, 368, 380, 384, 387
Rutherford, Ann **210**, 300, 390
Ryerson, Florence 125, 378, 381

Salt Water 27-28, 105, 362, 376
Sandy Gets Her Man **230**, 230, 392
Saratoga 189-193, **190**, **191**, 194, 388
Schallert, Edwin 280, 407, 408
Schenck, Joseph M. 24, 28, 365, 366
Scheuer, Philip 75
Schneider, Alan 296, 363
Scott, Martha 296, 363
Secret of Madame Blanche, The 97-98, 374
"Secret of the Red Room, The" 312, 420
Secret Witness, The 59-60, 62, 65, 107, 369-370
Selznick, David O. 187, 208
Sennett, Mack 271
She Wanted a Millonaire 59, 73, 370
Shearer, Douglas 142, 370, 371, 372, 373, 374, 375, 376, 377, 378, 379, 380, 381, 382, 383, 384, 385, 386, 387, 388, 390, 391, 398, 400, 401, 402
Shearer, Norma 65, 67, 138, 177, 370, 390
Sheldon, Sidney 282, 399
Sheridan, Ann 258, 307, 420
Sherman, Vincent 224
Sidney, Sylvia 25
Siegel, Sol 279, 288, 399
Silvers, Sid 160, **165**, 166-167, **167**, 169, 384, 385, 387
Simon, S. Sylvan 210, 390
Singin' in the Rain 295
Singleton, Penny 208
Six Cylinder Love 54, 367-368
Smith, Pete 118, 377, 390
Some Like it Hot (1939) 211-212, 390
Sothern, Ann 208

Speed 175-176, 386
Spewack, Sam 60, 369, 370, 374
Spinout 336, 407
Spoto, Donald 218
Stage Door Canteen 413
Stanton, Ernie 237
Stanwyck, Barbara 228, 281
Starr, Jimmy 40
Steele, Vernon **135**, 381
Stenn, David 187
Stewart, James xiv, **165**, 166, 168, 169, 175, 219, 345, 386, 387, 390, 391, 408, 423
"Stirring Blood, The" 269, 414
Stoloff, Benjamin 267, 397
Stone, Lewis 49, **51**, 369, 372
Stork Club 258
Storm, Jerome 12
Stowe, Leslie 19, 365
Stritch, Elaine 306
Studio One 300, 419
Sully, Frank 177, 178, 390, 393
Summer and Smoke xv, 280, 323-324, 326, **327**, 328-330, 363, 405-406
Summer Magic 331-332, **332**, 334, 406
Summerville, Slim 105, **107**, 376
Sweethearts of the U.S.A. **246**, 246-247, 396-397
Swift, David 324-325, 405
Sydes, Anthony 269, 397

Take Me Along 317-320, **318**, 323, 328, 364
Talbot, Nita 308, 386, 403
Tales of the City see *Willys Theatre Presenting Ben Hecht's Tales of the City*
Tarkington, Booth 27
Taurog, Norman 271, 282, 308, 312, 397, 399, 403, 404, 407
Taylor, Don 312, 363
Taylor, Robert xiv, 148, 158, **159**, 160, 163, 228, 384, 385, 402, 408
Terror by Night see *Secret Witness, The*
Texaco Star Theatre 209, 409-410
Thalberg, Irving 138, 171, 188, 370, 381, 382, 385
Thaxter, Phyllis 299, 419
They Call It Sin 93, 95, 97, 372-373
This is the Army 242-244, **243**, 395-396
This Side of Heaven 124-125, 378-379
Thomson, Kenneth 75, 371
Three is a Family 252-253, **253**, 257, 258, 362
Tiger Walks, A 335, 406-407
To Heir is Human 247-248, 396
Todd, Chokey 11
Tom, Dick, and Harry 308

Tone, Franchot 143, **144**, 146, 376, 377, 383
Tony Awards xv, 306, 344, 348, 420
Tracy, Lee 98, 99, 119, 120, 374, 377
Tracy, Spencer 54, 59, 73, 188, 189, 345, 368, 370, 386, 390
Treacy, Emerson 21, 31, 361
"Trucks Welcome" 301, 419
True Confession **204**, 204-206, 229, 389
True Story Magazine 18
Truex, Ernest 54, 87, **88**, 88, 90, 237, 373, 395
Tryon, Glenn 234, 235, 393
Turner Classic Movies 286, 349
Turner, Lana 292, 294, 401
Twin Beds 241-242, 395
Two By Two 20, 360
Two Girls Wanted 21, 361
"Two Little Minks" 300, 419

United Artists 24, 28, 29, 42, 44, 49, 54, 365, 366, 380, 395, 402, 404
United China Relief 240
United Service Organization (USO) 248-252, **249**
United States Steel Hour, The 313-314, 421

Vallee, Rudy 164-165, 228, 410, 411
Vallee's Varieties 228, 411
Van Dyke, Dick 317, 364
Vanderbilt, Gloria 314, 421

Wabash Avenue 279
Wadsworth, William **253**, 362
Walburn, Raymond **168**, 387, 401
Waldron, Charles 24, 362, 391
Walker, Charlotte 20, 360
Walker, Helen 274
Walley, Deborah 336, 406, 407
Wallis, Hal 324, 328-329, 371, 372, 374, 395, 405
Walton, Douglas 98, 374
Ware, Helen **43**, 360, 365, 367
Warren, Harry 101, 375
Warrick, Ruth 317
Watson, Bobs 212, **212**, 214, 391
Watts, Jr., Richard 120
Way Down East 12
Wayne, David 303, 305, 363, 399, 401
We Went to College 177-178, 386
Webster, Vera 348
Weiler, A.H. 278
Welk, Lawrence 242, 362

Wellman, William 108, 375
Welty, Eudora xv, 301, 303, 305, 363
West Side Story xv, 330
West, Roland 40, 41, 366
Westman, Nydia 21, 297, 360, 361
Wetherby, Lawrence W. 299
Wexler, Paul **307**, 403
Whale, James 69, 371
What Every Woman Knows 262
When My Baby Smiles at Me 279
Whistling in the Dark 87-88, **88**, 90, 373
White Rose, The 17-18
"Who Killed Cynthia Royal?" 334, 421
Wicked 58, 369
Wilcox, Grace 189, 194
Wilder, Patricia "Honey Chile" 175, 386
William, Warren 100
Williams, Guinn 180, 387
Williams, Tennesse xv, 280, 363, 405
Willys Theatre Presenting Ben Hecht's Tales of the City 299-300, 419
Winchell, Walter 159, 281, 319
Wing, Toby 102, 375, 389
Winninger, Charles 219, 220, 391
Winslowe, Paula 193, 409, 410
Winterhalter, Hugo 308, 403
With a Song in My Heart 286, 401
Withers, Jane 194-195, **196**, 389
Wolheim, Louis 17, 364
Women in His Life, The 123, 378
Wong, Anna May 81
Woolf, Edgar Allan 125, 376, 378, 379, 381, 383
World Shadows 12-13, 14, 16
Wright, Harold Bell 38, 366
Wright, Sr., Corina **246**, 397
Wynyard, Diana 104, 375

You and I see *Bargain, The*
You Belong to Me 281
Young, Loretta xiv, 93, 100, 107, **110**, 110, 372, 376, 381
Young, Robert 125, 380, 390, 408
Young, Roland 47, 48, 202, 367
"Youthful George Washington" (speech) 8

Zanuck, Darryl F. 100, 279, 288, 374, 381, 399, 401

Photo Credits

Every effort has been made to trace the copyright holders of the photographs included in this book; if any have been inadvertently overlooked, the author and publisher will be pleased to make necessary changes.

All Columbia photos. Columbia Pictures-Sony Entertainment.
 All Rights Reserved
All Eagle-Lion photos c.Eagle-Lion Films. All Rights Reserved
All MGM and United Artists photos. c.Metro-Goldwyn-Mayer Studio Inc.
 All Rights Reserved
All Monogram photos c.Allied Artists International Inc.
 All Rights Reserved
All Paramount photos c.Paramount Pictures. All Rights Reserved

All RKO photos. c.RKO Pictures LLC. All Rights Reserved.

All Tiffany photos. c.Tiffany-Stahl Productions. All Rights Reserved

All 20th Century-Fox photos. c.20th Century-Fox Film Corp.
   All Rights Reserved

All Universal photos c.Universal Studios. All Rights Reserved.

All Warner Bros./First National photos
   c.Warner Bros. Entertainment Inc. Co. All Rights Reserved

All Disney Productions photos. c.Walt Disney Company.
    All Rights Reserved.

All photos, unless otherwise noted, are from the author's collection.

About the Author

A native of West Virginia, Larry Sean Kinder currently resides in Bowling Green, Kentucky, where he works as an Associate Professor in the Department of Library Public Services at Western Kentucky University. When he is not indulging his love of classic films, he enjoys participating in church activities, reading, studying art history, learning new languages, and spending quality time with his loving wife and their three spoiled cats: Gracie, Shadow, and Lottie.

www.ingramcontent.com/pod-product-compliance
Lightning Source LLC
Chambersburg PA
CBHW050425240426
43661CB00055B/2271